Discover New York City

Experience the best of New York City

This edition written and researched by

Regis St Louis
Cristian Bonetto

Discover New York City

Lower Manhattan & the Financial District (p47)

Iconic monuments, river-front access and Wall St.

Don't Miss Statue of Liberty, Ellis Island

SoHo & Chinatown (p73)

Soup-dumpling parlors next door to cobblestone streets and big-name stores.

Don't Miss Chinatown

East Village & Lower East Side (p97)

Two of the city's hottest 'hoods that lure students, bankers and scruffier types alike.

Don't Miss St Marks Place

Greenwich Village, Chelsea & the Meatpacking District (p119)

Quaint, intimate streets plus trendy nightlife, shopping and art galleries galore.

Don't Miss The High Line

Union Square, Flatiron District & Gramercy (p143)

A bustling, vibrant park binds surrounding areas filled with good eats.

Don't Miss Union Square

Upper West Side & Central Park (p211)

Upper East Side (p189)

Midtown (p157)

Greenwich Village, Chelsea & the Meatpacking District (p119)

Union Square, Flatiron District & Gramercy (p143)

SoHo & Chinatown (p73)

East Village & Lower East Side (p97)

Lower Manhattan & the Financial District (p47)

Midtown (p157)

Times Square, Broadway theaters, canyons of skyscrapers, and bustling crowds that rarely thin.

Don't Miss Times Square & Broadway, Museum of Modern Art, Empire State Building

Upper East Side (p189)

High-end boutiques, sophisticated mansions and Museum Mile – one of the most cultured strips in the world.

Don't Miss Metropolitan Museum of Art, Guggenheim Museum

Upper West Side & Central Park (p211)

Home to the premier performing arts center and the park that helps define the city.

Don't Miss Central Park

Contents

Plan Your Trip

Discover New York City

In Focus

Survival Guide

This is New York City

Loud, fast and pulsing with energy, New York City (population 8.4 million) is symphonic, exhausting and always evolving. Maybe only a Walt Whitman poem cataloging typical city scenes – from the humblest hole-in-the wall to grand buildings – could begin to do the city justice.

It remains one of the world's creative and business centers. Fashion, theater, food, music, publishing, advertising and, of course, finance, all thrive here. As Groucho Marx once said, 'When it's 9:30 in New York, it's 1937 in Los Angeles.' Coming to NYC from anywhere else for the first time is like stepping into a movie; one you've probably been unknowingly writing; one that contains all imagined possibilities.

Almost every country in the world has a presence here. From Brooklyn's Russian enclave in Brighton Beach to the mini South America in Queens; from the middle of Times Square to the most obscure corner of the Bronx, you'll find extremes.

You can experience a little bit of everything. You can decide if you'd like your day to be filled with high culture in an uptown museum and trendy eating in the Village, or – if you like your city to be tougher – you can choose to spend an afternoon wandering through the twisting streets and art galleries of downtown. Just don't be too shocked if your day of high culture turns gritty when you come across a gifted jazz singer on the subway platform, or if your bohemian day gets fancy when a trendy boutique seduces you and you're shelling out for the perfect pair of shoes before you know it.

New York City is constantly in the process of reinventing itself. And so too are the successive waves of immigrants who have populated the city and the striving artists who have pinned their hopes and dreams on making it here.

> "Coming to NYC is like stepping into a movie containing all imagined possibilities"

Broadway, near Times Square

BILIZED
FOR 7 AVE SOUTH OF W 45 ST USE B'WAY
TARGET
ONE WAY
at&t
DISCOVER CARD
TDK
W 50 ST
ONE WAY
FOR 7 AVE SOUTH OF W 45 ST USE B'WAY
AREA AHEAD
B'WAY
BIKE ROUTE AHEAD
AERO NYC

New York City

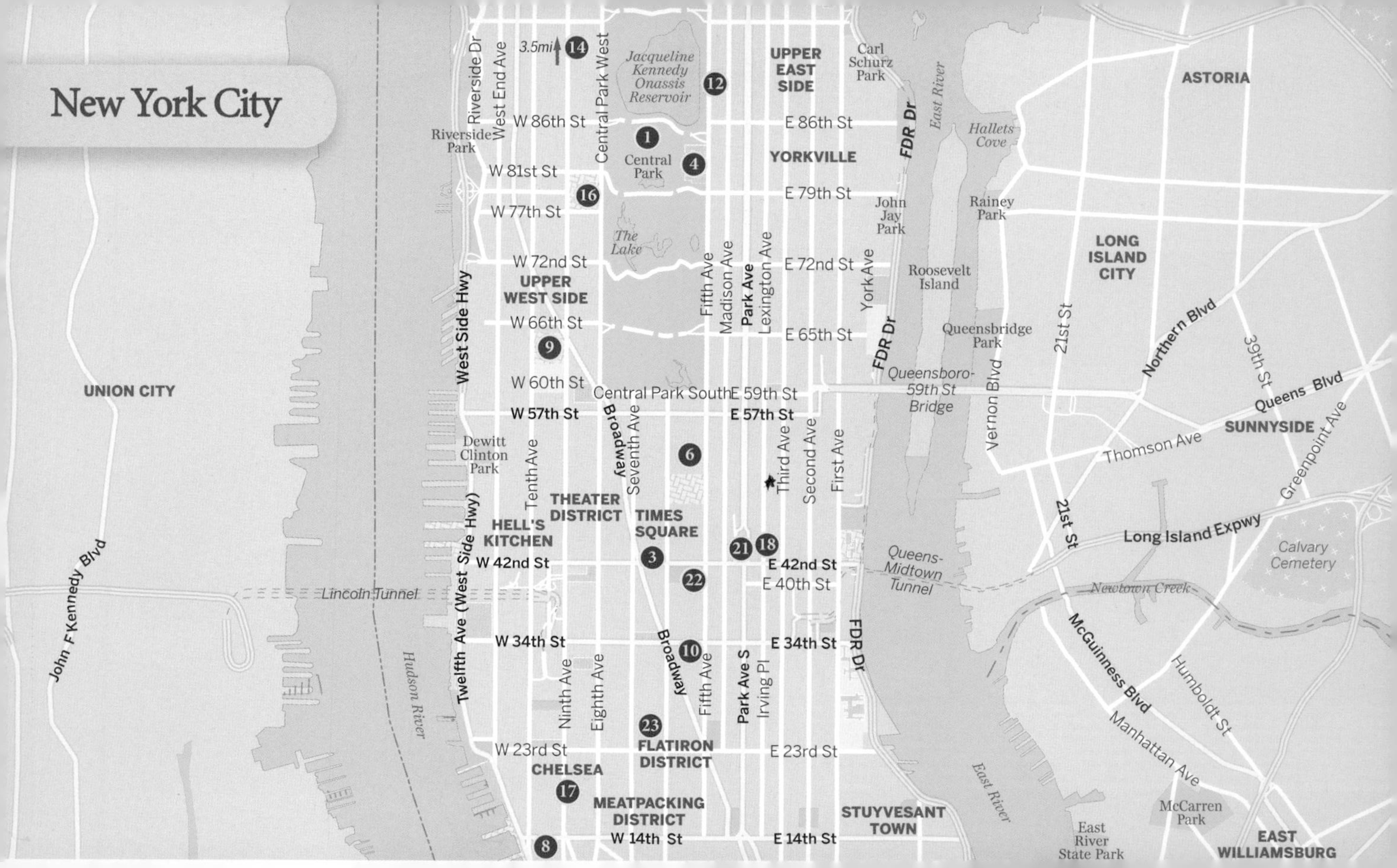

UNION CITY
John F Kennedy Blvd
Lincoln Tunnel
Hudson River
Riverside Park
Riverside Dr
West End Ave
3.5mi
14
W 86th St
W 81st St
W 77th St
W 72nd St
UPPER WEST SIDE
W 66th St
9
W 60th St
West Side Hwy
W 57th St
Dewitt Clinton Park
Tenth Ave
HELL'S KITCHEN
W 42nd St
Twelfth Ave (West Side Hwy)
W 34th St
Ninth Ave
Eighth Ave
W 23rd St
CHELSEA
17
8
MEATPACKING DISTRICT
W 14th St
Central Park West
16
Jacqueline Kennedy Onassis Reservoir
1
Central Park
4
12
The Lake
Central Park South
Broadway
Seventh Ave
THEATER DISTRICT
TIMES SQUARE
3
6
22
10
23
FLATIRON DISTRICT
Fifth Ave
Madison Ave
Park Ave
Lexington Ave
E 59th St
E 57th St
Third Ave
Second Ave
First Ave
21
18
E 42nd St
E 40th St
E 34th St
Park Ave S
Irving Pl
E 23rd St
E 14th St
STUYVESANT TOWN
UPPER EAST SIDE
E 86th St
YORKVILLE
E 79th St
E 72nd St
E 65th St
York Ave
Carl Schurz Park
John Jay Park
FDR Dr
East River
Roosevelt Island
Queensboro-59th St Bridge
Queens-Midtown Tunnel
Hallets Cove
Rainey Park
Queensbridge Park
Vernon Blvd
ASTORIA
LONG ISLAND CITY
21st St
Northern Blvd
39th St
Queens Blvd
SUNNYSIDE
Thomson Ave
Greenpoint Ave
Long Island Expwy
Calvary Cemetery
Newtown Creek
McGuinness Blvd
Humboldt St
Manhattan Ave
McCarren Park
East River State Park
EAST WILLIAMSBURG

25 Top Highlights

1. Central Park (p216)
2. Statue of Liberty (p52) & Ellis Island (p54)
3. Broadway & Times Square (p162)
4. Metropolitan Museum of Art (p194)
5. East Side Food Scene (p100)
6. Museum of Modern Art (p164)
7. Brooklyn Bridge (p66)
8. The High Line (p124)
9. Lincoln Center (p228)
10. Empire State Building (p166)
11. Strolling in the Village (p122)
12. Guggenheim Museum (p196)
13. Nightlife in the Lower East Side (p113)
14. Harlem Culture (p236)
15. National September 11 Memorial & Museum (p56)
16. American Museum of Natural History (p227)
17. Gallery Hopping in Chelsea (p138)
18. Midtown's Amazing Architecture (p168)
19. Hanging Out in Williamsburg (p243)
20. Washington Square Park (p131)
21. Grand Central Terminal (p174)
22. Bryant Park & the New York Public Library (p168)
23. Markets of Chelsea (p140)
24. Shopping in SoHo (p92)
25. New York Harbor (p63)

25 New York City's Top Highlights

Central Park (p216)

London has Hyde Park. Paris has the Bois de Boulogne. And New York City has Central Park. One of the world's most renowned green spaces, it checks in with 843 acres of rolling meadows, boulder-studded outcrops, elm-lined walkways, manicured European-style gardens, a lake and a reservoir – not to mention an outdoor theater, a memorial to John Lennon, an idyllic waterside eatery (the Loeb Boathouse) and one very famous statue of *Alice in Wonderland*. The big challenge? Figuring out where to begin.

1

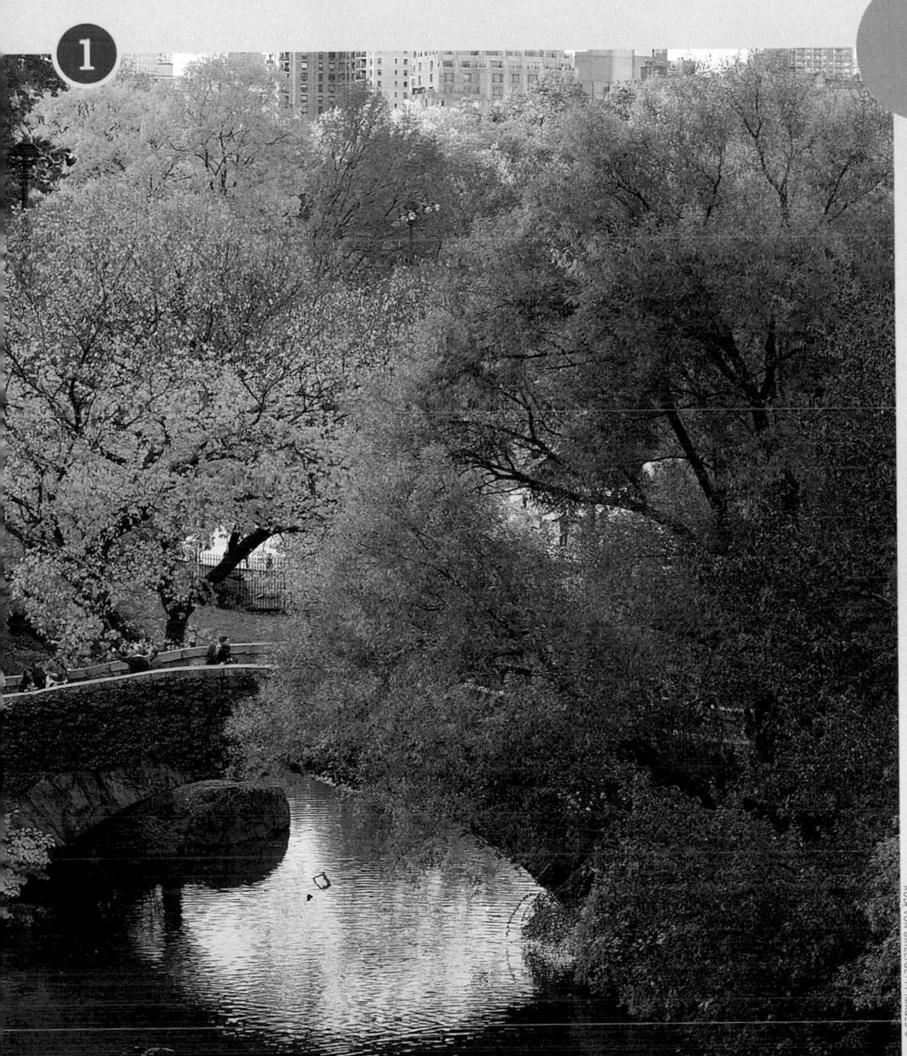

RUDI VON BRIEL/GETTY IMAGES ©

2

Statue of Liberty (p52) & Ellis Island (p54)

Since its unveiling in 1886, Lady Liberty has welcomed millions of immigrants sailing into New York Harbor in hope of a better life. It now welcomes millions of tourists, many of whom head up to her crown for one of New York City's finest views. Close by lies Ellis Island, the American gateway for more than 12 million new arrivals between 1892 and 1954. These days it's home to one of the city's most moving museums.

Broadway & Times Square (p162)

Sizzling lights, electrifying energy: this is the America of the world's imagination. Stretching from 40th St to 54th St, between Sixth and Eighth Aves, Broadway is NYC's dream factory – a place where romance, betrayal, murder and triumph come with dazzling costumes and stirring scores. The district's undisputed star is bright, blinding Times Square. More than the meeting point of Broadway and Seventh Ave, this is America in concentrate – an intense, intoxicating rush of Hollywood billboards, shimmering cola signs, and buffed topless cowboys. Welcome to the 'crossroads of the world.'

3

The Best... Free Activities

STATEN ISLAND FERRY
Hop on the ferry for postcard-perfect views of Manhattan's southern edge. (p71)

CHELSEA GALLERIES
Hundreds of galleries open to the public along Manhattan's West 20s. (p138)

NEW MUSEUM OF CONTEMPORARY ART ON THURSDAY NIGHTS
Contemporary art that's free for visitors on Thursday evenings. (p103)

GOVERNORS ISLAND
Take a quick ferry ride to explore this island with priceless views. (p69)

NEW YORK PUBLIC LIBRARY
Experience the stunning Reading Room, as well as diverse exhibits. (p168)

The Best... Restaurants

FORAGERS CITY TABLE
A triumph of farm-to-table cooking with flavorful sustainable recipes. (p133)

BALTHAZAR
A buzzing SoHo bistro with years of excellence. (p87)

ROSEMARY'S
A beautifully designed West Village spot with memorable cooking. (p127)

REDFARM
RedFarm's savvy Sino-fusion dishes boast bold flavors, but it doesn't take itself too seriously. (p127)

TANOSHI
The outrageously good chef's selection of sushi changes daily at this tiny, well-worn joint. (p206)

EATALY
Food emporium where you can eat and drink all things Italian. (p154)

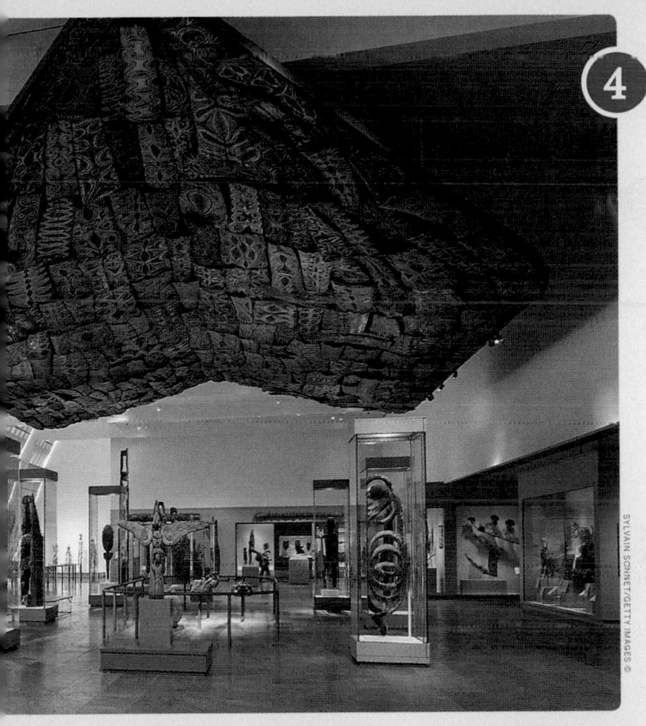

SYLVAIN SONNET/GETTY IMAGES ©

4 Metropolitan Museum of Art (p194)

With more than two million objects in its collections, the Met is simply dazzling. Its great works span the world, from the chiseled sculptures of ancient Greece to the evocative tribal carvings of Papua New Guinea. The Renaissance galleries are packed with old-world masters, while the relics of ancient Egypt fire the imagination – particularly the Temple of Dendur, with its 2000-year-old walls covered in hieroglyphics and carvings of papyrus seemingly growing from a pond.

GRAHAM CROUCH/GETTY IMAGES ©

5 East Side Food Scene (p100)

One of New York's greatest assets is the sheer variety of its restaurants. In a single neighborhood you'll find vintage-filled gastropubs, sushi counters, tapas bars, French bistros, barbecue joints, pizza parlors, vegan cafes and good old-fashioned delis, whipping up toasted bagels with lox and cream cheese. You can snack your way from China to Israel to Mexico in a few blocks in the East Village.

Museum of Modern Art (p164)

Quite possibly the greatest hoarder of modern masterpieces on earth, the MoMA is a cultural promised land. It's here that you'll see Van Gogh's *The Starry Night*, Cézanne's *The Bather*, Picasso's *Le Demoiselles d'Avignon*, Pollock's *One: Number 31, 1950* and Warhol's *Campbell's Soup Cans*.

SYLVAIN SONNET/GETTY IMAGES ©

Brooklyn Bridge (p66)

Completed in 1873, this Gothic Revival masterpiece – crafted entirely from granite – has inspired poetry (Jack Kerouac's 'Brooklyn Bridge Blues'), music (Frank Sinatra's 'Brooklyn Bridge') and plenty of art (Walker Evans' 1920s photography). A stroll over the graceful bridge, linking lower Manhattan and Brooklyn, is a rite of passage for New Yorkers and visitors alike. Nighttime is especially cinematic when the city lights reflect off the waters below and the bustling streets seem like a distant memory.

The High Line (p124)

A resounding triumph of urban renewal, the High Line is – without a doubt – New York's proudest testament to the continuous effort to transform scarring vestiges of the city's industrial past into eye-pleasing spaces that foster comfortable city-center living. Once an unsightly elevated train track that snaked between butcheries and low-end domestic dwellings, today the High Line is an unfurled emerald necklace of park space that encourages calm and crowds alike.

8

The Best... Skyline Views

BROOKLYN BRIDGE PARK
Expansive views of downtown Manhattan and the Brooklyn Bridge. (p241)

TOP OF THE STRAND
Enjoy resplendent views of the Empire State Building with a cocktail in hand. (p181)

STANDARD
Mesmerizing downtown views from the upper-floor lounge of this style maven. (p136)

ROOSEVELT ISLAND
River and skyscraper views from Franklin D Roosevelt Four Freedoms Park. (p206)

METROPOLITAN MUSEUM ROOF GARDEN CAFÉ & MARTINI BAR
Admire the sweep of Central Park after a day's art-gazing. (p207)

TOP OF THE ROCK
Probably the city's best views await atop this art-deco gem. (p183)

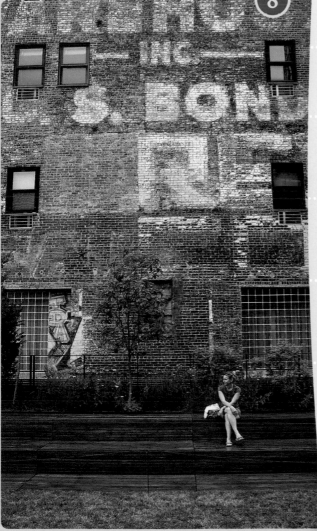

Lincoln Center (p228)

With the billion-dollar-plus redevelopment virtually complete, the world's largest performing-arts center is in stunning shape. The dramatically redesigned Alice Tully Hall anchors one end; other venues surround a massive fountain and public space. Every top-end genre has a stage here: the New York Philharmonic, the Chamber Music Society of Lincoln Center and the New York City Ballet. Two theaters present great drama, but the biggest draws are the Metropolitan Opera and American Ballet Theater. Below: Alice Tully Hall Lincoln Center

9

The Best... Cultural Experiences

METROPOLITAN OPERA HOUSE
Lavish productions and world-class performers in a magical setting. (p229)

JOYCE THEATER
An innovative line-up of contemporary ballet, flamenco and theatrical modern dance. (p139)

NEW YORK CITY BALLET
All the great works are here, from *Swan Lake* to *The Nutcracker*. (p230)

LA MAMA ETC
East Village icon continues to push boundaries in its genre-defying performances. (p114)

BROOKLYN ACADEMY OF MUSIC
An array of cutting-edge fare in theater, dance and music. (p247)

ANGELIKA FILM CENTER
Foreign and indie films in an unfancy but much-loved setting. (p92)

10 Empire State Building (p166)

The striking art-deco skyscraper is one of New York's most recognizable icons. The ESB has appeared in dozens of films and still provides one of the best views in town – particularly around sunset when the twinkling lights of the city (and neighboring states) switch on. The beloved landmark hasn't stopped turning heads, especially since the addition of LED lights which create more than 16 million color possibilities. Keep your eye to the sky on big holidays, when dramatic displays light up the night.

11 Strolling in the Village (p122)

One of the best ways to see New York is to pick a neighborhood, lace on your walking shoes and spend the day exploring. Greenwich Village is a fine place to start, with picturesque cobblestone streets dotted with sunlit shops, narrow sidewalk cafes and quaint restaurants that beckon you inside. For a different take on New York, head over to the bohemian East Village, overload your senses down in Chinatown, or take in the local scene in gallery-filled Chelsea. This is a city that invites endless wandering.

JEAN-PIERRE LESCOURRET/GETTY IMAGES ©

12 Guggenheim Museum (p196)

This museum's organic shape and sweeping spiral staircase – the inspired work of architect Frank Lloyd Wright – is a superb sculpture in its own right. Inside are 20th-century paintings by modern heavy hitters such as Picasso, Pollock, Chagall and Kandinsky in its permanent collection. But it's at least as well known for its temporary exhibits, which run the gamut from massive retrospectives and large-scale installations to in-depth national surveys.

NISIAN HUGHES/GETTY IMAGES ©

13 Nightlife in the Lower East Side (p113)

Trendy all-night lounges tucked behind a crumby Chinese restaurant; taco shops that clandestinely host late-night tranny cabarets; stadium-size discotheques that clang to the thump of DJ-ed beats; and after-after-after-parties on the roof as the sun rises – an alternate universe lurks between the cracks of everyday life. One of the best places to start the night is on the bar-lined streets of the Lower East Side.

Harlem Culture (p236)

A nexus of African American culture, Harlem is steeped in history. This is where the great artists, writers and musicians of the Harlem Renaissance transformed the neighborhood into an international icon. Today, there's much to experience, from real-deal soul food restaurants to riotously joyful gospel churches. Tomorrow's greats take the stage at the Apollo Theater while new beer gardens and cocktail dens ensure buzzing entertainment late into the night. For an introduction to the area's legendary culture, head to the Studio Museum in Harlem (p236).

14

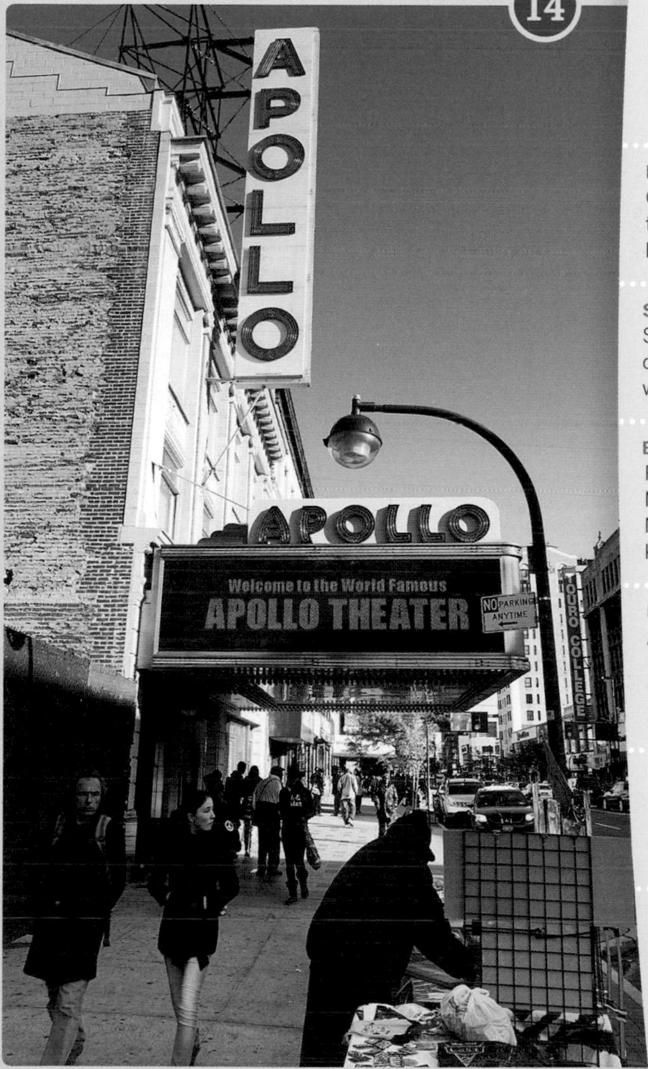

The Best... Gay & Lesbian Venues

MARIE'S CRISIS
One-time hooker hangout turned show-tune piano bar. (p135)

STONEWALL INN
Scene of rioting drag queens during the Stonewall riots of '69. (p136)

BRUNCH ON NINTH AVENUE
Pick a sidewalk table at Marseille and do your bit for Neighborhood Watch, Hell's Kitchen–style. (p180)

INDUSTRY
As night deepens, this Hell's Kitchen hit turns from buzzing bar to thumping club. (p182)

G LOUNGE
Always a fun night out at this Chelsea party spot. (p136)

LESLIE-LOHMAN MUSEUM OF GAY & LESBIAN ART
The world's first LGBT art museum. (p81)

The Best... With Kids

HUDSON RIVER PARK
Loads of kiddy excitement, including playgrounds and room to run free. (p132)

CONEY ISLAND
Hot dogs. Ice cream. Amusement park rides. Coney Island is just the ticket for some low-brow excitement. (p243)

CHILDREN'S MUSEUM OF THE ARTS
Hands-down the best museum for the under-six crowd. (p81)

AMERICAN MUSEUM OF NATURAL HISTORY
With dinosaurs, a marine world, planetarium and IMAX films, this one should not be missed. (p227)

15

National September 11 Memorial & Museum (p56)

Rising from the ashes of Ground Zero, the National September 11 Memorial and Museum is a beautiful, dignified response to the city's darkest chapter. Where the Twin Towers once soared, two reflecting pools now weep like dark, elegant waterfalls. Framing them are the names of those who lost their lives on September 11 and in the 1993 World Trade Center bombing. Deep below lies the Memorial Museum, a powerful, poignant exploration of these catastrophic events.

American Museum of Natural History (p227)

16

Delve into the great wonders of our world at this sprawling museum of natural history. Dinosaurs, mammoths, IMAX films and otherworldly temporary exhibitions will fire up the imagination, particularly for young visitors. Just gazing at the Rose Center for Earth & Space – a massive glass box containing a silver globe, home to space-show theaters and the planetarium – is mesmerizing, especially at night, when all of its otherworldly features are aglow.

BARRY WINIKER/GETTY IMAGES ©

17

Gallery Hopping in Chelsea (p138)

Dozens of galleries pack the streets of Chelsea, an industrial 'hood turned art mecca. Opening nights, usually on Thursdays, bring out avant-loving crowds, style hounds and wannabe players. And while the neighborhood's allure is undeniable, smaller pockets of edgier galleries have popped up in other neighborhoods, mainly the Lower East Side, Williamsburg in Brooklyn and Long Island City.

Midtown's Amazing Architecture (p168)

New York has been the drawing board of some of the world's leading architects – Richard Meier, Frank Gehry and Renzo Piano among others – who continue to create groundbreaking new works in the urban landscape. Get a panoramic view from atop one of the world's most famous skyscrapers, the Empire State Building (p166), or gaze up at the shiny gargoyles of art-deco icon, the Chrysler Building (p169). Below: View of the Chrysler Building

18

The Best... Must-See Architecture

CHRYSLER BUILDING
Manhattan's most elegant skyscraper. (p169)

EMPIRE STATE BUILDING
This Depression-era skyscraper never ever gets old. (p166)

GRAND CENTRAL TERMINAL
A classic beaux-arts stunner, with an astronomical pattern on the ceiling. (p174)

NEW MUSEUM OF CONTEMPORARY ART
A sexy stacked-cube structure with a translucent aluminum exterior. (p103)

FLATIRON BUILDING
An elegant triangular masterpiece that never fails to captivate. (p148)

Hanging Out in Williamsburg (p243)

19

Retro cocktail lounges peddling a Depression-era vibe. Artsy eateries dishing out everything from barbecue ribs to Michelin-starred gastronomy. And enough music halls and rowdy beer gardens to keep the most dedicated night owls up for weeks. Prefer the daylight hours? Williamsburg is stocked with an array of designer homeware shops, in addition to fashion outposts of all stripes, from vintage thrift emporiums to high-design boutiques. Just one subway stop from downtown Manhattan, this is the city's trendiest hangout.

MICHAEL MARQUAND/GETTY IMAGES ©

The Best... Live Music

CARNEGIE HALL
The world's greatest musicians have worked this hallowed stage. (p184)

SMALLS
A jazz basement with emerging talents and late-night jam fests. (p137)

PIANOS
A hipster-loving music hall with up-and-coming rock bands. (p115)

LE POISSON ROUGE
A 'multimedia art cabaret' with a staggering variety of music. (p137)

BROOKLYN BOWL
Converted iron works in Williamsburg with great bands, bowling and craft beer. (p246)

DENNIS K. JOHNSON/GETTY IMAGES ©

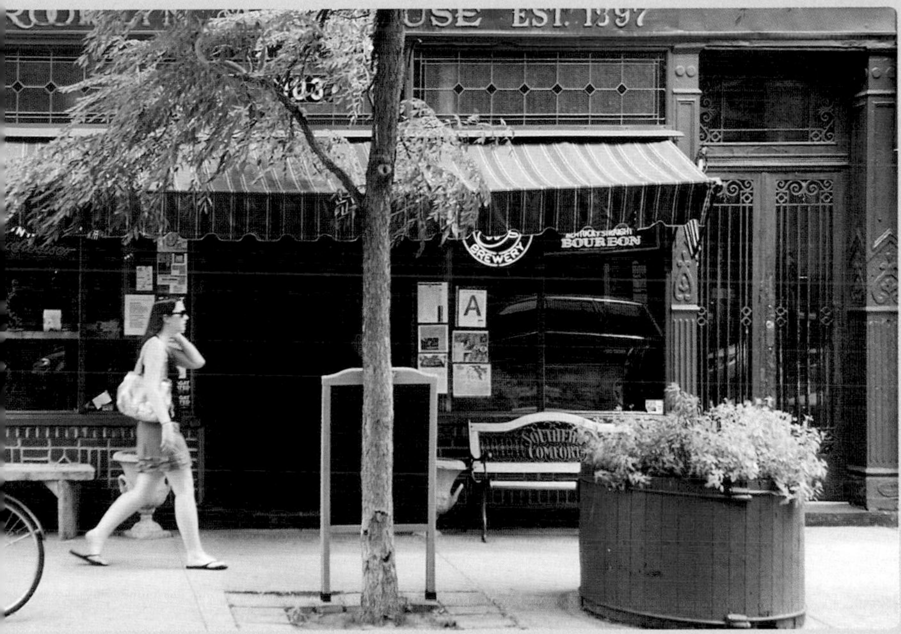

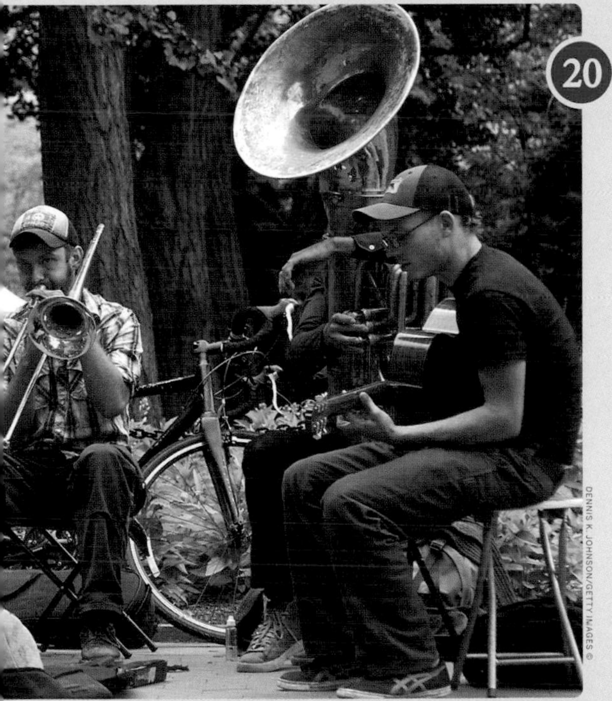

20 Washington Square Park (p131)

One of New York's liveliest green spaces, Washington Square Park is always a hive of activity, with jazz bands and krumpers, sleepy-eyed students and frolicking tots, footsore tourists and the odd folk singer. Surrounded by architectural gems of NYU, this leafy 10-acre park is looking lovelier than ever following a $16-million, five-year renovation completed in 2014. It's also a great spot for taking a break after exploring the Village. Left: Musicians in Washington Square Park

21 Grand Central Terminal (p174)

Even if you're not boarding a train to the 'burbs, it's worth exploring the grand, vaulted main concourse at Grand Central Terminal. The lower floor houses a truly excellent array of eateries, bringing the idea of 'food court' to grand new levels. The balconies overlooking the main concourse afford an expansive view; perch yourself here around 5pm on a

22 Bryant Park & the New York Public Library (p168)

Amid soaring skyscrapers and gridlocked sidewalks, Bryant Park feels like an oasis in the concrete desert of Midtown. There's year-round appeal with open-air film screenings in summer, a skating rink and festive Christmas market in winter, and basking on the lawn whenever the weather is nice. At the east end of the park is the stately New York Public Library. Free exhibitions tap into city lore, while its main reading room is a stunning work of grand design.

Markets of Chelsea (p140)

New York's markets are packed with treasures. On weekends, one parking garage in Chelsea transforms into an antique-lover's paradise, with vintage clothes, Victorian houseware, mid-century furniture, and hundreds of other curios from the past. Foodies meanwhile focus on Chelsea's sprawling food market (p126), an ideal spot for snacking, dining and browsing gourmet grocery sellers. Other good markets around the city include the Union Square Greenmarket (p148) and the Brooklyn Flea (p243), with its mash-up of antiques, food and artisanal goods and crafts. Below: Chelsea Market

23

The Best... Green Spaces

CENTRAL PARK
The city's most famous park has more than 800 acres of rolling meadows and boulder-topped hillocks. (p216)

BROOKLYN BRIDGE PARK
A brand new park lines the waterfront along Dumbo to Atlantic Ave. (p241)

THE HIGH LINE
A thin strip of green that unfurls up the western slice of downtown. (p124)

RIVERSIDE PARK
A 100-block park alongside the Hudson on Manhattan's west side – ideal spot for a bike ride. (p221)

Shopping in SoHo (p92)

Take it from the likes of Holly Golightly and Carrie Bradshaw, New York is a beacon of the material world. Hundreds of creators – both local and international – descend upon the city with alacrity to display their wares, and SoHo is a great place to begin your retail fix. But across the city you'll find dozens of ways to empty your coffers, and at the end of the day shopping in New York isn't about collecting a closet full of items, it's about accessing the city's myriad subcultures through their art and artifacts.

24

The Best... Old-School New York

RUSSIAN & TURKISH BATHS
Steam your stress away in this East Village classic, now more than 120 years old. (p117)

BOATING IN CENTRAL PARK
Bust out your seersucker and parasol for a rowboat hired from Loeb Boathouse. (p226)

BARNEY GREENGRASS
After a century in the business, BG still serves up some of the best smoked fish in the city. (p226)

ZABAR'S
An emporium for Upper West Side foodaholics since the 1930s. (p220)

MCSORLEY'S OLD ALE HOUSE
Abraham Lincoln and Boss Tweed are among the many who've raised a glass at this sawdust-covered pub. (p111)

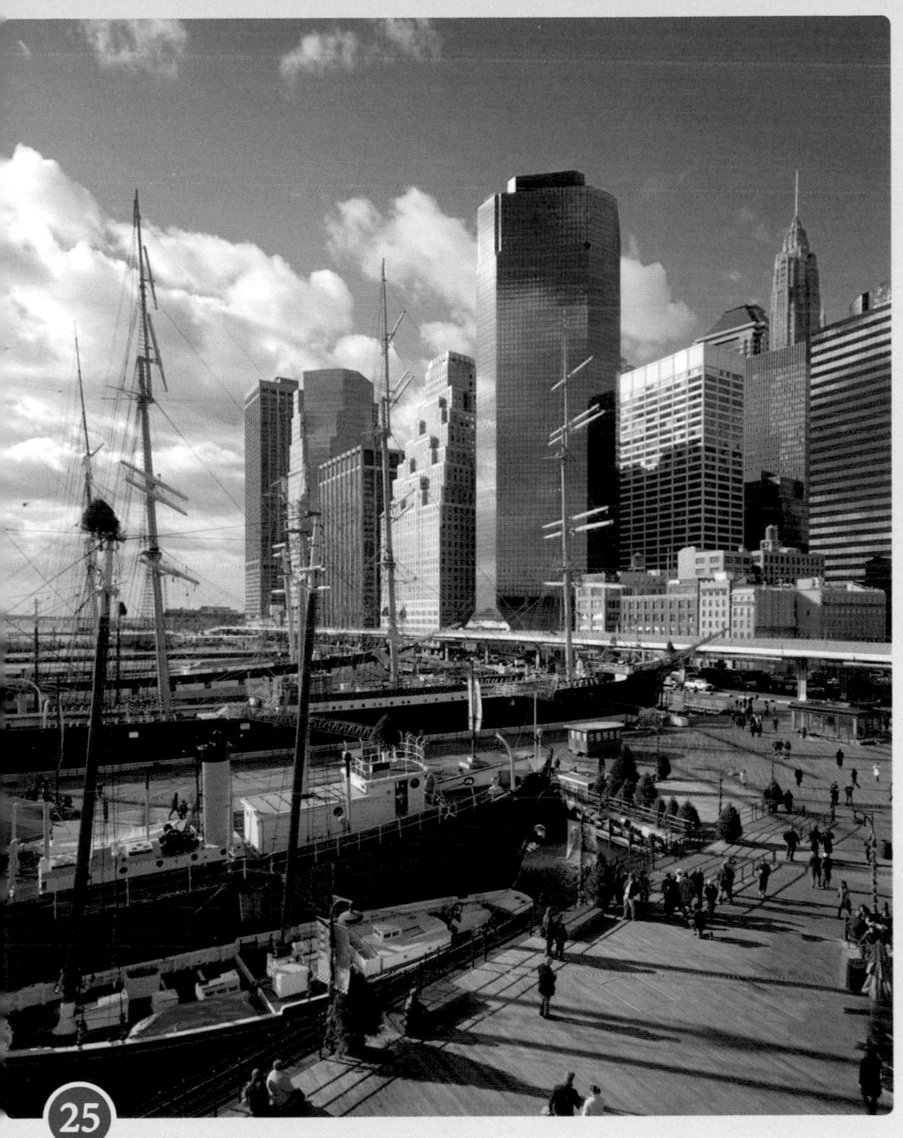

25

New York Harbor (p63)

Step off the island of Manhattan onto a ferry and you'll have a new appreciation for those pedestrian-clogged streets as the city skyline rises slowly into view. Governors Island (p69) makes a fine destination, with new parkland, art exhibitions and peaceful, car-free lanes to stroll or cycle along. You can also hop across to Brooklyn aboard the East River Ferry. The dock near the Brooklyn Bridge Park (p241) makes an excellent entry point to the borough. The free Staten Island Ferry (p71) provides another scenic panorama of the city skyline. Above: South Street Seaport (p64)

Top Days in New York City

Midtown & Uptown Icons

Landmarks, highlights, big-ticket items: on this itinerary you will experience the NYC of everyone's collective imagination, including the city's most famous museum and park. Take in the mythic landscape of Midtown's concrete and skyscrapers, from the street and amid the clouds.

1 Metropolitan Museum of Art (p194)

Start uptown at the big daddy of museums. Check out the Egyptian Wing and the European paintings on the 2nd floor.

METROPOLITAN MUSEUM OF ART ➔ CENTRAL PARK

Walk into Central Park at the 79th St entrance.

2 Central Park (p216)

Get some fresh air in Central Park, the city's spectacular public backyard. Walk south to the Conservatory Pond where toy boats ply the waters.

CENTRAL PARK ➔ TIMES SQUARE

Exit the park on Fifth Ave however far south you'd like, and grab a cab for Times Square.

3 Times Square (p162)

Soak up the Vegas-like atmosphere of Times Square from the TKTS Booth and get discounted tickets for that night. Head to the pedestrian plaza at the southern end where you can take in the dazzling tableau.

TIMES SQUARE ➔ ROCKEFELLER CENTER

For more elbow room walk up Sixth Ave to 49th St.

4 Top of the Rock (p183)

Ride to the open-air observation deck at the Top of the Rock in Rockefeller Center for stunning vistas.

ROCKEFELLER CENTER ➔ MARSEILLE

It's probably quickest to walk crosstown to Ninth Ave at 44th St (or the weary can grab a taxi).

5 Dinner at Marseille (p180)

For Broadway-goers, do an early dinner at this theatrically designed and buzzing French brasserie.

MARSEILLE ➔ BROADWAY THEATER

Walk east to the theater where you've already purchased tickets.

6 Broadway Theater (p184)

Check out a blockbuster musical for an only-in-New-York spectacle. Afterwards, swig cocktails late into the night at the Hotel Edison's restored piano bar, Rum House (p182).

View from the Top of the Rock, Rockefeller Center

DAY 2

Lower Manhattan

Surprisingly for this part of downtown dominated by the canyons of Wall St, this day takes in broad horizons and river views, not to mention an iconic historic sight. This itinerary requires a little planning – book your tickets for the Statue of Liberty and Ellis Island, as well as the 9/11 Memorial, in advance on the websites.

1 Statue of Liberty & Ellis Island (p52)

Time your arrival with your booked ferry's departure. Ellis Island will likely occupy most of the morning, unless you've also arranged a trip to the statue's crown.

ELLIS ISLAND ➔ BATTERY PARK CITY

Walk from Castle Clinton north and west to the riverfront promenade.

2 Battery Park City (p49)

This residential area backed by apartment towers offers unobstructed views of the Hudson River and New Jersey. Grab a bench and watch a parade of runners, office workers and other visitors.

BATTERY PARK CITY ➔ 9/11 MEMORIAL

Walk north until you reach the World Financial Center. Enter the atrium and cross the West Side Hwy through the covered walkway.

3 9/11 Memorial (p48)

This is the former World Trade Center site. Visit the WTC Tribute Visitor Center for photographs, artifacts and a historical context before lining up (online reservations in advance required).

9/11 MEMORIAL ➔ JOE'S SHANGHAI

S Take the N from the Cortlandt St station to Canal St; walk east on Canal and turn south on Mott St. Cross Bayard and turn left on Pell St.

4 Lunch at Joe's Shanghai (p87)

Savor soup dumplings at Joe's Shanghai, a Chinatown staple and Flushing transplant. After lunch, enjoy the neighborhood's bustling streets and Buddhist temples.

JOE'S SHANGHAI ➔ BROOKLYN BRIDGE

Walk south on Bowery and turn west on Worth St and then south again on Centre St; the access road to the bridge is on your left.

5 Brooklyn Bridge (p66)

Join the Brooklynites and hordes of other visitors making this magical pilgrimage on one of the city's most beautiful landmarks.

BROOKLYN BRIDGE ➔ EMPIRE FULTON FERRY STATE PARK

Walk over the bridge from Manhattan to Brooklyn. Take the stairs and turn left at the bottom. Walk downhill to the waterfront.

6 Empire Fulton Ferry State Park (p241)

This lovely park has staggering views of Manhattan, the Brooklyn Bridge and a fully restored 1922 carousel. The atmospheric brick streets behind are sprinkled with cafes, shops and 19th-century warehouses.

EMPIRE FULTON FERRY STATE PARK ➔ JULIANA'S

Walk up Old Fulton St to the corner of Front St.

7 Dinner at Juliana's (p243)

Don't miss the legendary thin-crust pies by famed pizza maestro Patsy Grimaldi. The classic margherita is one of New York's best.

JULIANA'S ➔ VILLAGE VANGUARD

S Walk up Old Fulton St to the High St A train stop. Take the A to W 4th St. Go north on Waverly to Seventh Ave.

8 Village Vanguard (p137)

End your day in the West Village with some of the world's best jazz beats.

Dumplings at Joe's Shanghai

West Side Culture

A famed green way, galleries, market adventures and one spectacular museum set the stage for a fun day's ramble on the West Side. Cap off the day at Lincoln Center, the stunning campus of some of the country's top performance spaces.

DAY 3

1 The High Line (p124)

Take a taxi to the stroll-worthy High Line, an abandoned railway 30ft above the street, now one of New York's favorite downtown destinations. Enter at 30th St and walk the meandering path for views of the Hudson River and city streets below.

THE HIGH LINE ➜ CHELSEA GALLERIES

Exit at the 26th St stairway and explore the surrounding neighborhood on foot.

2 Chelsea Galleries (p138)

One of the hubs of the city's art-gallery scene, here you can ogle works by up-and-comers and established artists alike, and maybe even take home an expensive souvenir. Some of the blue-chip galleries to check out are Gagosian, David Zwirner and Barbara Gladstone.

CHELSEA GALLERIES ➜ CHELSEA MARKET

Walk to Ninth Ave and south to 15th St.

3 Lunch at Chelsea Market (p126)

This building, a former cookie factory, has a huge concourse packed with shops selling fresh-baked goods, wines, vegetables, imported cheeses and other temptations.

CHELSEA MARKET ➜ AMERICAN MUSEUM OF NATURAL HISTORY

S Grab an uptown C train at Eighth Ave and 14th St and take it to 86th and Central Park West.

4 American Museum of Natural History (p227)

No matter what your age, you'll experience childlike wonder at the exceptional American Museum of Natural History. Be sure to save time for the Rose Center for Earth & Space, a unique architectural gem in its own right.

AMERICAN MUSEUM OF NATURAL HISTORY ➜ BARCIBO ENOTECA

Walk west to Amsterdam Ave and turn south; veer left on Broadway at 71st St.

5 Drink at Barcibo Enoteca (p229)

Stop in for a pre-show glass of expertly curated Italian wine, or go for some grub if you're seeing a full-length show.

BARCIBO ENOTECA ➜ LINCOLN CENTER

Walk south on Broadway to 63rd St.

6 Lincoln Center (p229)

Head to the Lincoln Center for opera at the Metropolitan Opera House (p229), the largest in the world, a symphony in Avery Fisher Hall, or a play at one of its two theaters – a promise of a great show in an architecturally mesmerizing setting. Don't miss the choreographed 'water shows' at the plaza fountain.

LINCOLN CENTER ➜ PJ CLARKE'S

Walk 300 paces to 44 W 63rd St and Columbus Ave.

7 PJ Clarke's (p181)

After a show, head across the street to this buzzing gastropub for an enjoyable post-performance dinner (it's open till 2am). Feast on oysters, crab cakes, black Angus steaks, fish and chips and other well-executed pub fare.

The High Line

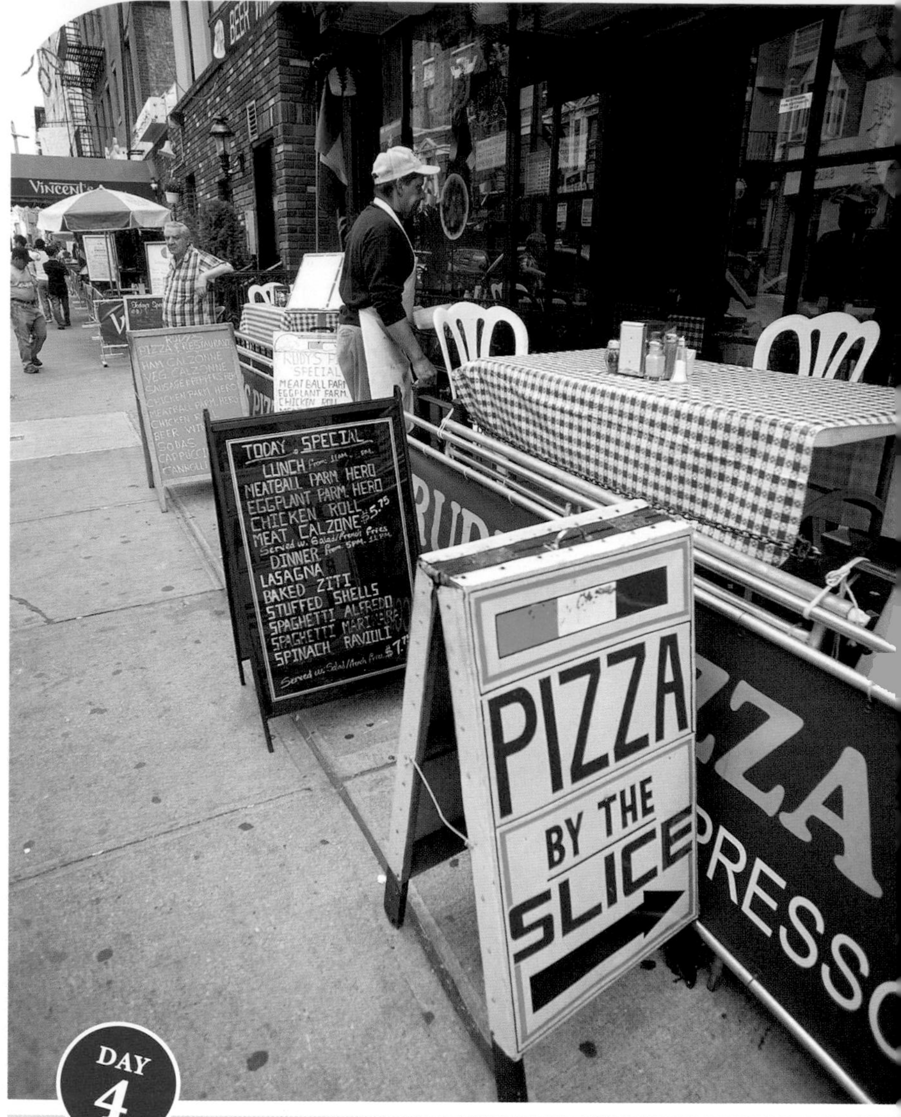

DAY
4

Eastside & Down

Gain insight into immigrant history, grab ethnic eats, check out cutting-edge art and theater as well as cheap booze and live music; walk up and down the tiny blocks and peek into stylish boutiques. As a general rule, the further east you go the looser things get.

1 Lower East Side Tenement Museum (p110)

Gain a fantastic insight into the life and shockingly cramped living conditions of immigrants during the 19th and early 20th centuries at this brilliantly curated museum. Sign up for a walking tour for more thorough exploration.

LOWER EAST SIDE TENEMENT MUSEUM ➲ LITTLE ITALY

Walk west on Delancey St through Sara D Roosevelt Park to Mulberry St.

2 Little Italy (p90)

Although it feels more like a theme park than an authentic Italian strip, Mulberry St is still the heart of the 'hood. Drop into Ferrara Cafe & Bakery (p90) brimming with classic Italian pastries and old-school ambience.

LITTLE ITALY ➲ LA ESQUINA

Walk two blocks east to Centre St and two blocks north to Kenmare.

3 Lunch at La Esquina (p85)

Grab some lunch at this funky and popular Mexican eatery housed in a former old-school diner. Standouts include fish tacos and mango and jicama salads, among other authentic and delicious options.

LA ESQUINA ➲ NEW MUSEUM OF CONTEMPORARY ART

Walk several blocks east to Bowery and turn north.

4 New Museum of Contemporary Art (p103)

Symbolic of the once-gritty Bowery's transformation, this uber contemporary museum has a steady menu of edgy works in new forms. Stop by the bookstore with an eclectic mix of cutting-edge publications.

NEW MUSEUM OF CONTEMPORARY ART ➲ ST MARKS PLACE

Turn right on Houston and then left up Second Ave until you reach 9th St.

5 St Marks Place (p105)

Stroll this famous street past the cheesy T-shirt shops, tattoo parlors, punk-rock stores and sake bars, then head to the neighboring streets for a quieter round of nibbling and boutique-ing.

ST MARKS PLACE ➲ NEW YORK THEATER WORKSHOP

Head to 4th St between Bowery and Second Ave.

6 New York Theater Workshop (p114)

A showcase for contemporary and cutting-edge fare, this much lauded performance space is a great spot to see a show.

NEW YORK THEATER WORKSHOP ➲ KATZ'S DELICATESSEN

Walk or cab it down First Ave to Houston St and turn left two blocks to Ludlow St.

7 Dinner at Katz's Delicatessen (p109)

The quintessential old-school Jewish Lower East Side eatery serves up smoked-meat sandwiches that will please even the biggest *kvetchers* (grumblers).

Restaurants in Little Italy

Month by Month

February

Winter Restaurant Week

Celebrate dreary February with slash-cut meal deals at some of the city's finest eating establishments during New York's Winter Restaurant Week, which actually runs for about three weeks.

Lunar New Year

One of the biggest Chinese New Year (www.explorechinatown.com) celebrations in the country, this display of fireworks and dancing dragons draws mobs of thrill seekers into the streets of Chinatown.

April

Tribeca Film Festival

You'll have to make some tough choices: more than 150 films are screened during the 10-day fest (p70).

May

Cherry Blossom Festival

Held on one weekend in late April or early May, Sakura Matsuri celebrates the magnificent flowering of cherry trees in the Brooklyn Botanic Garden (www.bbg.org).

Fleet Week

For non-swabby visitors, this is a chance to take free tours of ships that have arrived from various corners of the globe. See them docked off Manhattan (around Midtown) and Brooklyn (just south of Brooklyn Bridge Park's pier 6).

June

Puerto Rican Day Parade

The second weekend in June attracts thousands of flag-waving revelers for the annual Puerto Rican Day Parade. Now in its fifth decade, it runs up Fifth Ave from 44th to 86th Sts.

SummerStage

Central Park's SummerStage (p221), which runs from June through August, features an incredible line-up of music and dance throughout the summer.

Gay Pride

June is Gay Pride Month, and it culminates in a major march down Fifth Ave on the last Sunday of the month.

HBO Bryant Park Summer Film Festival

Beginning in June and ending in August, Bryant Park (www.bryantpark.org) hosts Monday-night outdoor screenings of classic Hollywood films, which kick off after sundown.

Mermaid Parade

It's a flash of glitter and glamour, as elaborately

Rockefeller Center's Christmas tree
STEVEN GREAVES/GETTY IMAGES ©

costumed folks display their fishy finery along the Coney Island boardwalk.

July

Independence Day

America's Independence Day is celebrated on the 4th of July with dramatic fireworks and fanfare. The fiery show erupts over either the East River or the Hudson River.

Shakespeare in the Park

The much-loved Shakespeare in the Park (p221) pays tribute to the Bard, with free performances in Central Park. The catch? You'll have to wait hours in line to score tickets, or win them in the online lottery.

August

Fringe Festival

This annual mid-August theater festival (www.fringenyc.org) presents two weeks of performances from companies all over the world.

September

BAM! Next Wave Festival

Celebrated for 30 years in 2012, the Brooklyn Academy of Music's Next Wave Festival (www.bam.org), which runs September through December, showcases world-class avant-garde theater, music and dance.

Electric Zoo

Celebrated over Labor Day Weekend, Electric Zoo (www.electriczoofestival.com) is New York's electronic music festival held in sprawling Randall's Island Park.

October

Open House New York

The country's largest architecture and design event, Open House New York (www.ohny.org) features special, architect-led tours as well as lectures, design workshops, studio visits and site-specific performances all over the city.

Village Halloween Parade

October 31 brings riotous fun to the city, as New Yorkers don their wildest costumes for a night of revelry. See the wildest, most outrageous displays at the Village Halloween Parade (www.halloween-nyc.com) that runs up Sixth Ave in the West Village.

November

NYC Marathon

Held in the first week of November, this annual 26-mile run draws thousands of athletes from around the world, and just as many excited viewers line the streets to cheer the runners on (www.nycmarathon.org).

Macy's Thanksgiving Day Parade

Massive helium-filled balloons soar overhead, high school marching bands rattle their snares and millions of onlookers bundle up with scarves and coats to celebrate Thanks-giving with Macy's (p187) world-famous 2.5-mile-long parade.

Oh, Christmas Tree

The flick of a switch ignites the massive Christmas tree in Rockefeller Center (p183), officially ushering in the holiday season.

December

New Year's Eve

The ultimate place to ring in the New Year in the northern hemisphere, Times Square (p162) swarms with millions of gatherers who come to witness the annual dropping of the ball.

What's New

For this new edition of Discover New York City, our authors hunted down the fresh, the transformed, the hot and the happening. Here are a few of our favorites. For up-to-the-minute recommendations, see lonelyplanet.com/usa/new-york-city.

1 BROOKLYN PRIDE
If you haven't heard, the Brooklyn renaissance is well under way. This epicenter of creativity boasts some of the city's best locavore-loving restaurants, cocktail bars, artisan shops and coffee roasters; it even has a buzzing new hotel scene. Brooklyn now has a pro basketball team (the Nets), a grand arena and new theaters and cultural spaces. (p240)

2 REMEMBERING SEPTEMBER 11
Within the memorial grounds of the World Trade Center site, the National September 11 Museum delves into the tragic events that forever changed NYC. (p56)

3 LESLIE-LOHMAN MUSEUM OF GAY & LESBIAN ART
This SoHo gem, which gained its museum charter in 2011 is finally poised to draw in the crowds. It's the first LGBT-specific art museum in the world. (p81)

4 THE COFFEE SCENE
Artisanal roasters and celebrated coffee makers have opened shop, transforming NYC's once humble java scene. Kaffe 1668 and La Colombe are fine starting points on the caffeinated odyssey. (p68)

5 QUEENS IS BACK
After a $70-million renovation, the Queens Museum is back – bigger and better than ever. It's quickly becoming an icon of NY's most ethnically diverse borough. (p248)

6 GOVERNORS ISLAND PARK
A new 30-acre park has been added to the wonderful car-free island in New York's harbor, bringing a hammock grove, ball fields, a formal garden and climbable play areas for kids. (p69)

7 FRANKLIN D ROOSEVELT FOUR FREEDOMS PARK
On Roosevelt Island, Louis Kahn's arresting memorial pays homage to one of America's greatest presidents. Striking skyline views link FDR with the UN, one of his most visible achievements. (p206)

8 ONE WORLD TRADE CENTER
The soaring, 104-story icon – costing some $4 billion, and eight years in the making – has at last arrived. Its observation deck should open in early 2015. (p57)

9 HIGH LINE 3.0
The celebrated green space opens its final section in late 2014, bringing a lush new design courtesy of Diller Scofidio + Renfro. Up next? The $15-billion commercial development of the Hudson Yards, adjoining the final section. (p124)

10 GREENER DAYS IN BROOKLYN
The magnificent 1.3-mile-long Brooklyn Bridge Park, with its staggering views of Manhattan, has transformed a once inaccessible waterfront into a green oasis. (p241)

Get Inspired

 Books

Go Tell It on the Mountain (James Baldwin) A lyrical novel of a day in the life of a 14-year-old set in Depression-era Harlem.

Bonfire of the Vanities (Tom Wolfe) A gripping novel of an uptown investment banker's entanglement with the black South Bronx.

Fortress of Solitude (Jonathan Lethem) A ballad to the Brooklyn streets and a lyrical journey into race relations and pop culture from the 1970s to the '90s.

Lush Life (Richard Price) A pitch-perfect exploration of the conflict between project residents and interloping hipsters.

 Films

Taxi Driver Martin Scorsese's film is a reminder of how much grittier NYC used to be.

Saturday Night Fever John Travolta is the hottest thing in bell bottoms in this tale of a streetwise Brooklyn kid.

Manhattan A divorced New Yorker falls for his best friend's mistress in what is essentially a Woody Allen love letter to NYC.

American Gangster A Harlem-based drug drama, inspired by a true story.

♫ Music

Autumn In New York (Billie Holiday) Why *does* it seem so inviting?

Walk on the Wild Side (Lou Reed) Groovy 1972 classic from NY's good ol' days of hustlers, drugs, transsexualism and street life.

Empire State of Mind (Jay Z) An instant classic – 'These streets will make you feel...'

Lullaby of Broadway (*42nd Street* musical-cast recording) A timeless favorite capturing all the hip-hooray and ballyhoo.

 Websites

New York Magazine (www.nymag.com) Comprehensive current listings for bars, restaurants, entertainment and shopping.

Time Out (www.timeout.com/newyork) Exhaustive event listings for art, theater, music, restaurants and more.

Gothamist (www.gothamist.com) Keen insight into everything New York.

Short on time?

This list will give you an instant insight into New York.

Read Dip into any chapter of *Gotham: A History of New York City to 1898*, a hugely entertaining, Pulitzer prize–winning tome.

Watch Cary Grant and Deborah Kerr make a pact to seal their love atop the Empire State Building in *An Affair to Remember*.

Listen Frank Sinatra's 'New York, New York' is the ultimate manifesto of NYC exceptionalism.

Log on For comprehensive tourist information check out NYC: The Official Guide (www.nycgo.com).

Wall mural in Harlem (p236)

BARRY WINIKER/GETTY IMAGES ©

Need to Know

Currency
US dollar (US$)

Language
English

Visas
Thirty-seven countries have a visa-waiver agreement with the US (see http://travel.state.gov); citizens of these countries can enter for stays of 90 days or less.

Cell Phones
Most US cell phones, apart from the iPhone, operate on CDMA, not the European standard GSM; check compatibility with your provider.

Time
Eastern Standard Time (GMT/UTC minus five hours)

Wi-Fi
Many cafes, restaurants, public parks and public libraries offer free wi-fi. Most hotels have wi-fi, though some charge per hour.

Tipping
In restaurants tip at least 15% unless the service is terrible; in taxis tip around 10%.

For more information, see Survival Guide (p280).

When to Go

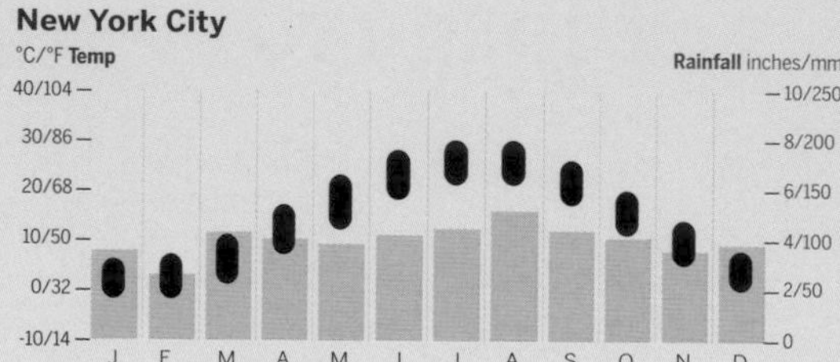

Spring (March–May) Brings blossoming trees.

Summer (June–August) Free cultural events but it can be beastly hot.

Winter (December–February) Buildings are festooned with lights; you'll get snow, sleet and cold.

Advance Planning

Two months before Book your hotel reservations as soon as possible. Snag tickets to a Broadway blockbuster.

Three weeks before Score a table at your favorite high-end restaurant.

One week before Surf the web for the latest openings. Join email news blasts as well.

Your Daily Budget

Budget less than $100

- Dorm bed at Chelsea Hostel $40–70
- Pizza slice around $2.50
- Walking the High Line (free)
- Drinks at an East Village dive bar $4

Midrange $100–$300

- Affordable digs at Chelsea Lodge from $140
- Brunch for two at Cafe Mogador $65–90
- Two cocktails at speakeasy-style Death + Co $32
- A discount TKTS ticket to a Broadway show from $80

Top end more than $300

- Luxury stay at the Gramercy Park Hotel $350–$800
- Dinner for two at RedFarm $120–160
- Metropolitan Opera orchestra seats $100–$390

Arriving in New York City

John F Kennedy International Airport (JFK) The AirTrain ($5) links to the subway ($2.50) or speedier LIRR, which goes to Penn Station ($7 to $10). Shared vans to Manhattan are $20 to $25. Taxis cost a flat rate of $52 excluding tolls and tip.

LaGuardia Airport (LGA) Taxis range from $26 to $48 (excluding tolls and tip) depending on traffic. Express bus to Midtown costs $13. By bus, take the Q70 express bus to the 74th St-Broadway subway station.

Newark Liberty International Airport (EWR) Take the AirTrain to Newark Airport rail station, and board any train bound for New York's Penn Station ($12.50). Express bus to Port Authority or Grand Central costs $16. Shared shuttles to Midtown cost $20 to $26. Taxis range from $60 to $80 (excluding the unavoidable $13 toll and tip).

Getting Around

Check out the **Metropolitan Transportation Authority** (www.mta.info) website for public transportation information (buses and subway), including a handy travel planner and regular notifications of delays.

- **Walking** New York, down deep, can't be seen until you've taken the time to hit the sidewalks. Crossing the East River over the Brooklyn Bridge is a New York classic, and Central Park trails can get you to wooded pockets.
- **Subway** It's inexpensive, mostly efficient and open around the clock, though it can be confusing to the uninitiated. A single ride is $2.50 with a MetroCard ($1). A 7-Day Unlimited Pass costs $30.
- **Taxi** Meters start at $2.50 and increase roughly $4 for every 20 blocks. Look for one with its roof light illuminated – this means it's available.
- **Cycling** Use one of Citi Bike's 330 stations for a speedy 30-minute jaunt across town. Pedaling on the sidewalk is illegal.
- **Ferries** The free Staten Island Ferry runs from Lower Manhattan. The more useful East River Ferry travels between Lower Manhattan and E 34th St stopping in Brooklyn and Queens.
- **Buses** Slow but scenic. Useful for getting 'crosstown' (going east–west or west–east). Same price as the subway (use a MetroCard).

Sleeping

In general, accommodation prices in New York City do not abide by any high-season or low-season rules; wavering rates usually reflect availability. With more than 50 million tourists visiting annually, you can expect that hotel rooms fill up quickly – especially in summer.

Useful Websites

- **newyorkhotels.com** (www.newyorkhotels.com) The self-proclaimed official website for hotels in NYC.
- **airbnb** (www.airbnb.com) Choose furnished apartments or rooms in a New Yorker's house.
- **Jetsetter** (www.jetsetter.com) Sales on luxury NYC hotels.

What to Bring

- **Walking shoes** Get on your feet and go green. New York City's streets, like Nancy Sinatra's boots, are made for walking.
- **Extra suitcase** To bring home all the newly bought goodies – from fashion-forward clothes to that kitschy Times Square snow globe.
- **Swanky clothing** Dress to the nines for a night out at the opera or a five-star dining room.

Be Forewarned

- **Public restrooms** Few and far between; your best bet is to pop into a Starbucks.
- **Restaurants** Large parties will have trouble getting seated without reservations.
- **Subways** Because of constant track work, weekend schedule changes are confusing.

Citi Bikes

To use a Citi Bike, here's how it works: purchase a 24-hour or seven-day access pass (around $11 or $28 including tax) at any Citi Bike kiosk. You will then be given a five-digit code to unlock a bike. Return the bike to any station within 30 minutes to avoid extra fees. Reinsert your credit card (you won't be charged) and follow the prompts to check out a bike again. You can make an unlimited number of 30-minute check-outs during those 24 hours or seven days.

I ♥ NY

Lower Manhattan & the Financial District

This area packs in a diverse wallop of sights. The borough comes to a pencil point at its southern tip, forming the general swath known as Lower Manhattan. This area is teeming with iconic sights that include the National September 11 Memorial, Wall St, the Brooklyn Bridge and City Hall and, offshore in the near distance, the Statue of Liberty.

The area has come back to life slowly and surely, despite seriously delayed redevelopment plans related to the former World Trade Center site. The whole area, in fact, has gone through a recent renaissance, bringing newness in many forms – museums, hotels and trendy restaurants – which has in turn lured more and more visitors. Add those elements to the area's geographic narrowness – waterfront parks and sweeping views are an intimate part of the fabric here – and you've got quite a lively little city corner.

National September 11 Memorial
ANADOLU AGENCY/GETTY IMAGES ©

Lower Manhattan & the Financial District Highlights

Walking the Brooklyn Bridge (p66)

The Brooklyn Bridge pedestrian walkway begins just east of City Hall and affords a wonderful view of Lower Manhattan. Observation points offer histories of the waterfront. Take care to stay on the side of the walkway marked for folks on foot – frustrated cyclists, who use it en masse for commuting and pleasure, have been known to get nasty with oblivious tourists.

1

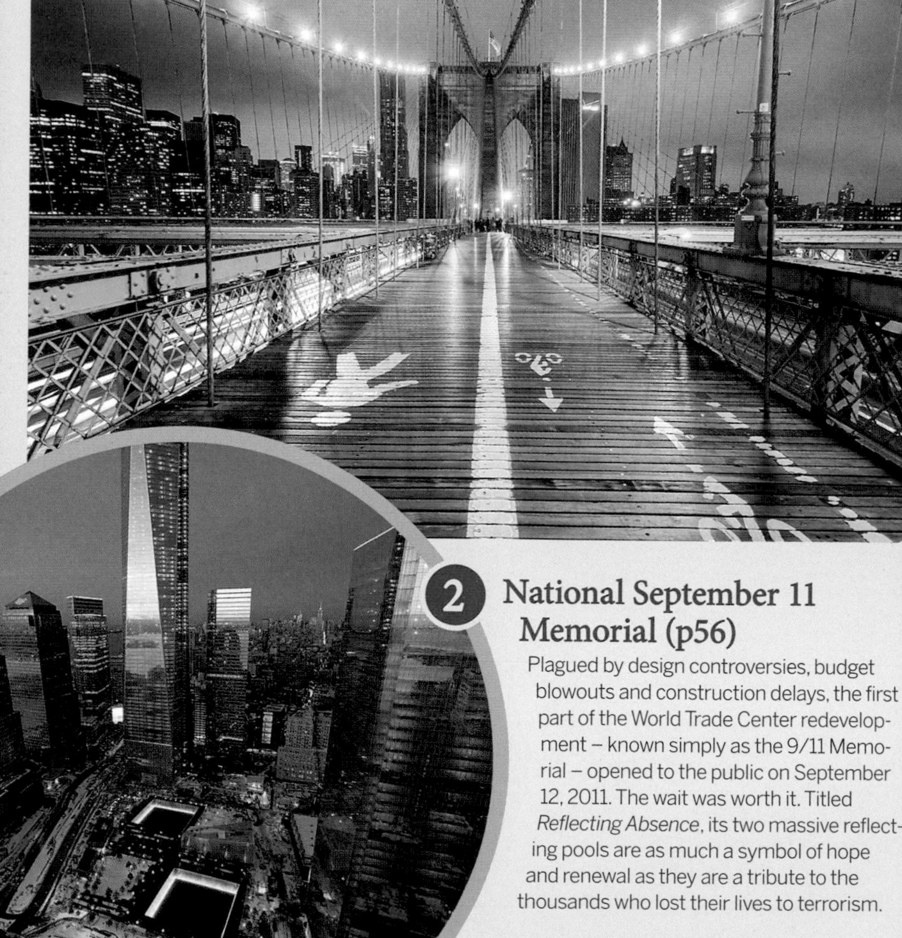

ANDREW C MACE/GETTY IMAGES ©

2 National September 11 Memorial (p56)

Plagued by design controversies, budget blowouts and construction delays, the first part of the World Trade Center redevelopment – known simply as the 9/11 Memorial – opened to the public on September 12, 2011. The wait was worth it. Titled *Reflecting Absence*, its two massive reflecting pools are as much a symbol of hope and renewal as they are a tribute to the thousands who lost their lives to terrorism.

TONY SHI PHOTOGRAPHY/GETTY IMAGES ©

NIMU1956/GETTY IMAGES ©

Battery Park City (p63)

There's a surreal sense to this corner of the city, its clutch of gleaming, modern high-rises and lovely promenades and parks cut off from the rest of town. Its position at sunset makes it feel like the hovering towers are quietly aglow. By day, you can find peace here, thanks to the 30-acre waterfront stretch of parkland along the Hudson River, making it one of downtown's great opportunities for escape.

3

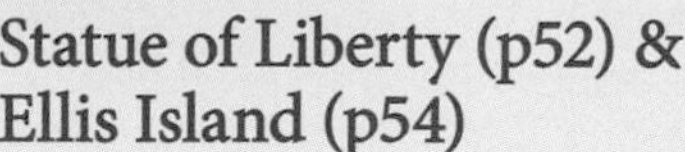

GLOW IMAGES, INC/GETTY IMAGES ©

4

Statue of Liberty (p52) & Ellis Island (p54)

No place in America has quite the same power to evoke the immigrant experience. These neighboring islands are home to two of NYC's historic treasures. The boat ride and long lines are all part of the experience – just a taste of what the immigrants endured. Take your time exploring, as you contemplate the monumental journey from old world into new.

5

Wall Street (p58)

Both an actual street and the metaphorical home of US commerce, Wall St is named for the wooden barrier built by Dutch settlers in 1653 to protect New Amsterdam from Native Americans and the British. Though the New York Stock Exchange (p59) has been closed to visitors indefinitely, tourists still gather on the sidewalk to gawk at harried traders who scurry out for cigarettes and food.

Lower Manhattan & the Financial District Walk

Anchored by the mile-long and world-famous Wall St and the reborn World Trade Center site, this area is steeped in history.

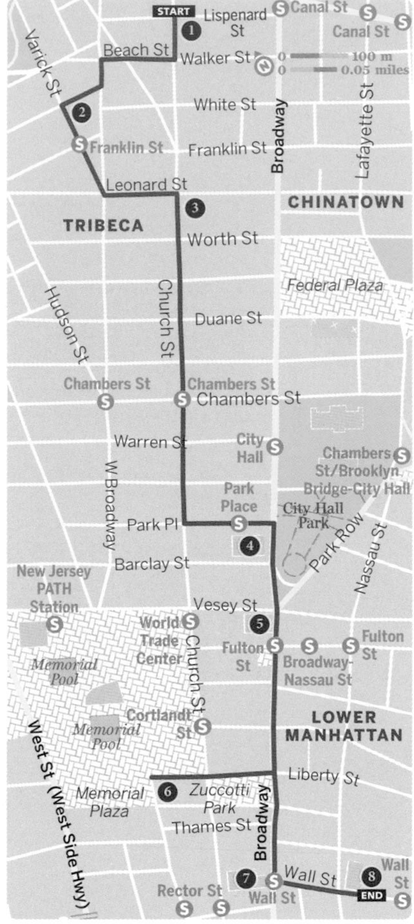

WALK FACTS

- **Start** La Colombe
- **End** Wall St
- **Distance** 2.5 miles
- **Duration** 2½ to three hours

❶ La Colombe

Start with coffee at La Colombe (p68). In the 19th century, the site was a stop on the antislavery 'underground railway,' a secret network of routes and safe houses allowing African Americans to reach free states and Canada. A plaque on the Lispenard St side of the building commemorates the fact.

❷ 8 Hook & Ladder

Further west, the intersection of Varick and N Moore Sts is where you'll find 8 Hook & Ladder, better known as ghost-control headquarters in '80s film *Ghostbusters*.

❸ Textile Building

Continue south on Varick St, turn left into Leonard St and stop at the intersection with Church St. On the southeast corner stands the Textile Building, built in 1901. Its architect, Henry J Hardenbergh, would go on to design Midtown's monumental Plaza Hotel.

❹ Woolworth Building

Head further south on Church St, turning left into Park Pl and right into Broadway. Before you is the neo-Gothic Woolworth Building (p65), which was the world's tallest skyscraper upon its completion in 1913. Security is tight, but you can usually poke your head in to inspect the opulent lobby and blue-and-gold-tiled ceiling.

❺ St Paul's Chapel

Heading south on Broadway, cross Vesey St and you'll see St Paul's Chapel (p59) on your right – it's the only pre–Revolutionary War church left intact in the city.

6 National September 11 Memorial & Museum

Walk up to Liberty St and head west to the memorial site. The museum (p56) houses artifacts relating to the 2001 terrorist attacks, while the memorial itself features two giant reflecting pools set in the footprints of the collapsed towers. Soaring above them is the 1776ft One World Trade Center, America's tallest skyscraper.

7 Trinity Church

Further south on Broadway, Trinity Church (p59) was the city's tallest building upon completion in 1846 and its peaceful cemetery is the final resting place of steamboat inventor Robert Fulton. Designed by English architect Richard Upjohn, the church helped launch the picturesque neo-Gothic movement in America.

8 Wall Street

Head east onto Wall St, home of the New York Stock Exchange (p59) and the Federal Hall (p59). You can visit the latter, in which John Peter Zenger was acquitted of seditious libel in 1735 – the first step, historians say, in establishing a democracy committed to a free press. Just across the street at the southeast corner of Wall and Broad Sts is the former headquarters of the JP Morgan Bank. Examine the pockmarks on its limestone facade on the Wall St side – they're the remnants of the 1920 Morgan Bank bombing.

The Best...

PLACES TO EAT

Locanda Verde Simple and relaxed urban Italian. (p67)

Les Halles Meat lovers head downtown to this Anthony Bourdain–owned restaurant. (p67)

North End Grill Danny Meyer's American grill serves up delectable fare. (p67)

PLACES TO DRINK

Macao Downstairs den with eclectic global decor and seriously delicious cocktails. (p69)

Dead Rabbit First-rate cocktails in a fun, vintage-laden setting. (p68)

Ward III Old-school ambiance and top-notch bar grub. (p69)

Weather Up Effortlessly cool. (p68)

PLACES TO TRACE HISTORY

Federal Hall Site where George Washington took the oath of office as first US president. (p59)

Trinity Church Originally founded by King William III. (p59)

St Paul's Chapel George Washington worshipped here. (p59)

Fraunces Tavern Museum Time-travel back to the 18th century. (p58)

Trinity Church

Don't Miss
Statue of Liberty

Lady Liberty has been gazing sternly across the waters to 'unenlightened Europe' since 1886. Dubbed the 'Mother of Exiles,' the statue serves as an admonishment to the rigid social structures of the old world. 'Give me your tired, your poor, Your huddled masses yearning to breathe free, The wretched refuse of your teeming shore. Send these, the homeless, tempest-tost to me, I lift my lamp beside the golden door!' she declares in Emma Lazarus' famous 1883 poem 'The New Colossus.' These famous words were added to the statue's base only in 1903, more than 15 years after the poet's death.

Map p60

☎877-523-9849

www.nps.gov/stli

Liberty Island

adult/child incl Ellis Island $17/9, incl crown & Ellis Island $20/12

⏲9.30am-5.30pm, check website for seasonal changes

S 1 to South Ferry, 4/5 to Bowling Green

Visiting Lady Liberty

Folks who reserve their tickets in advance are able to climb the (steep) 354 steps to Lady Liberty's crown, from where the city and harbor are breathtaking. That said, crown access is extremely limited, and the only way in is to reserve your spot in advance; the further in advance you can do it, the better, as a six-month lead time is allowed. Each customer may only reserve a maximum of four crown tickets, and children must be at least 4ft tall to access the crown.

If you miss out on crown tickets, you may have better luck with tickets to the pedestal, which also offers commanding views. Like crown tickets, pedestal tickets are limited and should be reserved in advance, either online or by phone. Only crown and pedestal ticket holders have access to the Statue of Liberty museum in the pedestal.

If you don't have crown or pedestal tickets, don't fret. All ferry tickets to Liberty Island offer basic access to the grounds, including guided ranger tours or self-guided audio tours. The grounds also host a gift shop and cafeteria. (Tip: Bring your own snacks and enjoy them by the water, the Manhattan skyline stretched out before you.)

Creating the Lady

One of America's most powerful symbols of kinship and freedom, 'Liberty Enlightening the World' was a joint effort between America and France to commemorate the centennial of the Declaration of Independence. It was created by commissioned sculptor Frédéric-Auguste Bartholdi. The artist spent most of 20 years turning his dream – to create the hollow monument and mount it in the New York Harbor – into reality. Along the way it was hindered by serious financial problems, but was helped in part by the fund-raising efforts of newspaper publisher Joseph Pulitzer. Lending a further hand was poet Emma Lazarus, whose aforementioned ode to Lady Liberty was part of a fund-raising campaign for the statue's pedestal, designed by American architect Richard Morris Hunt. Bartholdi's work on the statue was also delayed by structural challenges – a problem resolved by the metal framework mastery of railway engineer Gustave Eiffel (of, yes, the famous tower). The work of art was finally completed in France in 1884 (a bit off schedule for that centennial). It was shipped to NYC as 350 pieces packed into 214 crates, reassembled over a span of four months and placed on a US-made granite pedestal. Its spectacular October 1886 dedication included New York's first ticker-tape parade, and a flotilla of almost 300 vessels. Put under the administration of the National Park Service in 1933, a restoration of the Lady's oxidized copper began in 1984, the same year the monument made it onto the UN's list of World Heritage Sites.

Need to Know

Although the ferry ride from Battery Park in Lower Manhattan lasts only 15 minutes, a trip to both the Statue of Liberty and Ellis Island is an all-day affair, and only those setting out on the ferry by 1pm will be allowed to visit both sites. Security screening at the ferry terminal can take up to 90 minutes. Reservations to visit the grounds and pedestal are strongly recommended, as they give you a specific visit time and a guarantee you'll get in.

Don't Miss
Ellis Island

Ellis Island is America's most famous and historically important gateway – the very spot where old-world despair met new-world promise. Between 1892 and 1954, more than 12 million immigrants passed through this processing station, their dreams in tow. Among them were Hungarian Erik Weisz (Harry Houdini), Rodolfo Guglielmi (Rudolph Valentino) and British Archibald Alexander Leach (Cary Grant). An estimated 40% of Americans today have at least one ancestor who was processed here, confirming the major role this tiny harbor island has played in the making of modern America.

Map p60

212-363-3200

www.nps.gov/elis

admission free, ferry incl Statue of Liberty adult/child $17/9

9.30am-5.30pm, check website for seasonal changes

S 1 to South Ferry, 4/5 to Bowling Green

Main Building Architecture

After a $160 million restoration, the center was reopened to the public in 1990. Now anybody who rides the ferry to the island can experience a cleaned-up, modern version of the historic new-arrival experience at the impressive Immigration Museum, whose interactive exhibits pay homage to the hope, jubilation and sometimes bitter disappointment of the millions who came here in search of a new beginning.

With their Main Building, architects Edward Lippincott Tilton and William A Boring created a suitably impressive and imposing 'prologue' to America. The designing duo won the contract after the original wooden building burnt down in 1897. The building evokes a grand train station, with majestic triple-arched entrances, decorative Flemish bond brickwork, and granite quoins (cornerstones) and belvederes. Inside, it's the second-floor, 338ft-long Registry Room (also known as the Great Hall) that takes the breath away. It was under this beautiful vaulted ceiling that the newly arrived lined up to have their documents checked, and that the polygamists, paupers, criminals and anarchists were turned back. The original plaster ceiling was severely damaged by an explosion of munition barges at nearby Black Tom Wharf. It was a blessing in disguise – the rebuilt version was adorned with striking, herringbone-patterned tiles by Rafael Guastavino.

Immigration Museum Exhibits

The three-level Immigration Museum is a poignant tribute to the immigrant experience. To get the most out of your visit, opt for the 50-minute self-guided audio tour ($8, available from the museum lobby). Featuring narratives from a number of sources, including historians, architects and the immigrants themselves, the tour brings to life the museum's hefty collection of personal objects, official documents, photographs and film footage. It's an evocative experience to relive personal memories – both good and bad – in the very halls and corridors in which they occurred.

The collection itself is divided into a number of permanent and temporary exhibitions. On the second floor you'll find two of the most fascinating exhibitions. The first, 'Through America's Gate,' examines the step-by-step process faced by the newly arrived, including the chalk-marking of those suspected of illness, a wince-inducing eye examination, and 29 questions in the beautiful, vaulted Registry Room. The second must-see exhibition, 'Peak Immigration Years,' explores the motives behind the immigrants' journeys and the challenges they faced once they were free to begin their new American lives. For a history of the rise, fall and resurrection of the building itself, make time for the 'Restoring a Landmark' exhibition on the third floor; its tableaux of trashed desks, chairs and other abandoned possessions are strangely haunting. Best of all, the audio tour offers optional, in-depth coverage for those wanting to delve deeper into the collections and the island's history.

Need to Know

To be sure you get onto a ferry, you should make advance reservations. However, if you're not one for planning in advance, you can take your chances by going for one of a limited number of time passes available to walkups on a first-come-first-served basis. During the especially busy summer months, there is a less crowded approach to Ellis Island, via ferry from New Jersey's Liberty State Park. If you plan on exploring the museum in detail, set aside a good three hours.

Don't Miss

National September 11 Memorial & Museum

After years of delays, the National September [illegible]um has finally opened to [illegible]ing reflecting pools are as much a symbol of hope and renewal as they are a tribute to the thousands who lost their lives to terrorism. Beside them stands the state-of-the-art Memorial Museum, a solemn space documenting that tragic day in 2001.

Map p60

www.911memorial.org

cnr Greenwich & Albany Sts

admission $24

9am-8pm Mon-Sun, to 7pm winter

S A/C/E to Chambers St, R to Rector St, 2/3 to Park Pl

Reflecting Pools

Surrounded by a plaza planted with 400 swamp white oak trees, the National September 11 Memorial's reflecting pools occupy the very footprints of the ill-fated twin towers. From their rim, a steady cascade of water pours 30ft down towards a central void. The flow of the water is richly symbolic, beginning as hundreds of smaller streams, merging into a massive torrent of collective confusion, and ending with a slow journey towards an abyss. Bronze panels frame the pools, inscribed with the names of those who died in the terrorist attacks of September 11, 2001, and in the World Trade Center car bombing on February 26, 1993. Designed by Michael Arad and Peter Walker, the pools are both striking and deeply poignant.

Memorial Museum

The contemplative energy of the monument is further enhanced by the **National September 11 Memorial Museum** (www.911memorial.org/museum). Standing between the reflective pools, the museum's glass entrance pavilion subtly, yet eerily, evokes a toppled tower. Inside, a gently sloping ramp leads to the museum's subterranean exhibition galleries. On the descent, visitors stand in the shadow of two 70ft high steel tridents, originally embedded in the bedrock at the base of the North Tower. Looking like giant, rusty forks, these scorched survivors are but two of many artifacts that bear silent witness to the attacks. Among them is the so-called 'survivors staircase', used by hundreds of workers to flee the WTC site. There's the last steel column removed from the clean-up, adorned with the messages and mementos of recovery workers, responders and loved ones of the victims. And then there's the New York City Fire Department's Engine Company 21, its burnt out cab a piercing testament to the inferno faced by those at the scene.

One World Trade Center

Soaring skywards at the northwest corner of the WTC site is architect David M Childs' 104-floor **One World Trade Center** (Vesey St), pictured below, third building from the left – a redesign of Daniel Libeskind's original 2002 concept. Not only the loftiest building in America, this tapered giant is currently the tallest building in the Western Hemisphere, not to mention the fourth tallest in the world by pinnacle height. Topped by a cable-stayed antenna co-designed by sculptor Kenneth Snelson, the building's total height of 1776ft is a symbolic reference to the year of American independence. Symbolism feeds several aspects of the building: the tower's footprint is equal to those of the original towers, while the observation decks will match the heights of those in the destroyed buildings. Scheduled to open to the public in 2015, these observation decks will span floors 100 to 102, delivering unparalleled 360-degree views. Unlike the original towers, however, One WTC was built with a whole new level of safety in mind, its precautionary features including a 200ft-high blast-resistant base and 1m-thick concrete walls encasing all elevators, stairwells, and communication and safety systems. One thing that wasn't foreseen by the architects and engineers was the antenna's noisy disposition: the strong winds that race through its lattice design producing a haunting, howling sound known to keep locals up at night.

Angel of 9/11

One of the Memorial Museum's most curious (and famous) artifacts is the so-called 'Angel of 9/11', the eerie outline of a woman's anguished face on a twisted girder believed to originate from the point where American Airlines Flight 11 slammed into the North Tower. Experts have a more prosaic explanation: natural corrosion and sheer coincidence.

Discover Lower Manhattan & the Financial District

Getting There & Away

- **Subway** The Financial District is well serviced by subway lines, connecting the area to the rest of Manhattan, Brooklyn, Queens and the Bronx. Fulton St is the main interchange station, servicing the A/C, J/Z, 2/3 and 4/5 lines. The 1 train terminates at South Ferry, from where the Staten Island Ferry departs.
- **Boat** The Staten Island Ferry Terminal is at the southern end of Whitehall St. Ferries to Governors Island leave from the adjacent Battery Maritime Building. Services to Liberty and Ellis Islands depart from nearby Battery Park.

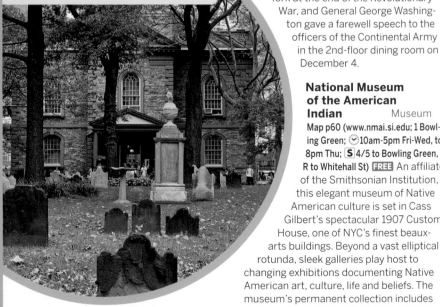

St Paul's Chapel
KEVIN CLOGSTOUN/GETTY IMAGES ©

Sights

Wall Street & the Financial District

National September 11 Memorial & Museum (p56)

Fraunces Tavern Museum Museum
Map p60 (www.frauncestavernmuseum.org; 54 Pearl St, btwn Broad St & Coenties Slip; adult/child $7/free; noon-5pm; S J/Z to Broad St, 4/5 to Bowling Green) Combining five early-18th-century structures, this unique museum/restaurant/bar combo pays homage to the nation-shaping events of 1783, when the British relinquished control of New York at the end of the Revolutionary War, and General George Washington gave a farewell speech to the officers of the Continental Army in the 2nd-floor dining room on December 4.

National Museum of the American Indian Museum
Map p60 (www.nmai.si.edu; 1 Bowling Green; 10am-5pm Fri-Wed, to 8pm Thu; S 4/5 to Bowling Green, R to Whitehall St) FREE An affiliate of the Smithsonian Institution, this elegant museum of Native American culture is set in Cass Gilbert's spectacular 1907 Custom House, one of NYC's finest beaux-arts buildings. Beyond a vast elliptical rotunda, sleek galleries play host to changing exhibitions documenting Native American art, culture, life and beliefs. The museum's permanent collection includes stunning decorative arts, textiles and ceremonial objects that document the diverse native cultures across the Americas.

Trinity Church Church

Map p60 (www.trinitywallstreet.org; Broadway at Wall St; church 7am-6pm Mon-Fri, 8am-4pm Sat, 7am-4pm Sun, churchyard 7am-4pm Mon-Fri, 8am-3pm Sat, 7am-3pm Sun; S R to Rector St; 2/3, 4/5 to Wall St) New York City's tallest building upon completion in 1846, Trinity Church features a 280ft-high bell tower, an arresting stained-glass window over the altar, and a small museum of historical church artifacts. Famous residents of its serene cemetery include Founding Father Alexander Hamilton, while its excellent music series includes Concerts at One (1pm Thursdays) and magnificent choir concerts, including an annual December rendition of Handel's *Messiah*.

St Paul's Chapel Church

Map p60 (www.trinitywallstreet.org; Broadway at Fulton St; 10am-6pm Mon-Fri, to 4pm Sat, 8am-4pm Sun; S A/C, J/Z, 2/3, 4/5 to Fulton St) Despite George Washington worshipping here after his inauguration in 1789, this classic revival brownstone chapel found new fame in the aftermath of September 11. With the World Trade Center destruction occurring just a block away, the mighty structure became a spiritual support and volunteer center, movingly documented in its exhibition 'Unwavering Spirit: Hope & Healing at Ground Zero.'

Federal Hall Museum

Map p60 (www.nps.gov/feha; 26 Wall St, entrance on Pine St; 9am-5pm Mon-Fri; S J/Z to Broad St, 2/3, 4/5 to Wall St) FREE A Greek Revival masterpiece, Federal Hall houses a museum dedicated to postcolonial New York. Themes include George Washington's inauguration, Alexander Hamilton's relationship with the city, and the struggles of John Peter Zenger – jailed, tried and acquitted of libel here for exposing government corruption in his newspaper. There's also a visitor information hall which covers downtown cultural happenings.

New York Stock Exchange Notable Building

Map p60 (www.nyse.com; 11 Wall St; closed to the public; S J/Z to Broad St, 2/3, 4/5 to Wall St) Home to the world's best-known stock exchange (the NYSE), Wall Street is an iconic symbol of US capitalism. About one billion shares change hands daily behind the portentous Romanesque facade, a sight no longer accessible to the

Blast from the Past

If you wander past the former headquarters of JP Morgan Bank on the southeast corner of Wall and Broad Sts, take a minute to examine its limestone facade on the Wall St side. The pockmarks you see are the remnants of the so-called Morgan Bank bombing – America's deadliest terrorist attack until the Oklahoma City bombing of 1995.

The fateful day was Thursday, September 16, 1920, when at exactly 12.01pm, 500 pounds of lead sash weights and 100 pounds of dynamite exploded from a horse-drawn carriage. Thirty-eight people were killed and around 400 injured. Among the latter was John F Kennedy's father, Joseph P Kennedy.

The bomb's detonation outside America's most influential financial institution at the time led many to blame anticapitalist groups, from Italian anarchists to stock-standard Bolsheviks. Yet the crime has yet to be solved, with the decision to reopen both the bank and New York Stock Exchange the following day leading to a swift clean-up of both debris and vital clues. Almost 100 years on, the shrapnel marks remain, purposely left by banker Jack Morgan as an act of remembrance and defiance.

Lower Manhattan & the Financial District

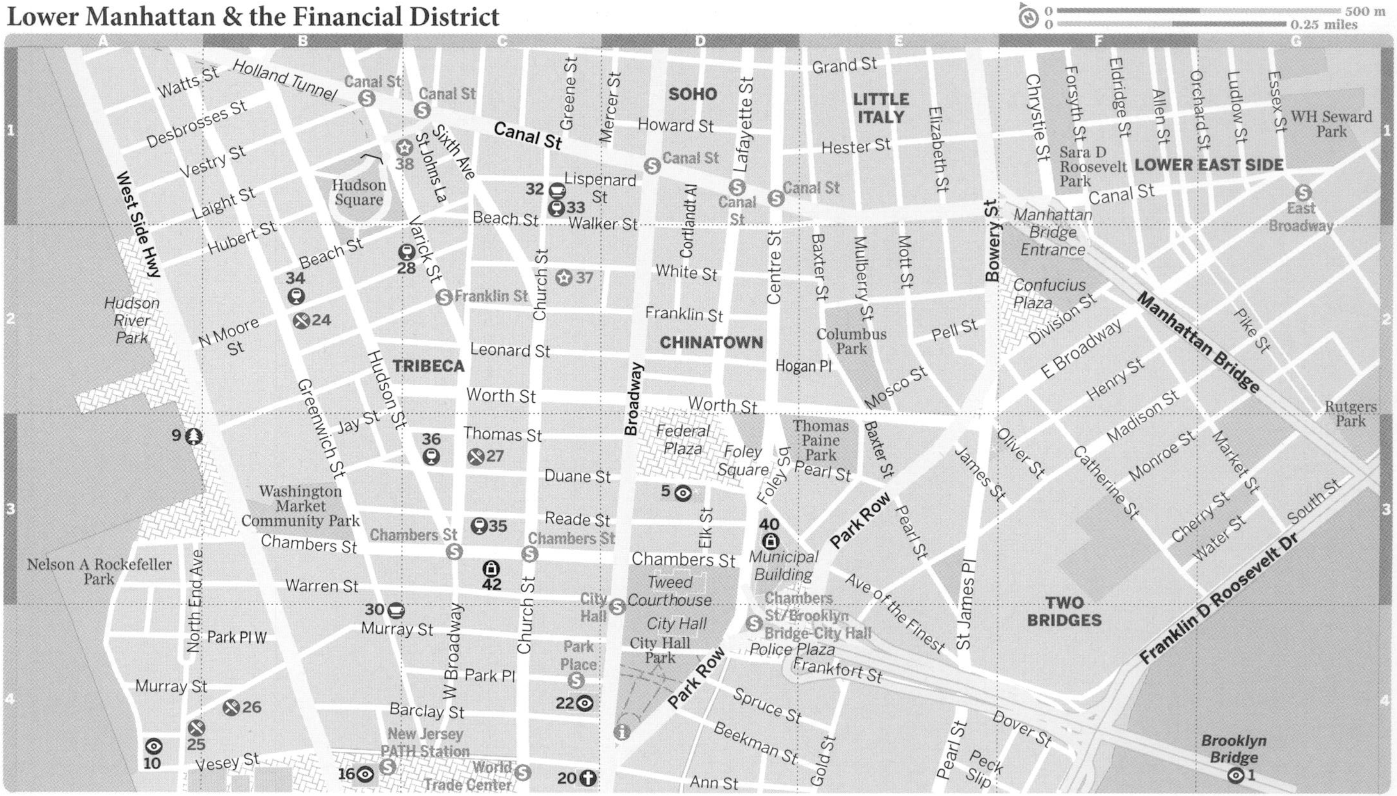

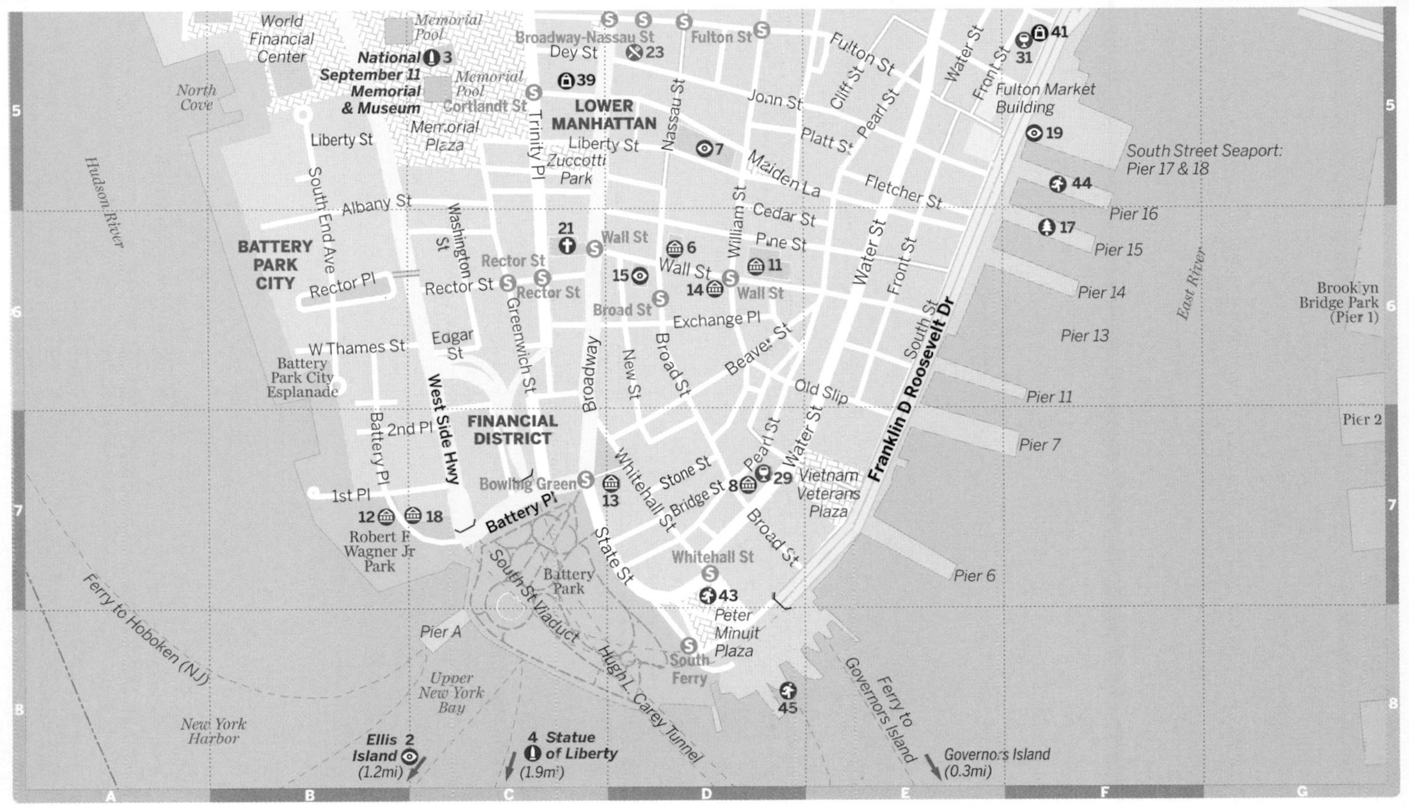
World Financial Center
North Cove
Hudson River
Memorial Pool
National September 11 Memorial & Museum 3
Memorial Pool
Cortlandt St
Memorial Plaza
Liberty St
South End Ave
Albany St
BATTERY PARK CITY
Rector Pl
W Thames St
Battery Park City Esplanade
Battery Pl
2nd Pl
1st Pl
12
18
Robert F Wagner Jr Park
West Side Hwy
Washington St
Rector St
Eagar St
Greenwich St
FINANCIAL DISTRICT
Bowling Green
Battery Pl
Trinity Pl
Broadway-Nassau St
Dey St
39
LOWER MANHATTAN
Liberty St
Zuccotti Park
21
Wall St
Broadway
23
Nassau St
7
Fulton St
John St
Maiden La
Cedar St
Pine St
William St
6
Wall St
14
15
Broad St
New St
Exchange Pl
11
Beaver St
Whitehall St
Stone St
Bridge St
13
8
29
State St
Battery Park
South St Viaduct
Hugh L Carey Tunnel
South Ferry
Whitehall St
43
Peter Minuit Plaza
Broad St
Pearl St
Water St
Old Slip
Vietnam Veterans Plaza
Front St
South St
Franklin D Roosevelt Dr
Fletcher St
Platt St
Cliff St
Pearl St
Fulton St
Water St
Front St
31
41
Fulton Market Building
19
44
17
South Street Seaport: Pier 17 & 18
Pier 16
Pier 15
Pier 14
Pier 13
Pier 11
Pier 7
Pier 6
Pier 2
Pier A
East River
Brooklyn Bridge Park (Pier 1)
45
Ferry to Governors Island
Governors Island (0.3mi)
4 Statue of Liberty (1.9mi)
Ellis Island 2 (1.2mi)
Upper New York Bay
New York Harbor
Ferry to Hoboken (NJ)

Lower Manhattan & the Financial District

Don't Miss Sights
1 Brooklyn Bridge ... G4
2 Ellis Island ... B8
3 National September 11 Memorial & Museum ... C5
4 Statue of Liberty ... C8

Sights
5 African Burial Ground ... D3
6 Federal Hall ... D6
7 Federal Reserve Bank of New York ... D5
8 Fraunces Tavern Museum ... D7
9 Hudson River Park ... A3
10 Irish Hunger Memorial ... A4
11 Museum of American Finance ... D6
12 Museum of Jewish Heritage ... B7
13 National Museum of the American Indian ... D7
14 New York City Police Museum ... D6
15 New York Stock Exchange ... D6
16 One World Trade Center ... B4
17 Pier 15 ... F6
18 Skyscraper Museum ... C7
19 South Street Seaport ... F5
20 St Paul's Chapel ... C4
21 Trinity Church ... C6
22 Woolworth Building ... C4

Eating
23 Les Halles ... D5
24 Locanda Verde ... B2
25 North End Grill ... A4
26 Shake Shack ... B4
27 Tiny's & the Bar Upstairs ... C3

Drinking & Nightlife
28 Brandy Library ... C2
29 Dead Rabbit ... D7
30 Kaffe 1668 ... B4
31 Keg No 229 ... F5
32 La Colombe ... C1
33 Macao ... C1
34 Smith & Mills ... B2
35 Ward III ... C3
36 Weather Up ... C3

Entertainment
37 Flea Theater ... C2
38 Tribeca Cinemas ... C1

Shopping
39 Century 21 ... C5
40 Citystore ... D3
41 Pasanella & Son ... F5
42 Philip Williams Posters ... C3

Sports & Activities
43 Bike & Roll Bike Rentals ... D7
44 Pioneer ... F5
45 Staten Island Ferry ... D8

public due to security concerns. Feel free to gawk outside the building, protected by barricades and the hawk-eyed NYPD (New York Police Department).

Museum of American Finance — Museum

Map p60 (www.moaf.org; 48 Wall St btwn Pearl & William Sts; adult/child $8/free; 10am-4pm Tue-Sat; S 2/3, 4/5 to Wall St) Money makes this museum go round, its focus on historic moments in American financial history. Permanent collections include rare historic currency (including Confederate currency used by America's southern states during the Civil War), stock and bond certificates from the Gilded Age, the oldest known photograph of Wall St and a stock ticker from circa 1875.

Once the headquarters for the Bank of New York, the building itself is a lavish spectacle, with 30ft ceilings, high arched windows, a majestic staircase to the mezzanine, glass chandeliers, and murals depicting historic scenes of banking and commerce.

New York City Police Museum — Museum

Map p60 (www.nycpolicemuseum.org; 45 Wall St at William St; admission $5; 10am-5pm Mon-Sat, noon-5pm Sun; ; S J/Z to Broad St; 2/3, 4/5 to Wall St) Until its Sandy-damaged landmark location at 100 Old Slip reopens sometime in 2015, this tribute to 'New York's Finest' will remain on Wall St. Exhibitions span both past and present aspects of city crime fighting, from the mug shots and weapons of notorious New York mobsters, to historic NYPD uniforms, to rare photographic images documenting the September 11 terrorist attacks.

Federal Reserve Bank of New York — Notable Building

Map p60 (212-720-6130; www.newyorkfed.org; 33 Liberty St at Nassau St, entry via 44 Maiden Lane; reservation required; guided tours 11:15am, noon, 12:45pm, 1:30pm, 2:15pm & 3pm

Mon-Fri, museum 10am-3pm; S A/C, J/Z, 2/3, 4/5 to Fulton St) FREE The best reason to visit the Federal Reserve Bank is the chance to (briefly) ogle at its high-security vault – more than 10,000 tons of gold reserves reside here, 80ft below ground. You'll only see a small part of that fortune, but signing on to a free tour (the only way down; book several months ahead) is worth the effort.

While you don't need to join a guided tour to browse the bank's interactive museum, which delves into the bank's history and research, you will still need to book a time online. Bring your passport or other official ID.

New York Harbor

Statue of Liberty (p52)

Ellis Island (p54)

Battery Park City

Museum of Jewish Heritage — Museum

Map p60 (www.mjhnyc.org; 36 Battery Pl; adult/child $12/free, 4-8pm Wed free; 10am-5:45pm Sun-Tue & Thu, to 8pm Wed, to 5pm Fri Apr-Sep, to 3pm Fri Oct-Mar; S 4/5 to Bowling Green) This evocative waterfront museum explores all aspects of modern Jewish identity, with often poignant personal artifacts, photographs and documentary films. Its outdoor Garden of Stones – created by artist Andy Goldsworthy – in which 18 boulders form a narrow pathway for contemplating the fragility of life is dedicated to those who lost loved ones in the Holocaust.

Skyscraper Museum — Museum

Map p60 (www.skyscraper.org; 39 Battery Pl; admission $5; noon-6pm Wed-Sun; S 4/5 to Bowling Green) Fans of phallic architecture will appreciate this compact, high-gloss gallery, examining skyscrapers as objects of design, engineering and urban renewal. Temporary exhibitions dominate the space, with one recent exhibition exploring New York's new generation of super-slim residential towers. Permanent fixtures include information on the design and construction of the Empire State Building and World Trade Center.

Irish Hunger Memorial — Memorial

Map p60 (290 Vesey St at North End Ave; S 2/3 to Park Place) FREE Artist Brian Tolle's compact labyrinth of low limestone walls and patches of grass pays tribute to the Great Irish Famine and Migration (1845–52),

Irish Hunger Memorial

STEVEN GREAVES/GETTY IMAGES ©

Below: Woolworth Building; **Right:** South Street Seaport
(BELOW) FRANZ MARC FREI/GETTY IMAGES ©; (RIGHT) BARRY WINIKER/GETTY IMAGES ©

which prompted hundreds of thousands of immigrants to leave Ireland for better opportunities in the New World. Representing abandoned cottages, stone walls and potato fields, the work was created with stones from each of Ireland's 32 counties.

Hudson River Park Park
Map p60 (www.hudsonriverpark.org; Manhattan's west side from Battery Park to 59th St; S 1 to Franklin St, 1 to Canal St) Stretching from Battery Park to Hell's Kitchen, the 5-mile, 550-acre Hudson River Park runs along the lower western side of Manhattan. Diversions include a bike/run/skate path that snakes along its entire length, community gardens, playgrounds, sculpture exhibitions, and renovated piers reinvented as riverfront esplanades, miniature golf courses, al fresco summertime movie theaters and concert venues. Visit the website for a detailed map.

East River Waterfront

South Street Seaport Neighborhood
Map p60 (www.southstreetseaport.com; S A/C, J/Z, 2/3, 4/5 to Fulton St) This 11-block enclave of cobbled streets, maritime warehouses and shops combines the best and worst in historic preservation. It's not on the radar for most New Yorkers, but tourists are drawn to the nautical air, the frequent street performers and the mobbed restaurants.

The iron-hulled **Pioneer** (**212-742-1969; www.nywatertaxi.com; Pier 16, South Street Seaport; adult/child $45/35**) at Pier 16 is a 19th-century vessel that offers wonderful two-hour sailing journeys through the warmer months. Happy times also await at neighboring **Pier 15** (**South St btwn Fletcher & John Sts; 6am-dusk**), a striking, two-level pier with swathes of soothing lawn and spectacular water views.

City Hall & Civic Center

Woolworth Building Notable Building

Map p60 (http://woolworthtours.com; 233 Broadway at Park Pl; 30-/90-min tours $15/45; S R to City Hall, 4/5/6 to Brooklyn Bridge-City Hall) The world's tallest building upon completion in 1913, Cass Gilbert's 60-story, 792ft-tall Woolworth Building is a neo-Gothic marvel, elegantly clad in masonry and terracotta. Surpassed in height by the Chrysler Building in 1930, its landmarked lobby is a breathtaking spectacle of dazzling, Byzantine-like mosaics. The lobby is only accessible on prebooked guided tours, which also offer insight into the building's more curious original features, among them a dedicated subway entrance and a secret swimming pool.

African Burial Ground Memorial

Map p60 (www.nps.gov/afbg; 290 Broadway btwn Duane & Elk Sts; memorial 9am-5pm daily, visitor center 10am-4pm Tue-Sat; S 4/5 to Wall St) FREE In 1991, construction workers here uncovered more than 400 stacked wooden caskets, just 16ft to 28ft below street level. The boxes contained the remains of enslaved Africans (nearby Trinity Church graveyard had banned the burial of Africans at the time). Today, a memorial and visitors center honors an estimated 15,000 Africans buried here during the 17th and 18th centuries.

Eating

Frenzied lunch rushes for financial types fuel two extremes in Lower Manhattan: fast-food storefronts and masculine dining rooms catering to steak-chomping bigwigs. Both genres offer plenty of satisfying experiences, whether it's faux filet Bercy at Les Halles or frozen custard at Shake Shack. Head north into Tribeca and the vibe is hipper and more fashion-forward, with a string of celeb-chef favorites.

Shake Shack Burgers $

Map p60 (www.shakeshack.com; 215 Murray St btwn West St & North End Ave; burgers from

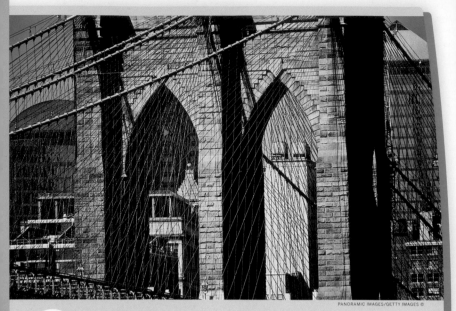

PANORAMIC IMAGES/GETTY IMAGES ©

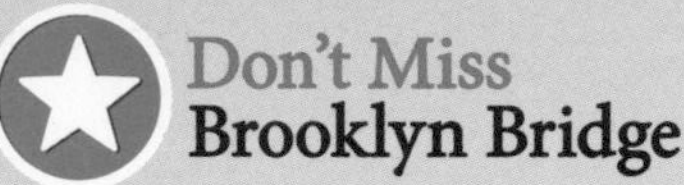

Don't Miss Brooklyn Bridge

A New York icon, the Brooklyn Bridge (**Map p60**) was the world's first steel suspension bridge. When it opened in 1883, the 1596ft span between its two support towers was the longest in history. Although its construction was fraught with disaster, the bridge became a magnificent example of urban design, inspiring poets, writers and painters. Today, the Brooklyn Bridge continues to dazzle – many regard it as the most beautiful bridge in the world.

The Prussian-born engineer John Roebling, who was knocked off a pier in Fulton Landing in June 1869, designed the bridge, which spans the East River from Manhattan to Brooklyn; he died of tetanus poisoning before construction of the bridge even began. His son, Washington Roebling, supervised construction of the bridge, which lasted 14 years and managed to survive budget overruns and the deaths of 20 workers. The younger Roebling himself suffered from the bends while helping to excavate the riverbed for the bridge's western tower and remained bedridden for much of the project; his wife Emily oversaw construction in his stead. There was one final tragedy to come in June 1883, when the bridge opened to pedestrian traffic. Someone in the crowd shouted, perhaps as a joke, that the bridge was collapsing into the river, setting off a mad rush in which 12 people were trampled to death.

$3.60; 11am-11pm; S A/C, 1/2/3 to Chambers St) Danny Meyer's cult burger chain is fast food at its finest: cotton-soft burgers made with prime, freshly ground mince; Chicago-style hot dogs in poppy-seed potato buns; and seriously good cheesy fries. Leave room for the legendary frozen custard and drink local with a beer from Brooklyn brewery Sixpoint.

North End Grill American $$

Map p60 (☎646-747-1600; www.northendgrill-nyc.com; 104 North End Ave at Murray St; 3-course lunch $39, dinner mains $17-34; ⏰11:30am-2pm & 5:30-10pm Mon-Thu, to 10:30pm Fri, 11am-2pm & 5:30-10:30pm Sat, 11am-2:30pm & 5:30-9pm Sun; S 1/2/3, A/C to Chambers St, E to World Trade Center) Handsome, smart and friendly, this is celeb chef Danny Meyer's take on the American grill. Top-tier produce (including stuff from the restaurant's own rooftop garden) forms the basis for modern takes on comfort grub, happily devoured by suited money-makers and a scattering of more casual passersby.

Les Halles French $$

Map p60 (☎212-285-8585; www.leshalles.net; 15 John St btwn Broadway & Nassau St; mains $14.50-32; ⏰7am-midnight; 📶; S A/C, J/Z, 2/3, 4/5 to Fulton St) Vegetarians need not apply at Anthony Bourdain's serious brasserie. Among the elegant light-fixture balls, dark-wood paneling and stiff white tablecloths, you'll find a buttoned-up, meat-lovin' crowd who've come for rich and decadent favorites such as *cote de boeuf* and steak au poivre.

Locanda Verde Italian $$$

Map p60 (☎212-925-3797; www.locandaverde-nyc.com; 377 Greenwich St at Moore St; lunch $19-29, dinner mains $28-34; ⏰7am-11pm Mon-Fri, from 8am Sat & Sun; S A/C/E to Canal St, 1 to Franklin St) Step through the velvet curtains into a sassy scene of loosened Brown Brothers' shirts, black dresses and slick barmen behind a long, crowded bar. Part of the **Greenwich Hotel** (**☎212-941-8900; www.greenwichhotelny.com; 377 Greenwich St, btwn N Moore & Franklin Sts; r from $635; ❄📶🏊; S 1 to Franklin St, A/C/E to Canal St**), this brasserie is owned by celebrity chef Andrew Carmellini, whose modern Italian grub sees pumpkin agnolotti get it on with sage and amaretti, or roasted scallops join forces with Sicilian cauliflower, pine nuts and capers.

Tiny's & the Bar Upstairs American $$$

Map p60 (☎212-374-1135; 135 W Broadway btwn Duane & Thomas Sts; mains $22-36; ⏰11:30am-11pm Mon-Thu, to midnight Fri, 10:30am-midnight Sat, 10:30am-11pm Sun; S A/C, 1/2/3 to Chambers St) Snug and adorable (book ahead!), Tiny's comes with a crackling fire in the back room and an intimate bar upstairs.

Lunch at Locanda Verde

THE WASHINGTON POST/GETTY IMAGES ©

Served on vintage porcelain, dishes are soulful, subtly re-tweaked delights; think burrata with date puree, lemon honey glaze and pistachios, or pan-seared scallops getting zesty with grapefruit and Thai chili-ginger coconut sauce.

Drinking & Nightlife

Corporate types don't always bolt for the 'burbs when 5pm hits, many loosening their ties in the smattering of wine bars and pubs around Stone St, Wall St and South Street Seaport. Tribeca keeps its cool with artisan coffee shops and plush cocktail dens.

La Colombe — Cafe

Map p60 (www.lacolombe.com; 319 Church St at Lispenard St; 7:30am-6:30pm Mon-Fri, from 8:30am Sat & Sun; S A/C/E to Canal St) Coffee and a few baked treats is all you'll get at this roaster but, man, are they good. The espresso is dark and intense, brewed by hipster baristas and swilled by an endless stream of cool kids and clued-in Continentals.

Kaffe 1668 — Cafe

Map p60 (www.kaffe1668.com; 275 Greenwich St btwn Warren & Murray Sts; 6:30am-10pm Mon-Fri, 7am-9pm Sat & Sun; ; S A/C, 1/2/3 to Chambers St) A coffee-geek mecca, with espresso machine, Steampunk, coffee urns and dual synessos pumping out single-origin magic. There's a large communal table speckled with suits and laptop-tapping creatives, and more seating downstairs. For a hair-raising thrill, order a triple ristretto.

Dead Rabbit — Cocktail Bar

Map p60 (www.deadrabbitnyc.com; 30 Water St; 11am-4am; S R to Whitehall St, 1 to South Ferry) Far from dead, this new kid on the cocktail block has wasted no time swagging awards, among them World's Best New Cocktail Bar, Best Cocktail Menu and International Bartender of the Year at the 2013 Tales of the Cocktail Festival.

During the day, hit the sawdust-sprinkled taproom for specialty beers, historic punches and pop-inns (lightly hopped ale spiked with different flavors). Come evening, scurry upstairs to the cozy Parlour for your choice of 72 meticulously researched cocktails.

Weather Up — Cocktail Bar

Map p60 (www.weatherupnyc.com; 159 Duane St btwn Hudson St & W Broadway; 5pm-2am; S 1/2/3 to Chambers St) Softly lit subway tiles, amiable barkeeps, and seductive cocktails make for a bewitching trio at Weather Up. Sweet talk the staff over a Whizz Bang (scotch whisky, dry vermouth, house made grenadine, orange bitters and absinthe).

Governors Island

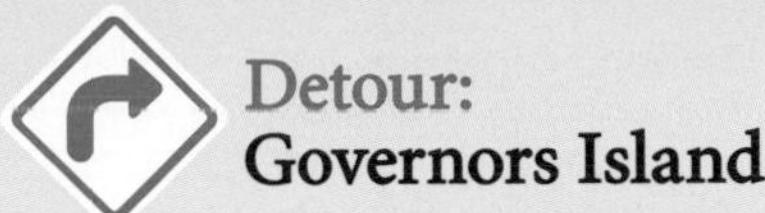

Detour: Governors Island

Off-limits to the public for 200 years, former military outpost **Governors Island** (☎212-514-8285; www.nps.gov/gois; admission free; ⏲10am-7pm Sat & Sun late May-late Sep; ferries leave from Battery Maritime Bldg, Slip 7, hourly 10am-3pm Fri & every 30min 10am-5pm Sat & Sun May-Oct; S 4, 5 to Bowling Green, 1 to South Ferry) is now one of New York's most popular seasonal playgrounds. Each summer, free ferries make the seven-minute trip from Lower Manhattan to the 172-acre oasis. In 2014, 30 new acres of island parkland opened to the public, with features including the six-acre, art-studded Liggett Terrace; the 10-acre Hammock Grove (complete with 50 hammocks); and the 14-acre Play Lawn, with a duo of natural turf ball fields for adult softball and Little League baseball.

Art is the focus at Figment (www.figmentproject.org), a one-weekend-only interactive art festival in June, while inspiring views are also on tap along the Great Promenade. Running for 2.2 miles along the island's perimeter, the path takes in everything from Lower Manhattan and Brooklyn, to Staten Island and New Jersey. Those who want to hit the pedal can rent bikes from Bike & Roll for $20 per half a day.

Ward III — Cocktail Bar

Map p60 (www.ward3tribeca.com; 111 Reade St btwn Church St & W Broadway; ⏲4pm-4am Mon-Fri, 5pm-4am Sat & Sun; S A/C, 1/2/3 to Chambers St) Dark and bustling, Ward III channels old-school jauntiness with its elegant libations, vintage vibe (including old Singer sewing tables behind the bar), and gentlemanly house rules (No 2: 'Don't be creepy').

Macao — Cocktail Bar

Map p60 (☎212-431-8750; www.macaonyc.com; 311 Church St btwn Lispenard & Walker Sts; ⏲bar 4pm-5am; S A/C/E to Canal St) Though we love the '40s-style 'gambling parlor' bar/restaurant, it's the downstairs 'opium den' (open Thursday to Saturday) that gets our hearts racing. A Chinese-Portuguese fusion of grub and liquor, both floors are a solid spot for late-night sipping and snacking, especially if you've got a soft spot for sizzle-on-the-tongue libations.

Brandy Library — Bar

Map p60 (www.brandylibrary.com; 25 N Moore St at Varick St; ⏲5pm-1am Sun-Wed, 4pm-2am Thu, 4pm-4am Fri & Sat; S 1 to Franklin St) When sipping means serious business, settle in at this uber-luxe 'library', its handsome club chairs facing floor-to-ceiling, bottle-lined shelves.

Keg No 229 — Beer Hall

Map p60 (www.kegno229.com; 229 Front St btwn Beekman St & Peck Slip; ⏲noon-midnight Sun-Wed, to 2am Thu-Sat; S A/C, J/Z, 1/2, 4/5 to Fulton St) If you know that a Flying Dog Raging Bitch is a craft beer – not a nickname for your ex – this curated beer bar is for you. From Mother's Milk Stout to Abita Purple Haze, its battalion of drafts, bottles and cans are a who's who of boutique American brews. Across the street, sibling Bin No 220 is its wine-loving sibling.

Smith & Mills — Cocktail Bar

Map p60 (www.smithandmills.com; 71 N Moore St btwn Hudson & Greenwich Sts; ⏲11am-2am Mon-Wed, to 3am Thu-Sat, to 1am Sun; S 1 to Franklin St) Petite Smith & Mills ticks all the cool boxes: unmarked exterior, kooky industrial interior and expertly crafted cocktails – the 'Carriage House' is a nod to the space's previous incarnation.

Broadway Tickets

After cheap tickets to Broadway shows? Ditch the TKTS Booth in Times Square for the TKTS Booth at South Street Seaport. Queues usually move a little faster and you can purchase tickets for next-day matinees (something you can't do at the Times Square outlet). The TKTS Smartphone app offers real-time listings of what's on sale.

Entertainment

Flea Theater Theater

Map p60 (www.theflea.org; 41 White St btwn Church St & Broadway; S 1 to Franklin St, A/C/E, N/Q/R, J/Z, 6 to Canal St) One of NYC's top off-Broadway companies, Flea is famous for performing innovative, timely new works in its two performance spaces.

Tribeca Cinemas Cinema

Map p60 (www.tribecacinemas.com; 54 Varick St at Laight St; S A/C/E, N/Q/R, J/Z, 6 to Canal St) This is the physical home of the **Tribeca Film Festival** (p40), founded in 2003 by Robert De Niro and Jane Rosenthal. Throughout the year, the space hosts a range of screenings and educational panels, including festivals dedicated to themes such as architecture and design.

Shopping

Century 21 Fashion

Map p60 (www.c21stores.com; 22 Cortlandt St btwn Church St & Broadway; 7:45am-9pm Mon-Wed, to 9:30pm Thu & Fri, 10am-9pm Sat, 11am-8pm Sun; S A/C, J/Z, 2/3, 4/5 to Fulton St, N/R to Cortlandt St) For penny-pinching fashionistas, this giant, cut-price department store is dangerously addictive. Raid the racks for designer duds at up to 70% off.

Philip Williams Posters Vintage

Map p60 (www.postermuseum.com; 122 Chambers St btwn Church St & W Broadway; 11am-7pm Mon-Sat; S A/C, 1/2/3 to Chambers St) You'll find more than half a million posters in this cavernous treasure trove, from oversized French advertisements for perfume and cognac to Soviet film posters and retro-fab promos for TWA.

Pasanella & Son Wine

Map p600 (www.pasanellaandson.com; 115 South St btwn Peck Slip & Beekman St; 10am-9pm Mon-Sat, noon-7pm Sun; S A/C, J/Z, 2/3, 4/5 to Fulton St) Oenophiles adore this savvy wine peddler, with its 400-plus drops both inspired and affordable. The focus is on small producers, with a number of biodynamic and organic winemakers in the mix.

Century 21 department store
KEVIN CLOGSTOUN/GETTY IMAGES ©

Citystore Souvenirs
Map p60 (www.nyc.gov/citystore; Municipal Bldg, North Plaza, 1 Centre St; ⏲10am-5pm Mon-Fri; S J/Z to Chambers St, 4/5/6 to Brooklyn Bridge-City Hall) Score all manner of New York memorabilia, including authentic taxi medallions, manhole coasters, Brooklyn Bridge posters, NYPD baseball caps, and actual streets signs ('No Parking,' 'Don't Feed the Pigeons').

Sports & Activities

Staten Island Ferry Ferry
Map p60 (www.siferry.com; Whitehall Terminal at Whitehall & South Sts; ⏲24hr; S 1 to South Ferry) FREE Staten Islanders know these hulking, dirty-orange ferryboats as commuter vehicles, while Manhattanites like to think of them as their secret, romantic vessels for a spring-day escape. Yet many a tourist is clued into the charms of the Staten Island Ferry, whose 5.2-mile journey between Lower Manhattan and the Staten Island neighborhood of St George is one of NYC's finest free adventures.

Bike & Roll Bike Rentals Bicycle Rental
Map p60 (☎212-260-0400; www.bikenewyorkcity.com; State & Water Sts; rentals per day from $44, tours from $50; ⏲varies, check website; S 4/5 to Bowling Green, 1 to South Ferry) Located just north of the Staten Island Ferry terminal, this is one of several Bike & Roll Bike Rental outlets in the city. It also leads bike tours, including across the Brooklyn Bridge and along the Hudson River.

Battery Park City Parks Conservancy Course, Tour
(☎212-267-9700; www.bpcparks.org) Offers a range of free and payable activities, from drawing classes and walking tours, to parent and baby yoga, storytelling sessions, and volunteer gardening. Check the website for upcoming events.

SOHO
475

SoHo & Chinatown

Head here to explore ethnic neighborhoods and cool shopping corridors. SoHo (SOuth of HOuston), NoHo (NOrth of HOuston) and Nolita (NOrth of Little ITAly) are known for their tangled thickets of hipness in the form of boutiques, bars and eateries. Real estate is through the roof in all three spots, and nights out (or days shopping) can prove to be expensive propositions. But in the end you'll be won over by the unique blend of industrial starkness and cobblestone coziness that lends these areas their character. There's a palpable anything-goes spirit that wafts up like stall smoke in Chinatown, where frenzied crowds and hawkers mingle under the winking lights of aging billboards. This, the largest Chinese community outside of Asia (there's a substantial Vietnamese presence as well), is a feast for the senses.

West Broadway, SoHo

SoHo & Chinatown Highlights

Shopping in SoHo (p92)

Hundreds of stores – big and small – are scattered along SoHo's streets. Broadway is lined with less-expensive chain stores. West along the tree-lined streets are pricier boutiques. Street vendors hawk jewelry, art, T-shirts, hats and other crafts on warm days. On Lafayette, shops cater to the DJ and skate crowds with indie labels and vintage shops thrown into the mix. Further east, Nolita is home to tiny jewel-box boutiques.

1

2

Chow Down in Chinatown (p87)

Duck into a produce market and check out various oddly shaped fruits and vegetables. Buy three luscious turnip cakes for $1 from a street vendor. Sip bubble teas and slurp noodles. With cuisine from Shanghai, Vietnam and Malaysia, from holes-in-the-wall to banquet-sized dining rooms, Chinatown is a true culinary adventure. Come with a handful of friends and eat 'family-style.'

STEPHEN J. BOITANO/GETTY IMAGES ©

Little Italy (p90)

Once known as a truly authentic pocket of Italian people, culture and eateries, Little Italy today is constantly shrinking (a growing Chinatown keeps moving in). Still, the old-world feels like it's hanging on when you take a nighttime stroll down Mulberry St, past turn-of-the-century tenements; loyal Italian Americans still flock here to gather around red-and-white-checkered tablecloths at a handful of long-standing red-sauce restaurants.

3

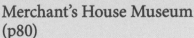

SLAVEN VLASIC/GETTY IMAGES ©

4

Merchant's House Museum (p80)

Walking through the doors of this perfectly preserved mansion is like stepping into a time machine that has transported you 150 years into the past. Everything in the house – from the polished floors to the crown molding – is as it was during a bygone era. It remains to this day the most authentic Federal house in New York City.

5

Independent Movie Theaters (p92)

Cinephiles can't beat the selection of classic, avant-garde, foreign and themed films on offer at the Film Forum on Houston St. Showings are often combined with director talks or filmic discussions. Listen for the roar of the subway under your seat at the Angelika Film Center (p92), where contemporary art-house, independent and occasionally Hollywood movies are screened.

Angelika Film Center

SoHo Walk

This walk through the land of acronyms and concrete catwalks of SoHo takes in some neighborhood architectural landmarks. However, the biggest attraction is the simple beauty of the small tangle of streets that feels like you're walking through an elegant village (with the exception of busy Broadway).

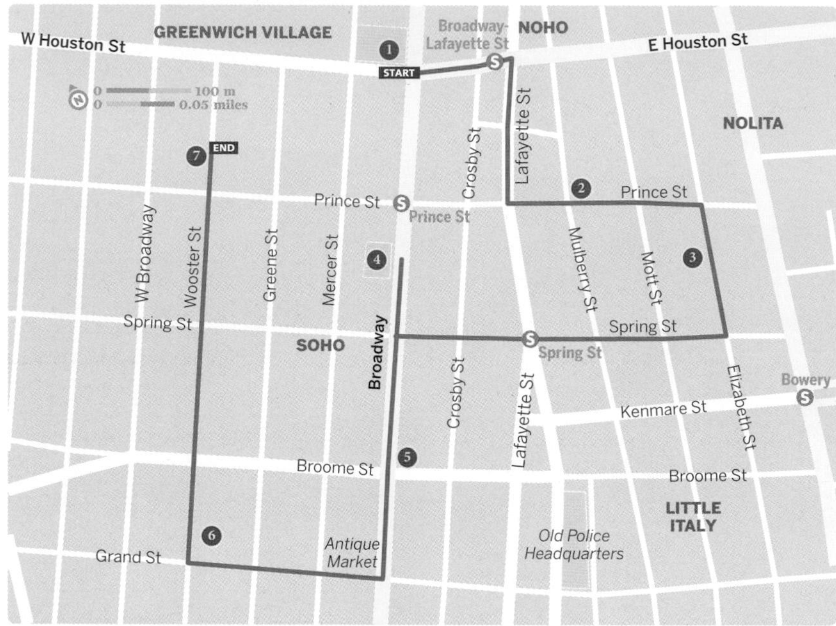

WALK FACTS

- **Start** Cable Building
- **End** New York Earth Room
- **Distance** 1.5 miles
- **Duration** One hour

❶ Cable Building

Pop out of the B, D, F, V train and get an immediate sense of old-meets-new with this NoHo beaux-arts building built by famed architects McKim, Mead and White in 1894. Originally used as the power plant for the Broadway Cable Car (the nation's first), the Cable Building features an oval window and caryatids on its Broadway facade. Today it houses the Angelika Film Center (p92).

❷ St Patrick's Old Cathedral

Head east across Houston St and make a right on Lafayette St. Turn left on Prince St and you'll be approaching St Patrick's Old Cathedral, which dates from 1809 and is the original location for the famous Fifth Ave cathedral's congregation. Don't miss the ancient, peaceful cemetery.

❸ Elizabeth Street Gallery

Continue along Prince St. If you're hungry, you can stop to fuel up at Café Gitane (p86) on Mott St. Otherwise, turn right onto Elizabeth St, where you can pause to admire the fenced-in garden of the curious Elizabeth Street Gallery, at No 210, part of a fireplace, fountain and garden-ornament shop for the well-off home owner.

4 Little Singer Building

Turn right on Spring St and walk until you hit Broadway. Just half a block north is the Little Singer Building, one of the post–Civil War buildings that gave this area its 'Cast-Iron District' nickname. This one used to be the main warehouse for the famous sewing-machine company of the same name.

5 Haughwout Building

Head south down Broadway and you'll come to a rather generic Staples store with a surprising history: it's located in the Haughwout Building, the first structure to use the exotic steam elevator developed by Elisha Otis. Known as the 'Parthenon of Cast-Iron Architecture,' the Haughwout (pronounced how-out) is considered a rare structure for its two sided design. Don't miss the iron clock that sits on the Broadway facade.

6 Drawing Center

Continue another block south on Broadway and then turn right onto Grand St and continue three blocks before turning right onto Wooster St. On your right is the Drawing Center (p80), the only nonprofit institute in the country to focus solely on drawings, using works by masters as well as unknowns to show the juxtaposition of various styles.

7 New York Earth Room

Continue north on Wooster St and head several blocks up to the New York Earth Room, where artist Walter De Maria's gallery filled with cool, moist soil will either thrill you or leave you scratching your head (or maybe a bit of both).

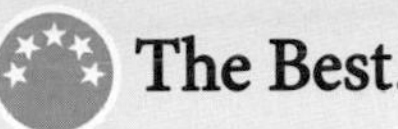

The Best...

PLACES TO EAT

Dutch 'Roots-inspired' locavore American at this award-winning restaurant. (p87)

Balthazar Buzzing SoHo brasserie with great food and ambiance. (p87)

Lovely Day Good-value Thai cooking in a sweet Nolita setting. (p84)

Café Gitane A touch of Europe with Franco-Moroccan dishes and a très cool downtown crowd. (p86)

PLACES TO DRINK

Apothéke It takes a little effort to track down this former opium den-turned-apothecary bar. (p91)

Pegu Club Intimate setting for an expertly crafted libation. (p89)

Spring Lounge Divey spot that always draws a fun-loving crowd. (p91)

Mulberry Project Enticing cocktail parlor with a backyard retreat. (p91)

PLACES TO SHOP

Rag & Bone Stylish, well-tailored wears for men and women. (p92)

McNally Jackson This literary haunt makes a fine retreat in bad weather. (p93)

Opening Ceremony Unique handsomely designed apparel you won't find elsewhere. (p94)

Balthazar brasserie
ANGUS OBORN/GETTY IMAGES ©

Don't Miss Chinatown

Endless exotic moments await in New York City's most colorfully cramped community, where a walk through the neighborhood is never the same no matter how many times you pass through. Catch the whiff of fresh fish and ripe persimmons, hear the clacking of mah-jongg tiles on makeshift tables, witness dangling duck roasts swinging in store windows and shop for anything imaginable from rice-paper lanterns and 'faux-lex' watches to [illegible] of pressed nutmeg. Amer-[illegible]on of Chinese immigrants is your oyster – dipped in soy sauce, of course.

Map p86

www.explorechinatown.com

south of Canal St & east of Broadway

S N/Q/R, J/Z, 6 to Canal St, B/D to Grand St, F to East Broadway

Culinary Adventure

The most rewarding experience for Chinatown neophytes is to access this wild and wonderful world through their taste buds. More than any other area of Manhattan, Chinatown's menus sport wonderfully low prices, uninflated by ambience or reputation. But more than cheap eats, the neighborhood is rife with family recipes passed between generations and continents. Food displays and preparation remain unchanged and untempered by American norms; it's not unusual to walk by storefronts sporting a tangled array of lacquered animals – chicken, rabbit and duck, in particular – ready to be chopped up and served at a family banquet.

Buddhist Temples

Chinatown is home to Buddhist temples large and small, public and obscure. They are easily stumbled upon during a full-on stroll of the neighborhood, and at least two such temples are considered landmarks. The **Eastern States Buddhist Temple** Map p86 (64 Mott St, btwn Bayard & Canal Sts; 9am-6pm; S J, M, Z, 6 to Canal St) is filled with hundreds of Buddhas, while the **Mahayana Buddhist Temple** Map p86 (133 Canal St, at Manhattan Bridge Plaza; 8am-6pm; S B/D to Grand St, J/Z, 6 to Canal St) holds one golden, 16ft-high Buddha, sitting on a lotus and edged with offerings of fresh oranges, apples and flowers.

Canal Street

Walking down Canal St is like a game of Frogger played on the streets of Shanghai. This is Chinatown's main artery, where you'll dodge oncoming human traffic as you scurry into back alleys to scout treasures from the Far East. You'll pass stinky seafood stalls hawking slippery fish; herb shops displaying a witch's cauldron's worth of roots and potions; storefront bakeries with the tastiest 50-cent pork buns you've ever had; restaurants with whole, roasted ducks hanging by their skinny necks in the windows; produce markets piled high with fresh lychees and Asian pears; and street vendors selling every iteration of knock-off designer goods.

Local Knowledge

Chinatown

RECOMMENDATIONS FROM HELEN KOH, EXECUTIVE DIRECTOR OF THE MUSEUM OF CHINESE IN AMERICA

1 CHINESE OPERA

Local opera troupes gather to perform outdoors in the area of Columbus Park closest to Bayard St on any Saturday or Sunday afternoon in good weather. There are also periodic performances on weekends in the basement of the Chinese Consolidated Benevolent Association at 62 Mott St.

2 STREETS TO WANDER

Grand St is a good window on the transformation of the neighborhood: new condo developments and the influx of non-Asians. You walk past little fish and vegetable stores, Vietnamese noodle shops and Italian cafes. The intersection of Doyers and Pell Sts is Chinatown's historical heart; Ting's, at the corner, is a time-capsule curio shop, one of the last to survive. The block of Mott St between Hester and Grand, condensed with groceries, fish shops and meat markets, has lots of energy and is a chance to view a slice of life of local residents.

3 GOOD EATS

Definitely check out renovated Nam Wah, one of the only made-to-order dim sum places and the self-proclaimed first in Chinatown. Besides the food, Red Egg is interesting for the old disco balls in back reminiscent of Hong Kong style from another era. And for late-night noodles, congee and rice dishes, one of my favorites is **Great New York Noodle Town** (p88), open to around 4am.

4 GOOD TIME TO VISIT

The neighborhood is especially festive from mid- to late September during the mid-Autumn moon festival; families gather together and bakeries sell delicious mooncakes, pastries with a variety of fillings, from red-bean paste to duck egg yolks.

5 BOOKS

The hard-boiled detective novels of Ed Lin and Henry Chang are entertaining fictional tours of the Chinatown streets.

Discover SoHo & Chinatown

Getting There & Away

- **Subway** The subway lines dump off along various points of Canal St (J/Z, N/Q/R and 6). Once you arrive it's best to explore on foot. The neighborhood's downtown location makes it easy to access from Midtown and Brooklyn.
- **Bus & Taxi** Avoid taking cabs or buses – especially in Chinatown, as the traffic is full-on. For SoHo, have your taxi let you off along Broadway if you aren't fussed about your final destination. Don't take cabs south of Canal St if you're simply planning to wander around Chinatown.

New York City Fire Museum
BARRY WINIKER/GETTY IMAGES ©

Sights

SoHo, NoHo & Nolita

Merchant's House Museum Museum

Map p82 (212-777-1089; www.merchantshouse.org; 29 E 4th St, btwn Lafayette St & Bowery; adult/child $10/free; noon-5pm Thu-Mon, guided tours 2pm; S 6 to Bleecker St) This elegant, red-brick row house is a family home dating from 1832 – and it's perfectly preserved both inside and out. Home to a prosperous merchant family, the place is in mint condition, allowing you to wander through formal Greek Revival parlors featuring mahogany pocket doors, bronze gasoliers and marble mantelpieces. Bedrooms reveal plenty of other luxuries, from fine antique furniture to a display of dresses, shoes and parasols.

Drawing Center Gallery

Map p82 (212-219-2166; www.drawingcenter.org; 35 Wooster St, btwn Grand & Broome Sts; adult/child $5/free; noon-6pm Wed & Fri-Sun, to 8pm Thu; S A/C/E, 1 to Canal St) America's only nonprofit institute focused solely on drawings, the Drawing Center uses work by masters as well as unknowns to juxtapose the medium's various styles. Historical exhibitions have included work by Michelangelo, James Ensor and Marcel Duchamp, while contemporary shows have showcased heavyweights such as Richard Serra, Ellsworth Kelly and Richard Tuttle.

New York City Fire Museum Museum

Map p82 (212-219-1222; www.nycfiremuseum.org; 278 Spring St, btwn Varick & Hudson Sts; adult/child $8/5; 10am-5pm; ; S C/E to Spring St)

SoHo & Chinatown

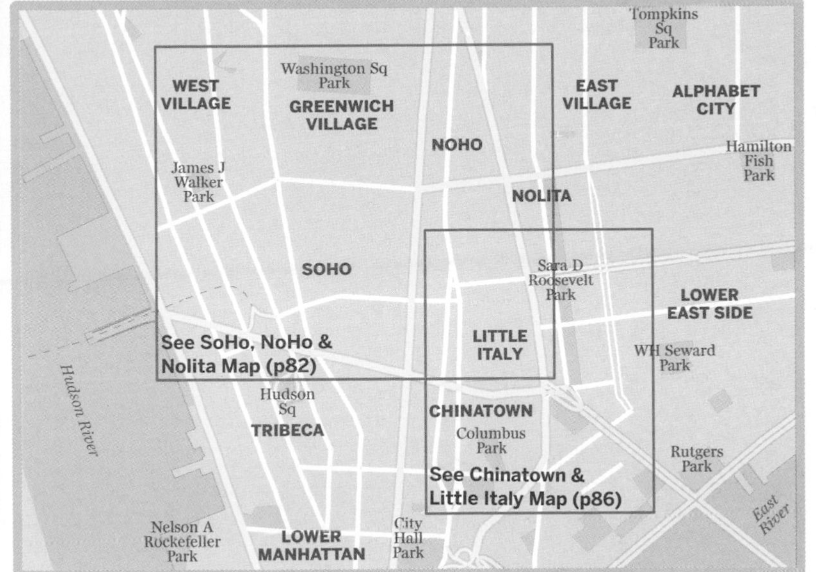

In a grand old firehouse dating from 1904, this ode to fire fighters includes a fantastic collection of historic equipment, from gold, horse-drawn firefighting carriages to early rescue gear like stovepipe firefighter hats. Exhibits trace the development of the NYC firefighting system, and the museum's friendly staff (and the heavy equipment) make this a great spot to bring kids.

Leslie-Lohman Museum of Gay & Lesbian Art Museum

Map p82 (212-431-2609; www.leslielohman.org; 26 Wooster St, btwn Grand & Canal Sts; noon-6pm Tue-Sat; S A/C/E to Canal St) FREE The world's first museum dedicated to LGBT themes stages six to eight annual exhibitions of both homegrown and international art. To date, offerings have included solo-artist retrospectives to themed shows exploring the likes of art and sex along the New York waterfront.

Artists Space Gallery

Map p82 (212-226-3970; www.artistsspace.org; 38 Greene St, 3rd fl, btwn Grand & Broome Sts; noon-6pm Wed-Sun; S A/C/E, J/Z, N/Q/R, 1, 6 to Canal St) FREE One of the first alternative spaces in New York, Artists Space made its debut in 1972. More than 40 years on, it remains a solid choice for those seeking crisp, provocative and experimental creativity.

Children's Museum of the Arts Museum

Map p82 (212-274-0986; www.cmany.org; 103 Charlton St, btwn Greenwich & Hudson Sts; admission $11, suggested donation 4-6pm Thu; noon-5pm Mon & Wed, noon-6pm Thu & Fri, 10am-5pm Sat & Sun; ; S 1 to Houston St; C/E to Spring St) This small but worthy stop exhibits paintings, drawings and photographs by local school kids, with adorable exhibit titles like 'Beyond the Refrigerator Door.' For more hands-on activities, check out the museum's vast offering of public programs for kids of all ages, including guided workshops on art forms ranging from sculpture to collaborative mural painting, as well as movie nights and other special treats.

SoHo, NoHo & Nolita

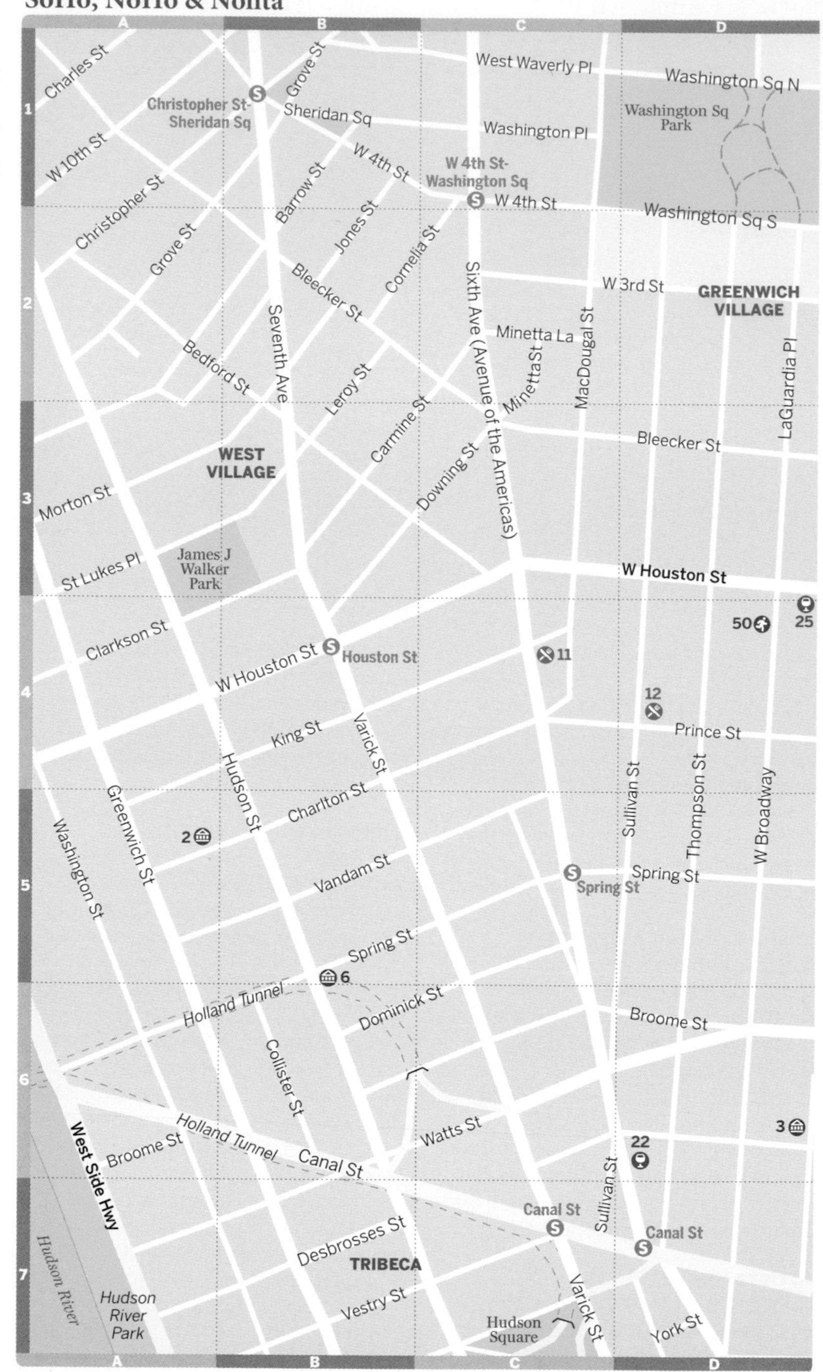

Charles St
W 10th St
Christopher St
Grove St
Christopher St-Sheridan Sq
Sheridan Sq
Barrow St
Jones St
W 4th St
Cornelia St
W 4th St-Washington Sq
W 4th St
West Waverly Pl
Washington Pl
Washington Sq N
Washington Sq Park
Washington Sq S
Bleecker St
Bedford St
Seventh Ave
Leroy St
Carmine St
Sixth Ave (Avenue of the Americas)
Minetta La
Minetta St
MacDougal St
W 3rd St
GREENWICH VILLAGE
LaGuardia Pl
Bleecker St
WEST VILLAGE
Downing St
Morton St
St Lukes Pl
James J Walker Park
W Houston St
Clarkson St
W Houston St
Houston St
King St
Varick St
Hudson St
Prince St
Charlton St
Greenwich St
Washington St
Sullivan St
Thompson St
W Broadway
Vandam St
Spring St
Spring St
Spring St
Holland Tunnel
Dominick St
Broome St
Collister St
West Side Hwy
Broome St
Holland Tunnel
Canal St
Watts St
Sullivan St
Canal St
Canal St
Desbrosses St
TRIBECA
Vestry St
Varick St
Hudson Square
York St
Hudson River
Hudson River Park
SOHO & CHINATOWN

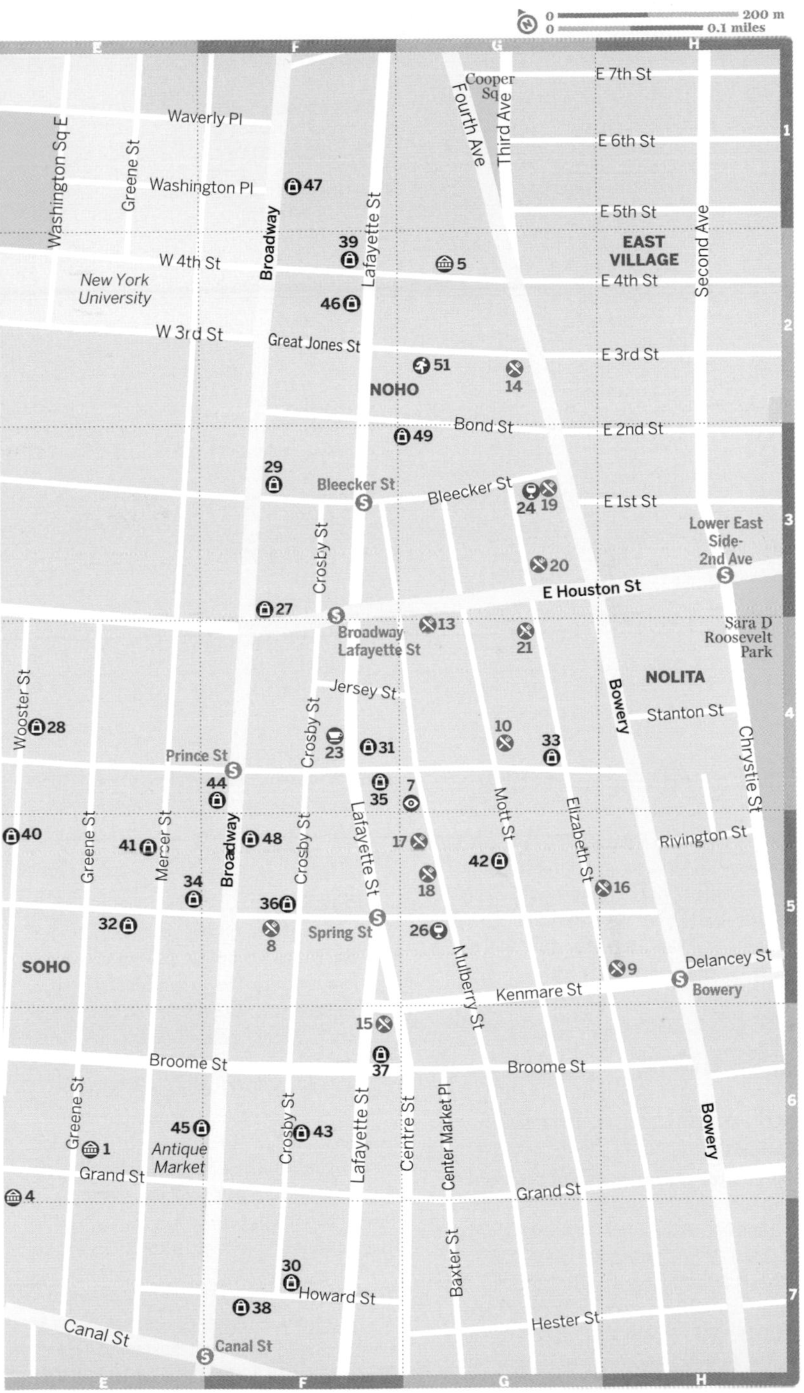

E 7th St
E 6th St
E 5th St
E 4th St
E 3rd St
E 2nd St
E 1st St
E Houston St
Cooper Sq
Fourth Ave
Third Ave
Second Ave
EAST VILLAGE
Waverly Pl
Washington Pl
Washington Sq E
Greene St
W 4th St
W 3rd St
New York University
Broadway
Lafayette St
Great Jones St
NOHO
Bond St
Bleecker St
Crosby St
Lower East Side-2nd Ave
Broadway Lafayette St
Sara D Roosevelt Park
NOLITA
Jersey St
Bowery
Stanton St
Wooster St
Prince St
Mott St
Elizabeth St
Chrystie St
Mercer St
Rivington St
Spring St
Mulberry St
SOHO
Delancey St
Kenmare St
Broome St
Centre St
Center Market Pl
Antique Market
Grand St
Baxter St
Howard St
Hester St
Canal St
0 200 m
0 0.1 miles

SoHo, NoHo & Nolita

Sights

1 Artists Space ... E6
2 Children's Museum of the Arts ... A5
3 Drawing Center ... D6
4 Leslie-Lohman Museum of Gay & Lesbian Art ... E6
5 Merchant's House Museum ... G2
6 New York City Fire Museum ... B5
7 Ravenite Social Club ... G4

Eating

8 Balthazar ... F5
9 Butcher's Daughter ... H5
10 Café Gitane ... G4
11 Charlie Bird ... C4
12 Dutch ... D4
13 Estela ... G4
14 Il Buco Alimentari & Vineria ... G2
15 La Esquina ... F6
16 Lovely Day ... H5
17 Rubirosa ... G5
18 Ruby's ... G5
19 Saxon + Parole ... G3
20 Siggi's ... G3
21 Tacombi ... G4

Drinking & Nightlife

22 Jimmy ... D6
23 La Colombe ... F4
24 Madam Geneva ... G3
25 Pegu Club ... D4
26 Spring Lounge ... G5

Shopping

27 Adidas ... F3
28 Adidas Originals ... E4
29 Atrium ... F3
30 De Vera ... F7
31 Etiqueta Negra ... F4
32 Evolution ... E5
33 INA Men ... G4
34 Kiosk ... E5
35 McNally Jackson ... F4
36 MoMA Design Store ... F5
37 Odin ... F6
38 Opening Ceremony ... F7
39 Other Music ... F2
40 Piperlime ... E5
41 Rag & Bone ... E5
42 Resurrection ... G5
43 Saturdays ... F6
44 Scholastic ... F4
45 Scoop ... E6
46 Screaming Mimi's ... F2
47 Shakespeare & Co ... F1
48 Uniqlo ... F5
49 United Nude ... G3

Sports & Activities

50 Bunya Citispa ... D4
51 Great Jones Spa ... G2

Chinatown & Little Italy

Columbus Park Park

Map p86 (Mulberry & Bayard Sts; S J/Z, N/Q/R, 6 to Canal St) Mah-jongg meisters, slow-motion tai chi practitioners and old aunties gossiping over homemade dumplings: it might feel like Shanghai, but this leafy oasis is core to NYC history.

Eating

SoHo, NoHo & Nolita

Tacombi Mexican $

Map p82 (www.tacombi.com; 267 Elizabeth St, btwn E Houston & Prince Sts; tacos from $4; 11am-late Mon-Fri, from 9am Sat & Sun; S B/D/F/M to Broadway-Lafayette St, 6 to Bleecker St) Festively strung lights, foldaway chairs and Mexican men flipping tacos in an old VW Kombi: if you can't make it to the Yucatan shore, here's your Plan B. Casual, convivial and ever-popular, Tacombi serves up fine, fresh tacos, including breakfast numbers such as *huevos con chorizo* (eggs with chorizo).

Lovely Day Thai $

Map p82 (www.lovelydaynyc.com; 196 Elizabeth St, btwn Spring & Prince Sts; dishes $5.50-15; 11am-11pm Sun-Thu, to midnight Fri & Sat; S 6 to Spring St, J to Bowery, N/R to Prince St) With a look best described as doll house–meets–retro diner, super-cute Lovely Day seems like an incongruous setting for cheap, scrumptious Thai-inspired grub. But life is full of surprises, and you'll find a steady stream of fans chowing down competent pad thai, spicy green curry or salty-sweet Thai chow fun (flat-rice noodles, Chinese broccoli and hoisin sauce).

Ruby's Cafe $

Map p82 (www.rubyscafe.com; 219 Mulberry St, btwn Spring & Prince Sts; breakfast $5-12, lunch & dinner dishes $9.50-13.50; 9:30am-10:30pm;

S 6 to Spring St, N/R to Prince St) Good things come in small packages, including this five-table, cash-only, Aussie-inspired cafe. All bases are covered, from 'breakie' friendly avo toast (mashed avocado and fresh tomato on seven-grain toast) and buttermilk pancakes, to posh panini and pastas, vibrant salads and lusty burgers named after Australian surf beaches.

Estela Modern American, Mediterranean **$$**

Map p82 (212-219-7693; www.estelanyc.com; 47 E Houston St, btwn Mulberry & Mott Sts; dishes $12-32; 5:30-11pm Mon-Thu, to 11:30pm Fri & Sat, to 10:30pm Sun; S B/D/F/M to Broadway-Lafayette St, 6 to Bleecker St) Estela might be hopeless at hide-and-seek (its sneaky location up some nondescript stairs hardly tricks the hipster masses), but this busy, skinny wine-bar kicks butt in the kitchen. Pick and graze from a competent string of sharing plates, market driven and Mediterranean inspired.

Il Buco Alimentari & Vineria Italian **$$**

Map p82 (www.ilbucovineria.com; 53 Great Jones St, btwn Bowery & Lafayette St; lunch $15-32, dinner mains $19-42; cafe 7am-late Mon-Fri, from 9am-late weekends; restaurant noon-3pm & 5:30pm-late Mon- Fri, 11am-3pm & 5:30pm-late weekends; ; S 6 to Bleecker St, B/D/F/M to Broadway-Lafayette St) Whether it's wham-bam espresso at the front bar, a panino to go from the deli, or long-and-lazy Italian feasting in the sunken dining room, Il Buco's trendier spin-off delivers the goods. Brickwork, hessian and giant industrial lamps set a hip-n-rustic tone, echoed in the menu's bold, nostalgic flavors.

Rubirosa Pizzeria **$$**

Map p82 (212-965-0500; www.rubirosanyc.com; 235 Mulberry St, btwn Spring & Prince Sts; pizzas $16-26, mains $12-28; 11:30am-late; S N/R to Prince St, B/D/F/M to Broadway-Lafayette St, 6 to Spring St) Rubirosa's infallible family recipe for the perfect, whisper-thin pie crust lures a steady stream of patrons from every corner of the city.

Chinese Immigrants

The history of Chinese immigrants in New York City is a long and tumultuous one. The first Chinese people to arrive in America came to work under difficult conditions on the Central Pacific Railroad; others were lured to the West Coast in search of gold. When prospects dried up, many moved east to NYC to work in factory assembly lines and in the laundry houses of New Jersey.

Butcher's Daughter Vegetarian **$$**

Map p82 (www.thebutchersdaughter.com; 19 Kenmare St, at Elizabeth St; meals $9-16; 8am-3:45pm Mon, to late Tue-Sat; ; S J to Bowery, 6 to Spring St) While healthy it is, boring it's not: everything from the organic muesli, to the spicy kale Caesar salad with almond Parmesan, to the dinnertime Butcher's burger (kasha portobello patty with cashew cheddar cheese) is devilishly delish.

La Esquina Mexican **$$**

Map p82 (646-613-6700; www.esquinanyc.com; 114 Kenmare St, at Petrosino Sq; tacos from $3.25, mains $12-32; noon-late; S 6 to Spring St) This mega-popular and quirky little spot is three places really: a stand-while-you-eat taco window (open till 2am), a casual Mexican cafe and, downstairs, a dim, slinky, cavernous brasserie requiring reservations. Standouts include chorizo tacos, rubbed pork tacos, and mango and jicama salad, among other authentic and delicious options (many of which are also available upstairs at the anyone-welcome area).

Siggi's Cafe **$$**

Map p82 (www.siggysgoodfood.com; 292 Elizabeth St, btwn E Houston & Bleecker Sts; dishes $10-22; 11am-10:30pm Mon-Sat; ; S 6 to Bleecker St, B/D/F/M to Broadway-Lafayette St) Organic deliciousness awaits at this casual, art-slung cafe (bonus points for the wintertime fireplace). All bases are

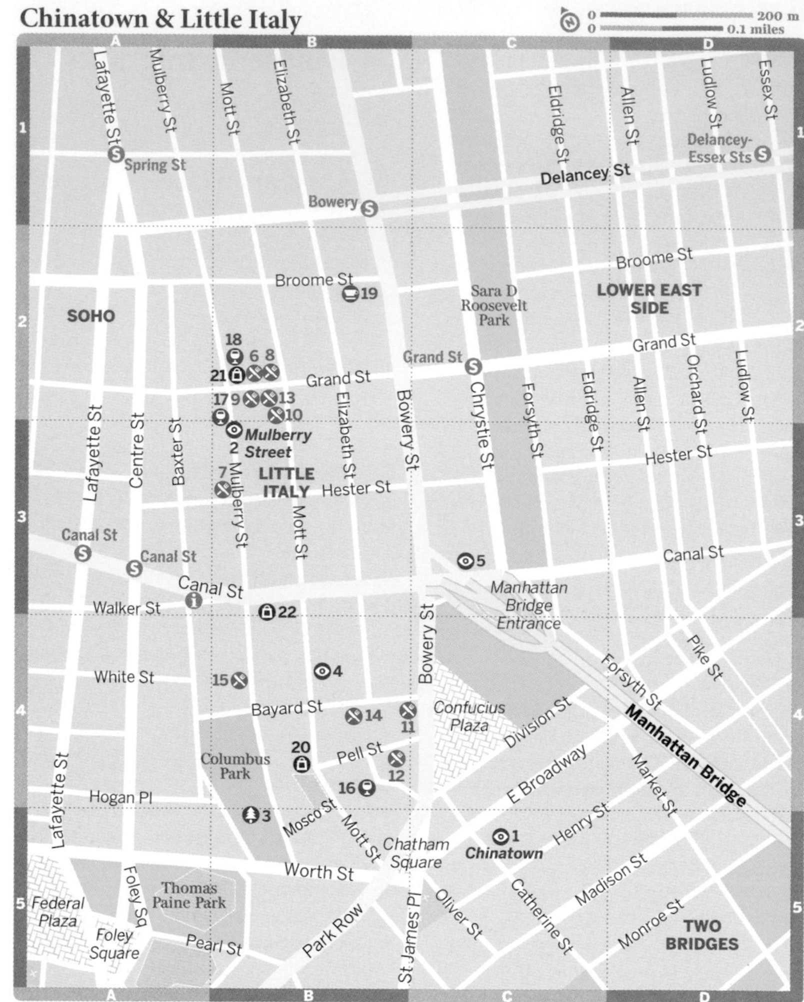

covered, from soups and salads, to made-from-scratch burgers, vegetarian lasagna, even slow-cooked organic stews.

Café Gitane Mediterranean **$$**

Map p82 (212-334-9552; www.cafegitanenyc.com; 242 Mott St, at Prince St; mains $14-16; 8:30am-midnight Sun-Thu, to 12:30am Fri & Sat; S N/R to Prince St, 6 to Spring St) Join the beautiful and their mignons for a fashionable nibble on the likes of blueberry and almond *friands* (small French cake), heart-of-palm salad or Moroccan couscous with organic chicken.

Saxon + Parole Modern American **$$$**

Map p82 (212-254-0350; www.saxonandparole.com; 316 Bowery, at Bleecker St; lunch $8-17, dinner mains $18-37; 5-11pm Mon-Thu, noon-midnight Fri, 10:30am-midnight Sat, 10:30am-10pm Sun; S 6 to Bleecker St, B/D/F/M to Broadway-Lafayette St) A fun, fashionable bistro-bar named in honor of two 19th-century racing horses, Saxon and Parole (pronounced

Chinatown & Little Italy

Don't Miss Sights

1 Chinatown C5
2 Mulberry Street B3

Sights

3 Columbus Park B5
4 Eastern States Buddhist Temple B4
5 Mahayana Temple C3

Eating

6 Bánh Mì Saigon Bakery B2
7 Da Gennaro B3
8 Di Palo B2
9 Ferrara Cafe & Bakery B2
10 Golden Steamer B2
11 Great New York Noodle Town B4
12 Joe's Shanghai B4
13 Nyonya B2
14 Original Chinatown Ice Cream Factory B4
15 Pho Viet Huong B4

Drinking & Nightlife

16 Apothéke B4
17 Mulberry Project B2
18 Mulberry Street Bar B2
19 Randolph B2

Shopping

20 Aji Ichiban B4
21 Alleva B2
22 Kam Man B3

'pearl') leads the charge with competent twists on comfort surf and turf. You might tuck into tuna tartare paired with *yuzu* (citrus fruit), avocado-wasabi and root chips, or an extraordinary Long Island duck, smoked to bacon-sweet perfection.

Belly full, trot through the secret door and kick on at cocktail den **Madam Geneva** **Map p82 (www.madamgeneva-nyc.com; 4 Bleecker St, at Bowery; 6pm-2am; S 6 to Bleecker St, B/D/F/M to Broadway-Lafayette St).**

Balthazar French **$$$**
Map p82 (212-965-1414; www.balthazarny.com; 80 Spring St, btwn Broadway & Crosby St; mains $17-45; 7:30am-late Mon-Fri, from 8am Sat & Sun; S 6 to Spring St, N/R to Prince St) Still the king of bistros, bustling (OK, *loud*) Balthazar is never short of a discriminating mob. That's all thanks to three winning details: its location in SoHo's shopping-spree heartland; the uplifting Paris-meets-NYC ambience; and, of course, the stellar something-for-everyone menu.

Dutch Modern American **$$$**
Map p82 (212-677-6200; www.thedutchnyc.com; 131 Sullivan St, btwn Prince & Houston Sts; mains $19-52; 11:30am-3pm & 5:30pm-late Mon-Fri, from 10am Sat & Sun; S C/E to Spring St, N/R to Prince St, 1 to Houston St) Whether perched at the front bar or dining snugly in the back room, you can always expect smart, farm-to-table soul grub at this see-and-be-seen stalwart. Slurp on silky Maine oysters, warm up with the juicy dry-aged burger, or keep it light with the likes of pillow-soft sea scallops spiked with arbol and chili salsa. Reservations are recommended.

Charlie Bird Italian, Modern American **$$$**
Map p82 (www.charliebirdnyc.com; 5 King St, entrance on Sixth Ave; small plates $12-16, mains $27-39; 5:30pm-late; S C/E to Spring St, 1 to Houston St) Tweeting away on SoHo's western fringe, loud-n-skinny Charlie Bird is winning regulars with its passion of local produce, rustic Italian know-how, and clever homespun twists. Mingle at the marble bar, or slip into a hand-sewn leather chair for artful dishes like grilled peach with prosciutto and fresh basil, or guanciale-spiked (Italian cured meat) duck-egg spaghetti, the latter a subtle play on Rome's classic carbonara.

Chinatown & Little Italy

Joe's Shanghai Chinese **$**
Map p86 (212-233-8888; www.joeshanghairestaurants.com; 9 Pell St btwn Bowery & Doyers St; mains $5-26; 11am-11pm; S N/Q/R, J/Z, 6 to Canal St, B/D to Grand St) Gather a gaggle of friends and descend upon this Flushing transplant en masse to spin the plastic lazy Susans and gobble down some of the juiciest *xiao long bao* in town. Dumplings aside, charge your chopsticks at budget-friendly thrills like spicy buffalo carp fish belly or jalapeno-sautéed pork and squid with dry bean curd. Cash only.

Di Palo
Deli $

Map p86 (☎212-226-1033; www.dipaloselects.com; 200 Grand St, at Mott St; sandwich from $7; 9am-6:30pm Mon-Sat to 4pm Sun; S B/D to Grand St, N/Q/R, J/Z, 6 to Canal St) Food bloggers revere the *porchetta* sandwich from this family-run deli; a crusty baguette stuffed with melt-in-your-mouth roast pork seasoned with garlic, fennel and herbs. Normally available from 1:30pm, the prized meat sells out in 20 minutes, so get there at 1:15pm or call ahead. Not available Mondays.

Pho Viet Huong
Vietnamese, Chinese $

Map p86 (☎212-233-8988; www.phoviethuong.com; 73 Mulberry St, btwn Bayard & Walker Sts; mains $5.50-17.50; 11am-10:30pm; S N/Q/R, J/Z, 6 to Canal St) Feast on slurp-worthy bowls of *pho* and dripping *bánh mì* (Vietnamese roast-pork sandwiches served on fat baguettes with piles of sliced cucumber, pickled carrots, hot sauce and cilantro), all to the sound of loose change in your pocket.

Bánh Mì Saigon Bakery
Vietnamese $

Map p86 (☎212-941-1514; www.banhmisaigonnyc.com; 198 Grand St, btwn Mulberry & Mott Sts; sandwiches $3.50-5.75; 8am-6pm; S N/Q/R, J/Z, 6 to Canal St) This no-frills storefront doles out some of the best *bánh mì* in town – we're talking crisp, toasted baguettes generously stuffed with hot peppers, pickled carrots, daikon, cucumber, cilantro and your choice of meat. Top billing goes to the classic BBQ pork version.

Great New York Noodle Town
Chinese $

Map p86 (☎212-349-0923; www.greatnynoodletown.com; 28 Bowery St, at Bayard St; dishes $3.50-16; 9am-4am; S N/Q/R, J/Z, 6 to Canal St) This Chinatown stalwart peddles endless incarnations of the long and slippery strands, from noodle soup with roast pork or duck, beef *chow fun* (wide rice noodles), spicy Singapore *mai fun* (rice vermicelli), wide Cantonese noodles with shrimp and egg or Hong Kong–style *lo mein* (wheat flour noodles) with ginger and onions.

Left: Salad Niçoise at Balthazar (p87); **Below:** Mah-jongg in Columbus Park (p84)
(LEFT) BLOOMBERG/GETTY IMAGES ©; (BELOW) MARK DAFFEY/GETTY IMAGES ©

Golden Steamer Chinese $

Map p86 (143a Mott St, btwn Grand & Hester Sts; buns from $0.70; 7am-7:30pm; S B/D to Grand St, N/Q/R, 6 to Canal St, J to Bowery) Squeeze into this hole-in-the-wall for the fluffiest, tastiest *bao* (steamed buns) in Chinatown.

Original Chinatown Ice Cream Factory Ice Cream $

Map p86 (212-608-4170; www.chinatownicecreamfactory.com; 65 Bayard St; scoop $4; 11am-10pm; ; S N/Q/R, J/Z, 6 to Canal St) Chinatown's favorite ice-cream peddler keeps it local with flavors such as green tea, ginger, durian and lychee sorbet.

Nyonya Malaysian $$

Map p86 (212-334-3669; 199 Grand St, btwn Mott & Mulberry Sts; mains $7-24; 11am-late; S N/Q/R, J/Z, 6 to Canal Street, B/D to Grand St) Take your palate to steamy Melaka at this bustling, cash-only temple to Chinese-Malay Nyonya cuisine. Savor the sweet, the sour and the spicy in classics including pungent *kangkung belacan* (sautéed water spinach spiked with spicy Malaysian shrimp paste), rich beef *randang* (spicy dry curry) and refreshing *rojak* (savory fruit salad tossed in a piquant tamarind dressing).

Drinking & Nightlife

La Colombe Cafe

Map p82 (www.lacolombe.com; 270 Lafayette St, btwn Prince & Jersey Sts; 7:30am-6:30pm Mon-Fri, from 8:30am Sat & Sun; S N/R to Prince St, 6 to Spring St) Spent SoHo shoppers reboot at this pocket-sized espresso bar. The brews are strong, full-bodied and worthy of any bar in Italy (note the cool Rome wall mural).

DAN HERRICK/GETTY IMAGES ©

Don't Miss
Mulberry Street

Named for the mulberry farms that once stood here, Mulberry St is now better known as the meat in Little Italy's sauce. It's an animated strip, packed with smooth-talking restaurant hawkers (especially between Hester and Grand Sts), wisecracking baristas and a healthy dose of kitschy souvenirs.

Despite the neighborhood's many changes over the years, history looms large. It was inside restaurant **Da Gennaro** Map p86 (129 Mulberry St, at Hester St), formerly Umberto's Clam House, that 'Crazy Joe' Gallo was gunned down on April 2, 1972, an unexpected birthday surprise for the Brooklyn-born mobster. One block further north stands fourth-generation **Alleva** Map p86 (188 Grand St, at Mulberry St), one of the city's original cheese shops and famed for its mozzarella. Across the street on Grand lies another veteran, **Ferrara Cafe & Bakery** Map p86 (195 Grand St; S B/D to Grand St), celebrated for its classic Italian pastries and gelati. Back on Mulberry, old-time **Mulberry Street Bar** Map p86 (☎212-226-9345; 176½ Mulberry St , btwn Broome & Grand Sts; S B/D to Grand St) was a favorite haunt of the late Frank Sinatra; its own TV cameos include *Law & Order* and *The Sopranos*. Take a gander at what was once the **Ravenite Social Club** Map p82 (247 Mulberry St; S 6 to Spring St, N/R to Prince St) to see how things have really changed around here. Now a designer shoe store, it was once a mobster hangout (originally known as the Alto Knights Social Club). Indeed, it was right here that big hitters such as Lucky Luciano and John Gotti (as well as the FBI, who kept a watchful eye from the building across the street) logged time.

NEED TO KNOW

Map p86; S N/Q/R, J/Z, 6 to Canal St, B/D to Grand St

Pegu Club

Cocktail Bar

Map p82 (www.peguclub.com; 77 W Houston St, btwn W Broadway & Wooster St; ⏲5pm-2am Sun-Wed, to 4am Thu-Sat; S B/D/F/M to Broadway-Lafayette St, C/E to Spring St) Elegant Pegu Club (named after a legendary gentleman's club in colonial-era Rangoon) is an obligatory stop for cocktail connoisseurs. Sink into a velvet lounge and savor seamless libations from award-winning bartender Kenta Goto.

Spring Lounge

Dive Bar

Map p82 (www.thespringlounge.com; 48 Spring St, at Mulberry St; ⏲8am-4am Mon-Sat, from noon Sun; S 6 to Spring St, N/R to Prince St) This neon-red rebel has never let anything get in the way of a good time. Fueling the fun are cheap drinks and free grub (hot dogs on Wednesdays from 5pm, bagels on Sundays from noon, while they last).

Mulberry Project

Cocktail Bar

Map p86 (☎646-448-4536; www.mulberryproject.com; 149 Mulberry St, btwn Hester & Grand Sts; ⏲6pm-1am Sun-Thu, to 4am Fri & Sat; S N/Q/R, J/Z, 6 to Canal St) Lurking behind an unmarked door is this intimate, cavernous cocktail den, with its festive, 'garden-party' backyard one of the best spots to chill in the hood.

Jimmy

Cocktail Bar

Map p82 (☎212-201-9118; www.jimmysoho.com; James Hotel, 15 Thompson St, at Grand St; ⏲5pm-1am Sun-Wed, to 2am Thu-Sat; S A/C/E, 1 to Canal St) Lofted atop the James Hotel in SoHo, Jimmy is a sky-high hangout with sweeping views of the city below. The summer months teem with tipsy patrons who spill out onto the open deck; in cooler weather, drinks are slung indoors from the centrally anchored bar guarded by floor-to-ceiling windows.

Apothéke

Cocktail Bar

Map p86 (☎212-406-0400; www.apothekenyc.com; 9 Doyers St; ⏲6:30pm-2am Mon-Sat, 8pm-2am Sun; S J to Chambers St, 4/5/6 to Brooklyn Bridge-City Hall) It takes a little effort to track down this former opium den–turned–apothecary bar on Doyers St. Inside, skilled barkeeps work like careful chemists, using local and organic produce from greenmarkets or the rooftop herb garden to produce intense, flavorful 'prescriptions.'

Apothéke

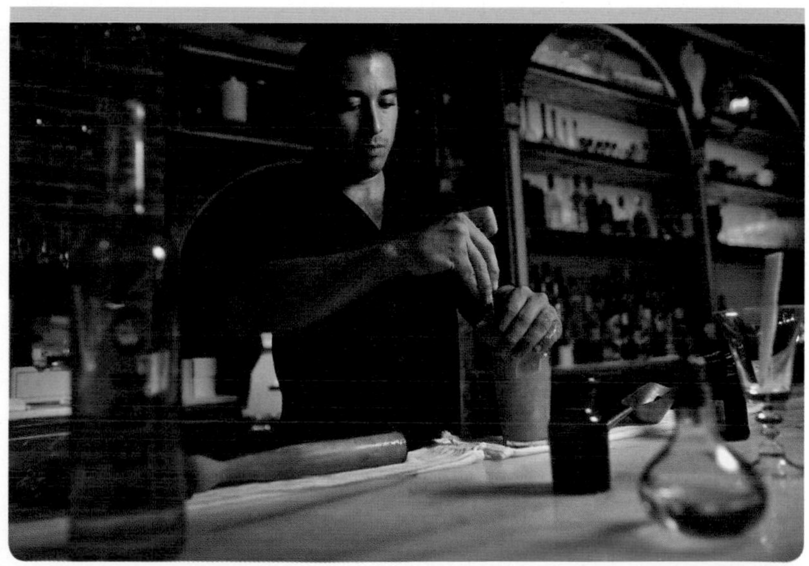

BLOOMBERG/GETTY IMAGES ©

Randolph Cafe, Cocktail Bar

Map p86 (www.randolphnyc.com/broome; 349 Broome St, btwn Bowery & Elizabeth St; ⌚10am-2am Mon-Wed, to 4am Thu-Sat, to midnight Sun; 📶; S J to Bowery) Laidback Randolph brews coffee by day and swirls cocktails by night. Beans are sourced from top-notch roasters like Intelligentsia, while cocktails focus on the seasonal and the creative.

Entertainment

Angelika Film Center Cinema

(☎212-995-2570; www.angelikafilmcenter.com; 18 W Houston St at Mercer St; tickets $10-14; 👪; S B/D/F/M to Broadway-Lafayette St) Angelika specializes in foreign and independent films and has some quirky charms (the rumble of the subway, long lines and occasionally bad sound). But its roomy cafe is a great place to meet and the beauty of its Stanford White–designed, beaux-arts building is undeniable.

Shopping

SoHo

Rag & Bone Fashion

Map p82 (www.rag-bone.com; 119 Mercer St, btwn Prince & Spring Sts; ⌚11am-8pm Mon-Sat, noon-7pm Sat; S N/R to Prince St) Downtown label Rag & Bone is a hit with many of New York's coolest, sharpest dressers, both men and women. Detail-orientated pieces range from clean-cut shirts and blazers, to graphic tees, feather-light strappy dresses, leathergoods and Rag & Bone's highly prized jeans.

MoMA Design Store Homewares, Gifts

Map p82 (☎646-613-1367; www.momastore.org; 81 Spring St, at Crosby St; ⌚10am-8pm Mon-Sat, 11am-7pm Sun; S N/R to Prince St, 6 to Spring St) The Museum of Modern Art's downtown retail space carries a huge collection of sleek, smart and clever objects for the home, office and wardrobe.

Saturdays Fashion, Accessories

Map p82 (www.saturdaysnyc.com; 31 Crosby St, btwn Broome & Grand Sts; ⌚8:30am-7pm

Angelika Film Center

LONELY PLANET/GETTY IMAGES ©

Mon-Fri, from 10am Sat & Sun; S N/Q/R, J/Z, 6 to Canal St) SoHo's version of a surf shop sees boards, wax and wetsuits paired up with designer grooming products, graphic art and surf tomes, and Saturdays' own line of high-quality, fashion-literate threads for dudes.

Adidas Originals Shoes, Fashion

Map p82 (212-673-0398; 136 Wooster St, btwn Prince & W Houston Sts; 11am-7pm Mon-Sat, noon-6pm Sun; S N/R to Prince St) Iconic triple-striped sneakers, many referencing Adidas' halcyon days from the '60s to the '80s, is what you get here. You can even custom-design your own. For the big-box retail experience, head to the 29,500-sq-ft **Adidas** **Map p82 (212-529-0081; 610 Broadway, at Houston St; 10am-10pm Mon-Sat, to 8pm Sun; S N/R to Prince St; B/D/F/M to Broadway-Lafayette St)** sneaker emporium a few blocks back.

Piperlime Fashion, Shoes

Map p82 (www.piperlime.com; 121 Wooster St, btwn Prince & Spring Sts; 10am-8pm Mon-Sat, 11am-7pm Sun; S N/R to Prince St, C/E to Spring St) Known for giving newer designers exposure, the store's stock is organized by categories such as 'Shortcut to Chic', 'Girl on a Budget' and 'Guest Editor's Picks,' the latter handpicked by the likes of stylist Rachel Zoe and actor/model Jessica Alba.

INA Men Vintage

Map p82 (www.inanyc.com; 19 Prince St, at Elizabeth St; noon-8pm Mon-Sat, to 7pm Sun; S 6 to Spring St, N/R to Prince St) Male style-meisters love INA for pre-loved, luxury clothes, shoes and accessories. Edits are high quality across the board, with sought-after items including the likes of Rag & Bone jeans, Alexander McQueen wool pants, Burberry shirts and Church's brogues. Next door is the women's store.

McNally Jackson Books

Map p82 (212-274-1160; www.mcnallyjackson.com; 52 Prince St, btwn Lafayette & Mulberry Sts; 10am-10pm Mon-Sat, to 9pm Sun; S N/R to Prince St; 6 to Spring St) Bustling, indie MJ stocks an excellent selection of magazines and books covering contemporary fiction, food writing, architecture and design, art and history. The in-store cafe is a fine spot to settle in with some reading material or to catch one of the frequent readings and book signings held here.

Scholastic Books, Children

Map p82 (www.scholastic.com/sohostore; 557 Broadway, btwn Prince & Spring Sts; 10am-7pm Mon-Sat, 11am-6pm Sun; S N/R to Prince St) Bright and sprawling, this bookstore is a wonderland for young readers (and the young at heart). Check the store's website for free weekly events like storytime sessions, character visits and sing-a-longs.

Kiosk Gifts

Map p82 (212-226-8601; www.kioskkiosk.com; 2nd fl, 95 Spring St, btwn Mercer St & Broadway; noon-7pm Mon-Sat; S N/R to Prince St, B/D/F/M to Broadway-Lafayette St) Kiosk's owners scour the planet for the most interesting and unusual items (from books and lampshades, to toothpaste), which they bring back to SoHo and proudly vend with museum-worthy acumen.

Uniqlo Fashion

Map p82 (917-237-8811; www.uniqlo.com; 546 Broadway, btwn Prince & Spring Sts; 10am-9pm Mon-Sat, 11am-8pm Sun; S N/R to Prince St, 6 to Spring St) This enormous, three-story Japanese emporium owes its popularity to good-looking, good-quality apparel at discount prices. You'll find Japanese denim, Mongolian cashmere, graphic T-shirts, svelte skirts and endless racks of colorful ready-to-wear – with most things at the sub-$100 mark.

United Nude Shoes

Map p82 (212-420-6000; www.unitednude.com; 25 Bond St, btwn Lafayette St & Bowery; noon-7pm Sun & Mon, 11am-7pm Tue-Thu, 11am-8pm Fri & Sat; S 6 to Bleecker St, B/D/F/M to Broadway-Lafayette St) The flagship store is stocked with improbably beautiful, statement-making footwear – flamboyant, classical, business-smart and sporty.

Other Music Music

Map p82 (212-477-8150; www.othermusic.com; 15 E 4th St, btwn Lafayette St & Broadway; 11am-9pm Mon-Fri, noon-8pm Sat, noon-7pm Sun; S 6 to Bleecker St) This indie-run CD store feeds its loyal fan base with a clued-in selection of, well, other types of music: offbeat lounge, psychedelic, electronica, indie rock etc, available new and used.

Etiqueta Negra Fashion, Shoes

Map p82 (212-219-4015; www.etiquetanegra.us; 273 Lafayette St, at Prince St; 11am-7pm Mon-Sat, from noon Sun; S N/R to Prince St, B/D/F/M to Broadway-Lafayette St) While we love the open-topped Bugatti race car parked near the cash register, the real reason to hit this Argentine boutique is for its timeless, well-priced threads for men.

Atrium Fashion, Shoes

Map p82 (212-473-3980; www.atriumnyc.com; 644 Broadway, at Bleecker St; 10am-9pm Mon-Sat, 11am-8pm Sun; S 6 to Bleecker St, B/D/F/M to Broadway-Lafayette St) Head here for interesting, unisex edits of detail-orientated designer wear – including shoes and accessories – from labels such as Drome, Canada Goose and T by Alexander Wang.

De Vera Antiques

Map p82 (212-625-0838; www.deveraobjects.com; 1 Crosby St, at Howard St; 11am-7pm Tue-Sat; S N/Q/R, J/Z, 6 to Canal St) Federico de Vera travels the globe in search of rare and exquisite jewelry, carvings, lacquerware and other *objets d'art* for this jewel-box of a store.

Odin Clothing, Accessories

Map p82 (212-966-0026; www.odinnewyork.com; 199 Lafayette St, btwn Kenmare & Broome Sts; 11am-8pm Mon-Sat, noon-7pm Sun; S 6 to Spring St, N/R to Prince St) Named after the mighty Norse god, Odin's flagship men's boutique carries hip downtown labels like 3.1 Phillip Lim, Rag & Bone and Death to Tennis. It's also a good place to browse for up-and-coming designers.

Opening Ceremony Fashion

Map p82 (212-219-2688; www.openingceremony.us; 35 Howard St, btwn Broadway & Lafayette St; 11am-8pm Mon-Sat, noon-7pm Sun; S N/Q/R, J/Z, 6 to Canal St) Opening Ceremony is famed for its never-boring edit of indie labels. The place showcases a changing roster of names from across the globe, complimented by Opening Ceremony's own creations.

Screaming Mimi's Vintage

Map p82 (212-677-6464; 382 Lafayette St, btwn E 4th & Great Jones Sts; noon-8pm Mon-Sat, 1-7pm Sun; S 6 to Bleecker St, B/D/F/M to Broadway-Lafayette St) This funtastic shop carries an excellent selection of yesteryear pieces – organized, ingeniously, by decade, from the '50s to the '90s (ask to see the small, stashed-away collection of clothing from the '20s, '30s and '40s).

SoHo streets
LATITUDESTOCK/GETTY IMAGES ©

Resurrection Vintage
Map p82 (212-625-1374; www.resurrection vintage.com; 217 Mott St, btwn Prince & Spring Sts; 11am-7pm Mon-Sat, noon-7pm Sun; S 6 to Spring St; N/R to Prince St) Boudoir-red Resurrection gives new life to cutting-edge designs from past decades. Striking, mint-condition pieces cover the eras of mod, glam-rock and new-wave design, and design deities like Marc Jacobs have dropped by for inspiration.

Shakespeare & Co Books
Map p82 (212-529-1330; www.shakeandco.com; 716 Broadway, at Washington Pl; 10am-9pm Mon-Sat, noon-7pm Sun; S N/R to 8th St; 6 to Astor Pl) You'll find a wide array of contemporary fiction and nonfiction, art books and tomes about NYC, not to mention a steady stream of aspiring actors and directors seeking out the perfect playscript downstairs.

Scoop Fashion
Map p82 (212-925-3539; www.scoopnyc.com; 473 Broadway, btwn Broome & Grand Sts; 11am-8pm Mon-Sat, to 7pm Sun; S N/Q/R to Canal St, 6 to Spring St) Scoop up contemporary threads from the likes of Theory, Diane Von Furstenberg, Michael Kors and J Brand at this handy one-stop shop.

Evolution Gifts
Map p82 (212-343-1114; www.theevolution store.com; 120 Spring St, btwn Mercer & Greene Sts; 11am-7pm; S N/R to Prince St, 6 to Spring St) Evolution keeps things quirky with natural-history collectibles usually seen in museum cabinets. This is the place to buy – or simply gawk at – framed beetles and butterflies, bugs frozen in amber-resin cubes, stuffed parrots, zebra hides and shark teeth, as well as stony wonders, from meteorites and fragments from Mars to 100-million-year-old fossils.

Chinatown

Aji Ichiban Food
Map p86 (212-233-7650; 37 Mott St, btwn Bayard & Mosco Sts; 10am-8pm; S N/Q/R, J/Z, 6 to Canal St) In Japanese, the name means 'awesome,' and it's exactly what sweet-tooths think once inside this Hong Kong candy shop. Defy your dentist with sesame-flavored marshmallows, Thai durian milk candy, preserved plums, mandarin peel, blackcurrant gummies and dried guava.

Kam Man Homewares
Map p86 (212-571-0330; 200 Canal St, btwn Mulberry & Motts Sts; 9am-8.30pm; S N/Q/R, J/Z, 6 to Canal St) Head past hanging ducks to the basement of this classic Canal St food store for cheap Chinese and Japanese tea sets, plus kitchen products such as chopsticks, bowls, stir-frying utensils and rice cookers.

Sports & Activities

Great Jones Spa Day Spa
Map p82 (212-505-3185; www.greatjonesspa.com; 29 Great Jones St, btwn Lafayette St & Bowery; 4-10pm Mon, from 9am Tue-Sun; S 6 to Bleecker St; B/D/F/M to Broadway-Lafayette St) Don't skimp on the services at this downtown feng shui master, complete with three-story indoor waterfall. If you spend more than $100 (not hard: hour-long massages start at $140, hour-long facials start at $130), you get two-hour access in the water lounge's hot tub, rock sauna, chakra-light steam room and cold pool. Swimwear is essential.

Bunya Citispa Day Spa
Map p82 (212-388-1288; www.bunyacitispa.com; 474 W Broadway, btwn Prince & W Houston Sts; 10am-10pm Mon-Sat, to 9pm Sun; S N/R to Prince St; C/E to Spring St) Ex-models and fatigued shoppers retreat to this chic, Asian-inspired spa for a little Eastern pampering. Tension-soothing solutions include reflexology, head massage with green-tea hair treatment, hot stone massage and the popular 'Oriental herbal compress' Thai massage (one hour, $120).

East Village & Lower East Side

Old meets new on every block of this downtown duo. These are two of the city's hottest 'hoods for nightlife and cheap eats that lure students, bankers and scruffier types alike.

No longer the edgy radical area of decades past, the East Village is still very cool – filled with endless boutiques, bars, restaurants and characters. These days, however, it's developers who are truly shaping the physical landscape. Stick to the area around Tompkins Square Park, and the lettered avenues (known as Alphabet City) to its east, for interesting nooks – as well as a collection of little community gardens that provide leafy respites.

Originally a settlement for Jews and then Latinos, the Lower East Side (LES) has become the place to be seen. It's either about cramming yourself into low-lit lounges and live-music clubs or about snagging a table at a pricey restaurant. A bunch of luxury high-rise condominiums and hip boutique hotels coexist with large public-housing projects and blocks of tenement-style buildings.

Street mural in the East Village

East Village & Lower East Side Highlights

Bar Scene (p109)

From cocktail bars to dirty dives filled with NYU students or lounges pulling in outsiders wanting to booze in NY punk rock's old HQ, the East Village is the ideal neighborhood for a tippling tour. Meanwhile, the Lower East Side is hipster central. In a relatively concentrated area there are dozens of pick-up spots, low-key hangouts, re-created speakeasies, ironically themed dives, and up-towners wanting 'in' on the cool side of town.

1

2

Art Spaces (p115)

A recent anchor in Manhattan's ever-spinning art world, the stacked-box architecture of the New Museum of Contemporary Art (p103) offers a transformative take on the typical gallery experience. Exhibitions are mind-bending iterations of art across myriad media. A handful of galleries, including Sperone Westwater (p115), have also thrown open their doors in the Lower East Side, offering cutting-edge fare. New Museum of Contemporary Art

LONELY PLANET/GETTY IMAGES ©

3

Tenement Museum (p110)

There's no museum in New York that humanizes the city's colorful past quite like the Lower East Side Tenement Museum, which puts the neighborhood's heartbreaking but inspiring heritage on full display in several re-creations of turn-of-the-20th-century tenements. Always evolving and expanding, the museum also has a variety of tours and talks beyond the museum's walls – a must for any curious visitor interested in old New York.

GARDEL BERTRAND/GETTY IMAGES ©

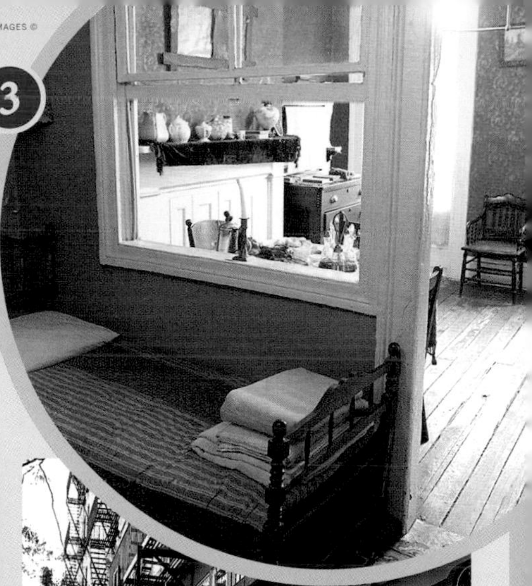

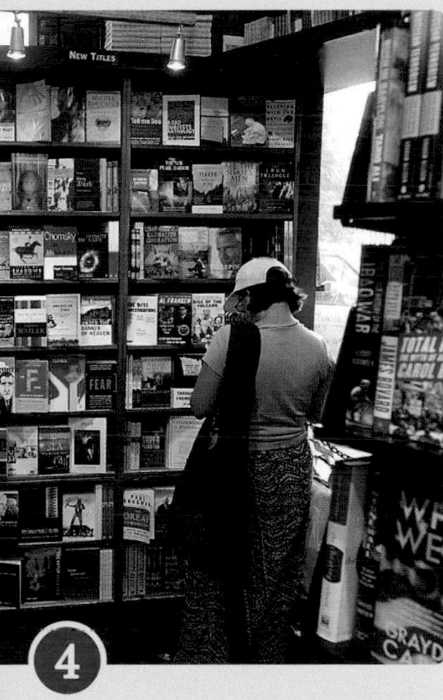

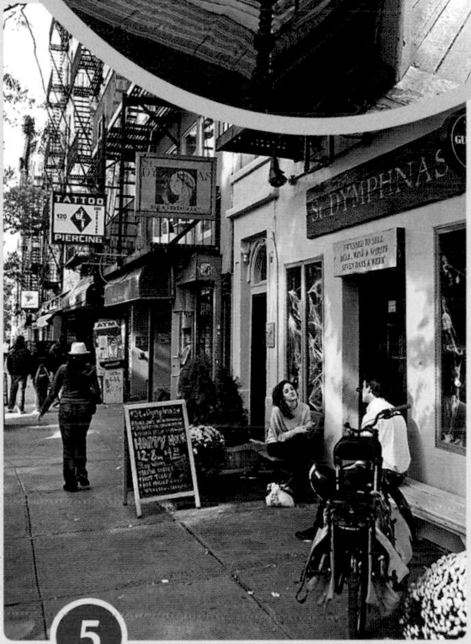

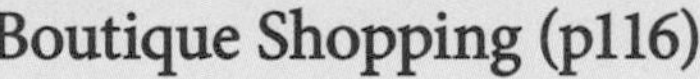

4

Boutique Shopping (p116)

The downtown fashion crowd looking for that edgy, experimental or old-school hip-hop look head to the Lower East Side. Sprinkled throughout are stores selling vintage apparel, vegan shoes, one-of-a-kind sneakers, sex toys, left-wing books and more. In the East Village, you'll still find punk-rock T-shirt shops, tattoo parlors and dusty stores selling vintage clothing alongside new local designers and even chain stores.

5

St Marks Place (p105)

In New York City almost every street tells a story, from the action unfurling before your eyes to the dense history hidden behind colorful facades. St Marks Place is one of the best strips of pavement in the city for storytelling, as almost every building on these hallowed blocks is rife with tales from a time when the East Village embodied a far more lawless spirit.

Snacking on the Lower East Side

You'll find a mind-blowing variety of foods on this snacking tour around the Lower East Side. The best time to go is around lunchtime. Arrive with an empty stomach, start off slow, and pace yourself. You can always get a few items for takeaway to eat later.

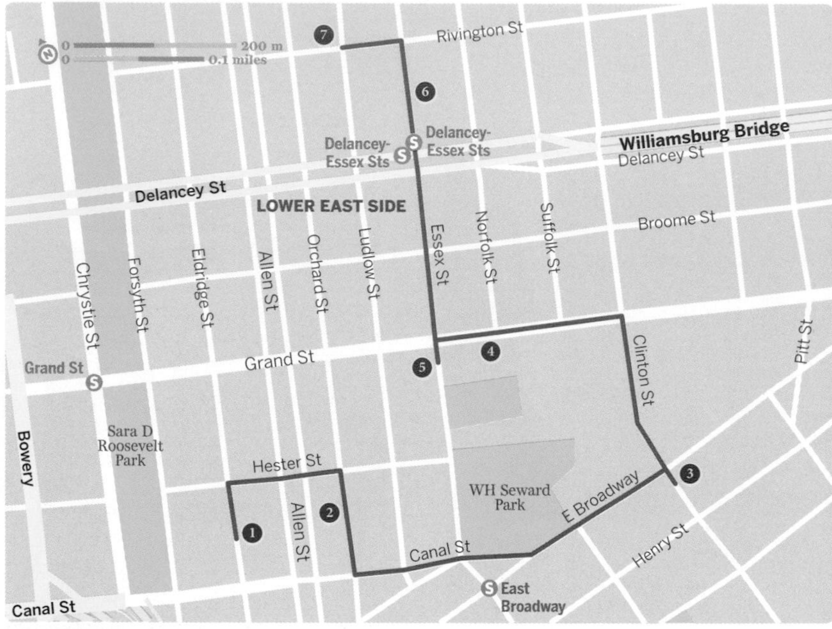

WALK FACTS

- **Start** Prosperity Dumplings
- **End** 'inoteca
- **Distance** 1 mile
- **Time** Two hours

❶ Prosperity Dumpling

Being on the edge of Chinatown, it's only fitting to start off at Prosperity Dumpling (46 Eldridge St), serving delectably plump pockets filled with chives and pork, chicken or vegetables. And the prices are unreal (eight dumplings will set you back $2).

❷ Cheeky Sandwiches

One block over is Cheeky Sandwiches (35 Orchard St), a ramshackle little eatery that looks like it's been airlifted in from New Orleans. The homemade biscuits, biscuit sandwiches and bread pudding are outstanding.

❸ Eastwood

Afterwards stroll down to Eastwood (200 Clinton St), which is a curious hybrid of Scottish and Israeli cooking. To see what it's all about, try the Israeli Scotch egg – which is like a hardboiled egg encased in a falafel. Exquisite.

4 Donut Plant

Loop back up to Grand St and stroll into the Donut Plant (379 Grand St). True to name, this place cranks out beautifully crafted donuts in flavors such as pistachio, tres leches and Valhrona chocolate, plus daily and seasonal specials.

5 Pickle Guys

Around the corner, you'll find the Pickle Guys (49 Essex St), an open storefront crammed with vats of pickled products of all kinds: cukes of all varieties, olives, sweet peppers, beets and more. Pickles have been around the Lower East Side since the early 1900s, and this place feels like the real deal.

6 Essex Street Market

Next, it's time to tackle the granddaddy of snack spots: the Essex Street Market (120 Essex St), home to smoked salmon, first-rate bagels, gourmet cheeses, produce stands and various ethnic food stalls. Our favorites: Brooklyn Taco Company for *chilorio* beef brisket tacos, Boubouki for spinach pie and baklava, and ice cream at Luca & Bosco (try the spicy cashew caramel).

7 'inoteca

The market is a good place to end for the day, though if you're ready for a drink after all that eating, head around the corner to 'inoteca (98 Rivington St), a great little wine bar that stocks more than 600 different wines, including 25 by the glass.

The Best...

PLACES TO EAT

Cafe Mogador Neighborhood classic serving delicious tagines and celebrated brunches. (p104)

Westville East New American comfort food; our favorite of the three downtown locations. (p105)

Kuma Inn Charming, secretive spot for creative pan-Asian cooking. (p108)

Clinton Street Baking Company Best breakfasts in town. (p108)

PLACES TO DRINK

McSorley's Old Ale House Sawdust floors, cobweb-covered fixtures and old-time ambiance. (p111)

Wayland Jaunty spot for rye whiskey, 'moonshine' cocktails and bluegrass. (p110)

Ten Bells Charming candelit bar with great wines and mouth-watering Spanish tapas. (p113)

Immigrant Twin narrow bars doling out excellent microbrews and wines by the glass. (p112)

CULTURAL SPACES

Anthology Film Archives Unique cinema you won't see elsewhere. (p115)

La MaMa ETC Venerable theater that stages thought-provoking and experimental works. (p114)

Restaurant kitchen in the East Village

Discover East Village & Lower East Side

Getting There & Away

- **Subway** Trains don't go far enough east to carry you to most East Village locations, but it's a quick walk (and even quicker cab or bus ride) from the 6 at Astor Pl, the F, V at Lower East Side-Second Ave or the L at First or Third Aves. The subway's F line (Lower East Side-Second Ave or Delancey St stops) will let you off in the thick of the Lower East Side.
- **Bus** If you're traveling from the west side, it's better to take the M14 (across 14th St) or the M21 (down Houston).

Sights

East Village

Tompkins Square Park Park

Map p112 (www.nycgovparks.org; E 7th & 10th Sts, btwn Aves A & B; 6am-midnight; S 6 to Astor Pl) This 10.5-acre park is like a friendly town square for locals, who gather for chess at concrete tables, picnics on the lawn on warm days and spontaneous guitar or drum jams on various grassy knolls. It's also the site of basketball courts, a fun-to-watch dog run (a fenced-in area where humans can unleash their canines), frequent summer concerts and an always-lively kids' playground.

The annual Howl! Festival of East Village Arts brings Allen Ginsberg–inspired theater, music, film, dance and spoken-word events to the park and various neighborhood venues each September. The Charlie Parker Jazz Festival is also held here, bringing some of the biggest jazz names to the 'hood each August.

St Mark's in the Bowery Church

Map p112 (212-674-6377; www.stmarksbowery.org; 131 E 10th St, at Second Ave; 10am-6pm Mon-Fri; S L to 3rd Ave, 6 to Astor Pl) Though it's most popular with East Village locals for its cultural offerings – such as poetry readings hosted by the Poetry Project or cutting-edge dance performances from Danspace and the Ontological Hysteric Theater – this is also a historic site.

East River Park

DAN HERRICK/GETTY IMAGES ©

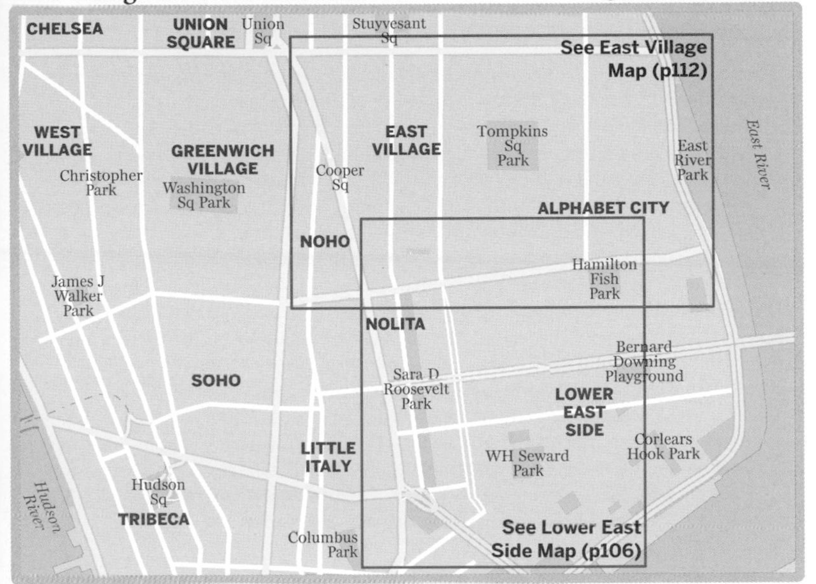

Lower East Side

New Museum of Contemporary Art — Museum

Map p106 (212-219-1222; www.newmuseum.org; 235 Bowery, btwn Stanton & Rivington Sts; adult/child $16/free, 7-9pm Thu free; 11am-6pm Wed & Fri-Sun, to 9pm Thu; S N/R to Prince St, F to 2nd Ave, J/Z to Bowery, 6 to Spring St) A recent addition to the neighborhood, the New Museum of Contemporary Art is a sight to behold: a seven-story stack of off-kilter, white, ethereal boxes, designed by Tokyo-based architects Kazuyo Sejima and Ryue Nishizawa of SANAA and the New York–based firm Gensler. The thrills don't stop when you step inside, either, as the city's sole museum dedicated to contemporary art has brought a steady menu of edgy works in new forms.

Museum at Eldridge Street Synagogue — Museum

Map p106 (212-219-0302; www.eldridgestreet.org; 12 Eldridge St, btwn Canal & Division Sts; adult/child $10/6; 10am-5pm Sun-Thu, to 3pm Fri; S F to East Broadway) This landmarked house of worship, built in 1887, was once the center of Jewish life, before falling into squalor in the 1920s. Left to rot, it has only recently been reclaimed, and now shines with original splendor. Its onsite museum gives tours every half hour, with the last one departing at 4pm.

East River Park — Park

Map p112 (FDR Dr & E Houston St; S F to Delancey-Essex Sts) In addition to the great ballparks, running and biking paths, 5000-seat amphitheater for concerts and expansive patches of green, this park has cool, natural breezes and stunning views of the Williamsburg, Manhattan and Brooklyn Bridges.

Eating

East Village

Tacos Morelos — Mexican $

Map p112 (438 E 9th St, btwn First Ave & Ave A; tacos from $2.50; noon-midnight Sun-Thu, to 2am Fri & Sat; S L to 1st Ave) This famed food truck put down roots in a no-frills East Village storefront in 2013, quickly becoming

Community Gardens

After a stretch of arboreal abstinence in New York City, the community gardens of Alphabet City are breathtaking. A network of gardens was carved out of abandoned lots to provide low-income neighborhoods with a communal backyard. Trees and flowers were planted, sandboxes were built, found-art sculptures erected and domino games played – all within green spaces wedged between buildings or even claiming entire blocks. You can visit most on weekends, when the gardens tend to be open to the public; many gardeners are activists within the community and are a good source of information about local politics.

Le Petit Versailles Map p112 (http://lpvtv.blogspot.com; 346 E Houston St, at Ave C; S F to Delancey St, J/M/Z to Essex St) is a unique marriage of a verdant oasis and an electrifying arts organization, offering a range of quirky performances and screenings to the public. The **6th & B Garden** Map p112 (www.6bgarden.org; E 6th St & Ave B; 1-6pm Sat & Sun; S 6 to Astor Pl) is a well-organized space that hosts free music events, workshops and yoga sessions; check the website for details. Three dramatic weeping willows, an odd sight in the city, grace the twin plots of **9th St Garden** and **La Plaza Cultural** Map p112 (www.laplazacultural.com; E 9th St, at Ave C; noon-5pm Sat & Sun Apr-Oct). Also check out the **All People's Garden** Map p112 (E 3rd St, btwn Aves B & C) and **Brisas del Caribe** Map p112 (237 E 3rd St).

one of Manhattan's favorite tacos. Tip: pay the $0.50 extra for the homemade tortilla.

Minca Noodles $

Map p112 (212-505-8001; www.newyorkramen.com; 536 E 5th St btwn Aves A & B; ramen $11-14; noon-11:30pm; S F to Second Ave, J/M/Z to Essex St, F to Delancey St) The epitome of an East Village hole-in-the-wall, Minca focuses all of its attention on the food: cauldron-esque bowls of steaming ramen served with a recommended side order of fried gyoza.

Kanoyama Sushi $

Map p112 (212-777-5266; www.kanoyama.com; 175 Second Ave, near E 11th St; rolls from $5; 5:30-11pm; ; S L to Third Ave; L, N/Q/R/W, 4/5/6 to 14th St-Union Sq) Providing no-fuss sushi with fresh daily specials in the heart of the East Village, Kanoyama is a local favorite that has so far been overlooked by the city's big-name food critics (that might explain its unpretentious air).

Veselka Ukrainian $

Map p112 (212-228-9682; www.veselka.com; 144 Second Ave, at 9th St; mains $10-18; 24hr; S L to 3rd Ave, 6 to Astor Pl) A bustling tribute to the area's Ukrainian past, Veselka dishes out *varenyky* (handmade dumplings) and veal goulash amid the usual suspects of greasy comfort food.

Angelica Kitchen Vegan, Cafe $$

Map p112 (212-228-2909; www.angelicakitchen.com; 300 E 12th St, btwn First & Second Aves; dishes $11-19; 11:30am-10:30pm; ; S L to 1st Ave) This enduring herbivore classic has a calming vibe – candles, tables both intimate and communal, and a mellow, longtime staff – and enough creative options to make your head spin.

Cafe Mogador Moroccan & Middle Eastern $$

Map p112 (212-677-2226; 101 St Marks Pl; mains lunch $8-14, dinner $17-21; 9am-1am Sun-Thu, to 2am Fri & Sat; S 6 to Astor Pl) Family-run Mogador is a long-running NYC classic, serving fluffy piles of couscous, char-grilled lamb and merguez sausage over basmati rice and satisfying mixed platters of hummus and baba ghanoush. Brunch (served weekends 9am to 4pm) is excellent.

GARDEL BERTRAND/GETTY IMAGES ©

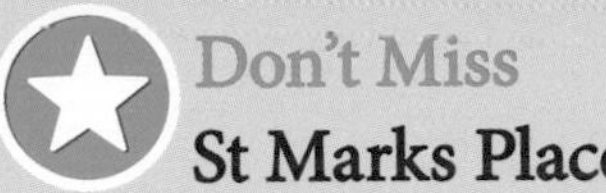

Don't Miss
St Marks Place

Easily one of NYC's most famous streets, St Marks Place is also one of the city's smallest, occupying only three blocks between Astor Pl and Tompkins Square Park. The road, however, is jam-packed with historical tidbits that would delight any trivia buff. Some of the most important addresses include number 2, 4, 96 and 98, and 122 St Marks Place. Number 2 St Marks Place is known as the St Mark's Ale House, but for a time it was the famous Five-Spot, where jazz fiend Thelonious Monk got his start in the 1950s.

A cast of colorful characters have left their mark at 4 St Marks Place: Alexander Hamilton's son built the structure, James Fenimore Cooper lived here in the 1830s and Yoko Ono's Fluxus artists descended upon the building in the 1960s.

The buildings at 96 and 98 St Marks Place are immortalized on the cover of Led Zeppelin's *Physical Graffiti* album. Though it closed in the 1990s, number 122 St Marks Place was the location of a popular cafe called Sin-é, where Jeff Buckley and David Gray often performed.

NEED TO KNOW

Map p112 St Marks Pl, Ave A to Third Ave; S N/R/W to 8th St-NYU, 6 to Astor Pl

Westville East Modern American **$$**
Map p112 (☎212-677-2033; www.westvillenyc.com; 173 Ave A; mains $11-22; ⏲10am-11pm; S L to 1st Ave, 6 to Astor Pl) Market-fresh veggies and mouthwatering mains is the name of the game at Westville, and it doesn't hurt that the cottage-chic surrounds are undeniably charming.

Luzzo's Pizzeria **$$**
Map p112 (☎212-473-7447; 211-213 First Ave, btwn 12th & 13th Sts; pizzas from $20; ⏲noon-11pm Tue-Sun, 5-11pm Mon; S 1st Ave)

Lower East Side

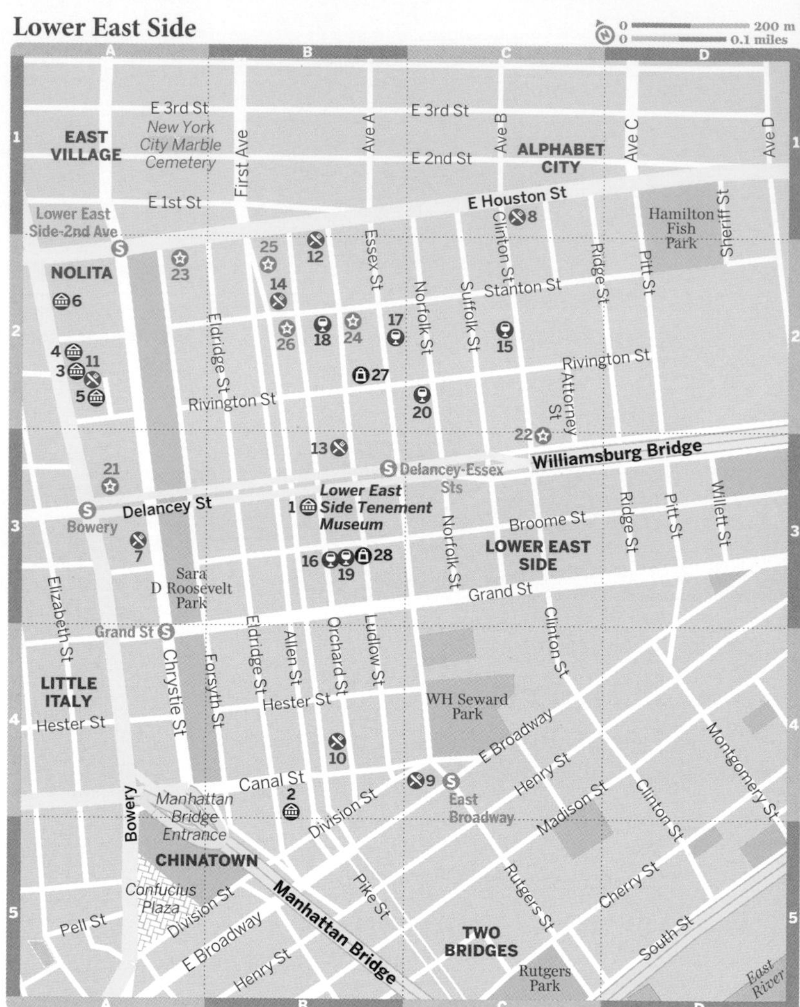

Fan-favorite Luzzo's occupies a thin sliver of real estate in the East Village, which gets stuffed to the gills each evening as discerning diners feast on thin-crust pies, kissed with ripe tomatoes and cooked in a coal-fired stove.

Redhead — Southern $$

Map p112 (☎212-533-6212; www.theredheadnyc.com; 349 E 13th St, btwn First & Second Aves; mains $12-24; ⏰5:30pm-1am Mon-Sat, 5-10pm Sun; S L to First Ave; L to Third Ave; 6 to Astor Pl) Cozy corners of exposed brick and warm smiles from the staff mirror the home-style comfort food, which has a distinctly Southern bent.

Motorino — Pizzeria $$

Map p112 (www.motorinopizza.com; 349 E 12th St btwn First & Second Aves; individual pizza $15-18; ⏰11am-midnight Sun-Thu, to 1am Fri & Sat; 🍴; S L to First Ave; 4/5/6 to 14th St-Union Sq) Crusts that are both chewy and pillowy at this intimate East Village restaurant.

Lower East Side

MUD Cafe **$$**

Map p112 (212-228-9074; www.themudtruck.com; 307 E 9th St, btwn Second & First Aves; brunch $15; 8am-midnight; S L to Third Ave; L to First Ave; 4/6 to Astor Pl) Offering trustworthy beans and a foolproof brunch that'll put some hair on the dog, this 9th St nook is a favorite among East Villagers looking for a quick caffeine fix or a friendly place to loiter with a book.

Brick Lane Curry House Indian **$$**

Map p112 (306 E 6th St, btwn First & Second Aves; mains $16-25; noon-11pm Sun-Thu, to 1am Fri & Sat) Modeled on the curry houses of East London, Brick Lane serves authentic tikka massala, vindaloo and tandoori that far surpasses the neighboring Indian joints lining E 6th St (though the bill certainly reflects this).

Upstate Seafood **$$**

Map p112 (www.upstatenyc.com; 95 First Ave, btwn 5th & 6th Sts; mains $15-30; 5-11pm; S F to 2nd Ave) Small and often overlooked, Upstate nevertheless serves outstanding seafood dishes and craft beers. The small always-changing menu features the likes of beer-steamed mussels, seafood stew, scallops over mushroom risotto, softshell crab and wondrous oyster selections.

Prune American **$$$**

Map p112 (212-677-6221; www.prunerestaurant.com; 54 E 1st St, btwn First & Second Aves; mains brunch/dinner from $12/25; 5:30-11pm daily & 10am-3:30pm Sat & Sun; S F/V to Lower East Side-Second Ave) Expect lines around the block on the weekend, when the hungover show up to cure their ills with Prune's brunches and excellent Bloody Marys (in 10 varieties). The small room is always busy as diners pour in for pan-roasted bass with melted leeks, seared duck breast and rich sweetbreads. Reservations available for dinner only.

Lower East Side

Dimes Cafe **$**

Map p106 (212-240-9410; 143 Division St, btwn Canal & Ludlow Sts; mains $8-12; 8am-4pm Mon-Fri, from 9am Sat & Sun;) A design-minded group crowds in for eggy breakfasts (served all day), bowls of açaí (that richly flavored, vitamin-rich Amazonian berry), creative salads (with fennel, blood orange, Brussel sprouts, pumpkin seeds), roasted vegetables and pulled chicken or spicy roasted beat sandwiches.

Meatball Shop Italian **$**

Map p106 (212-982-8895; www.themeatballshop.com; 84 Stanton St, btwn Allen & Orchard Sts; mains from $10; noon-2am Sun-Thu,

to 4am Thu-Sat; **S** 2nd Ave; F to Delancey St; J/M/Z to Essex St)** Elevating the humble meatball to high art, the Meatball Shop serves up five varieties of juiciness (including a vegetable option). The LES branch boasts a rock-and-roll vibe, with tattooed waitstaff and prominent beats.

Clinton Street Baking Company — American $

Map p106 (646-602-6263; www.clintonstreetbaking.com; 4 Clinton St, btwn Stanton & Houston Sts; mains from $9-17; 8am-4pm & 6-11pm Mon-Sat, 9am-6pm Sun; S J/M/Z to Essex St, F to Delancey St, F to Second Ave) Mom-and-pop shop extraordinaire, Clinton Street Baking Company gets the blue-ribbon in so many categories – best pancakes (blueberry! swoon!), best muffins, best po'boys (southern-style sandwiches), best biscuits etc – that you're pretty much guaranteed a stellar meal no matter what time of day (or night) you stop by.

Kuma Inn — Asian $$

Map p106 (212-353-8866; 113 Ludlow St, btwn Delancey & Rivington Sts; small dishes $8-14; dinner Tue-Sun; S F, J/M/Z to Delancey-Essex Sts) Reservations are a must at this popular spot in a secretive 2nd-floor location (look for a small red door with 'Kuma Inn' painted the concrete side). The Filipino- and Thai-inspired tapas runs the gamut, from vegetarian summer rolls (with jicama) to spicy drunken shrimp, and pan-roasted scallops with bacon and sake. Bring your own beer, wine or sake (corkage fee applies).

Boil — Seafood $$

Map p106 (139 Chrystie St, btwn Delancey & Broome Sts; shrimp/crab from $12/30 per pound; 5-11pm Mon-Fri, to midnight Sat & Sun) Crustaceans, of course, are the reason you're here and you'll make an ungodly mess tearing into succulent Dungeness crab, lobster, crawfish, shrimp and clams (hence the gloves). Craft beers go down nicely with the proceedings. Cash only.

Left: Katz's Delicatessen; **Below:** Classic New York pizzas
(LEFT) RACHEL LEWIS/GETTY IMAGES ©; (BELOW) JUANMONINO/GETTY IMAGES ©

Katz's Delicatessen Deli **$$**
Map p106 (☎212-254-2246; www.katzsdelicatessen.com; 205 E Houston St, at Ludlow St; pastrami on rye $17; ⏰8am-10:45pm Mon-Wed & Sun, to 2:45am Thu-Sat; Ⓢ F to 2nd Ave) Though visitors won't find many remnants of the classic, old-world-Jewish Lower East Side dining scene, there are a few stellar holdouts, among them the famous Katz's Delicatessen, where Meg Ryan faked her orgasm in the 1989 Hollywood flick *When Harry Met Sally*, and where, if you love classic deli grub such as pastrami and salami on rye, it just might have the same effect on you.

Fat Radish Modern British **$$$**
Map p106 (17 Orchard St, btwn Hester & Canal Sts; mains $18-28; ⏰noon-3:30pm daily, 5:30pm-midnight Mon-Sat, to 10pm Sun; 🥕; Ⓢ F to East Broadway, B/D to Grand St) The young and fashionable pack into this dimly lit dining room with exposed white brick and industrial touches. There's a loud buzz and people checking each other out but the mains, typical of the local-seasonal-haute-pub-fare fad, are worth your attention.

Freemans American **$$$**
Map p106 (☎212-420-0012; www.freemansrestaurant.com; end of Freeman Alley; mains lunch $12-19, dinner $22-32; ⏰11am-11:30pm Mon-Fri, from 10am Sat & Sun; Ⓢ F to 2nd Ave) Tucked down a back alley, the charmingly located Freeman's draws a mostly hipster crowd who let their chunky jewelry clang on the wooden tables as they lean over to sip overflowing cocktails.

Drinking & Nightlife

East Village

Ost Cafe Cafe
Map p112 (441 E 12th St, cnr Ave A; ⏰7:30am-10pm Mon-Fri, from 8:30am Sat & Sun; Ⓢ L to

WENDY CONNETT/ALAMY ©

Don't Miss
Lower East Side Tenement Museum

This museum puts the neighborhood's heartbreaking but inspiring heritage on full display in three re-creations of turn-of-the-20th-century tenements, including the late-19th-century home and garment shop of the Levine family from Poland, and two immigrant dwellings from the Great Depressions of 1873 and 1929.

The visitor center shows a video detailing the difficult life endured by the people who once lived in the surrounding buildings, which more often than not had no running water or electricity. Museum visits are available only as part of scheduled tours (the price of which is included in the admission), which typically operate daily. But call ahead or check the website for the schedules, as they change frequently. The museum also leads other tours, from one that explores various Lower East Side sites and their role in the neighborhood's immigration history to another that visits the restored home of Irish immigrants who dealt with the death of a child in the 1800s.

NEED TO KNOW

Map p106 ✆212-982-8420; www.tenement.org; 103 Orchard St, btwn Broome & Delancey Sts; admission $22; ⌚10am-6pm; Ⓢ B/D to Grand St, J/M/Z to Essex St, F to Delancey St

First Ave) With exposed brick walls, pressed tin ceiling, velvety armchairs and marble-topped cafe tables, Ost Cafe has class. It also has excellent coffee drinks (the kind that are topped with foam art) and wines by the glass (around $11).

Wayland Bar

Map p112 (700 E 9th St, cnr Ave C; ⌚5pm-4am; Ⓢ L to 1st Ave) Whitewashed walls, weathered floorboards and salvaged lamps give this urban outpost a Mississippi flair, which goes just right with the live music on weekdays (bluegrass, jazz, folk).

Proletariat
Bar

Map p112 (102 St Marks Pl, btwn First Ave & Ave A; ⏲5pm-2am; S L to 1st Ave) The cognoscenti of NYC's beer world pack this tiny, 10-stool bar just west of Tompkins Square Park.

Golden Cadillac
Bar

Map p112 (13 First Ave, cnr 1st St; ⏲5pm-2am Sun-Wed, to 4am Thu-Sat; S 2nd Ave) This enticing new drinking spot pays homage to grittier, hard-drinking days of the 1970s, with glorious wood paneling, patterned wallpaper and groove-heavy '70s tunes (disco, funk) playing overhead – plus 1970s Playboy covers in the bathroom.

ABC Beer Co
Bar

Map p112 (96 Ave C, btwn 6th & 7th Sts; ⏲noon-midnight Sun-Thu, to 2am Fri & Sat) At first glance, ABC looks like a dimly lit beer shop (indeed bottles are available for purchase); but venture deeper inside and you'll find a small indie-rock-playing gastropub in back, with a long communal table and a few plush leather sofas and chairs set against the brick walls.

Terroir
Wine Bar

Map p112 (☎646-602-1300; www.wineisterroir.com; 413 E 12th St, btwn First Ave & Ave A; ⏲5pm-2am Mon-Sat, to midnight Sun; S L to 1st Ave, 6 to Astor Pl) Removing the pretension from the wine bar experience, Terroir spins vino by the tome-ful on smooth communal tables made from large scraps of wood.

McSorley's Old Ale House
Bar

Map p112 (☎212-474-9148; 15 E 7th St, btwn Second & Third Aves; ⏲11am-1am Mon-Sat, from 1pm Sun; S 6 to Astor Pl) Around since 1854, McSorley's feels far removed from the East Village veneer of cool: you're more likely to drink with firemen, Wall St refugees and a few tourists.

Death + Co
Lounge

Map p112 (☎212-388-0882; www.deathandcompany.com; 433 E 6th St, btwn First Ave & Ave A; ⏲6pm-1am Mon-Thu & Sun, to 2am Fri & Sat; S F to 2nd Ave, L to 1st Ave, 6 Astor Pl) Relax amid dim lighting and thick wooden slatting and let the bartenders – with their PhDs in mixology – work their magic as they shake, rattle and roll some of the most perfectly concocted cocktails ($14 to $16) in town.

Angel's Share
Bar

Map p112 (☎212-777-5415; 2nd fl, 8 Stuyvesant St, near Third Ave & E 9th St; ⏲5pm-midnight; S 6 to Astor Pl) Show up early and snag a seat at this hidden gem, behind a Japanese restaurant on the same floor. It's quiet and elegant with creative cocktails, but you can't stay if you don't have a table or a seat at the bar, and they tend to go fast.

McSorley's Old Ale House

MARTIN THOMAS PHOTOGRAPHY/ALAMY ©

East Village

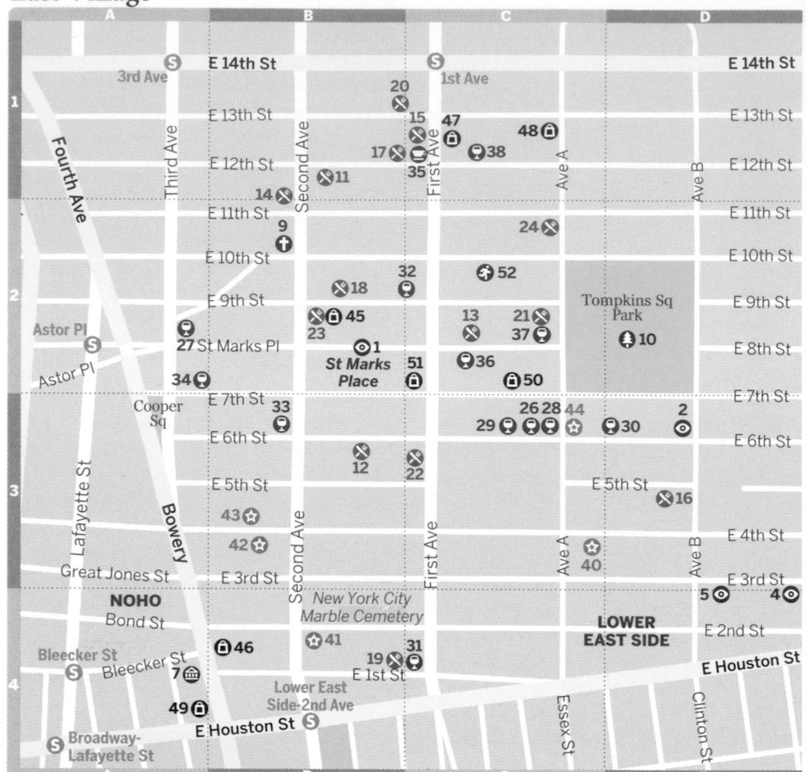

Eastern Bloc Gay

Map p112 (☎222-777-2555; www.easternblocnyc.com; 505 E 6th St, btwn Aves A & B; ⏱7pm-4am; **S** F to 2nd Ave) Though the theme may be 'Iron Curtain,' the drapery is most definitely velvet and taffeta at this East Village gay bar.

Ten Degrees Bar Wine Bar

Map p112 (☎212-358-8600; www.10degreesbar.com; 121 St Marks Pl, btwn First Ave & Ave A; ⏱noon-4am Mon-Sun; **S** F to Second Ave, L to First Ave, L to Third Ave) This small candle-lit St Marks charmer is a great spot to start out the night with leather couches, friendly bartenders and an excellent wine and cocktail list.

Immigrant Wine & Beer

Map p112 (☎212-677-2545; www.theimmigrantnyc.com; 341 E 9th St, btwn First & Second Aves; ⏱5pm-1am Mon-Wed & Sun, to 2am Thu, to 3am Fri & Sat; **S** L to 1st Ave, 4/6 to Astor Pl) Wholly unpretentious, these twin boxcar-sized bars could easily become your neighborhood local if you decide to stick around town. The staff are knowledgeable and kind, mingling with faithful regulars while dishing out tangy olives and topping up glasses with imported snifters.

Cienfuegos Bar

Map p112 (☎212-614-6818; www.cienfuegosny.com; 95 Ave A, btwn 6th & 7th Sts; ⏱6pm-2am Sun-Thu, to 3am Fri & Sat; **S** F to Second Ave, L to First Ave, 4/6 to Astor Pl) If Fidel Castro had a stretched Cadillac, its interior would look something like the inside of New York's foremost rum-punch joint. If you like this place, then make a pit stop at the connected **Amor y Amargo** Map p112 (www.amoryamargo.com; 443 E 6th St, btwn Ave

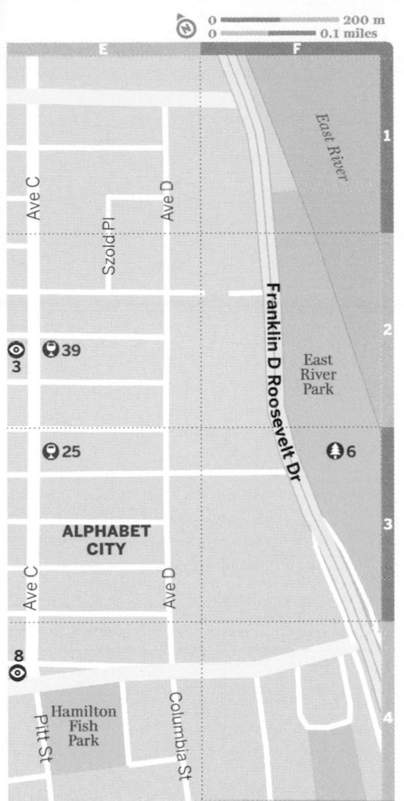

A & First Ave; ⌚Mon-Wed & Sun 5pm 11pm, Thu to midnight, Fri-Sat to 1am; S F to 2nd Ave, L to 1st Ave, 4/6 to Astor Pl) – Cienfuegos' tiny bitters-centric brother.

Mayahuel Cocktail Bar

Map p112 (☎212-253-5888; 304 E 6th St, at Second Ave; ⌚6pm-2am; S L to 3rd Ave, L to 1st Ave, 6 to Astor Pl) Devotees of the fermented agave can seriously indulge themselves experimenting with dozens of varieties (all cocktails $14); in between drinks, snack on quesadillas and tamales.

Lower East Side

Ten Bells Tapas Bar

Map p106 (☎212-228-4450; 247 Broome St, btwn Ludlow & Orchard Sts; ⌚5pm-2am Mon-Fri, from 3pm Sat & Sun; S F to Delancey St, J/M/Z to Essex St) This charmingly tucked-away tapas bar has a grotto-like design, with flickering candles, dark tin ceilings, brick walls and a U-shaped bar that's an ideal setting for conversation with a new friend. The unsigned entrance is easy to miss. It's right next to the shop Top Hat.

Stanton Social Lounge

Map p106 (99 Stanton St, btwn Orchard & Ludlow Sts; ⌚5pm-1am) Skip the uninspired restaurant on the first floor, and head upstairs to the stylish lounge with a somewhat speakeasy vibe – a nondescript steel door leads into the unmarked space. Here you'll find a well-dressed downtown crowd mingling over craft cocktails ($13 each) and groovy DJs.

Beauty & Essex Bar

Map p106 (☎212-614-0146; www.beautyandessex.com; 146 Essex St, btwn Stanton & Rivington Sts; ⌚5pm-1am; S F to Delancey St, J/M/Z to Essex St) This newcomer's glamour is concealed behind a tawdry pawnshop front space. Beyond lies 10,000-sq-ft of sleek lounge space, complete with leather sofas and banquettes, dramatic amber-tinged lighting and a curved staircase that leads to yet another lounge and bar area.

Barrio Chino Cocktail Bar

Map p106 (☎212-228-6710; 253 Broome St, btwn Ludlow & Orchard Sts; ⌚11:30am-4:30pm & 5:30pm-1am; S F, J/M/Z to Delancey-Essex Sts) An eatery that spills easily into a party scene, with an airy Havana-meets-Beijing vibe and a focus on fine sipping tequilas. Or stick with fresh blood-orange or black-plum margaritas, guacamole and chicken tacos.

Welcome to the Johnsons Bar

Map p106 (☎212-420-9911; 123 Rivington St, btwn Essex & Norfolk Sts; ⌚4:30pm-4am Mon-Fri, from 1pm Sat & Sun; S F, J/M/Z to Delancey-Essex Sts) Set up like a '70s game room – a bit sleazier than the one on *That '70s Show* – the Johnsons' irony still hasn't worn off for the devoted 20-something crowd. It could have something to do with the cheap beer, the pool table, the blasting garage-rock jukebox or the plastic-covered sofas.

East Village

Don't Miss Sights

1 St Marks Place ... B2

Sights

2 6th and B Garden ... D3
3 9th St Garden & La Plaza Cultural ... E2
4 All People's Garden ... D4
5 Brisas del Caribe ... D4
6 East River Park ... F3
7 Hole ... A4
8 Le Petit Versailles ... E4
9 St Mark's in the Bowery ... B2
10 Tompkins Square Park ... D2

Eating

11 Angelica Kitchen ... B1
12 Brick Lane Curry House ... B3
13 Cafe Mogador ... C2
14 Kanoyama ... B1
15 Luzzo's ... C1
16 Minca ... D3
17 Motorino ... B1
18 MUD ... B2
19 Prune ... B4
20 Redhead ... B1
21 Tacos Morelos ... C2
22 Upstate ... C3
23 Veselka ... B2
24 Westville East ... C2

Drinking & Nightlife

25 ABC Beer Co ... E3
26 Amor y Amargo ... C3
27 Angel's Share ... A2
28 Cienfuegos ... C3
29 Death + Co ... C3
30 Eastern Bloc ... D3
31 Golden Cadillac ... C4
32 Immigrant ... C2
33 Mayahuel ... B3
34 McSorley's Old Ale House ... A2
35 Ost Cafe ... C1
36 Proletariat ... C2
37 Ten Degrees Bar ... C2
38 Terroir ... C1
39 Wayland ... E2

Entertainment

40 Amore Opera ... C3
41 Anthology Film Archives ... B4
42 La MaMa ETC ... B3
43 New York Theater Workshop ... B3
44 Sidewalk Café ... C3

Shopping

45 Dinosaur Hill ... B2
46 John Varvatos ... B4
47 No Relation Vintage ... C1
48 Obscura Antiques ... C1
49 Patricia Field ... A4
50 Still House ... C2
51 Tokio 7 ... C2

Sports & Activities

52 Russian & Turkish Baths ... C2

Barramundi Lounge

Map p106 (212-529-6999; 67 Clinton St, btwn Stanton & Rivington Sts; 6pm-4am; S F, J/M/Z to Delancey-Essex Sts) This Australian-owned arty place fills an old tenement building with convivial booths, reasonably priced drinks (including some Aussie imports) and some cool tree-trunk tables.

Entertainment

East Village

Sidewalk Café Country, Folk

Map p112 (212-473-7373; www.sidewalkmusic.net; 94 Ave A, at 6th St; S F/V to Lower East Side-Second Ave; 6 to Astor Pl) Anti-folk forever! Never mind the Sidewalk's burger-bar appearance outside; inside is the home of New York's 'anti-folk' scene, where the Moldy Peaches carved out their legacy before Juno got knocked up. The open-mic 'anti-hootenanny' is Monday night. Poetry slams happen most Tuesdays.

La MaMa ETC Theater

Map p112 (212-475-7710; www.lamama.org; 74A E 4th St; admission $10-20; S F to Second Ave) A long-standing home for onstage experimentation (the ETC stands for Experimental Theater Club), La MaMa is now a three-theater complex with a cafe, an art gallery and a separate studio building that features cutting-edge dramas, sketch comedy and readings of all kinds.

New York Theater Workshop Theater

Map p112 (212-460-5475; www.nytw.org; 79 E 4th St, btwn Second & Third Aves; S F to 2nd Ave) Recently celebrating its 25th year, this innovative production house is a treasure to those seeking cutting-edge, contemporary plays with purpose. It was the originator of two big Broadway hits, *Rent* and *Urinetown*, and offers a constant supply of high-quality drama.

Anthology Film Archives Cinema

Map p112 (212-505-5181; www.anthologyfilmarchives.org; 32 Second Ave, at 2nd St; S F to 2nd Ave) Opened in 1970, this theater is dedicated to the idea of film as an art form. It screens indie works by new filmmakers and also revives classics and obscure oldies, from Luis Buñuel to Ken Brown's psychedelia.

Amore Opera Opera

Map p112 (www.amoreopera.org; Connelly Theater, 220 E 4th St, btwn Aves A & B; tickets $40; S F to 2nd Ave) This company, formed by several members of the now defunct Amato Opera, presents well-known works such as *The Magic Flute, La Bohème, The Mikado* and *Hansel and Gretel*, performed at its East Village theater.

Lower East Side

Slipper Room Burlesque

Map p106 (www.slipperroom.com; 167 Orchard St, entrance on Stanton St; admission $7-15; S F to 2nd Ave) The two-story club hosts a wide range of performances, including Seth Herzog's popular variety show *Sweet* and several weekly burlesque shows, which feature a mash-up of acrobatics, sexiness, comedy and absurdity – generally well worth the admission. Tickets available online.

Bowery Ballroom Live Music

Map p106 (212-533-2111; www.boweryballroom.com; 6 Delancey St, at Bowery St; S J/Z to Bowery) This terrific, medium-sized venue has the perfect sound and feel for more blown-up indie-rock acts (The Shins, Stephen Malkmus, Patti Smith).

Delancey Live Music

Map p106 (212-254-9920; www.thedelancey.com; 168 Delancey St at Clinton St; S F to Delancey St, J/M/Z to Essex St) Surprisingly stylish for the Lower East Side, the Delancey hosts some popular local bands for doting indie-rock crowds.

Pianos Live Music

Map p106 (212-505-3733; www.pianosnyc.com; 158 Ludlow St, at Stanton St; cover $8-10; noon-4am; S F to 2nd Ave) Nobody's bothered to change the sign at the door, a leftover from the location's previous incarnation as a piano shop. Now it's a musical mix of genres and styles, leaning more toward pop, punk and new wave, but throwing in some hip-hop and indie for good measure.

Lower East Side Galleries

Though Chelsea may be the heavy hitter when it comes to the New York gallery scene, the Lower East Side has dozens of quality showplaces. One of the early pioneers, the **Sperone Westwater gallery** (www.speronewestwater.com; 257 Bowery St), opened in 1975, represents heavy hitters such as William Wegman and Richard Long. Nearby the avant-garde **Salon 94** has two Lower East Side outposts: one secreted away on Freeman Alley and another on Bowery near the New Museum. A few blocks north is the 4000-sq-ft **Hole** – known as much for its art as it is for its rowdy openings that gather both scenesters of the downtown art circuit and well-known faces like Courtney Love and Salman Rushdie.

Broome St between Chrystie and Bowery is quickly becoming the nexus of the Lower East Side art scene, with major galleries including **White Box**, **Canada**, **Jack Hanley** and **Marlborough** right next door to one another. Another buzzing strip of galleries runs down Orchard St between Rivington and Canal St.

Rockwood Music Hall Live Music
Map p106 (212-477-4155; www.rockwoodmusichall.com; 196 Allen St, btwn Houston & Stanton Sts; S F/V to Lower East Side-Second Ave) Opened by indie rocker Ken Rockwood, this breadbox-sized concert space has three stages that see a rapid-fire flow of bands and singer/songwriters. With no cover, and a max of one hour per band (die-hards can see five or more a night), what's to lose? Music kicks off at 3pm on weekends, 6pm on weeknights.

Landmark Sunshine Cinema Cinema
Map p106 (212-260-7289; www.landmarktheatres.com; 143 E Houston St, btwn Forsyth & Eldridge Sts; S F/V to Lower East Side-Second Ave) A renovated Yiddish theater, the wonderful Landmark shows foreign and first-run mainstream art films on massive screens. It also has much-coveted stadium style seating, so it doesn't matter what giant sits in front of you after the lights go out.

Shopping

East Village

Dinosaur Hill Children
Map p112 (212-473-5850; www.dinosaurhill.com; 306 E 9th St; 11am-7pm; S 6 to Astor Pl) A small, old-fashioned toy store that's inspired more by imagination than Disney movies, this shop has loads of great gift ideas.

Still House Glassware
Map p112 (212-539-0200; 117 E 7th St; noon-8pm; S 6 to Astor Pl) Step into this petite and peaceful boutique to browse sculptural glassware and pottery: hand-blown vases, geometric tabletop objects, ceramic bowls and cups and other finery for the home.

No Relation Vintage Vintage Clothing
Map p112 (212-228-5201; 204 First Ave, btwn 12th & 13th Sts; noon-8pm Sun-Thu, to 9pm Fri & Sat; S L to First Ave) Among the many vintage shops of the East Village, No Relation is a winner for its wide-ranging collections that run the gamut from

Russian & Turkish Baths

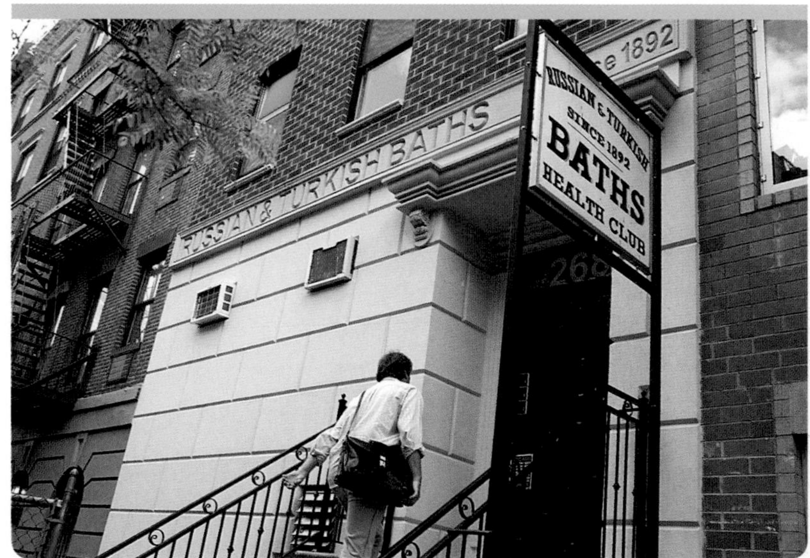

denim and leather jackets to flannels, sneakers, plaid shirts, Levi's aplenty, candy-colored T-shirts, varsity jackets, clutches and more.

Tokio 7 Consignment Store
Map p112 (☎212-353-8443; www.tokio7.net; 83 E 7th St, near First Ave; ⏲noon-8pm; S 6 to Astor Pl) This revered, hip consignment shop on a shady stretch of E 7th St, has good-condition designer labels for men and women at some fairly hefty prices.

Patricia Field Fashion
Map p112 (☎212-966-4066; 306 Bowery St, at 1st St; ⏲11am-8pm Sun-Thu, to 9pm Fri & Sat; S F to 2nd Ave) The fashion-forward stylist for *Sex and the City*, Patricia Field isn't afraid of flash, with feather boas, pink jackets, disco dresses, graphic and color-block T-shirts and leopard-print heels, plus colored frizzy wigs, silver spandex and some wacky gift ideas for good measure.

Obscura Antiques Antiques
Map p112 (☎212-505-9251; 207 Ave A, btwn 12th & 13th Sts; ⏲noon-8pm Mon-Sat, to 7pm Sun; S L to 1st Ave) This small cabinet of curiosities pleases both lovers of the macabre and inveterate antique hunters.

John Varvatos Fashion, Shoes
Map p112 (☎212-358-0315; 315 Bowery, btwn 1st & 2nd Sts; ⏲noon-8pm Mon-Sat to 6pm Sun; S F to 2nd Ave, 6 to Bleecker St) Set in the hallowed halls of former punk club CBGB, the John Varvatos Bowery store goes to great lengths to tie fashion with rock-and-roll, with records, '70s audio equipment and even electric guitars for sale alongside JV's denim, leather boots, belts and graphic tees.

Lower East Side

Top Hat Accessories
Map p106 (☎212-677-4240; 245 Broome St, btwn Ludlow & Orchard Sts; ⏲noon-8pm; S B/D to Grand St) Sporting curios from around the globe, this whimsical little shop is packed with intrigue: from vintage Italian pencils and handsomely miniaturized leather journals to beautifully carved wooden bird whistles.

Edith Machinist Vintage
Map p106 (☎212-979-9992; 104 Rivington St, at Essex St; ⏲noon-7pm Tue-Sat, to 6pm Sun; S F to Delancey St, J/M/Z to Essex St) To properly strut about the Lower East Side, you've got to dress the part. Edith Machinist can help you get that rumpled but stylish look in a hurry – a bit of vintage glam via knee-high soft suede boots, 1930s silk dresses and ballet-style flats.

Sports & Activities

Russian & Turkish Baths Bathhouse
Map p112 (☎212-674-9250; www.russianturkishbaths.com; 268 E 10th St, btwn First Ave & Ave A; per visit $35; ⏲noon-10pm Mon-Tue & Thu-Fri, from 10am Wed, from 9am Sat, from 8am Sun; S L to First Ave; 6 to Astor Pl) Since 1892, this has been the spa for anyone who wants to get naked (or stay in their swimsuit) and romp in steam baths, an ice-cold plunge pool, a sauna and on the sundeck. The baths are open to both men and women most hours (wearing shorts is required at these times), though at some times it's men or women only.

Greenwich Village, Chelsea & the Meatpacking District

There's a good reason why this area is known as the Village.
Quaint, quiet lanes carve their way between brown-brick town houses offering endless strolling fodder. New York University (NYU) dominates much of the central Village, but the vibe turns mellow west of the park. Nestled in the few circuitous blocks just below 14th St is the Meatpacking District – once filled with slaughterhouses and now brimming with sleek boutiques and roaring nightclubs.

Chelsea, just a smidge to the north, bridges the gap between the West Village and Midtown, importing bits and bobs from both. It's the de facto neighborhood for the city's sociable gay community, and its broad avenues are lined with breezy cafes, themed bars and sweaty clubs. The neighborhood's massive gallery scene can be found in the West 20s, with starkly contrasting mega-mart retailers orbiting Sixth Ave.

Brownstones in Greenwich Village
GREGORY OLSEN/GETTY IMAGES ©

Greenwich Village, Chelsea & the Meatpacking District Highlights

Gallery Hopping (p138)

Chelsea is home to the highest concentration of art galleries in the entire city – and the cluster continues to grow with each season. Most lie in the 20s, on the blocks between Tenth and Eleventh Aves. With hundreds of galleries peppering the area's westernmost avenues and streets it can be difficult to figure out which showcase to visit when; fortunately a casual wander can reveal interesting installations that capture the imagination. Pace Gallery

1

2

Washington Square Park (p131)

Despite its recent makeover, Washington Square Park is still the Village's town square. The same odd characters still dance around the fountain, NYU undergrads still flip through used editions of Nietzsche, and shifty amateur chess masters still hustle for games. Only now it's among immaculately landscaped gardens and grounds.

LUIS DAVILLA/GETTY IMAGES ©

3 Live Music (p137)

Greenwich Village is the unofficial headquarters of the world's jazz club scene. Here you'll find some of the city's most iconic music spaces: the Blue Note, Village Vanguard and Smalls. Le Poisson Rouge, a relative newcomer, houses a staggering variety of music: jazz, hip-hop, folk, plus global sounds (from Africa, Iceland, Japan) favored by the multi-culti-loving crowd. Blue Note (p139)

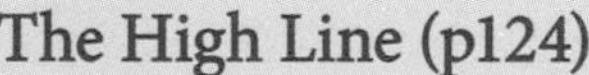

MICHELLE BENNETT/GETTY IMAGES ©

4 The High Line (p124)

Refurbished rail tracks have been transformed into grassy catwalks in the sky. It's the paradigm of urban renewal gone right, enjoying its status as one of the city's most beloved public green spaces. Strolling above the city's streets offers some unusual vantage points over the metropolis, and wild native plants and flowers add to the raw beauty of this unusual setting.

5 Chelsea Market (p126)

In a former factory, this vast shopping emporium is a must for the food-minded. Exposed brick walls and industrial details form the backdrop to a wide range of shops selling fresh-baked breads, seafood, wine, fresh veggies and desserts. There are plenty of places to snack or even have a sit-down meal, though the market's proximity to the High Line and the waterfront make it a good spot to assemble a picnic.

Greenwich Village Walk

Of all the neighborhoods in New York City, Greenwich Village is the most pedestrian-friendly, with its cobbled corners that stray from the signature gridiron that unfurls across the rest of the island.

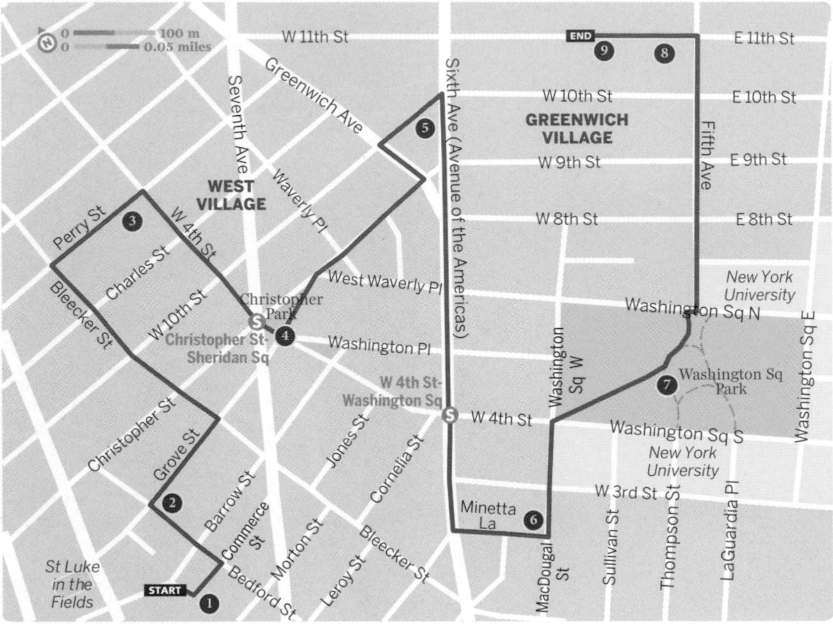

WALK FACTS

- **Start** Cherry Lane Theater
- **End** Oscar Wilde's House
- **Distance** 1 mile
- **Duration** One hour and 15 minutes

1 Cherry Lane Theater

Start your walkabout at the small Cherry Lane Theater. Established in 1924, it is the city's longest continuously running off-Broadway establishment and a center of creative activity during the 1940s.

2 90 Bedford St

Make a left on Bedford and you'll find 90 Bedford St on the right hand side at the corner of Grove St. You might recognize the apartment block as the fictitious home of the cast of *Friends*. (Sadly, Central Perk was just a figment of the writers' imaginations.)

3 66 Perry St

For another iconic TV landmark, wander up Bleecker St and make a right on Perry St stopping at 66 Perry St, which was used as the facade and stoop of the city's 'It Girl,' Carrie Bradshaw, in *Sex and the City*.

4 Christopher Park

Make a right on W 4th St until your reach Christopher Park, where two white, life-sized statues of same-sex couples stand guard. On the north side of the green space is the legendary Stonewall Inn (p136), where a clutch of fed-up drag queens rioted for their civil rights in 1969, signaling the start of the gay revolution.

5 Jefferson Market Library

Follow Christopher St to Sixth Ave to find this building straddling a triangular plot of land. The 'Ruskinian gothic' spire was once a fire lookout tower; today it houses a branch of the public library.

6 Café Wha?

Stroll down Sixth Ave taking in the flurry of passers-by, then make a left on Minetta Lane to swing by Café Wha?, the notorious institution where many young musicians and comedians – such as Bob Dylan and Richard Pryor – got their start.

7 Washington Square Park

Wander further along MacDougal St until you reach Washington Square Park (p131), the Village's unofficial town square, which plays host to loitering NYU students, buskers and a regular crowd of protesters. Pass under the iconic arch and head up Fifth Ave.

8 Weatherman House

Make a left on W 11th St, where you'll find two notable town houses. First is the infamous Weatherman house at No 18, used in 1970 as a hideout and bomb factory for the radical anti-government group, the Weatherman, until an accidental explosion killed three members and destroyed the house; it was rebuilt in 1978.

9 Oscar Wilde's House

A bit further west, the tour ends at the former, albeit brief, home of Oscar Wilde (at No 48). The famed Irish wit lived here for a few weeks in 1882.

The Best...

PLACES TO EAT

RedFarm Savvy Sino fusion is this cottage-style restaurant's signature. (p127)

Chelsea Market Perfect for picnic fare: grab a bottle of wine, cheese, sandwich and gourmet cupcake. (p133)

Jeffrey's Grocery Lively West Village haunt famed for its seafood. (p130)

Tía Pol Feast on Spanish tapas and wine after visiting the Chelsea galleries. (p133)

PLACES TO DRINK

Bell Book & Candle Low-lit spot for cocktails and oysters, with spacious booths hidden in back. (p134)

Buvette Charming little wine bar in the West Village. (p135)

Little Branch West Village hideout with a speakeasy vibe. (p134)

Marie's Crisis The ultimate cramped piano bar where no one's afraid to be themselves. (p135)

PERFORMANCE SPACES

Le Poisson Rouge Diverse and exciting line up across musical genres. (p137)

Village Vanguard Venerable institution for jazz stars. (p137)

Joyce Theater NYC's premier space for modern dance. (p139)

Gay Liberation monument in Christopher Park

Don't Miss
The High Line

In the early 1900s, the western area around the Meatpacking District and Chelsea was the largest industrial section of Manhattan and a set of elevated tracks were created to move freight off the cluttered streets below. As NYC evolved, the rails eventually became obsolete, and in 1999 a plan was made to convert the scarring strands of metal into a public green space. On June 9, 2009, part one of the city's most beloved urban renewal project opened with much ado, and it has been one of New York's star attractions ever since.

212-500-6035

www.thehighline.org

Gansevoort St

7am-7pm

M11 to Washington St; M11, M14 to 9th Ave; M23, M34 to 10th Ave, S L, A/C/E to 14th St-8th Ave; C/E to 23rd St-8th Ave

More Than Just a Public Space

As the West Village and Chelsea continue to embrace their new-found residential nature, the High Line is making a dedicated move towards becoming more than just a public place but an inspired meeting point for families and friends. As you walk along the High Line you'll find dedicated staffers wearing shirts with the signature double-H logo who can point you in the right direction or offer you additional information about the converted rails.

'Spike' level members of the High Line (https://thehighline.org/get-involved/membership) receive a variety of discounts at the establishments in the neighborhood below, from Diane von Furstenberg's boutique under her imaginative geodesic dome, to Amy's Bread, a tasty food outlet in the uberpopular Chelsea Market.

Industrial Past

It's hard to believe that the High Line – a shining example of brilliant urban renewal – was once a dingy rail line that anchored a rather unsavory district of thugs, trannies and slaughterhouses. The tracks that would one day become the High Line were commissioned in the 1930s when the municipal government decided to raise the street-level tracks after years of accidents that gave Tenth Ave the nickname 'Death Avenue.' The project drained more than $150 million in funds (equivalent to about $2 billion by today's dime) and took roughly five years to complete. After two decades of effective use, a rise in truck transportation and traffic led to the eventual decrease in usage, and finally, in the 1980s, the rails became obsolete. Petitions were signed by local residents to remove the eyesores, but in 1999 a committee called the Friends of the High Line – founded by Joshua David and Robert Hammond – was formed to save the rusting iron and transform the tracks into a unique elevated green space.

Local Knowledge

The High Line

RECOMMENDATIONS FROM ROBERT HAMMOND, COFOUNDER AND EXECUTIVE DIRECTOR OF FRIENDS OF THE HIGH LINE.

1 HIGHLINE HIGHLIGHTS

To me, the West Village is a reminder of New York's industrial past and residential future. What I love most about the High Line are its hidden moments, like at the Tenth Ave cut-out near 17th St; most people sit on the bleachers, but if you turn the other way you can see the Statue of Liberty far away in the harbor. Architecture buffs will love looking down 18th St, and up on 30th is my favorite moment – a steel cut-out where you can see the cars underneath.

2 STOP-OFFS

For lunch near the High Line, I recommend **Hector's Café & Diner** (44 Little W 12th St; mains $8-12.95; 2am-10pm Mon-Sat). It's cheap, untouristy and not at all a see-and-be-seen spot – the cookies are great. If you're in the area, you have to visit the galleries in Chelsea – there are more than 300, and check out **Printed Matter** Map p134 (212-925-0325; 195 Tenth Ave btwn 21st & 22nd Sts; 11am-7pm Sat & Mon-Wed, to 8pm Thu-Fri; S C/E to 23rd St), with its artist-made books. Check out the **Hôtel Americano** (p276) in northern Chelsea – it's very up-and-coming. For an evening out on the town, head to the Boom Boom Room at the **Top of the Standard** (p136) – go early and book ahead.

3 FAMILY-FRIENDLY ACTIVITIES

The High Line is also great for kids, with scheduled programming for kids on Saturdays and Wednesdays. Group tours for children can be organized on a variety of topics from the plant life of the high-rise park to the area's history.

Discover Greenwich Village, Chelsea & the Meatpacking District

Getting There & Away

- **Subway** Sixth Ave, Seventh Ave and Eighth Ave are graced with convenient subway stations, but public transportation slims further west. Take the A/C/E or 1/2/3 lines to reach this colorful clump of neighborhoods – disembark at 14th St (along either service) if you're looking for a good place to make tracks.
- **Bus** Try M14 or the M8 if you're traveling across town and want to access the westernmost areas of Chelsea and the West Village by public transportation.

Sights

Greenwich Village & the Meatpacking District

The High Line (p124)

New York University University

Map p128 (NYU; ☎212-998-2222; www.nyu.edu; 50 W 4th St (information center); S A/C/E, B/D/F/M to W 4th St-Washington Sq; N/R to 8th St-NYU) In 1831 Albert Gallatin, formerly Secretary of the Treasury under President Thomas Jefferson, founded an intimate center of higher learning open to all students, regardless of race or class background. Some of its crevices are charming, such as the leafy courtyard at its School of Law, or impressively modern, such as the Skirball Center for the Performing Arts, where top-notch dance, theater, music, spoken-word and other performers wow audiences at the 850-seat theater.

Chelsea

Chelsea Market Market

Map p134 (www.chelseamarket.com; 75 Ninth Ave at 15th St; ⏰7am-10pm Mon-Sat, 8am-9pm Sun; S A/C/E to 14th St; L to 8th Ave) In a shining example of redevelopment and preservation, the Chelsea Market has taken a former factory of cookie giant Nabisco (creator of the Oreo) and turned it into an 800ft-long shopping concourse that caters to foodies. The prime draw for shoppers, though, are the more than two dozen food shops, including Amy's Bread, Fat Witch Bakery, the Lobster Place, Hale & Hearty Soup, Ronnybrook Dairy and the Nutbox.

Rubin Museum of Art
STEVEN GREAVES/GETTY IMAGES ©

Greenwich Village, Chelsea & the Meatpacking District

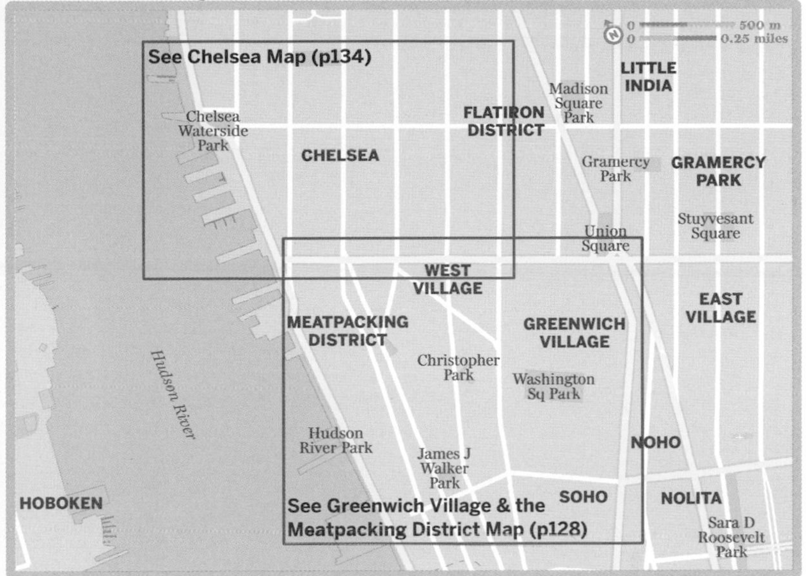

Rubin Museum of Art Museum

Map p134 (☎212-620-5000; www.rmanyc.org; 150 W 17th St at Seventh Ave; adult/child $10/free, 6-10pm Fri free; ⏰11am-5pm Mon & Thu, to 9pm Wed, to 10pm Fri, to 6pm Sat & Sun; S 1 to 18th St) This is the first museum in the Western world to dedicate itself to the art of the Himalayas and surrounding regions. Its impressive collections include embroidered textiles from China, metal sculptures from Tibet, Pakistani stone sculptures and intricate Bhutanese paintings, as well as ritual objects and dance masks from various Tibetan regions, spanning from the 2nd to the 19th centuries.

Eating

Greenwich Village & the Meatpacking District

Moustache Middle Eastern $

Map p128 (☎212-229-2220; moustachepitza.com; 90 Bedford St btwn Grove & Barrow Sts; mains $8-17; ⏰noon-midnight; S 1 to Christopher St-Sheridan Sq) Small and delightful Moustache serves up rich, flavorful sandwiches (leg of lamb, merguez sausage, falafel), thin-crust pizzas, tangy salads and hearty specialties including *ouzi* (filo stuffed with chicken, rice and spices) and moussaka.

RedFarm Fusion $$$

Map p128 (☎212-792-9700; www.redfarmnyc.com; 529 Hudson St btwn 10th & Charles Sts; mains $19-49; ⏰5pm-11:45pm Mon-Sat, to 11pm Sun & 11am-2:30pm Sat & Sun; S A/C/E, B/D/F/M to W 4th St; 1 to Christopher St-Sheridan Sq) RedFarm transforms Chinese cooking into pure, delectable artistry at this small, buzzing space on Hudson St. Fresh crab and eggplant bruschetta, juicy rib steak (marinated overnight in papaya, ginger and soy) and pastrami egg rolls are among the many creative dishes that brilliantly blend east with west.

Rosemary's Italian $$

Map p128 (☎212-647-1818; rosemarysnyc.com; 18 Greenwich Ave at W 10th St; mains $12-26; ⏰8am-midnight; S 1 to Christopher St-Sheridan Sq) Currently one of the West Village's hottest restaurants, Rosemary's serves

Greenwich Village & the Meatpacking District

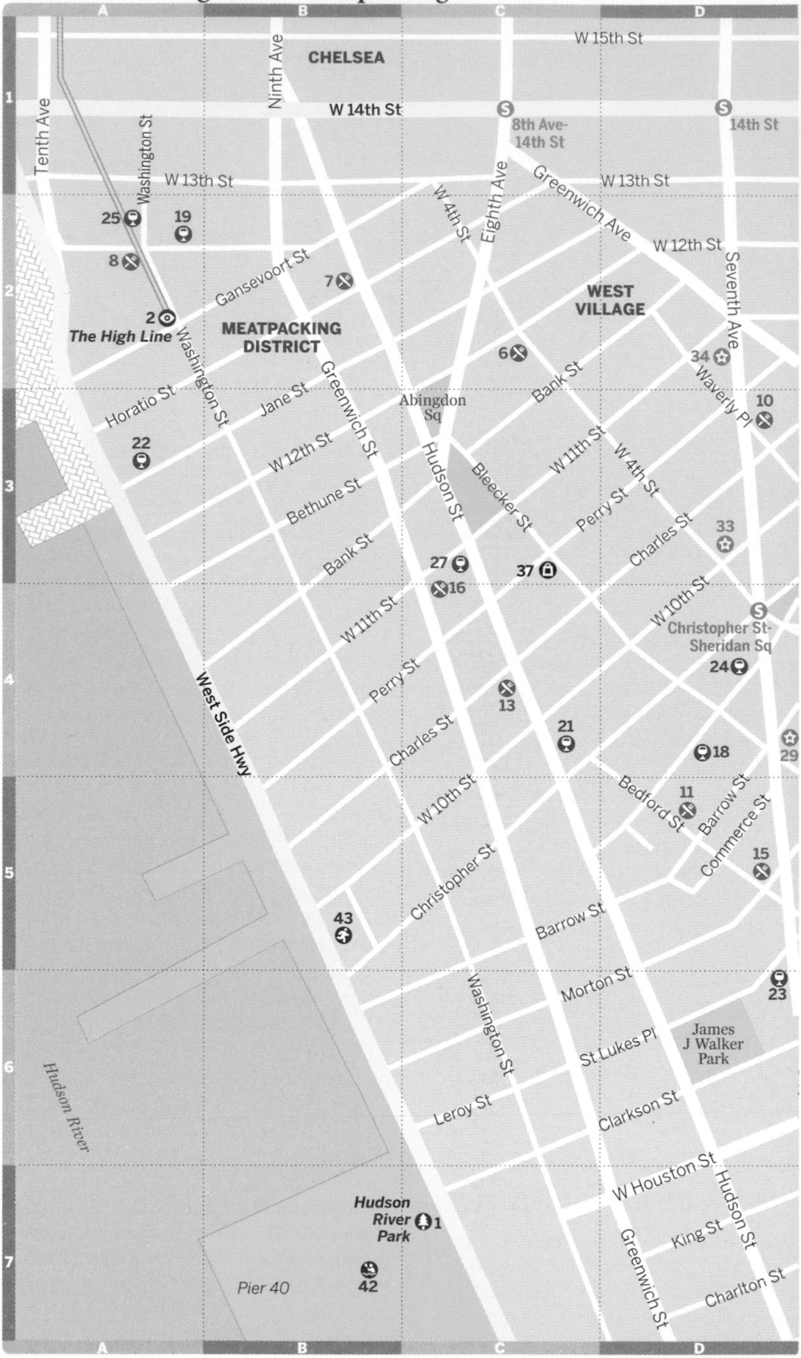
A
B
C
D
1
2
3
4
5
6
7
W 15th St
CHELSEA
Ninth Ave
W 14th St
8th Ave-
14th St
14th St
Tenth Ave
Washington St
W 13th St
W 13th St
Greenwich Ave
W 4th St
Eighth Ave
W 12th St
Seventh Ave
Gansevoort St
WEST
VILLAGE
The High Line
Washington St
MEATPACKING
DISTRICT
Horatio St
Jane St
Greenwich St
Abingdon
Sq
Bank St
Waverly Pl
W 12th St
Hudson St
Bleecker St
W 11th St
W 4th St
Bethune St
Perry St
Charles St
Bank St
W 11th St
W 10th St
Christopher St-
Sheridan Sq
Perry St
West Side Hwy
Charles St
Bedford St
Barrow St
W 10th St
Commerce St
Christopher St
Barrow St
Morton St
Washington St
St Lukes Pl
James
J Walker
Park
Hudson River
Leroy St
Clarkson St
W Houston St
Hudson St
Hudson
River
Park
King St
Greenwich St
Charlton St
Pier 40
1
2
6
7
8
10
11
13
15
16
18
19
21
22
23
24
25
27
29
33
34
37
42
43

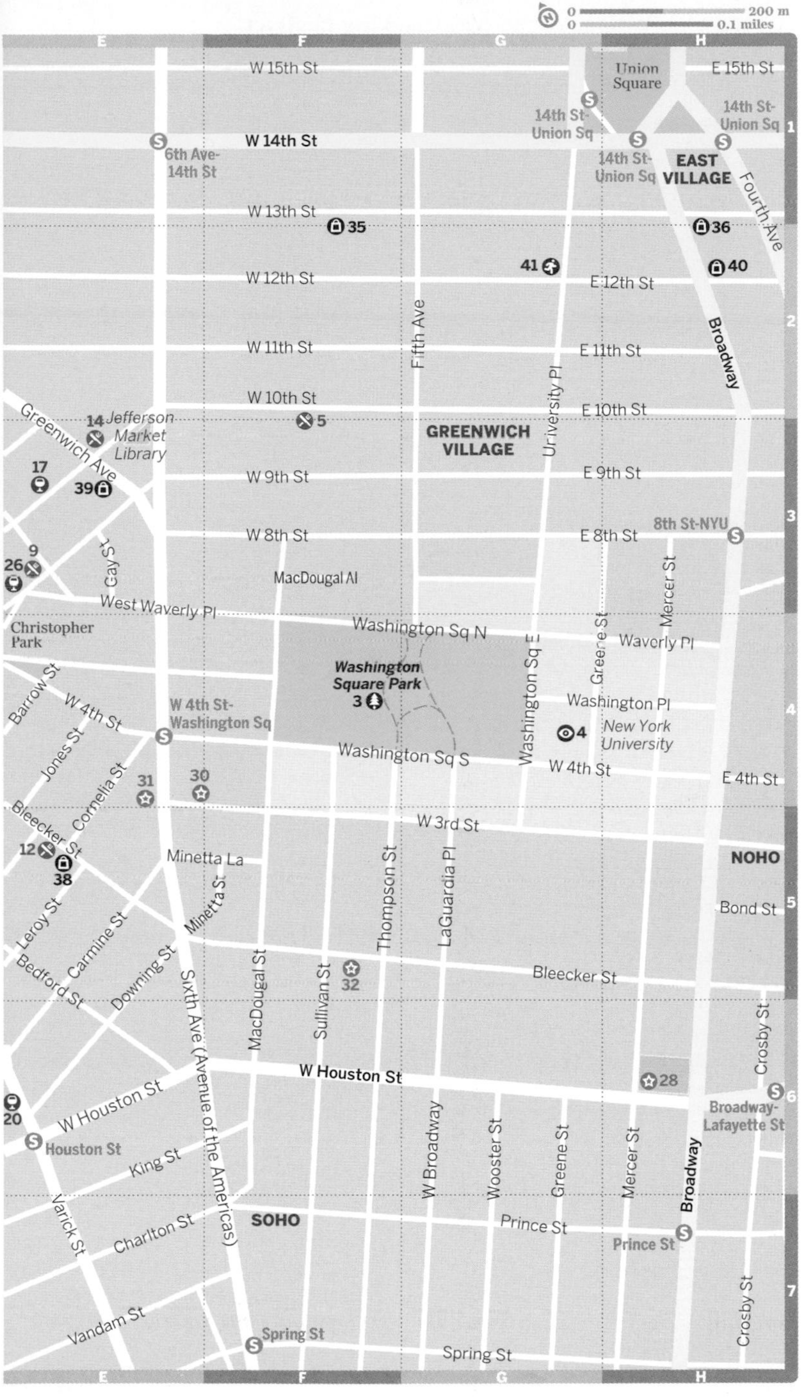

GREENWICH VILLAGE, CHELSEA & THE MEATPACKING DISTRICT

Greenwich Village & the Meatpacking District

high-end Italian fare that more than lives up to the hype. In a vaguely farmhouse-like setting, diners tuck into generous portions of housemade pastas, rich salads and cheese and *salumi* (cured meat) boards. Current favorites include the *acqua pazza* (seafood stew) and braised pork shoulder with roasted vegetables.

Jeffrey's Grocery — Modern American $$

Map p128 (646-398-7630; jeffreysgrocery.com; 172 Waverly Pl at Christopher St; mains $18-35; 8am-11pm Sun-Wed, to 2am Thu-Sat; S 1 to Christopher St-Sheridan Sq) A West Village classic, Jeffrey's is a lively eating and drinking spot that hits all the right notes. Seafood is the focus: there's an oyster bar and beautifully executed seafood selections such as razor clams with caviar and dill, whole roasted dourade with curry, and seafood platters to share.

Morandi — Italian $$

Map p128 (212-627-7575; www.morandiny.com; 211 Waverly Place btwn Seventh Ave & Charles St; mains $17-30; 8am-midnight Mon-Fri, 10am-midnight Sat, 10am-11pm Sun; S 1 to Christopher St-Sheridan Sq) Run by celebrated restaurateur Keith McNally, Morandi is a warmly lit space where the hubbub of garrulous diners resounds amid brick walls, wide plank floors and rustic chandeliers.

Spotted Pig — Pub $$

Map p128 (212-620-0393; www.thespottedpig.com; 314 W 11th St at Greenwich St; mains $16-35; 11am-2am; S A/C/E to 14th St; L to 8th Ave) This Michelin-starred gastropub is a favorite of Villagers, serving an upscale blend of hearty Italian and British dishes. Its two floors are bedecked with old-timey trinkets that give the whole place an air of relaxed elegance.

Café Cluny — Bistro $$

Map p128 (212-255-6900; www.cafecluny.com; 284 W 12th St; mains lunch $14-24, dinner $18-34; 8am-11:30pm Mon-Fri, 9am-11pm Sat & Sun; S L to 8th Ave; A/C/E, 1/2/3 to 14th St) Café Cluny brings the whimsy of Paris to the West Village, with woven bistro-style bar

PATTI MCCONVILLE/GETTY IMAGES ©

Don't Miss Washington Square Park

What was once a potter's field and a square for public executions is now the unofficial town square of the Village and plays host to lounging NYU students, fire-eating street performers, curious canines and their owners, and legions of speed-chess pros. Encased in perfectly manicured brownstones and gorgeous twists of modern architecture (all owned by NYU) Washington Square Park is one of the most beautiful garden spaces in the city – especially as you are welcomed by the iconic Stanford White Arch on the north side of the green.

NEED TO KNOW

Map p128 Fifth Ave at Washington Sq **S** N A/C/E, B/D/F/M to W 4th St-Washington Sq; N/R to 8th St-NYU

chairs, light wooden upholstery, and a selection of joie-de-vivre-inducing platters such as *steak frîtes,* mixed green salads and roasted chicken.

Alta Tapas **$$**

Map p128 (212-505-7777; www.altarestaurant.com; 54 W 10th St btwn Fifth & Sixth Aves; small plates $5-19; 6-11pm, to midnight Fri & Sat; S A/C/E, B/D/F/V to W 4th St-Washington Sq) This gorgeous town house highlights the neighborhood's quaintness, with plenty of exposed brick, wood beams, flickering candles, massive mirrors and romantic fireplace glows. A small-plates menu of encyclopedic proportions cures indecision with the likes of succulent lamb meatballs, roasted snapper with artichoke puree, seared wild mushrooms, fried goat cheese, and squid ink paella.

Fatty Crab Pan-Asian **$$**

Map p128 (212-352-3590; www.fattycrab.com; 643 Hudson St btwn Gansevoort & Horatio Sts;

STEVEN GREAVES/GETTY IMAGES ©

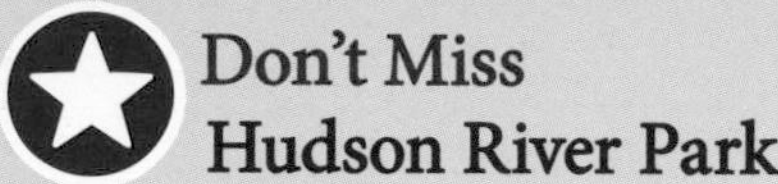

Don't Miss Hudson River Park

The High Line may be all the rage these days, but one block away there stretches a five-mile-long ribbon of green that has dramatically transformed the city over the past ten years.

Covering 550 acres, and running from Battery Park at Manhattan's southern tip to 59th St in Midtown, the Hudson River Park is Manhattan's wondrous backyard. The long riverside path is a great spot for **cycling** Map p128 (www.bikeshopny.com; 391 West St btwn W 10th & Christopher Sts; rentals per 1hr/4hr $10/20; 10am-7pm), running and strolling; several **boathouses** (p141) offer kayak hire and longer excursions for the more experienced. There's also beach volleyball, basketball courts, a skate park and tennis courts. Families with kids have loads of options including four sparkling new playgrounds, a carousel (off W 22nd St) and minigolf (Pier 25 off West St near N Moore St).

Those who simply need a break from the city, come here to loll on the grass for a bout of people-watching and river contemplation (those seeking something less sedate can join the sangria- and sun-loving crowds at the dockside **Frying Pan** (p137). The park is also a fine spot to come and watch the sunset.

mains $16-35; noon-11pm Sun-Wed, to midnight Thu-Sat; S L to 8th Ave; A/C/E, 1/2/3 to 14th St) The Fatty folks have done it again with their small Malaysian-inspired joint in the thick of things on the west side. It's super hip and always teeming with locals who swing by in droves to devour fish curries and pork belly accompanied by a signature selection of cocktails.

Snack Taverna Greek $$

Map p128 (212-929-3499; www.snacktaverna.com; 63 Bedford St; mains small plates $12-14, large plates $22-28; 7:30am-11pm Mon-Fri, 11am-11pm Sat, to 10pm Sun; S A/C/E, B/D to

W 4 St; 1/2 to Christopher St-Sheridan Sq)** So much more than your usual Greek restaurant, Snack Taverna eschews gyros for a seasonal selection of scrumptious small plates to accompany the flavorful selection of market mains. The regional wines are worth a miss, but the Med beers are surprisingly refreshing.

Murray's Cheese Bar Cheese **$$**
Map p128 (www.murrayscheesebar.com; 246 Bleecker St; mains $12-17, cheese platters $12-16; noon-10pm Sun-Tue, to midnight Wed-Sat; S A/C/E, B/D/F/M to W 4th St) Gourmet mac and cheese, melted cheese sandwiches, French onion soup, and other cheese-centric dishes dominate the menu at this tile-lined eat-and-drinkery. There's a nicely curated wine list (from $9 a glass), and suggested wine pairings for the cheese platters.

Chelsea

Chelsea Market (p126)

Heath Supper Club **$$**
Map p134 (212-564-1622; mckittrickhotel.com/theheath; 542 W 27th St btwn Tenth & Eleventh Aves; mains $24-32; 6pm-2am; S C/E to 23rd St) In late 2013, the creators of hit interactive theater piece *Sleep No More* opened a restaurant next door to their warehouse venue. Like the fictional McKittrick Hotel in the drama, the Heath is set in another place and time (vaguely Britain, 1920s), with suspenders-wearing barkeeps, period furnishings and (fake) smoke wafting over the dining room, as a jazz band performs on stage. Actors disguised as waitstaff interact with the diners, and soon you become part of the whole theatrical experience.

The menu features heritage English recipes – spit-turned leg of lamb, terrines, beef and ale pie, bay scallops – and is mostly unremarkable. But the evening is quite memorable, assuming you're up for a night of drama and surprises.

Foragers City Table Modern American **$$**
Map p134 (www.foragerscitygrocer.com; 300 W 22nd St, cnr Eighth Ave; mains $22-28; 6-10pm Tue-Sat, from 10:30am Sat & Sun; ; S C/E, 1 to 23rd St) Owners of this new restaurant in Chelsea run a 28-acre farm in the Hudson Valley, from which much of their menu is sourced (and true to name, some products are indeed 'foraged'). A few temptations: squash soup with Jerusalem artichokes and black truffles; roasted chicken with polenta; heritage pork loin; and the season's harvest featuring toasted quinoa and a flavorful mix of vegetables.

Cookshop Modern American **$$**
Map p134 (212-924-4440; www.cookshopny.com; 156 Tenth Ave btwn 19th & 20th Sts; mains $15-35; 11:30am-4pm & 5:30-11:30pm daily, from 10:30am Sat & Sun; S L to 8th Ave; A/C/E to 23rd St) Excellent service, eye-opening cocktails (good morning Bloody Maria!), a perfectly baked breadbasket and a selection of inventive egg mains make this a favorite in Chelsea on a Sunday afternoon. Dinner is a sure-fire win as well. Ample outdoor seating on warm days.

Co Pizzeria **$$**
Map p134 (212-243-1105; www.co-pane.com; 230 Ninth Ave at 24th St; pizza $15-20; 5-11pm Mon, 11:30am-11pm Tue-Sun; S C/E to 23rd St) Masterfully prepared pizza is served in trim wooden surrounds that lend a Scandinavian farmhouse vibe.

Tía Pol Tapas **$$**
Map p134 (212-675-8805; www.tiapol.com; 205 Tenth Ave btwn 22nd & 23rd Sts; small plates $4-16; noon-11pm Tue-Sun, from 5:30pm Mon; S C/E to 23rd St) Wielding Spanish tapas amid closet-sized surrounds, Tía Pol is the real deal, as the hordes of locals the entrance can attest. There's a great wine list and a tantalizing array of small plates.

Blossom Vegan **$$**
Map p134 (212-627-1144; www.blossomnyc.com; 187 Ninth Ave btwn 21st & 22nd Sts; mains lunch $12-18, dinner $19-23; lunch & dinner; ; S C/E to 23rd St) This Chelsea veg oasis – with a sinful wine and chocolate bar attached – is a peaceful, romantic dining room that offers imaginative tofu, seitan and vegetable creations, some raw, all kosher.

Chelsea

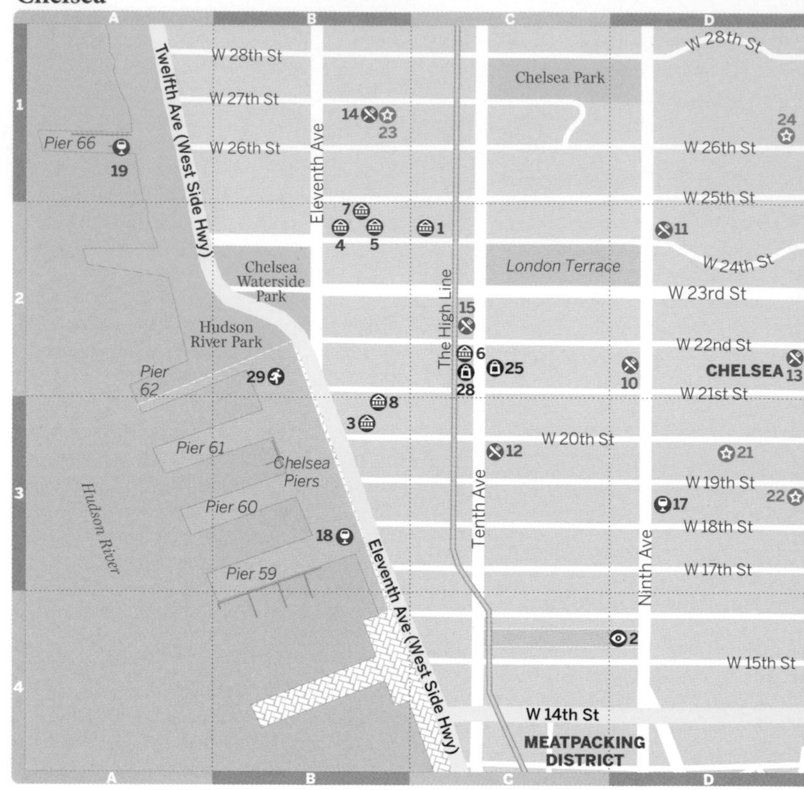

Drinking & Nightlife

Greenwich Village & the Meatpacking District

Clarkson Bar

Map p128 (225 Varick St at Clarkson St; 11am-1:30am Mon, to 2:30am Tue-Sat, to 10pm Sun; S 1 to Houston St) This stylish if spare newcomer has a polished wood, horseshoe-shaped bar – perfect for discreetly taking in the garrulous crowd that gathers here most nights. There's also a side room with tables set among zebra-painted columns, where folks come to dine on creative French bistro fare.

Bell Book & Candle Bar

Map p128 (141 W 10th St btwn Waverley & Greenwich Ave; S A/B/C, B/D/F/M to W 4th St; 1 to Christopher St-Sheridan Sq) Step down into this candle-lit gastropub for strong, inventive libations (try the canela margarita, with cinnamon-infused tequila), and hearty pub grub.

Jane Ballroom Lounge

Map p128 (113 Jane St cnr West St; S L to 8th Ave; A/C/E, 1/2/3 to 14th St) Inside the Jane Hotel, this spacious high-ceilinged lounge is an explosion of wild design: beneath an oversized disco ball is a mish-mash of leather sofas and velour chairs, animal print fabrics, potted palms and various taxidermied creatures (a peacock, a ram's head over the flickering fireplace).

Little Branch Cocktail Bar

Map p128 (212-929-4360; 22 Seventh Ave at Leroy St; 7pm-3am; S 1 to Houston St) If it weren't for the doorman, you'd never guess that a charming drinking den lurked beyond the plain metal door

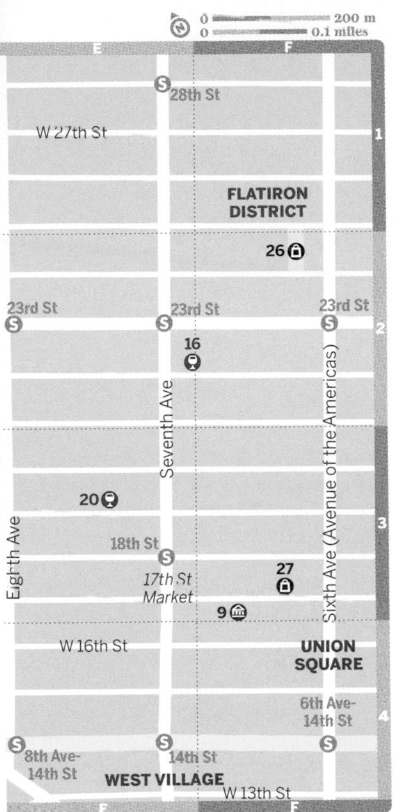

Chelsea

Sights
1 Barbara Gladstone Gallery C2
2 Chelsea Market D4
3 David Zwirner B3
4 Gagosian B2
5 Mary Boone Gallery B2
6 Matthew Marks Gallery C2
7 Pace Gallery B2
8 Paula Cooper Gallery B3
9 Rubin Museum of Art F3

Eating
10 Blossom D2
Chelsea Market .... (see 2)
11 Co D2
12 Cookshop C3
13 Foragers City Table D2
14 Heath B1
15 Tía Pol C2

Drinking & Nightlife
16 Barracuda E2
17 Bathtub Gin D3
18 Chelsea Brewing Company B3
19 Frying Pan A1
20 G Lounge E3
Gallow Green .... (see 14)

Entertainment
21 Atlantic Theater Company D3
22 Joyce Theater D3
23 Sleep No More B1
24 Upright Citizens Brigade Theatre D1

Shopping
25 192 Books C2
26 Antiques Garage Flea Market F2
27 Housing Works Thrift Shop F3
28 Printed Matter C2

Sports & Activities
29 Chelsea Piers Complex B2

positioned at this triangular intersection. When you get the go-ahead to enter, you'll find a basement bar that feels like a kickback to Prohibition times. Old-time jazz tunes waft overhead as locals clink glasses and sip inventive, artfully prepared cocktails.

Buvette Wine Bar

Map p128 (☎212-255-3590; www.ilovebuvette.com; 42 Grove St btwn Bedford & Bleecker Sts; ⏰8am-2am Mon-Fri, from 10am Sat & Sun; S 1 to Christopher St-Sheridan Sq; A/C/E, B/D/F/M to W 4th St) The rustic-chic decor here (think delicate tin tiles and a swooshing marble countertop) make it the perfect place for a glass of wine – no matter the time of day. For the full experience at this self-proclaimed *gastrotèque*, grab a seat at one of the surrounding tables, and nibble on small plates while enjoying the Old-World wines (mostly from France and Italy).

Marie's Crisis Bar

Map p128 (☎212-243-9323; 59 Grove St btwn Seventh Ave & Bleecker St; ⏰4pm-4am; S 1 to Christopher St-Sheridan Sq) Aging Broadway queens, wide-eyed out-of-town gay boys, giggly tourists and various other fans of musical theater assemble around the piano here and take turns belting out campy show tunes, often joined by the entire crowd. It's old-school fun, no matter how jaded you were when you went in.

Employees Only Bar
Map p128 (☎212-242-3021; 510 Hudson St near Christopher St; ⏰6pm-4am; Ⓢ1 to Christopher St-Sheridan Sq) Duck behind the neon 'Psychic' sign to find this hidden hangout. The bar gets busier as the night wears on. Bartenders are ace mixologists, fizzing up crazy, addictive libations such as the Ginger Smash and the Mata Hari. Great for late-night drinking, and eating, courtesy of the onsite restaurant that serves past midnight.

Standard Bar
Map p128 (☎212-645-4646, 877-550-4646; www.standardhotels.com; 848 Washington St; ⓈA/C/E to 14th St; L to 8th Ave) Rising on concrete stilts over the High Line, the Standard attracts an A-list crowd, with a chichi lounge and nightclub on the upper floors – the **Top of the Standard** Map p128 (☎212-645-4646; standardhotels.com/high-line; 848 Washington St btwn 13th & Little W 12th Sts; ⏰4pm-2am; ⓈL to 8th Ave; 1/2/3, A/C/E to 14th St) and **Le Bain** Map p128 (☎212-645-4646; 848 Washington St btwn 13th & Little W 12th Sts; ⏰10pm-4am Wed-Fri, 2pm-4am Sat & Sun; ⓈL to 8th Ave; 1/2/3, A/C/E to 14th St). There's also a grill, an eating-and-drinking plaza (that becomes a skating rink in winter) and an open-air beer garden with a classic German menu and frothy drafts.

Stonewall Inn Gay
Map p128 (53 Christopher St; Ⓢ1 to Christopher St-Sheridan Sq) Site of the Stonewall riots in 1969, this historic bar was losing its fan base to trendier spots until new owners came along several years back, gave it a facelift and opened it to a new and welcoming crowd. Since then, it's been pulling in varied crowds nightly for parties catering to everyone under the gay rainbow.

White Horse Tavern Bar
Map p128 (☎212-243-9260; 567 Hudson St at 11th St; Ⓢ1 to Christopher St-Sheridan Sq) It's a bit on the tourist trail, but that doesn't dampen the century-old, pubby dark-wood, tin-ceiling atmosphere of this bar, where Dylan Thomas had his last drink (too many beers led to his 1953 death) and a tipsy Jack Kerouac got kicked out. Sit at the long oak bar inside or on sidewalk tables.

Cielo Club
Map p128 (☎212-645-5700; www.cieloclub.com; 18 Little W 12th St; cover charge $15-25; ⏰10:30pm-5am Mon-Sat; ⓈA/C/E, L to 8th Ave-14th St) This long-running club boasts a largely attitude-free crowd and an excellent sound system.

Chelsea

Gallow Green Bar
Map p134 (☎212-564-1662; mckittrickhotel.com/gallowgreen; 542 W 27th St btwn Tenth & Eleventh Aves; ⏰May-Oct; ⓈC/E to 23rd St; 1 to 28th St) Run by the creative team behind **Sleep No More** (p139), Gallow Green is a rooftop bar festooned with vines, potted plants and fairy lights.

Bathtub Gin Cocktail Bar
Map p134 (☎646-559-1671; www.bathtubginnyc.com; 132 Ninth Ave btwn 18th & 19th Sts; ⏰6pm-1:30am Sun-Tue, to 3:30am Wed-Sat; ⓈA/C/E to 14th St; L to 8th Ave; A/C/E to 23rd St) Amid New York City's obsession with speakeasy-styled hangouts, Bathtub Gin manages to poke its head above the crowd with its super-secret front door, which doubles as a wall for an unassuming cafe. Inside, chill seating, soft background beats and kindly staff make it a great place to sling back bespoke cocktails with friends.

G Lounge Gay
Map p134 (☎212-929-1085; www.glounge.com; 225 W 19th St btwn Seventh & Eighth Aves; ⏰4pm-4am; Ⓢ1 to 18th St) For heavy drinking and dancing with no cover, you can't beat G, as locals call it – although you may have to wait in line to get in. The occasional burlesque or drag show adds to the good fun. Cash only.

Chelsea Brewing Company
Pub

Map p134 (212-336-6440; West Side Hwy at W 18th St, Chelsea Piers, Pier 59; noon-1am; S C/E to 23rd St) Enjoy a quality microbrew, waterside, in the expansive outdoor area of this beer haven. It's a perfect place to re-enter the world after a day of swimming, golfing or rock climbing at the **Chelsea Piers Complex** (p141).

Barracuda
Gay

Map p134 (212-645-8613; 275 W 22nd St at Seventh Ave; S C/E to 23rd St) This longtime favorite holds its own even as newer, slicker places come and go. That's because it's got a simple, winning formula: affordable cocktails, a cozy rec-room vibe and free entertainment from some of the city's top drag queens.

Frying Pan
Bar

Map p134 (212-989-6363; Pier 66 at W 26th St; noon-midnight; S C/E to 23rd St) Salvaged from the bottom of the sea (or at least the Chesapeake Bay), the Lightship *Frying Pan* and the two-tiered dockside bar where it's parked are fine go-to spots for a sundowner.

Entertainment

Greenwich Village & the Meatpacking District

Le Poisson Rouge
Live Music

Map p128 (212-505-3474; www.lepoissonrouge.com; 158 Bleecker St; S A/C/E, B/D/F/M to W 4th St-Washington Sq) This high-concept art space (complete with dangling fish aquarium) hosts a highly eclectic lineup of live music, with the likes of Deerhunter, Marc Ribot and Cibo Matto performing in past years. There's a lot of experimentation and cross-genre pollination between classical, folk music, opera and more.

Village Vanguard
Jazz

Map p128 (212-255-4037; www.villagevanguard.com; 178 Seventh Ave at 11th St; cover $25-30 plus 1-drink minimum; S 1/2/3 to 14th St) Possibly the city's most prestigious jazz club, the Vanguard has hosted literally every major star of the past 50 years.

Smalls
Jazz

Map p128 (212-252-5091; www.smallsjazzclub.com; 183 W 4th St; cover $20 from 7:30pm-12:30am, $10 after; S 1 to Christopher St-Sheridan Sq) Living up to its name, this cramped but appealing basement jazz den offers a grab-bag collection of jazz acts who take the stage nightly. Cover for the evening is $20, with a come-and-go policy if you need to duck out for a slice.

Smalls jazz club
ANGUS OBORN/GETTY IMAGES ©

LONELY PLANET/GETTY IMAGES ©

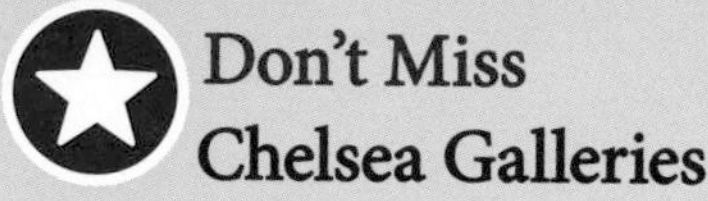

Don't Miss Chelsea Galleries

Chelsea is home to the highest concentration of art galleries in the entire city. Most lie in the 20s, on the blocks between Tenth and Eleventh Aves, and openings for their new shows are typically held on Thursday evenings. Pick up Art Info's Gallery Guide (with map) available for free at most galleries. Note that most galleries close on Monday.

If time is limited, the following galleries should be high on your itinerary:

Pace Gallery Map p134 (534 W 25th St btwn Tenth & Eleventh Aves; ⌚10am-6pm Tue-Sat; **S** C/E to 23rd St)

Gagosian Map p134 (☎212-741-1111; www.gagosian.com; 555 W 24th St; ⌚10am-6pm Tue-Sat; **S** C/E to 23rd St)

Mary Boone Map p134 (www.maryboonegallery.com; 541 W 24th St; ⌚10am-6pm Tue-Sat; **S** C/E, 1 to 23rd St)

Barbara Gladstone Map p134 (☎212-206-9300; www.gladstonegallery.com; 515 W 24th St btwn Tenth & Eleventh Aves; ⌚10am-6pm Tue-Sat, closed weekends Jul & Aug; **S** C/E, 1 to 23rd St)

Matthew Marks Map p134 (☎212-243-0200; www.matthewmarks.com; 522 W 22nd St; ⌚10am-6pm Tue-Sat; **S** C/E to 23rd St)

Paula Cooper Map p134 (534 W 21st St btwn Tenth & Eleventh Aves; ⌚10am-6pm Tue-Sat; **S** C/E to 23rd St)

David Zwirner Map p134 (www.davidzwirner.com; 537 W 20th St btwn Tenth & Eleventh Sts; ⌚10am-6pm Tue-Sat; **S** C/E to 23rd St)

Blue Note Jazz

Map p128 (☎212-475-8592; www.bluenote.net; 131 W 3rd St btwn Sixth Ave & MacDougal St; S A/C/E, B/D/F/M to W 4th St-Washington Sq) This is by far the most famous (and expensive) of the city's jazz clubs. Go on an off night, and be quiet – all attention is on the stage!

Barrow Street Theater Theater

Map p128 (☎212-243-6262; www.barrowstreettheatre.com; 27 Barrow St, btwn Seventh Ave & W 4th St; S 1/2 to Christopher St-Sheridan Sq; A/C/E, B/D/F/M to W 4th St; 1/2 to Houston St) A fantastic off-Broadway space in the heart of the West Village showcasing a variety of local and international theater.

IFC Center Cinema

Map p128 (☎212-924-7771; www.ifccenter.com; 323 Sixth Ave at 3rd St; S A/C/E, B/D/F/M to W 4th St-Washington Sq) This arthouse cinema in NYU land has a solidly curated lineup of new indies, cult classics and foreign films.

Chelsea

Sleep No More Theater

Map p134 (www.sleepnomorenyc.com; McKittrick Hotel, 530 W 27th St; tickets from $106; ⏰7pm-midnight Mon-Sat; S C/E to 23rd St) One of the most immersive theater experiences ever conceived, *Sleep No More* is a loosely based retelling of *Macbeth* set inside a series of Chelsea warehouses that have been redesigned to look like an abandoned hotel.

Joyce Theater Dance

Map p134 (☎212-242-0800; www.joyce.org; 175 Eighth Ave; S C/E to 23rd St; A/C/E to Eighth Ave-14th St; 1 to 18th St) A favorite among dance junkies because of its excellent sight lines and offbeat offerings, this is an intimate venue, seating 472 in a renovated cinema.

Atlantic Theater Company Theater

Map p134 (☎212-691-5919; www.atlantictheater.org; 336 W 20th St btwn Eighth & Ninth Aves; S C/E to 23rd St, 1 to 18th St) Founded by David Mamet and William H Macy in 1985, the Atlantic Theater is a pivotal anchor for the off-Broadway community, hosting many Tony Award and Drama Desk winners over the last 25-plus years.

Upright Citizens Brigade Theatre Comedy

Map p134 (☎212-366-9176; www.ucbtheatre.com; 307 W 26th St btwn Eighth & Ninth Aves; cover $5-10; S C/E to 23rd St) Pros of comedy sketches and outrageous improvisations reign at this popular 74-seat venue, which gets drop-ins from casting directors.

Bleecker St, Greenwich Village

Shopping

Greenwich Village & the Meatpacking District

Beacon's Closet — Thrift Store

Map p128 (10 W 13th St btwn Fifth & Sixth Aves; 11am-8pm; S L, N/R, 4/5/6 to Union Sq) You'll find a good selection of gently used clothing (which is of a decidedly downtown/Brooklyn hipster aesthetic) at only slightly higher prices than Beacon's sister store in Williamsburg.

Personnel of New York — Fashion, Accessories

Map p128 (9 Greenwich Ave btwn Christopher & W 10th St; 11am-8pm Mon-Sat, noon-7pm Sun; S A/C/E, B/D/F/M to W 4th St; 1 to Christopher St-Sheridan Sq) New in 2013, this small, delightful indie shop sells men's and women's designer clothing from unique labels from the East and West Coast and beyond.

Strand Book Store — Books

Map p128 (212-473-1452; www.strandbooks.com; 828 Broadway at 12th St; 9:30am-10:30pm Mon-Sat, from 11am Sun; S L, N/Q/R, 4/5/6 to 14th St-Union Sq) In operation since 1927, the Strand sells new, used and rare titles, spreading an incredible 18 miles of books (more than 2.5 million of them) among three labyrinthine floors.

Marc by Marc Jacobs — Fashion

Map p128 (212-924-0026; www.marcjacobs.com; 403-405 Bleecker St; noon-8pm Mon-Sat, to 7pm Sun; S A/C/E to 14th St; L to 8th Ave) With five small shops sprinkled around the West Village, Marc Jacobs has established a real presence in this well-heeled neighborhood.

Murray's Cheese — Food & Drink

Map p128 (212-243-3289; www.murrayscheese.com; 254 Bleecker St btwn Sixth & Seventh Aves; 8am-8pm Mon-Sat, 10am-7pm Sun; S 1 to Christopher St-Sheridan Sq) Founded in 1914, this is one of New York's best cheese shops.

Forbidden Planet — Comics

Map p128 (212-473-1576; 840 Broadway; 9am-10pm Sun-Wed, to midnight Thu-Sat; S L, N/Q/R, 4/5/6 to 14th St-Union Sq) Indulge your inner sci-fi and fantasy nerd. Find heaps of comics, manga, graphic novels, posters and figurines (ranging from *Star Trek* to *Doctor Who*).

Chelsea

Housing Works Thrift Shop — Vintage

Map p134 (718-838-5050; 143 W 17th St btwn Sixth & Seventh Aves; 10am-7pm Mon-Fri, to 6pm Sat, noon-5pm Sun; S 1 to 18th St) This shop, with its swanky window displays, looks more boutique than thrift, but its selections of clothes, accessories, furniture, books and records are great value.

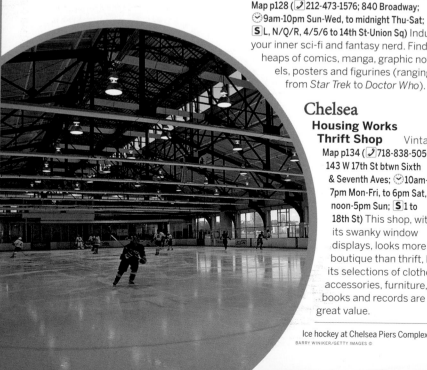

Ice hockey at Chelsea Piers Complex
BARRY WINIKER/GETTY IMAGES ©

192 Books Books

Map p134 (212-255-4022; www.192books.com; 192 Tenth Ave btwn 21st & 22nd Sts; 11am-7pm; S C/E to 23rd St) Located right in the gallery district is this small indie bookstore, with sections on fiction, history, travel, art and criticism.

Antiques Garage Flea Market Antiques

Map p134 (112 W 25th St at Sixth Ave; 9am-5pm Sat & Sun; S 1 to 23rd St) This weekend flea market is set in a two-level parking garage, with more than 100 vendors spreading their wares.

Sports & Activities

Chelsea Piers Complex Sports

Map p134 (212-336-6666; www.chelseapiers.com; Hudson River at end of W 23rd St; S C/E to 23rd St) This massive waterfront sports center caters to the athlete in everyone. You can set out to hit a bucket of golf balls at the four-level driving range, ice skate on the complex's indoor rink or rent in-line skates to cruise along the new bike path on the Hudson River Park – all the way down to Battery Park. The complex has a jazzy bowling alley, Hoop City for basketball, a sailing school for kids, batting cages, a huge gym facility with an indoor pool (day passes for nonmembers are $50), indoor rock-climbing walls – the works.

Bowlmor Lanes Bowling

Map p128 (212-255-8188; www.bowlmor.com; 110 University Pl; bowling per person from $12, shoe rental $6; 1pm-midnight Mon-Thu, noon-2am Fri & Sat, noon-midnight Sun; S L, N/Q/R, 4/5/6 to 14th St-Union Sq) Among retro-crazed New Yorkers, a night of bowling qualifies as quite a hoot. Maybe it's the shoes, or all the pitchers of beer.

Downtown Boathouse Kayaking

Map p128 (www.downtownboathouse.org; Pier 40 near Houston St; tours free; 10am-6pm Sat & Sun, 5-7pm Thu mid-May–mid-Oct; S 1 to Houston St) New York's most active public boathouse offers free walk-up 20-minute kayaking sessions (including equipment) in a protected embayment in the Hudson River on weekends and some weekday evenings. Longer weekend three-hour trips usually go from the Midtown location at **Clinton Cove** Map p178 (Pier 96 at W 56th St; 9am-6pm Sat & Sun, 5-7pm Mon-Fri mid-Jun–Aug; S A/C, B/D, 1 to 59th St-Columbus Circle); there's another boathouse at **Riverside Park** Map p222 (W 72nd St; 10am-5pm Sun; S 1/2/3 to 72nd St) on the Upper West Side; and a summer-only location on **Governor's Island** (www.downtownboathouse.org/governors-island/; 10:30am-4pm Sat Jun-Aug).

Union Square, Flatiron District & Gramercy

This trio of neighborhoods boasts lovely architecture and diverse public spaces. Although Union Square earned its moniker from rather practical and prosaic roots, it is much more than the junction of two roads. In many ways the neighborhood is the union of disparate parts of the city, acting as veritable urban glue linking unlikely cousins. Shops and eateries surround the park, whose interior hops with activity. To the northwest is the Flatiron District, loaded with loft buildings and boutiques, and doing a good imitation of SoHo without the pretensions, prices or crowds. The neighborhood takes its name from the Flatiron Building – a thin, gorgeous work of architecture that sits just south of Madison Square Park. The Gramercy area, loosely comprising the 20s blocks east of Park Ave South, is named after one of New York's loveliest parks and is primarily a residential area.

Sunset over the Flatiron District
TONY SHI PHOTOGRAPHY/GETTY IMAGES ©

Union Square, Flatiron District & Gramercy Highlights

Flatiron Building (p148)

At the intersection of Broadway, Fifth Ave and 23rd St, the famous (and absolutely gorgeous) 1902 Flatiron Building has a distinctive triangular shape to match its site. It was New York's first iron-frame high-rise, and the world's tallest building until 1909. The surrounding district is a fashionable area of boutiques and loft apartments. You can now enjoy the best views from a tiny plaza just north of 23rd St.

1

2

Madison Square Park (p148)

This green oasis halfway between downtown and midtown makes a pleasant respite from exploring the urban streets. Have a loll on the grass, grab a bite at Shake Shack (p149), or a picnic from Eataly across Broadway, and admire the changing art installations that pop up here every year. If you have kids in tow, don't miss the north-end playground. In the summertime, the park hosts an array of small concerts and other events. Shake Shack in Madison Square Park

DENNIS K. JOHNSON/GETTY IMAGES ©

ANGUS OBORN/GETTY IMAGES ©

Greenmarket Farmers Market (p148)

3

New York City has been on a market kick for the last two decades, but the biggest and best is still in Union Square. At this sprawling market, you can join chefs and gourmands to purchase organic and naturally grown products from farmers in the region (most comes from less than 100 miles from NYC). Afterwards, you can picnic on Union Square.

BARRY WINIKER/GETTY IMAGES ©

4

Eataly (p154)

A 50,000-sq-ft tribute to *la dolce vita*, Mario Batali's food-filled wonderland is a New York version of those dreamy Tuscan markets you find in Diane Lane films. Decked stem to stern with gourmet edibles, Eataly is a must for a picnic lunch – though make sure to leave room for some pork shoulder at the rooftop beer garden, Birreria (p152).

5

Union Square (p153)

The crossroads of the city, Union Square is one of the best places to simply sit and take it all in. Amid the tapestry of stone steps and fenced-in foliage, you'll find denizens of every ilk: suits gulping fresh air during their lunch breaks, rowdy college kids chowing down cheap take-out, skateboarding punks flipping tricks and throngs of protesters reaching out for various causes.

Union Square, Flatiron District & Gramercy Walk

You'll feel the Village vibe spilling over with the likes of quirky cafes, after-work watering holes, funky storefronts and dreadlocked buskers in the square.

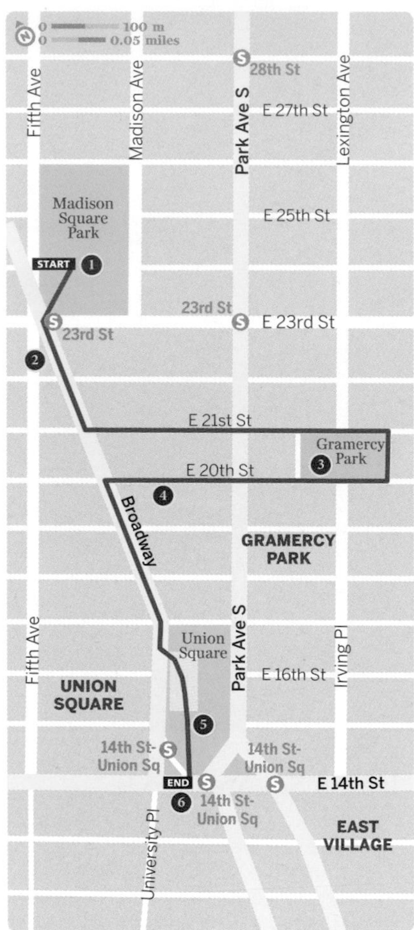

WALK FACTS

- **Start** Madison Square Park
- **End** DSW
- **Distance** 2 miles
- **Duration** Two hours

1 Madison Square Park

Start off in Madison Square Park (p148); this peaceful green space is dotted with 19th-century statues of folks including Senator Roscoe Conkling (who froze to death in a brutal 1888 blizzard) and Civil War admiral David Farragut. Between 1876 and 1882 the torch-bearing arm of the Statue of Liberty was on display here, and in 1879 the first Madison Square Garden arena was constructed at Madison Ave and 26th St. If you'd like to eat before the walk, hit up Shake Shack (p149) for a gourmet burger and fries.

2 Flatiron Building

Take in lovely views of the beaux-arts triangular masterpiece, the Flatiron Building (p148), before exiting the park at its southwest corner. Cross the street to stand up close and admire the city's oddest skyscraper from a whole new angle at Fifth Ave and Broadway. The construction of the building (originally known as the Fuller Building) coincided with the proliferation of mass-produced picture postcards – the partnership was kismet. Even before its completion, there were images of the soon-to-be tallest tower circulating the globe, creating much wonder and excitement.

3 Gramercy Park

Follow Broadway south to 21st St and take a left. Past Park Ave S you'll find yourself alongside Gramercy Park, which was created by Samuel Ruggles in 1831 after he drained the swamp in this area and laid out streets in an English style. You can't enter the park, as it's private, but go ahead and peer through the gate. Just across the street from the southwestern corner of the park is the National Arts Club (p149). Calvert Vaux, who was one of the creators of Central Park, designed the building, originally the private residence of Samuel J Tilden, governor of New York and failed presidential candidate in 1876.

4 Theodore Roosevelt's Birthplace

Head back west along 20th St, stopping at the reconstructed version of the Theodore Roosevelt birthplace (p149), run by the National Parks Service; hourly tours are offered.

5 Union Square

Once back on Broadway continue south and you'll soon find yourself at the northwest corner of Union Square (p153). Check out the produce, cheese, baked goods and flowers of the Greenmarket Farmers Market (p148) or amuse yourself by watching the skateboarders, visiting the Gandhi statue near the southwest corner, or grabbing some food at one of the surrounding eateries for a picnic in the park.

6 DSW

Standing like a beacon of retail on Union Sq South (14th St) is the massive warehouse, DSW, dedicated to heavily discounted designer shoes and accessories. Shop if you wish, but the real attraction is the store's massive, north-facing window, which lets you look down over the park and across to the top of the Empire State Building from a 4th-floor perch.

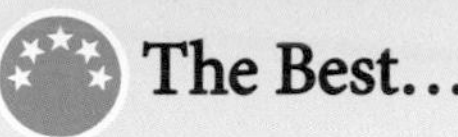

The Best...

PLACES TO EAT

Pure Food & Wine For fresh, creative and alarmingly delicious vegetarian cuisine. (p151)

ABC Kitchen Sustainable, modern American fare in an atmospheric setting. (p151)

Eataly The Macy's of food courts with a handful of specialty dining halls, all with a different focus. (p154)

PLACES TO DRINK

Raines Law Room Sink into a leather lounge chair and enjoy an artfully made cocktail. (p152)

Old Town Bar & Restaurant The classic, preserved decor here offers a turn-of-the-century vibe. (p153)

Flatiron Lounge Stylish, deco-inspired drinking den. (p152)

PLACES FOR VIEWS

Birreria Amazing roof deck. (p152)

Madison Square Park The south side offers a full-frontal of the Flatiron Building. (p148)

Burger from Shake Shack (p149)

Discover Union Square, Flatiron District & Gramercy

Getting There & Away

- **Subway** A slew of subway lines converge below Union Square, shuttling passengers up Manhattan's East Side on the 4/5/6 lines, straight across to Williamsburg on the L, or up and over to Queens on the N/Q/R lines.
- **Bus** The M14 and the M23 provide cross-town service along 14th St and 23rd St respectively. Go for the bus over the subway if you're traveling between two eastern points in Manhattan – it's not worth traveling over to Union Square to walk back to First Ave.

Greenmarket Farmers Market
MARCO VACCA/GETTY IMAGES ©

Sights

Madison Square Park Park
Map p150 (www.nycgovparks.org/parks/madisonsquarepark; 23rd to 26th Sts btwn Fifth & Madison Aves; 6am-11pm; S N/R, F/M, 6 to 23rd St) This park defined the northern reaches of Manhattan until the island's population exploded after the Civil War. These days, it's a much-welcome oasis from Manhattan's relentless pace, with locals unleashing their dogs in the popular dog-run area, children squealing giddily at the impressive playground, and the hungry lining up at on-site burger joint **Shake Shack** (p149).

Flatiron Building Landmark
Map p150 (Broadway cnr Fifth Ave & 23rd St; S N/R, F/M, 6 to 23rd St) Built in 1902, the 20-story Flatiron Building, designed by Daniel Burnham, has a uniquely narrow triangular footprint that resembles the prow of a massive ship, and a traditional beaux arts limestone facade, built over a steel frame, that gets more complex and beautiful the longer you stare at it.

Greenmarket Farmers Market Food Market
Map p150 (212-788-7476; www.grownyc.org; 17th St btwn Broadway & Park Ave S; 8am-6pm Mon, Wed, Fri & Sat) On most days, Union Square's north end hosts the most popular of the nearly 50 greenmarkets throughout the five boroughs, where even celebrity chefs come for just-picked rarities including fiddlehead ferns, heirloom tomatoes and fresh curry leaves.

Tibet House Cultural Center
Map p150 (212-807-0563; www.tibethouse.org; 22 W 15th St, btwn Fifth & Sixth Aves; suggested donation $5; 11am-6pm Mon-Fri, to 4pm Sun; S F to 14th St, L to 6th Ave) With the Dalai Lama as the patron of its board, this nonprofit cultural space is dedicated to presenting Tibet's ancient traditions through art exhibits, a research library and various publications.

Exhibits span a variety of subjects, from traditional Tibetan thangka painting and sculpture, to contemporary views of Tibetan Buddhist and Hindu tantric art.

Theodore Roosevelt Birthplace Historic Site
Map p150 (212-260-1616; www.nps.gov/thrb; 28 E 20th St, btwn Park Ave S & Broadway; adult/child $3/free; guided tours 10am, 11am, 1pm, 2pm, 3pm & 4pm Tue-Sat; S N/R/W, 6 to 23rd St) This National Historic Site is a bit of a cheat, since the physical house where the 26th president was actually born was demolished in his own lifetime. But this building is a worthy reconstruction by his relatives, who joined it with another family residence next door. Guided tours of the property last 30 minutes.

National Arts Club Cultural Center
Map p150 (212-475-3424; www.nationalartsclub.org; 15 Gramercy Park S; S 6 to 23rd St) Founded in 1898 to promote public interest in the arts, the National Arts Club boasts a beautiful, vaulted, stained-glass ceiling above the wooden bar in its picture-lined front parlor. The club holds art exhibitions, ranging from sculpture to photography, that are open to the public from 9am to 5pm Monday to Friday (check the website for upcoming shows).

Eating

Shake Shack Burgers $
Map p150 (212-989-6600; www.shakeshack.com; Madison Square Park, cnr 23rd St & Madison Ave; burgers from $3.60; 11am-11pm; S N/R, F/M, 6 to 23rd St) The flagship of chef Danny Meyer's gourmet burger chainlet, Shake Shack whips up hyper-fresh burgers, hand-cut fries and a rotating line-up of frozen custards. Veg-heads can dip into the crisp Portobello burger. Lines are long, but worth it.

Artichoke Basille's Pizza Pizzeria $
Map p150 (212-228-2004; www.artichokepizza.com; 328 E 14th St, btwn First & Second Aves; slice from $4.50; 11am-5am; S L to First Ave) Run by two Italian guys from Staten Island, the pizza here is authentic, tangy and piled high with all sorts of toppings.

Max Brenner Desserts $
Map p150 (Chocolate By the Bald Man; 646-467-8803; www.maxbrenner.com; 841 Broadway, btwn 13th & 14th Sts; desserts from $8.50; 9am-midnight Mon-Thu, to 2am Fri & Sat, to 11pm Sun; S L, N/Q/R, 4/5/6 to 14th St-Union Sq) Sweet-toothed Aussie Max Brenner is expanding waistlines in NYC with his cafe-cum-chocolate-bar.

City Bakery Bakery $
Map p150 (212-366-1414; www.thecitybakery.com; 3 W 18th St, btwn Fifth & Sixth Aves; pastries from $3, cafeteria lunch per pound $15; 7:30am-7pm Mon-Fri, 8am-7pm Sat, 9am-6pm Sun; S L, N/Q/R, 4/5/6 to 14th St-Union Sq) A happy marriage between gourmet entrées and cafeteria service, City Bakery is best known for its scrumptious drip coffee (look how they pour the milk in first – yum!) and homemade hot chocolate. Breakfast edibles include yogurt with fresh fruit, muffins, croissants and scrambled eggs, while the Sunday brunch is particularly popular.

Republic Asian $$
Map p150 (www.thinknoodles.com; 37 Union Sq W; mains $12-15; 11:30am-10:30pm Sun-Wed, to 11:30pm Thu-Sat; S L, N/Q/R, 4/5/6 to 14th St-Union Sq) Eat-and-go Republic feeds the masses with fresh 'n' tasty Asian staples. Slurp away on warming broth noodles, chomp on juicy pad thai or keep it light with a green papaya and mango salad. Located right on Union Square, it's a handy spot for a cheap, uncomplicated, walk-in bite.

Union Square, Flatiron District & Gramercy

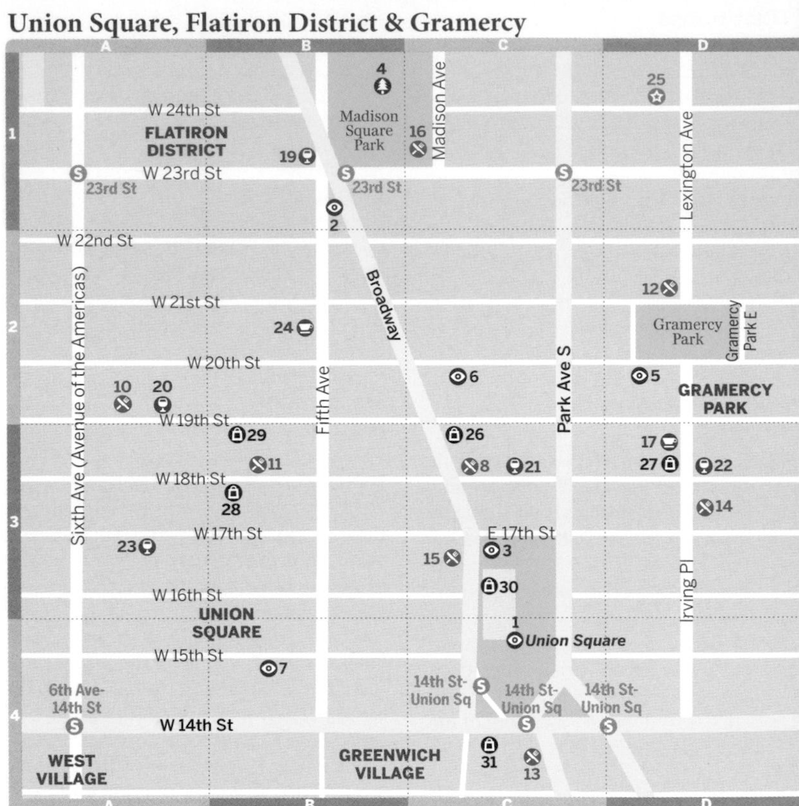

Union Square, Flatiron District & Gramercy

Don't Miss Sights

1 Union Square C4

Sights

2 Flatiron Building B1
3 Greenmarket Farmers Market C3
4 Madison Square Park B1
5 National Arts Club D2
6 Theodore Roosevelt Birthplace C2
7 Tibet House B4

Eating

8 ABC Kitchen C3
9 Artichoke Basille's Pizza F4
10 Boqueria Flatiron A2
11 City Bakery B3
12 Maialino D2
13 Max Brenner C4
14 Pure Food & Wine D3
15 Republic C3
16 Shake Shack C1

Drinking & Nightlife

17 71 Irving Place D3
18 Beauty Bar E4
19 Birreria B1
20 Flatiron Lounge A2
21 Old Town Bar & Restaurant C3
22 Pete's Tavern D3
23 Raines Law Room A3
24 Toby's Estate B2

Entertainment

25 Peoples Improv Theater D1

Shopping

26 ABC Carpet & Home C3
27 Bedford Cheese Shop D3
28 Books of Wonder B3
Eataly .... (see 19)
29 Idlewild Books B3
30 Union Square Greenmarket C3
31 Whole Foods C4

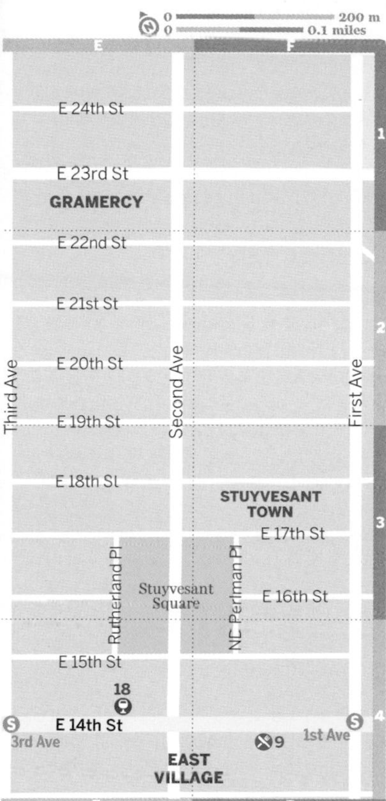

Boqueria Flatiron Tapas **$$**
Map p150 (☎212-255-4160; www.boquerianyc.com; 53 W 19th St, btwn Fifth & Sixth Aves; dishes $5-22; ⊙noon-10:30pm Sun-Wed, to 11:30pm Thu-Sat; S F/M, N/R, 6 to 23rd St) A holy union between Spanish-style tapas and market-fresh fare, Boqueria woos the after-work crowd with a brilliant line up of small plates and larger *raciones*.

Maialino Italian **$$$**
Map p150 (☎212-777-2410; www.maialinonyc.com; 2 Lexington Ave, at 21st St; mains lunch $19-26, dinner $28-72; ⊙7.30am-10.30pm Mon-Fri, from 10am Sat & Sun; S 6, N/R to 23rd St) Take your taste buds on a Roman holiday at this Danny Meyer must, humming away inside the forever-fashionable Gramercy Park Hotel. Created with Greenmarket produce from nearby Union Square, Maialino's iterations of rustic Italian fare are exquisite; one taste of the extraordinary *brodetto* (seafood stew), and we swear you'll agree.

ABC Kitchen Modern American **$$$**
Map p150 (☎212-475-5829; www.abckitchennyc.com; 35 E 18th St, at Broadway; pizzas $15-19, dinner mains $24-34; ⊙noon-3pm & 5:30-10:30pm Mon-Wed, to 11pm Thu, to 11:30pm Fri, 11am-3:30pm & 5:30-11:30pm Sat, to 10pm Sun; ✎; S L, N/Q/R, 4/5/6 to Union Sq) Looking part gallery, part rustic farmhouse, sustainable ABC Kitchen is the culinary avatar of chi-chi home goods department store ABC Carpet & Home. Organic gets haute in dishes such as vibrant raw diver scallops with market grapes and lemon verbena, or comforting roast suckling pig with braised turnips and smoked bacon marmalade. For a more casual bite, hit the scrumptious whole-wheat pizzas.

Pure Food & Wine Vegetarian **$$$**
Map p150 (☎212-477-1010; www.oneluckyduck.com/purefoodandwine; 54 Irving Pl, btwn 17th & 18th Sts; mains $19-26; ⊙noon-4pm & 5:30-11pm; ✎; S L, N/Q/R, 4/5/6 to 14th St-Union Sq) Smart and sophisticated, Pure achieves the impossible, churning out obscenely delicious creations made completely from raw organics put through blenders, dehydrators and the capable hands of its staff. The result is seductive, invigorating dishes including tomato-zucchini lasagna (sans cheese and pasta), Brazil-nut sea-vegetable croquettes, and a gorgeous lemon bar with almond coconut crust and zesty lemon custard.

Drinking & Nightlife

Toby's Estate Cafe
Map p150 (www.tobysestate.com; 160 Fifth Ave, btwn 20th & 21st Sts; ⊙7am-9pm Mon-Fri, 9am-9pm Sat, 10am-7pm Sun; S N/R, F/M, 6 to 23rd St) Sydney-born, Williamsburg-roasting Toby's Estate is further proof of Manhattan's evolving artisan coffee culture. Loaded with a custom-made Strada espresso machine, you'll find it tucked away in the Club Monaco store.

Curry Hill

It's not exactly politically correct, but a small four-block section north of Union Square and Gramercy, traditionally known as Murray Hill, is sometimes also referred to as Curry Hill – a nod to the numerous Indian restaurants, shops and delis that proliferate here. Starting around E 28th St and flowing north on Lexington Ave to about E 33rd St, you'll find some of the finest Indian eateries in town – and most at bargain prices. The all-time local fave? **Curry in a Hurry** (Map p170; 212-683-0900; www.curryinahurrynyc.com; 119 Lexington Ave, at E 28th St; 11am-10pm; S 6 to 28th St). It's not fancy, but even Bono of U2 fame has been spotted having a nosh here.

Eataly (p154) at lunchtime

BLOOMBERG /GETTY IMAGES ©

71 Irving Place Cafe

Map p150 (Irving Farm Coffee Company; www.irvingfarm.com; 71 Irving Pl, btwn 18th & 19th Sts; 7am-10pm Mon-Fri, from 8am Sat & Sun; S 4/5/6, N/Q/R to 14th St-Union Sq) Hand-picked beans are lovingly roasted on a farm in the Hudson Valley (about 90 miles from NYC), and imbibers can tell – this is one of the smoothest cups of joe you'll find in Manhattan.

Birreria Beer Hall

Map p150 (www.eataly.com/birreria; 200 Fifth Ave, at 23rd St; mains $17-26; 11:30am-midnight Sun-Wed, to 1am Thu-Sat; S N/R, F/M, 6 to 23rd St) The crown jewel of Italian food emporium **Eataly** (p154) is its rooftop beer garden tucked betwixt the Flatiron's corporate towers. A beer menu of encyclopedic proportions offers drinkers some of the best suds on the planet. If you're hungry, the signature pork shoulder is your frosty one's soul mate.

In case you can't find the sneaky access elevator, it's near the checkouts on the 23rd St side of the store.

Flatiron Lounge Cocktail Bar

Map p150 (www.flatironlounge.com; 37 W 19th St, btwn Fifth & Sixth Aves; 4pm-2am Mon-Wed, to 3am Thu, to 4am Fri, 5pm-4am Sat, 5pm-2am Sun; S F/M, N/R, 6 to 23rd St) Until time machines hit the market, this swinging cocktail den will do just fine. Head through a dramatic archway and into a dark, deco-inspired fantasy of lipstick-red booths, racy jazz tunes and sassy grown-ups downing seasonal drinks.

Raines Law Room Cocktail Bar

Map p150 (www.raineslawroom.com; 48 W 17th St, btwn Fifth & Sixth Aves; 5pm-2am Mon-Thu, to 3am Fri & Sat, 8pm-1am Sun; S F/M to 14th St, L to 6th Ave, 1 to 18th St) A sea of velvet drapes and

ALBERTO GUGLIELMI/GETTY IMAGES ©

Don't Miss
Union Square

Union Square is like the Noah's Ark of New York, rescuing at least two of every kind from the curling seas of concrete. In fact, one would be hard-pressed to find a more eclectic cross-section of locals gathered in one public place.

A walk around Union Square will reveal a string of whimsical, temporary sculptures. Of the permanent offerings is an imposing equestrian statue of George Washington (one of the first public pieces of art in New York City) and a statue of peacemaker Mahatma Gandhi.

NEED TO KNOW

Map p150; www.unionsquarenyc.org; 17th St btwn Broadway & Park Ave S; S L, N/Q/R, 4/5/6 to 14th St-Union Sq

overstuffed leather lounge chairs, tin-tiled ceilings, the perfect amount of exposed brick, and expertly crafted cocktails using perfectly aged spirits – these guys are about as serious as a mortgage payment when it comes to amplified atmosphere.

Beauty Bar Theme Bar

Map p150 (212-539-1389; http://thebeautybar.com/home-new-york; 531 E 14th St, btwn Second & Third Aves; 5pm-4am Mon-Fri, from 2pm Sat & Sun; S L to 3rd Ave) A kitschy favorite since the mid-'90s, this homage to old-fashioned beauty parlors pulls in a cool local crowd with its gritty soundtrack, nostalgic vibe and around $10 manicures (with a free Blue Rinse margarita thrown in) from 6pm to 11pm on weekdays, and 3pm to 11pm on weekends.

Old Town Bar & Restaurant Bar

Map p150 (212-529-6732; www.oldtownbar.com; 45 E 18th St, btwn Broadway & Park Ave S; 11:30am-11:30pm Mon-Fri, 10am-11:30pm Sat, 11am-11:30pm Sun; S L, N/Q/R, 4/5/6 to 14th St-Union Sq) It still looks like 1892 in here, with the original tile floors and tin ceilings – the Old Town is an 'old world' drinking-man's classic (and woman's: Madonna lit up at the bar here, when lighting up was still legal, in her 'Bad Girl' video). There are cocktails around, but most come for an afternoon beer and burger (from $11.50).

Pete's Tavern Bar

Map p150 (☎212-473-7676; www.petestavern.com; 129 E 18th St, at Irving Pl; ⏰11am-2am; S L, N/Q/R, 4/5/6 to 14th St-Union Sq) This dark and atmospheric watering hole has all the earmarks of a New York classic – pressed tin, carved wood and an air of literary history. You can get a respectable burger here and choose from 17 draft beers.

Entertainment

Peoples Improv Theater Comedy

Map p150 (PIT; ☎212-563-7488; www.thepit-nyc.com; 123 E 24th St, btwn Lexington & Park Aves; 📶; S 6, N/R, F/M to 23rd St) Aglow in red neon, this bustling comedy club serves up top-notch laughs at dirt-cheap prices (from free to a modest $20). The string of nightly acts ranges from stand-up to musical comedy, playing in either the main-stage theater or the basement lounge.

Shopping

Eataly Food & Drink

Map p150 (www.eatalyny.com; 200 Fifth Ave, at 23rd St; ⏰8am-11pm; S F/M, N/R, 6 to 23rd St) This sprawling food emporium stocks a wondrous assortment of Italian edibles: cheeses, olive oils, chocolates, bakery items, gelato, wines (around the corner on 23rd St), and even cookbooks. For diners, there are both snack stands and sit-down restaurants where you can feast on thin-crust pizzas, grilled bronzini, calf's tongue with leaks, oysters, antipasti and myriad other selections. There's also a rooftop restaurant and beer garden, **Birreria** (p152).

Eataly also runs on-site cooking and culinary appreciation classes. See the website for details.

ABC Carpet & Home Homewares, Gifts

Map p150 (☎212-473-3000; www.abchome.com; 888 Broadway, at 19th St; ⏰10am-7pm Mon-Wed, Fri & Sat, to 8pm Thu, noon-6pm Sun;

Pete's Tavern

S L, N/Q/R/, 4/5/6 to 14th St-Union Sq) A mecca for home designers and decorators brainstorming ideas, this beautifully curated, six-level store heaves with all sorts of furnishings, small and large. Shop for easy-to-pack knickknacks, designer jewelry, global gifts, as well as statement furniture, slinky lamps and antique carpets. Come Christmas season the shop is a joy to behold.

Bedford Cheese Shop Food

Map p150 (www.bedfordcheeseshop.com; 67 Irving Pl, btwn 18th & 19th Sts; 8am-9pm Mon-Sat, to 8pm Sun; S L, N/Q/R, 4/5/6 to 14th St-Union Sq) Whether you're after local raw cow-milk cheese washed in absinthe, or garlic-infused goat-milk cheese from Australia, chances are you'll find it among the 200-strong selection at this outpost of Brooklyn's most celebrated cheese vendor. Pair the cheesy goodness with artisanal charcuterie, deli treats, ready-to-eat sandwiches ($9), as well as a proud array of Made-in-Brooklyn edibles.

Idlewild Books Books

Map p150 (212-414-8888; www.idlewildbooks.com; 12 W 19th St, btwn Fifth & Sixth Aves; noon-7.30pm Mon-Thu, to 6pm Fri & Sat, to 5pm Sun; S L, N/Q/R, 4/5/6 to 14th St-Union Sq) Named after JFK Airport's original moniker, this indie travel bookshop gets feet seriously itchy. Books are divided by region, and cover guidebooks as well as fiction, travelogues, history, cookbooks and other stimulating fare for delving into different corners of the world.

Books of Wonder Books

Map p150 (212-989-3270; www.booksofwonder.com; 18 W 18th St, btwn Fifth & Sixth Aves; 11am-7pm Mon-Sat, to 6pm Sun; ; S F/M, L to 6th Ave-14th St) Devoted to children's and young-adult titles, it's a great place to take young ones on a rainy day, especially when a kids' author is giving a reading, or a storyteller is on hand.

Whole Foods Food & Drink

Map p150 (212-673-5388; www.wholefoodsmarket.com; 4 Union Sq S; 7.30am-11pm; ; S L, N/Q/R, 4/5/6 to 14th St-Union Sq) One of several locations of the healthy food emporium that has swept the city, Whole Foods is an excellent place to fill the picnic hamper.

THURSDAYS
project RUNWAY
LG
2012
TDK
MARY POPPINS
Kodak

Midtown

This is, in many ways, the heart of Manhattan. It's the New York most outsiders thrill over in films or daydream about before they ever set foot in the city. It's classic NYC, home to Broadway and larger-than-life billboards, crushing crowds, skyscraping icons and an inimitable, frenzied energy.

Midtown West is a general term that refers to any part of Midtown (between 34th and 59th Sts) that lies west of Fifth Ave. Its collection of neighborhoods includes the trendy far-west reaches of Hell's Kitchen, the office-worker crush of harried suit-wearers along Sixth Ave, and the bustle of Times Square.

From the sophisticated shops of storied Fifth Ave to a handful of iconic sights, Midtown East is the quieter side of Manhattan's full belly. It's where you'll find the Chrysler Building, the UN Building, St Patrick's Cathedral and the beaux-arts-style Grand Central train station – plus iconic stores such as Tiffany & Co and Saks Fifth Avenue.

Times Square
MITCHELL FUNK/GETTY IMAGES ©

Midtown Highlights

Rockefeller Center (p183)

A ritzy enclave full of media companies and wine bars, Rockefeller Center also doubles as a public art plaza: *Prometheus* overlooks the famous skating rink; there's *Atlas*, carrying the world on Fifth Ave; and the aptly named *News*, an installation by Isamu Noguchi, sits not far from NBC studios. Inside, you can zip up to its observation deck, Top of the Rock (p183), for absolutely amazing views. Prometheus

1

2 Skyscrapers (p166 & p169)

No matter where you are in the city, the jutting silhouette of the Empire State Building (p166) is the perfect landmark Just east of Grand Central Terminal, the Chrysler Building (p169), an art-deco masterpiece, is magnificent when viewed from a distance. However, Midtown's skyline has enough modernist and postmodern beauties to satisfy the wildest of high-rise dreams. Spire of th Chrysler Building

Grand Central (p174)

3

New York's most breathtaking beaux-arts building, Grand Central, more than just a station, is an enchanted time machine; its swirl of chandeliers, marble, and historic bars and restaurants are a porthole into an era where train travel and romance were not mutually exclusive. While the underground electric tracks serve only commuter trains en route to northern suburbs and Connecticut, Grand Central is one stop you cannot afford to miss.

4

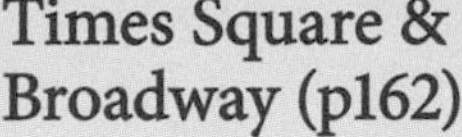

Times Square & Broadway (p162)

The buzzing, neon-lit epicenter of New York City, Times Square is an electrifying rush of glittering billboards, starstruck visitors and buffed topless cowboys. Step off the plaza in either direction to enter the Theater District, a place where romance, betrayal, murder and triumph come with dazzling costumes and stirring scores.

5

Museum of Modern Art (p164)

The shining star of the modern-art world is this hallowed institution, home to one of the most staggering collections of 20th- and 21st-century works on the planet. Come here to gaze at celebrated works by Cezanne, Picasso, Rousseau, Warhol and hundreds of others. Then catch your breath in the sculpture garden, followed by a bit of culinary decadence at the Modern, onsite.

Midtown Walk

This walk takes you through Bryant Park, a famed green refuge, then through the Diamond District, a world unto itself and a bit like Diagon Alley in Harry Potter; play spot the landmark at Top of the Rock, and hang out with Picasso, Warhol and Rothko at the Museum of Modern Art.

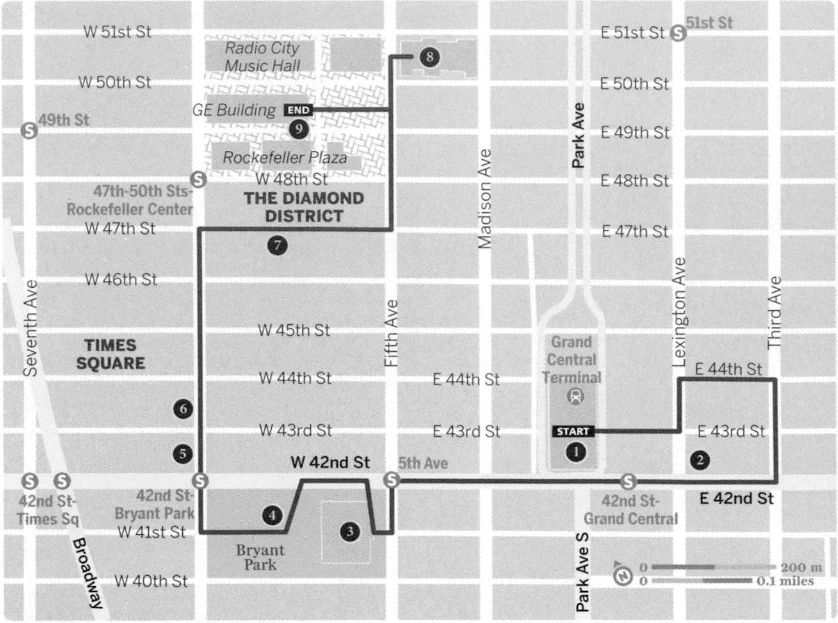

WALK FACTS

- **Start** Grand Central Terminal
- **End** Rockefeller Center
- **Distance** 1.8 miles
- **Duration** 3½ hours

❶ Grand Central Terminal

Start your Midtown saunter at beaux-arts marvel Grand Central Terminal (p174). Star gaze at the Main Concourse ceiling, share sweet nothings at the Whispering Gallery and pick up a gourmet treat at the Grand Central Market.

❷ Chrysler Building

Exit onto Lexington Ave and walk one block east along 44th St to Third Ave for a view of William Van Alen's 1930 masterpiece, the Chrysler Building (p169). Walk down Third Ave to 42nd St, turn right and slip into the Chrysler Building's sumptuous art-deco lobby, lavished with exotic inlaid wood, marble and purportedly the world's largest ceiling mural.

❸ New York Public Library

At the corner of 42nd St and Fifth Ave stands the stately New York Public Library (p168). Step in to peek at its spectacular Rose Main Reading Room and peruse exhibitions (always free) on the ground floor.

❹ Bryant Park

Behind the library lies Bryant Park (p168), the Midtown oasis that invites lingering. Have a seat at one of the cafe tables and enjoy the swirl of people – or create your own swirl, by going for a spin on the carousel (or a glide around the ice rink in winter).

❺ Bank of America Tower

On the northwest corner of 42nd St and Sixth Ave soars the Bank of America Tower, NYC's third-tallest building and one of its most ecofriendly.

❻ International Center of Photography

The next block north along Sixth Ave is home to the International Center of Photography (p173) at 43rd St. Head in to explore the two airy levels of top-notch images. Don't miss the excellent gallery shop, great for instant cameras and photography tomes, cool little gifts and NYC souvenirs.

❼ Diamond District

Continue north up Sixth Ave to 47th St, which features the Diamond District between Sixth and Fifth Aves, a wealth of diamond, gold, pearls and gemstones.

❽ St Patrick's Cathedral

Continue on to Fifth Ave and turn left – on 50th St is the Gothic stunner, St Patrick's Cathedral (p168), that looks as if it has been there since the Middle Ages while the city popped up around it. Check out the heavenly ceilings and its impressive rose window.

❾ Rockefeller Center & Top of the Rock

The last stop is Rockefeller Center (p183), a magnificent complex of art-deco skyscrapers and sculptures. Enter between 49th and 50th Sts to the main plaza and its golden statue of *Prometheus*, then head to the 70th-floor of the GE Building for an unforgettable vista at Top of the Rock (p183).

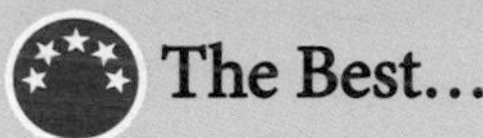

The Best...

PLACES TO EAT

NoMad Creative nouveau American cooking in a stylish setting. (p180)

Danji Masterfully prepared and wildly inventive 'Korean tapas.' (p177)

Smith An enticing eating and drinking spot in Midtown East. (p175)

PLACES TO DRINK

Rum House Vintage cocktails matched by live piano music nearly every night. (p182)

Terroir Upping Murray Hill's drinking scene with the third branch of this acclaimed wine bar. (p181)

PLACES FOR VIEWS

Top of the Rock Jaw-dropping observation deck with possibly the most expansive panorama in the city. (p183)

Empire State Building Nothing compares to this mesmerizing view over the city. (p166)

Top of the Strand Rooftop bar with fabulous views of New York's best-loved skyscraper, the Empire State Building. (p181)

Robert Floor-to-ceiling picture windows look out on Central Park from the ninth floor of the Museum of Arts & Design. (p173)

Top of the Rock

Times Square

The intersection of Broadway and Seventh Ave (better known as Times Square) is New York City's hyperactive heart. It's not hip, fashionable or in-the-know, and it couldn't care less. It's too busy pumping out iconic, mass-marketed NYC – yellow cabs, golden arches, soaring skyscrapers and razzle-dazzle Broadway marquees. This is the New York of collective fantasies – the place where Al Jolson 'makes it' in the 1927 film *The Jazz Singer*, where photojournalist Alfred Eisenstaedt famously captured a lip-locked sailor and nurse on V-J Day in 1945, and where Alicia Keys and Jay-Z waxed lyrically about this 'concrete jungle where dreams are made.'

Map p178

www.timessquare.com

Broadway at Seventh Ave

S N/Q/R, S, 1/2/3, 7 to Times Sq-42nd St

Cleaning the Square

For several decades, the dream here was a sordid, wet one. The economic crash of the early 1970s led to a mass exodus of corporations from Times Square. Billboard niches went dark, stores shut and once-grand hotels were converted into SROs (single-room occupancy) dives, attracting the poor and the destitute. What was once an area bathed in light and showbiz glitz became a dirty den of drug dealers and crime. While the adjoining Theater District survived, its respectable playhouses shared the streets with porn cinemas, strip clubs and adult bookstores. That all changed with tough-talking mayor Rudolph Giuliani, who, in the 1990s, forced out the skin flicks, boosted police numbers and lured a wave of 'respectable' retail chains, restaurants and attractions. By the new millennium, Times Square had gone from 'X-rated' to 'G-rated,' drawing almost 40 million annual visitors and raking in more than $1.8 billion annually from its 17,000 hotel rooms.

Broadway Classics

The Broadway of the 1920s was well known for its lighthearted musicals, commonly fusing vaudeville and music hall traditions, and producing classic tunes such as George Gershwin's *Rhapsody in Blue* and Cole Porter's *Let's Misbehave*. At the same time, Midtown's theater district was evolving as a platform for new American dramatists. One of the greatest was Eugene O'Neill. Born in Times Square at the long-gone Barrett Hotel (1500 Broadway) in 1888, the playwright debuted many of his works here, including Pulitzer Prize winners *Beyond the Horizon* and *Anna Christie*. O'Neill's success on Broadway paved the way for other American greats includingTennessee Williams, Arthur Miller and Edward Albee – a surge of serious talent that led to the establishment of the annual Tony Awards in 1947, Broadway's answer to Hollywood's Oscars.

Local Knowledge

Don't Miss List

BY TIM TOMPKINS, COMMUNICATIONS MANAGER AT TIMES SQUARE ALLIANCE.

1 DUFFY SQUARE RED STEPS

Home of the famous TKTS Booth, this dramatic all-glass structure rises over a fiberglass shell and includes a geothermal system and LEDs to illuminate the amphitheater-like steps. Crowds can sit and gaze at the blazing lights and spectacular signs of Times Square while taking in the diverse crowds on their way to restaurants and theaters.

2 MIDNIGHT MOMENT LIGHT SHOW

Each night from 11:57pm to midnight an artist takes over Times Square and transforms it into a virtual art gallery – an arresting sight for the late-night tourist or local trekking home. Midnight Moment is the largest coordinated effort in history by the sign operators of Times Square, and displays synchronized, cutting-edge creative content on the billboards and newspaper kiosks throughout the square.

3 BROADWAY (THE SHOWS AND THE STREET)

Nab a ticket to any of the shows playing at more than 40 Broadway theaters in the district, then wander the street to watch the second best show on Broadway – Times Square itself.

4 CHURCH OF ST MARY THE VIRGIN

Find calm amid the din of Times Square – St Mary's (Broadway, btwn 40th & 53rd Sts) is a stunning example of French Gothic design and is thought to be the first steel frame church in the United States. This oasis of quiet located in the heart of Times Square is open to the public daily.

5 CAFE EDISON

For more than 30 years, formica tables and aged vinyl booths loaded with sunny-side-up eggs and extra crispy bacon have inhabited the former Grand Ballroom of the Edison Hotel (228 W 47th St). Cafe Edison is one of the few remaining authentic diners left in New York City. A great spot for breakfast or lunch on-the-go, it is the epitome of great New York food with a side of New York attitude.

Don't Miss
Museum of Modern Art

Superstar of the modern art scene, MoMA's booty makes many other collections look...well... endearing. You'll find more A-listers here than at an Oscars after party: Van Gogh, Matisse, Picasso, Warhol, Lichtenstein, Rothko, Pollock, Bourgeois. Since its founding in 1929, the museum has amassed more than 150,000 artworks, documenting the emerging creative ideas and movements of the late 19th century through to those that dominate today. For art buffs, it's Valhalla. For the uninitiated, it's a thrilling crash course in all that is beautiful and addictive about art.

MoMA

Map p178

www.moma.org

11 W 53rd St, btwn Fifth & Sixth Aves

adult/child $25/ free, 4-8pm Fri free

10.30am-5.30pm Sat-Thu, to 8pm Fri, to 8pm Thu Jul-Aug

S E, M to 5th Ave-53rd St

Collection Highlights

It's easy to get lost in MoMA's vast collection. To maximize your time and create a plan of attack, download the museum's floor plan and visitor guide from the website beforehand. MoMA's permanent collection spans four levels, with prints, illustrated books and the unmissable Contemporary Galleries on level two; architecture, design, drawings and photography on level three; and painting and sculpture on levels four and five. Many of the big hitters are on these last two levels, so tackle the museum from the top down before the fatigue sets in. Must-sees include Van Gogh's *The Starry Night*, Cézanne's *The Bather*, Picasso's *Les Demoiselles d'Avignon*, and Henri Rousseau's *The Sleeping Gypsy*, not to mention iconic American works such as Warhol's *Campbell's Soup Cans* and *Gold Marilyn Monroe*, Lichtenstein's equally poptastic *Girl with Ball*, and Hopper's haunting *House by the Railroad*.

Abstract Expressionism

One of the greatest strengths of MoMA's collections is abstract expressionism, a radical movement that emerged in New York in the 1940s and boomed a decade later. Defined by its penchant for irreverent individualism and monumentally scaled works, this so-called 'New York School' helped turn the metropolis into the epicenter of western contemporary art. Among the stars are Rothko's *Magenta, Black, Green on Orange*, Pollock's *One (Number 31, 1950)* and de Kooning's *Painting*.

Modern Eats

MoMA's eateries have a stellar reputation. For communal tables and a super-casual vibe, nosh on Italian-inspired panini, pasta dishes, salads, salumi and cheeses at **Cafe 2** Map p178 (Museum of Modern Art, 11 W 53rd St, btwn Fifth & Sixth Aves; 11am-5pm Sat-Mon, Wed & Thu, to 7.30pm Fri; S E, M to Fifth Ave-53rd St). For table service, à la carte options and Danish design, opt for **Terrace Five** Map p178 (Museum of Modern Art, 11 W 53rd St, btwn Fifth & Sixth Aves; mains $11-18; 11am-5pm Sat-Mon, Wed & Thu, to 7.30pm Fri; S E, M to Fifth Ave-53rd St), which features an outdoor terrace overlooking the Sculpture Garden. If you're after a luxe feed, however, book a table at fine-dining **Modern** Map p178 (212-333-1220; www.themodernnyc.com; 9 W 53rd St, btwn Fifth & Sixth Aves; 3-/4-course lunch $62/76, 4-course dinner $108; restaurant noon-2pm & 5-10.30pm Mon-Fri, 5-10.30pm Sat; bar 11.30am-10.30pm Mon-Sat, to 9.30pm Sun; S E, M to Fifth Ave-53rd St), whose Michelin-starred menu serves up decadent, French-American creations such as 'pralines' of foie gras terrine with mango puree and balsamic vinegar. Fans of *Sex and the City* will be keen to know that it was here that scribe-about-town Carrie announced her impending marriage to Big. (If you're on a *real* writer's wage, you can always opt for simpler, cheaper Alsatian-inspired grub in the adjacent Bar Room.) The Modern has its own entrance on W 53rd St.

Gallery Conversations

To delve a little deeper into MoMA's collection, join one of the museum's daily 'Gallery Conversations,' which sees lecturers, graduate students and the odd curator offer expert insight into specific works and exhibitions on view. Talks take place each day at 11:30am and 1:30pm (except on Tuesdays, when the museum is closed). To check upcoming topics, click the 'Learn' link on the MoMA website.

Film Screenings

Not only a palace of visual art, MoMA screens an incredibly well-rounded selection of celluloid gems from its collection of more than 22,000 films, including the works of the Maysles Brothers and every Pixar animation film ever produced. Expect anything from Academy-nominated documentary shorts and Hollywood classics to experimental works and international retrospectives. Best of all, your museum ticket will get you in for free.

Don't Miss
Empire State Building

[illegible] may be prettier and One [illegible] now be taller, but the [illegible] New York skyline remains the Empire State Building. It's NYC's tallest star, enjoying more than its fair share of close-ups in around 100 films, from *King Kong* to *Independence Day*. No other building screams New York quite like it.

Map p170

www.esbnyc.com

350 Fifth Ave, at 34th St

86th-fl observation deck adult/child $27/21, incl 102nd-fl observation deck $44/38

8am-2am, last elevators up 1:15am

S B/D/F/M, N/Q/R to 34th St-Herald Sq

Skyscraper Facts

The statistics are astounding: 10 million bricks, 60,000 tons of steel, 6400 windows and 328,000 sq ft of marble. Built on the original site of the Waldorf-Astoria, construction took a record-setting 410 days, using seven million hours of labor and costing a mere $41 million. It might sound like a lot, but it fell well below its $50 million budget (just as well given it went up during the Great Depression). Coming in at 102 stories and 1472ft from top to bottom, the limestone phallus opened for business on May 1, 1931. Generations later, Deborah Kerr's words to Cary Grant in *An Affair to Remember* still ring true: 'It's the nearest thing to heaven we have in New York.'

Observation Decks

Unless you're Ann Darrow (the unfortunate blonde caught in King Kong's grip), heading to the top of the Empire State Building should leave you beaming. There are two observation decks. The open-air 86th-floor deck offers an alfresco experience, with coin-operated telescopes for close-up glimpses of the metropolis in action. Further up, the enclosed 102nd-floor deck is New York's second-highest observation deck, trumped only by the observation deck at One World Trade Center. Needless to say, the views over the city's five boroughs (and five neighboring states, weather permitting) are quite simply exquisite. The views from both decks are especially spectacular at sunset, when the city dons its nighttime cloak in dusk's afterglow. For a little of that *Arthur's Theme* magic, head to the 86th floor between 10pm and 1am from Thursday to Saturday, when the twinkling sea of lights is accompanied by a soundtrack of live sax (yes, requests are taken). Alas, the passage to heaven will involve a trip through purgatory: the queues to the top are notorious. Getting here very early or very late will help you avoid delays – as will buying your tickets online, ahead of time, where an extra $2 convenience fee is well worth the hassle it will save you.

An Ambitious Antenna

A locked, unmarked door on the 102nd-floor observation deck leads to one of New York's most outrageous pie-in-the-sky projects to date: a narrow terrace intended to dock zeppelins. Spearheading the dream was Alfred E Smith, who went from failed presidential candidate in 1928 to head honcho of the Empire State Building project. When architect William Van Alen revealed the secret spire of his competing Chrysler Building, Smith went one better, declaring that the top of the Empire State Building would sport an even taller mooring mast for transatlantic airships. While the plan looked good on paper, there was one major oversight: dirigibles require anchoring at both ends (not just at the nose as planned) and a steady wind knocking around a 40-ton craft over a heavily populated area ultimately seemed a bad idea. Regardless, it didn't stop them from trying. In September 1931, the *New York Evening Journal* threw sanity to the wind, managing to moor a zeppelin and deliver a pile of newspapers fresh out of Lower Manhattan. Years later, an aircraft met up with the building with less success: a B-25 bomber crashed into the 79th floor on a foggy day in 1945, killing 14 people.

Language of Light

Since 1976, the building's top 30 floors have been floodlit in a spectrum of colors each night, reflecting seasonal and holiday hues. Famous combos include red and pink sparkles for Valentine's Day; orange, white and green for St Patrick's Day; red and green for Christmas; and the rainbow colors for Gay Pride weekend in June. Adding to the tower's vibrant lighting spectacle is a new LED system, installed in 2012, that has nearly 17 million color combinations. Visit the website to see what colors will light up the ESB while you're in town.

Discover Midtown

Getting There & Away

- **Subway** Times Sq-42nd St, Grand Central-42nd St and 34th St-Herald Sq are Midtown's main interchange stations. A/C/E and 1/2/3 lines run north–south through Midtown West. The 4/5/6 lines run north–south through Midtown East. The central B/D/F/M lines run up Sixth Ave, while N/Q/R lines follow Broadway. The 7, E and M lines offer some crosstown service.

- **Bus** Routes include the M11 (running northbound on Tenth Ave and southbound on Ninth Ave), the M101, M102 and M103 (running northbound along Third Ave and southbound along Lexington Ave) and the M15 (running northbound on First Ave and southbound on Second Ave). Useful crosstown buses run along 34th and 42nd Sts.

Spire of the Chrysler Building

Sights

Fifth Avenue

Empire State Building (p166)

New York Public Library Cultural Building

Map p170 (Stephen A Schwarzman Building; 917-275-6975; www.nypl.org; Fifth Ave at 42nd St; 10am-6pm Mon & Thu-Sat, to 8pm Tue & Wed, 1-5pm Sun, guided tours 11am & 2pm Mon-Sat, 2pm Sun; S B/D/F/M to 42nd St-Bryant Park, 7 to 5th Ave) FREE Loyally guarded by 'Patience' and 'Fortitude' (the famous marble lions overlooking Fifth Ave), this beaux-arts show-off is one of NYC's best free attractions. When dedicated in 1911, New York's flagship library ranked as the largest marble structure ever built in the US, and to this day, its Rose Main Reading Room will steal your breath with its lavish, coffered ceiling.

Bryant Park Park

Map p170 (www.bryantpark.org; 42nd St btwn Fifth & Sixth Aves; 7am-midnight Mon-Fri, to 11pm Sat & Sun Jun-Sep, shorter hrs rest of yr; S B/D/F/M to 42nd St-Bryant Park, 7 to Fifth Ave) European coffee kiosks, alfresco chess games, summer film screenings and winter ice-skating: it's hard to believe that this leafy oasis was dubbed 'Needle Park' in the '80s. Nestled behind the show-stopping New York Public Library building, it's a whimsical spot for a little time-out from the Midtown madness.

St Patrick's Cathedral Church

Map p170 (www.saintpatrickscathedral.org; Fifth Ave btwn 50th & 51st Sts; 6:30am-8:45pm; S B/D/F/M to 47th-50th Sts-Rockefeller Center) When

Midtown

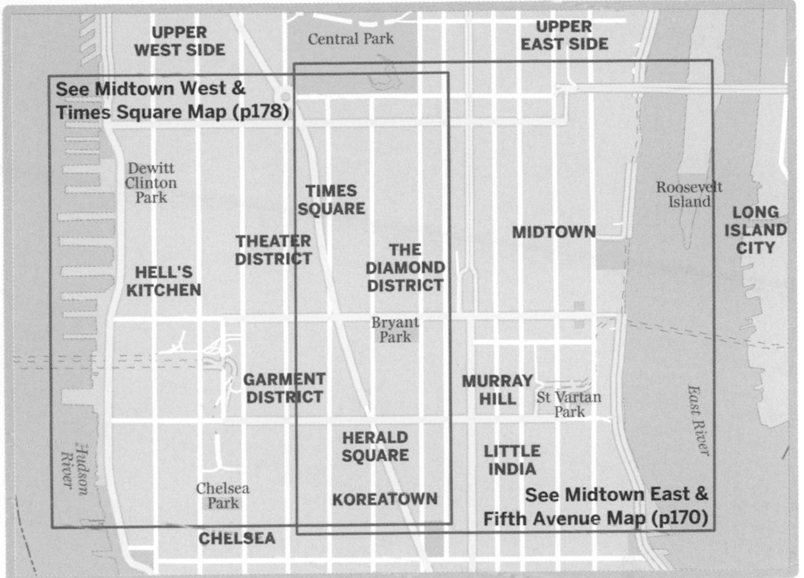

its face-lift is complete and the scaffolding comes down in late 2015, America's largest Catholic cathedral will once more grace Fifth Ave with its neo-Gothic splendor. Built at a cost of nearly $2 million during the Civil War, the building did not originally include the two front spires; those were added in 1888. Step inside to appreciate the Louis Tiffany–designed altar and Charles Connick's stunning Rose Window, the latter gleaming above a 7000-pipe church organ.

Paley Center for Media Cultural Building

Map p170 (www.paleycenter.org; 25 W 52nd St, btwn Fifth & Sixth Aves; adult/child $10/5; noon-6pm Wed & Fri-Sun, to 8pm Thu; S E, M to 5th Ave-53rd St) Pop culture repository Paley Center offers more than 150,000 TV and radio programs from around the world on its computer catalog. Reliving your favorite TV shows on one of the center's consoles is sheer bliss on a rainy day, and the radio-listening room is an unexpected pleasure – as are the excellent, regular screenings, festivals, speakers and performers.

Midtown East

Morgan Library & Museum Museum

Map p170 (www.morganlibrary.org; 29 E 36th St, at Madison Ave, Midtown East; adult/child $18/12; 10:30am-5pm Tue-Thu, to 9pm Fri, 10am-6pm Sat, 11am-6pm Sun; S 6 to 33rd St) Part of the 45-room mansion once owned by steel magnate JP Morgan, this sumptuous library features a phenomenal array of manuscripts, tapestries and books (with no fewer than three Gutenberg Bibles). There's a study filled with Italian Renaissance artwork, a marble rotunda and a program of top-notch rotating exhibitions.

Chrysler Building Notable Building

Map p170 (Lexington Ave at 42nd St, Midtown East; lobby 8am-6pm Mon-Fri; S S, 4/5/6, 7 to Grand Central-42nd St) The 77-floor Chrysler Building makes most other skyscrapers look like uptight geeks. Designed by Willian Van Alen in 1930, it's a dramatic fusion of art deco and Gothic aesthetics, adorned with stern steel eagles and topped by a spire that screams *Bride of Frankenstein*. More than 80 years on,

Midtown East & Fifth Avenue

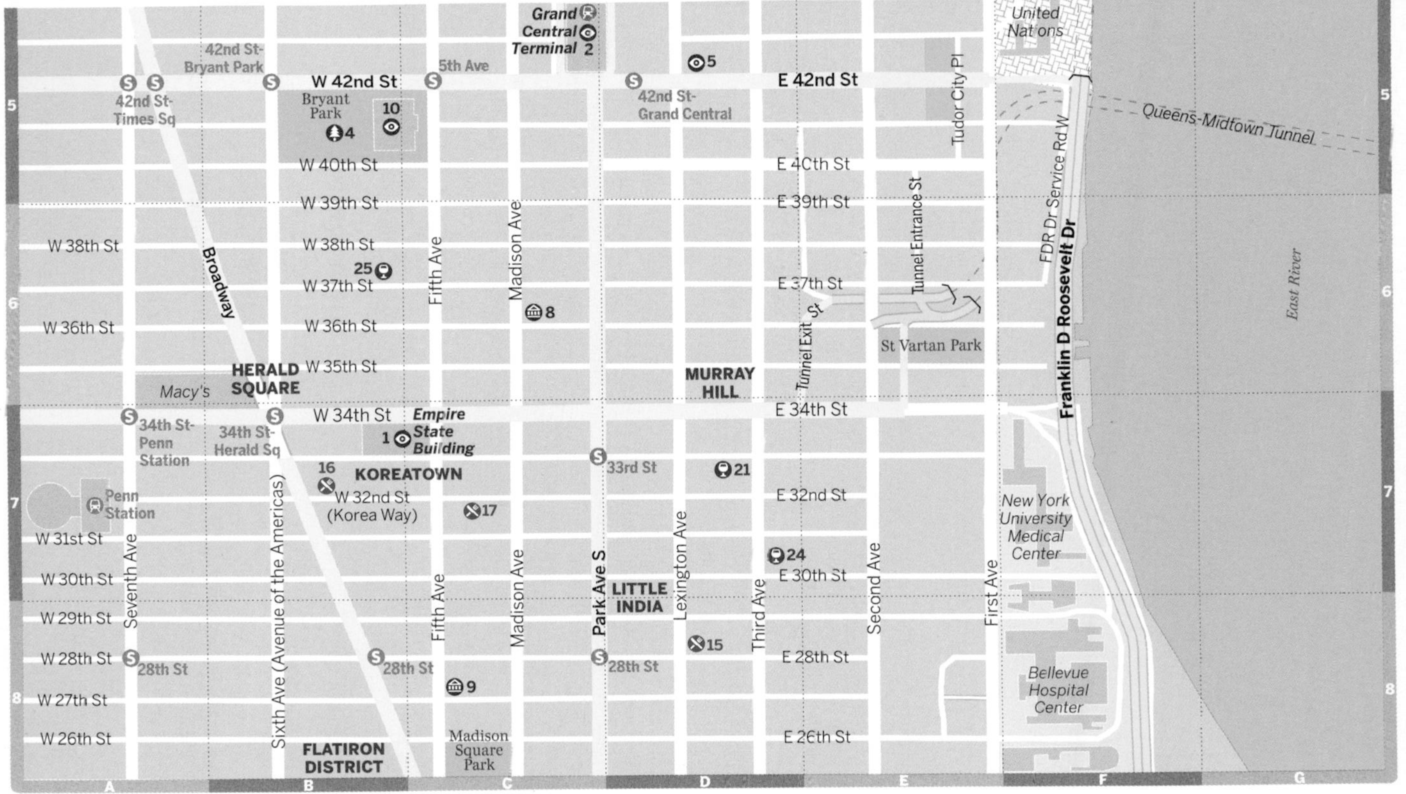
Grand Central Terminal
2
5
W 42nd St
E 42nd St
42nd St-Bryant Park
5th Ave
42nd St-Times Sq
Bryant Park
4
10
42nd St-Grand Central
Tudor City Pl
United Nations
Queens-Midtown Tunnel
FDR Dr Service Rd W
Franklin D Roosevelt Dr
East River
W 40th St
E 40th St
W 39th St
E 39th St
W 38th St
Broadway
Fifth Ave
Madison Ave
Tunnel Entrance St
25
W 37th St
E 37th St
W 36th St
8
Tunnel Exit St
St Vartan Park
W 35th St
HERALD SQUARE
Macy's
MURRAY HILL
W 34th St
E 34th St
34th St-Penn Station
34th St-Herald Sq
Empire State Building
1
16
KOREATOWN
33rd St
21
Penn Station
W 32nd St (Korea Way)
17
E 32nd St
New York University Medical Center
W 31st St
24
W 30th St
E 30th St
Seventh Ave
Sixth Ave (Avenue of the Americas)
Park Ave S
LITTLE INDIA
Lexington Ave
Third Ave
Second Ave
First Ave
W 29th St
15
W 28th St
28th St
E 28th St
9
Bellevue Hospital Center
W 27th St
W 26th St
FLATIRON DISTRICT
Madison Square Park
E 26th St
A
B
C
D
E
F
G
5
6
7
8

Midtown East & Fifth Avenue

Don't Miss Sights

1 Empire State Building B7
2 Grand Central Terminal C5
3 Rockefeller Center B3

Sights

4 Bryant Park B5
5 Chrysler Building D5
6 Franklin D Roosevelt Four Freedoms Park G4
7 Japan Society E4
8 Morgan Library & Museum C6
9 Museum of Sex C8
10 New York Public Library B5
11 Paley Center for Media B3
12 St Patrick's Cathedral C3
13 Top of the Rock B3
14 United Nations F4

Eating

15 Curry in a Hurry D8
16 Gahm Mi Oak B7
17 Hangawi C7
18 Rouge Tomate C1
19 Smith E3
20 Sparks D4

Drinking & Nightlife

21 Middle Branch D7
22 PJ Clarke's D2
23 Subway Inn D1
24 Terroir D7
25 Top of the Strand B6

Shopping

26 Barneys C1
27 Bergdorf Goodman C1
28 Bloomingdale's D1
29 Dylan's Candy Bar D1
30 FAO Schwarz C1
31 Tiffany & Co C2
32 Uniqlo C3

Chrysler's ambitious $15 million statement remains one of New York's most poignant symbols.

United Nations Notable Building
Map p170 (☎212-963-4475; http://visit.un.org/wcm/content; visitors' gate First Ave at 47th St, Midtown East; guided tour adult/child $20/11, children under 5yr not admitted, grounds access Sat & Sun free; ⌚tours 9:15am-4:15pm Mon-Fri, visitor center also open 10am-5pm Sat & Sun; S S, 4/5/6, 7 to Grand Central-42nd St) Welcome to the headquarters of the UN, a worldwide organization overseeing international law, international security and human rights. Weekday tours must be booked online (book at least two days ahead). Free walk-in access to the visitor center only is permitted on weekends (enter at 43rd Street).

Japan Society Cultural Center
Map p170 (www.japansociety.org; 333 E 47th St, btwn First & Second Aves, Midtown East; adult/child $12/free, 6-9pm Fri free; ⌚11am-6pm Tue-Thu, to 9pm Fri, to 5pm Sat & Sun; S S, 4/5/6, 7 to Grand Central-42nd St) Elegant exhibitions of Japanese art, textiles and design are the main draw at this cultural center. Its theater hosts a range of films and dance, music and theatrical performances, while those who want to dig deeper can browse through the 14,000 volumes of the research library or attend one of its myriad lectures.

Museum of Sex Museum
Map p170 (www.museumofsex.com; 233 Fifth Ave, at 27th St; adult $17.50; ⌚10am-8pm Sun-Thu, to 9pm Fri & Sat; S N/R to 23rd St) Get the lowdown on anything from online fetishes to homosexual necrophilia in the mallard duck at this slick, smallish ode to all things hot and sweaty. The rotating program of temporary exhibitions has included explorations of cyber sex and retrospectives of controversial artists, while the permanent collection showcases the likes of erotic lithographs and awkward anti-onanism devices.

Midtown West & Times Square

Times Square (p162)

Museum of Modern Art (p164)

Radio City Music Hall Notable Building
Map p178 (www.radiocity.com; 1260 Sixth Ave, at 51st St; tours adult/child $20/15; ⌚tours 11am-3pm; S B/D/F/M to 47th-50th Sts-Rockefeller Center) A spectacular art-deco

diva, this 5901-seat movie palace was the brainchild of vaudeville producer Samuel Lionel 'Roxy' Rothafel. Never one for understatement, Roxy launched his venue on December 23 1932 with an over-the-top extravaganza that included a *Symphony of the Curtains* (starring... you guessed it... the curtains), and the high-kick campness of precision dance troupe the Roxyettes (mercifully renamed the Rockettes).

As far as catching a show here goes, be warned: the vibe doesn't quite match the theater's splendor now that it's managed by the folks from Madison Square Garden. Still, there are often some fabulous talents in the lineup, with past performers including Rufus Wainwright, Aretha Franklin and Dolly Parton. And while the word 'Rockettes' provokes eye rolling from most self-consciously cynical New Yorkers, fans of glitz and kitsch might just get a thrill from the troupe's annual Christmas Spectacular (your secret is safe with us...promise!).

Museum of Arts & Design Museum

Map p178 (MAD; www.madmuseum.org; 2 Columbus Circle, btwn Eighth Ave & Broadway; adult/child $16/free; ⏲10am-6pm Tue, Wed, Sat & Sun, to 9pm Thu & Fri; S A/C, B/D, 1 to 59th St-Columbus Circle) MAD offers four floors of superlative design and handicrafts, from blown glass and carved wood to elaborate metal jewelry. Its temporary exhibitions are top notch and innovative; one past show explored the art of scent. On the first Sunday of the month, professional artists lead explorations of the galleries, followed by hands-on workshops inspired by the current exhibitions. The museum gift shop sells some fantastic contemporary jewelry, while the 9th-floor restaurant/bar **Robert (www.robertnyc.com; 2 Columbus Circle, btwn Eighth Ave & Broadway; 11:30am-10pm Mon, 11:30am-midnight Tue-Fri, 11am-midnight Sat, 11am-10pm Sun)** is perfect for panoramic cocktails.

International Center of Photography Gallery

Map p178 (ICP; www.icp.org; 1133 Sixth Ave, at 43rd St; adult/child $14/free, by donation Fri 5-8pm; ⏲10am-6pm Tue-Thu, Sat & Sun, to 8pm Fri; S B/D/F/M to 42nd St-Bryant Park) ICP is New York's paramount platform for photography, with a strong emphasis on photojournalism, and changing exhibitions

Radio City Music Hall

TETRA IMAGES/GETTY IMAGES ©

Don't Miss
Grand Central Terminal

Threatened by the opening of rival Penn Station (the majestic original, that is), shipping and railroad magnate Cornelius Vanderbilt set to work on transforming his 19th-century Grand Central Depot into a 20th-century showpiece. The fruit of his envy is Grand Central Terminal, New York's most breathtaking beaux-arts building. More than just a station, Grand Central is an enchanted time machine. Its swirl of chandeliers, marble and historic bars and restaurants a porthole into an era where train travel and romance were not mutually exclusive.

Grand Central's trump card is more akin to a glorious ballroom than a thoroughfare. The vaulted ceiling is (quite literally) heavenly, its turquoise and gold-leaf mural depicting eight constellations...backwards. A mistake? Apparently not. Its French designer, painter Paul César Helleu, wished to depict the stars from God's point of view – from the out, looking in.

The vaulted landing directly below the bridge linking the Main Concourse and Vanderbilt Hall harbors one of Grand Central's quirkier features, the so-called Whispering Gallery. If you're in company, stand facing the walls diagonally opposite each other and whisper something. If your partner proposes (it happens a lot down here), chilled champagne is just through the door at the Grand Central Oyster Bar & Restaurant. An elevator beside the restaurant leads up to another historic gem: the deliciously snooty bar Campbell Apartment.

NEED TO KNOW

Map p170; www.grandcentralterminal.com; 42nd St at Park Ave, Midtown East; 5:30am-2am; S S, 4/5/6, 7 to Grand Central-42nd St

on a wide range of themes. Past shows in the two-floor space have included work by Henri Cartier-Bresson, Man Ray and Robert Capa. The center is also a school, offering coursework (for credit) and a public lecture series.

Herald Square Square

Map p178 (cnr Broadway, Sixth Ave & 34th St; S B/D/F/M, N/Q/R to 34th St-Herald Sq) This crowded convergence of Broadway, Sixth Ave and 34th St is best known as the home of mammoth department store **Macy's** (p187), where you can still ride some of the original wooden elevators. As part of the city's 'traffic-free Times Square' plan, you can also (try to) relax in a lawn chair outside the store, slap-bang in the middle of Broadway.

Intrepid Sea, Air & Space Museum Museum

Map p178 (www.intrepidmuseum.org; Pier 86, Twelfth Ave at 46th St, Midtown West; Intrepid & Growler submarine adult/child $24/12, incl Space Shuttle Pavilion adult/child $31/17; 10am-5pm Mon-Fri, to 6pm Sat & Sun Apr-Oct, 10am-5pm Mon-Sun Nov-Mar; M42, M50 bus westbound, S A/C/E to 42nd St-Port Authority Bus Terminal) The USS *Intrepid* survived both a WWII bomb and kamikaze attacks. Thankfully, this hulking aircraft carrier is now a lot less stressed, playing host to a multimillion dollar interactive military museum that tells its tale through videos, historical artifacts and frozen-in-time living quarters. The flight deck features fighter planes and military helicopters, which might inspire you to try the museum's high-tech flight simulators.

Koreatown Neighborhood

Map p178 (31st to 36th Sts & Broadway to Fifth Ave; S B/D/F/M, N/Q/R to 34th St-Herald Sq) For kimchi and karaoke, it's hard to beat Koreatown (Little Korea). Mainly concentrated on 32nd St, with some spillover into the surrounding streets both south and north of this strip, it's a Seoul-ful jumble of Korean-owned restaurants, shops, salons and spas.

Eating

Midtown East & Fifth Avenue

Hangawi Korean **$$**

Map p170 (212-213-0077; www.hangawirestaurant.com; 12 E 32nd St, btwn Fifth & Madison Aves; mains lunch $10-16, dinner $16-26; noon-2:45pm & 5-10:15pm Mon-Thu, to 10:30pm Fri, 1-10:30pm Sat, 5-9:30pm Sun; ; S B/D/F/M, N/Q/R to 34th St-Herald Sq) Flesh-free Korean is the draw at high-achieving Hangawi. Leave your shoes at the entrance and slip into a soothing, Zen-like space of meditative music, low seating and clean, complex dishes. Show-stoppers include leek pancakes and a seductive tofu claypot in ginger sauce.

Smith American **$$**

Map p170 (212-644-2700; www.thesmithnyc.com; 956 Second Ave, at 51st St, Midtown East; mains $17-33; 7:30am-midnight Mon-Wed, to 1am Thu & Fri, 10am-1am Sat, 10am-midnight Sun; ; S 6 to 51st St) This cool, funky brasserie has sexed-up Midtown's far east with its industrial-chic interior, sociable bar and well-executed grub. Much of the food is made from scratch, the seasonal menu is a mix of nostalgic American and Italian inspiration.

Rouge Tomate Modern American **$$$**

Map p170 (646-237-8977; www.rougetomatenyc.com; 10 E 60th St, btwn Fifth & Madison Aves; dinner mains $29-42; noon-3pm & 5:30-10:30pm Mon-Sat; ; S N/Q/R to Fifth Ave-59th St, 4/5/6 to 59th St) Health-conscious, Michelin-starred Rouge Tomate puts the sexy in sustainable. To retain their maximum nutritional value, the mostly local, seasonal ingredients are never fried or grilled. This seeming limitation is no obstacle in creating complex, sophisticated marvels such as fleshy, textured eggplant tartare with garlic confit.

John Dory Oyster Bar Seafood **$$$**

Map p178 (www.thejohndory.com; 1196 Broadway, at 29th St; small plates $9-28; noon-midnight; S N/R to 28th St) Anchored to the **Ace Hotel** (p278) lobby, loud 'n' trendy John Dory is a

fine spot to sip bubbly and slurp on plump and salty creatures of the sea. Crudo gets clever in dishes such as Spanish mackerel with chili, cilantro and squid crackling, while the tapas-style 'small plates' harbor some equally creative morsels (chorizo stuffed squid with smoked tomato, anyone?).

Sparks Steakhouse **$$$**
Map p170 (212-687-4855; www.sparkssteakhouse.com; 210 E 46th St, btwn Second & Third Aves, Midtown East; dinner mains $36-53; 11:30am-11pm Mon-Thu, 11:30am-11:30pm Fri, 5-11:30pm Sat; ; S S, 4/5/6, 7 to Grand Central-42nd St) Get an honest-to-goodness New York steakhouse experience at this classic joint, a former mob hangout that's been around for nearly 50 years and still packs 'em in for a juicy carnivorous feed.

Midtown West & Times Square

Totto Ramen Japanese **$**
Map p178 (www.tottoramen.com; 366 W 52nd St, btwn Eighth & Ninth Aves, Midtown West; ramen from $10; noon-midnight Mon-Fri, noon-11pm Sat, 5-11pm Sun; S C/E to 50th St) Write your name and number of guests on the clipboard by the door and wait for your (cash-only) ramen revelation. Skip the chicken and go for the pork, which sings in dishes of miso ramen (with fermented soybean paste, egg, scallion, bean sprouts, onion and homemade chili paste).

Burger Joint Burgers **$**
Map p178 (www.burgerjointny.com; Le Parker Meridien, 119 W 56th St, btwn Sixth & Seventh Aves, Midtown West; burgers from $8; 11am-11:30pm Sun-Thu, to midnight Fri & Sat; S F to 57th St) With only a small neon burger as your clue, this cash-only, speakeasy-style burger hut lurks behind the lobby curtain in the Le Parker Meridien hotel. Though it might not be as 'hip' or as 'secret' as it once was, it still delivers the same winning formula of graffiti-strewn walls, retro booths and attitude-loaded staff slapping up beef 'n' patty brilliance.

Left: Herald Square (p175); Below: Macy's department store (p187)
(LEFT) PATTI MCCONVILLE/GETTY IMAGES ©; (BELOW) RICHARD CUMMINGS/GETTY IMAGES ©

El Margon
Cuban $
Map p178 (136 W 46th St, btwn Sixth & Seventh Aves, Midtown West; sandwiches from $4, mains $9-15; 🕗7am-5pm; S B/D/F/M to 47-50th Sts-Rockefeller Center) It's still 1973 at this ever-packed Cuban lunch counter, where orange Laminex and greasy goodness never went out of style.

Danji Korean $$
Map p178 (www.danjinyc.com; 346 W 52nd St, btwn Eighth & Ninth Aves, Midtown West; plates $6-20; 🕗noon-2:30pm & 5:15-11pm Mon-Thu, noon-2:30pm & 5:15pm-midnight Fri, 5:15pm-midnight Sat; S C/E to 50th St) Young-gun chef Hooni Kim makes tastebuds weep with his Michelin-starred Korean 'tapas.' Served in a snug-and-slinky contemporary space, his bite-sized marvels fall into one of two categories: 'traditional' or 'modern.'

ViceVersa Italian $$
Map p178 (☎212-399-9291; www.viceversanyc.com; 325 W 51st St, btwn Eighth & Ninth Aves, Midtown West; pasta dishes $10-22, mains $23-30; 🕗noon-2:30pm & 5-11pm Mon-Fri, 5-11pm Sat, 11:30am-3pm & 5-10pm Sun; S C/E to 50th St) ViceVersa is the quintessential Italian: suave and sophisticated, affable and scrumptious. Scan the menu for refined, cross-regional dishes such as arancini with black truffle and fontina cheese, or slow-roasted suckling pig with fennel pollen and grilled endives.

Gahm Mi Oak Korean $$
Map p170 (43 W 32nd St, btwn Broadway & Fifth Ave; dishes $10-22; 🕗24hr; S N/Q/R, B/D/F/M to 34th St-Herald Sq) If you're craving *yook hwe* (raw beef and Asian pear matchsticks) at 3am, this K-Town savior has you covered. The shtick here is authenticity, shining through in dishes such as the house speciality *sul long tang* (a milky broth of ox bones, boiled for 12 hours and pimped with brisket and scallion), which will cure the most evil of hangovers.

Midtown West & Times Square

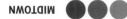

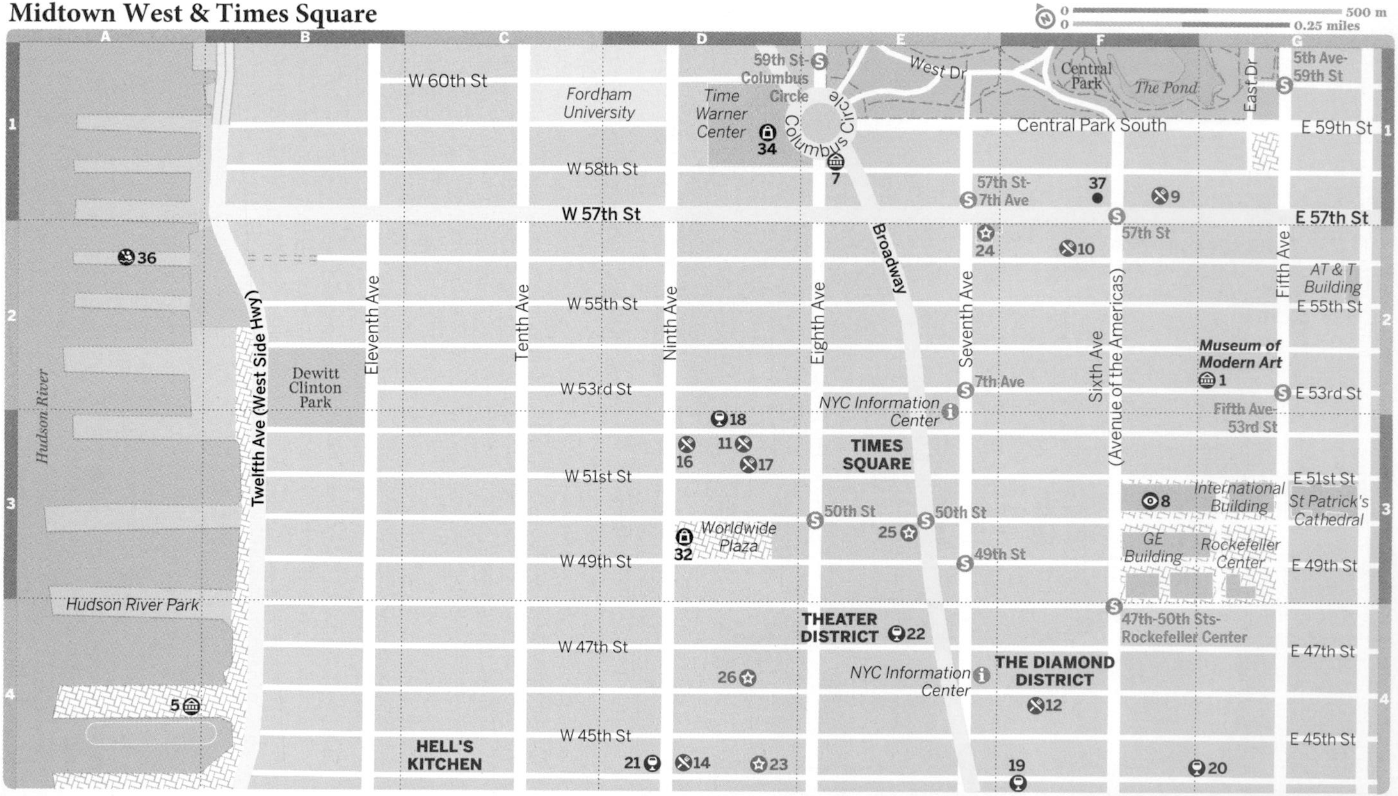

0 500 m
0 0.25 miles

A B C D E F G
1 2 3 4

Hudson River
Hudson River Park
Twelfth Ave (West Side Hwy)
Dewitt Clinton Park
Eleventh Ave
Tenth Ave
Ninth Ave
Eighth Ave
Broadway
Seventh Ave
Sixth Ave (Avenue of the Americas)
Fifth Ave
W 60th St
W 58th St
W 57th St
W 55th St
W 53rd St
W 51st St
W 49th St
W 47th St
W 45th St
E 59th St
E 57th St
E 55th St
E 53rd St
E 51st St
E 49th St
E 47th St
E 45th St
Fordham University
Time Warner Center
59th St-Columbus Circle
Columbus Circle
West Dr
East Dr
Central Park
The Pond
Central Park South
5th Ave-59th St
57th St-7th Ave
57th St
AT & T Building
Museum of Modern Art
7th Ave
Fifth Ave-53rd St
NYC Information Center
TIMES SQUARE
50th St
49th St
Worldwide Plaza
International Building
St Patrick's Cathedral
GE Building
Rockefeller Center
47th-50th Sts-Rockefeller Center
THEATER DISTRICT
THE DIAMOND DISTRICT
HELL'S KITCHEN
1 5 7 8 9 10 11 12 14 16 17 18 19 20 21 22 23 24 25 26 32 34 36 37

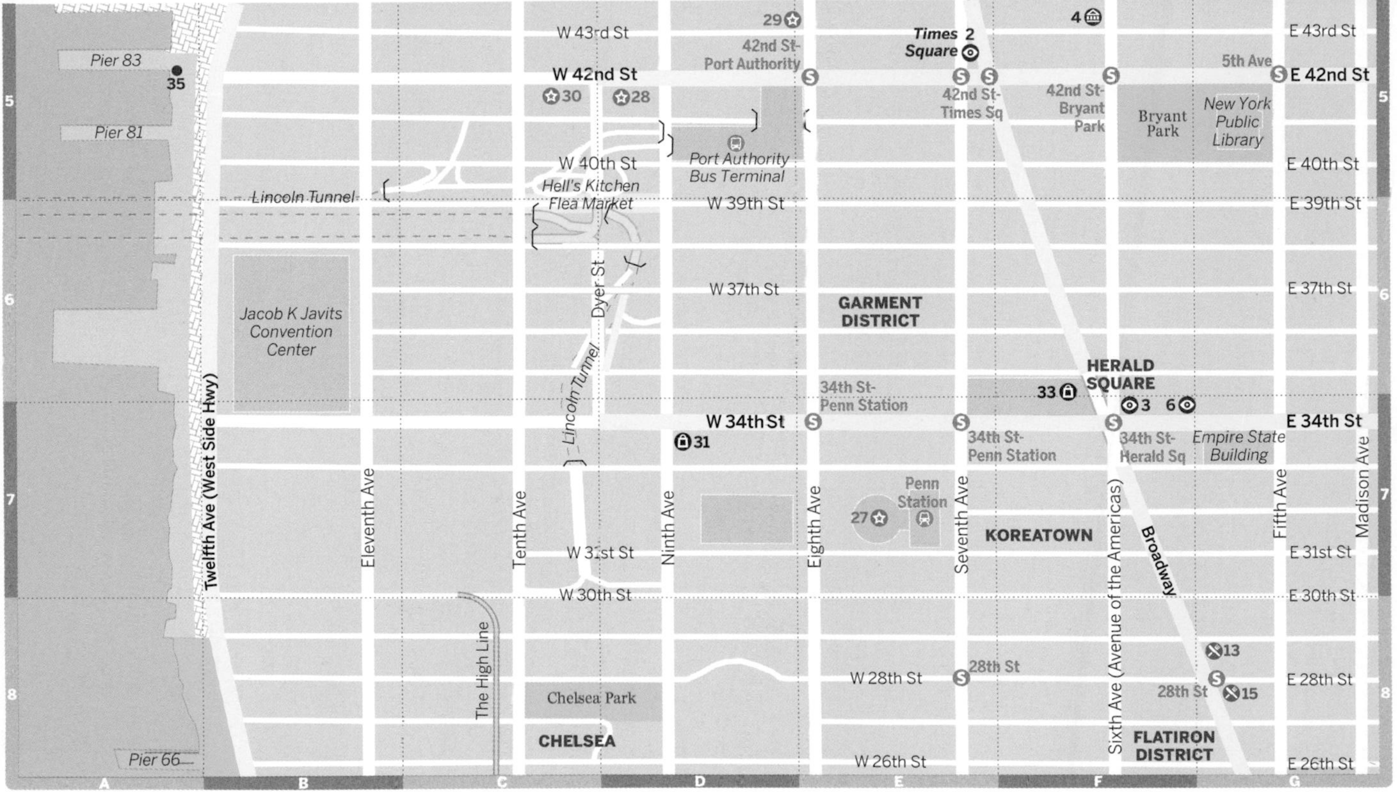

W 43rd St
E 43rd St
W 42nd St
E 42nd St
W 40th St
E 40th St
W 39th St
E 39th St
W 37th St
E 37th St
W 34th St
E 34th St
W 31st St
E 31st St
W 30th St
E 30th St
W 28th St
E 28th St
W 26th St
E 26th St
Twelfth Ave (West Side Hwy)
Eleventh Ave
Tenth Ave
Ninth Ave
Eighth Ave
Seventh Ave
Sixth Ave (Avenue of the Americas)
Fifth Ave
Madison Ave
Broadway
Dyer St
Lincoln Tunnel
The High Line
Pier 83
Pier 81
Pier 66
Jacob K Javits Convention Center
Hell's Kitchen Flea Market
Port Authority Bus Terminal
42nd St-Port Authority
Times Square
42nd St-Times Sq
42nd St-Bryant Park
Bryant Park
New York Public Library
5th Ave
GARMENT DISTRICT
HERALD SQUARE
34th St-Penn Station
34th St-Herald Sq
Empire State Building
Penn Station
KOREATOWN
28th St
Chelsea Park
CHELSEA
FLATIRON DISTRICT

Midtown West & Times Square

Don't Miss Sights
1 Museum of Modern Art.......................... G2
2 Times Square.. E5

Sights
3 Herald Square.. F7
4 International Center of Photography.... F5
5 Intrepid Sea, Air & Space Museum...... A4
6 Koreatown.. F7
7 Museum of Arts & Design..................... E1
8 Radio City Music Hall............................ F3

Eating
9 Betony.. F1
10 Burger Joint.. F2
Cafe 2... (see 1)
11 Danji.. D3
12 El Margon.. F4
13 John Dory Oyster Bar.......................... G8
14 Marseille.. D4
Modern... (see 1)
15 NoMad.. G8
Terrace Five................................. (see 1)
16 Totto Ramen.. D3
17 ViceVersa... D3

Drinking & Nightlife
18 Industry.. D3
19 Jimmy's Corner...................................... F4
20 Lantern's Keep...................................... G4
Robert.. (see 7)
21 Rudy's... D4
22 Rum House... E4

Entertainment
23 Birdland.. D4
24 Carnegie Hall... E2
25 Caroline's on Broadway........................ E3
26 Don't Tell Mama..................................... D4
Jazz at Lincoln Center................ (see 34)
27 Madison Square Garden....................... E7
28 Playwrights Horizons............................. D5
29 Second Stage Theatre........................... D5
30 Signature Theatre.................................. C5

Shopping
31 B&H Photo Video.................................... D7
32 Housing Works.. D3
33 Macy's.. F6
MoMA Design & Book Store........... (see 1)
34 Time Warner Center.............................. D1

Sports & Activities
35 Circle Line Boat Tours............................ A5
36 Downtown Boathouse (Midtown).......... A2
37 Municipal Art Society............................. F1

Betony Modern American **$$$**
Map p178 (212-465-2400; www.betony-nyc.com; 41 W 57th St, btwn Fifth & Sixth Aves; mains $27-38; 5-10pm Mon-Thu, to 10:30pm Fri & Sat; S F to 57th St) Thrilling menus, seamless service, and a slinky downtown vibe: welcome to Midtown's latest godsend. While industrial windows, exposed brickwork and a soaring bar make Betony's front section perfect for after-five cocktails, request a table in the intimate, baroque-esque back dining room to savor chef Bryce Shuman's sophisticated albeit playful dishes.

NoMad New American **$$$**
Map p178 (347-472-5660; www.thenomadhotel.com/#!/dining; NoMad Hotel, 1170 Broadway, at 28th St; mains $20-37; noon-2pm & 5:30-10:30pm Mon-Thu, to 11pm Fri, 11am-2pm & 5:30-11pm Sat, 11am-3pm & 5:30-10pm Sun; S N/R, 6 to 28th St; F/M to 23rd St) Sharing the same name as the 'It kid' hotel it inhabits, NoMad has sealed its rep as one of Manhattan's culinary highlights. Carved up into a series of distinctly different spaces – including a see-and-be-seen Atrium, Victoriana parlor and snacks-only Library – the restaurant is the hipper, (slightly) more relaxed sibling of Michelin-starred Eleven Madison Park. The menus are eclectic, Eurocentric and – true to chef Daniel Humm's reputation – just a little playful.

Marseille French, Mediterranean **$$$**
Map p178 (www.marseillenyc.com; 630 Ninth Ave at 44th St; mains $20-29; 11:30am-11pm Sun-Tue, to midnight Wed-Sat; S A/C/E to 42nd St-Port Authority) Looking somewhere between an old cinema lobby and an art-deco brasserie, this Hell's Kitchen classic is a fabulous spot to kick back with a Le Pamplemousse (Absolut Ruby Red Grapefruit vodka, Campari, elderflower and citrus) and nibble on flavor-packed French-Med fare such as Provençal goat cheese tart or Tuscan chicken with truffle jus.

Drinking & Nightlife

Midtown East & Fifth Avenue

PJ Clarke's — Bar

Map p170 (www.pjclarkes.com; 915 Third Ave, at 55th St, Midtown East; 11:30am-4am; S E, M to Lexington Ave-53rd St) A bastion of old New York, this lovingly worn wooden saloon has been straddling the scene since 1884; Buddy Holly proposed to his fiancée here and Ol' Blue Eyes pretty much owned table 20. Choose a jukebox tune, order the knockout burger and settle in with a come-one-and-all crowd of collar-and-tie colleagues, college students and nostalgia-craving urbanites.

Middle Branch — Cocktail Bar

Map p170 (154 E 33rd St, btwn Lexington & Third Aves, Midtown East; 5pm-2am; S 6 to 33rd St) Brainchild of cocktail deity Sasha Petraske, bi-level Middle Branch injects some much-needed drinking cred in beer-and-margarita-centric Murray Hill. Eye-candy bartenders whip up some of Midtown's sharpest libations, from faithful classics to playful reinterpretations such as the Enzoni (a lemon-and-grape-laced twist on the classic Negroni). Cash only.

Subway Inn — Dive Bar

Map p170 (143 E 60th St, btwn Lexington & Third Aves, Midtown East; 11am-4am Mon-Sat, from noon Sun; S 4/5/6 to 59th St; N/Q/R to Lexington Ave-59th St) Occupying its own world across from Bloomingdale's, this old-geezer watering hole is a vintage cheap-booze spot that, despite the classic rock and worn red booths, harkens to long-past days when Marilyn Monroe would drop in.

Terroir — Wine Bar

Map p170 (439 Third Ave, btwn 30th & 31st Sts, Midtown East; 5pm-1am Mon-Thu, to 2am Fri & Sat, to 11pm Sun; S 6 to 28th St) The well-versed, well-priced wine list is the size of your grandma's family photo album, with an impressive array of drops by the glass.

Midtown West & Times Square

Top of the Strand — Cocktail Bar

Map p170 (www.topofthestrand.com; Strand Hotel, 33 W 37th St, btwn Fifth & Sixth Aves; 5pm-midnight Mon & Sun, to 1am Tue-Sat; S B/D/F/M to 34th St) For that 'Oh my God, I'm in New York' feeling, head to the **Strand** (**212-448-1024; www.thestrandnyc.com; r $255-630;**) hotel's rooftop bar, order a martini (extra dirty) and drop your jaw (discreetly). Sporting slinky cabanas and a sliding glass roof, its view of the Empire State Building is unforgettable.

PJ Clarke's

Rum House Cocktail Bar

Map p178 (www.edisonrumhouse.com; 228 W 47th St, btwn Broadway & Eighth Ave, Midtown West; 1pm-4am; S N/Q/R to 49th St) Not long ago, this was Hotel Edison's crusty old piano bar. Enter the capable team from Tribeca bar Ward III, who ripped out the grubby carpet, polished up the coppertop bar and revived this slice of old New York. You'll still find a nightly pianist (Wednesday to Monday), now accompanied by well-crafted drinks and an enviable medley of whiskeys and rums.

Lantern's Keep Cocktail Bar

Map p178 (212-453-4287; www.thelanternskeep.com; Iroquois Hotel, 49 W 44th St, btwn Fifth & Sixth Aves; 5pm-midnight Mon-Fri, 6pm-1am Sat; S B/D/F/M to 42nd St-Bryant Park) Can you keep a secret? If so, cross the lobby of the **Iroquois Hotel (800-332-7220, 212-840-3080; www.iroquoisny.com; r $289-559;)** and slip into this dark, intimate cocktail salon. Its specialty is pre-Prohibition drinks, shaken and stirred by passionate, personable mixologists. Reservations are recommended.

Jimmy's Corner Dive Bar

Map p178 (140 W 44th St, btwn Sixth & Seventh Aves, Midtown West; 11:30am-4am Mon-Sat, from 3pm Sun; S N/Q/R, 1/2/3, 7 to 42nd St-Times Sq, B/D/F/M to 42nd St-Bryant Park) This welcoming, completely unpretentious dive off Times Square is run by an old boxing trainer – as if you wouldn't guess by all the framed photos of boxing greats (and lesser-known fighters, too). The jukebox covers Stax to Miles Davis (plus Lionel Ritchie's most regretful moments), kept low enough for post-work gangs to chat away.

Industry Gay

Map p178 (www.industry-bar.com; 355 W 52nd St, btwn Eighth & Ninth Aves, Midtown West; 4pm-4am; S C/E, 1 to 50th St) What was once a parking garage is now one of the hottest gay bars in Hell's Kitchen – a slick 4000-sq-ft watering hole with handsome lounge areas, a pool table and a stage for top-notch drag divas.

Rudy's Dive Bar

Map p178 (www.rudysbarnyc.com; 627 Ninth Ave, at 44th St, Midtown West; 8am-4am Mon-Sat, noon-4am Sun; S A/C/E to 42nd St-Port Authority

Bryant Park (p168)

LUIS DAVILLA/GETTY IMAGES ©

Don't Miss Rockefeller Center

This 22-acre 'city within a city' debuted at the height of the Great Depression. Taking nine years to build, it was America's first multiuse retail, entertainment and office space – a modernist sprawl of 19 buildings (14 of which are the original art-deco structures), outdoor plazas and big-name tenants. Developer John D Rockefeller Jr may have sweated over the cost (a mere $100 million), but it was all worth it. The Center was declared a National Landmark in 1987.

There are views, and then there's the view from the **Top of the Rock** Map p170 (www.topoftherocknyc.com; 30 Rockefeller Plaza, at 49th St, entrance on W 50th St btwn Fifth & Sixth Aves; adult/child $27/17, sunrise/sunset combo $40/22; 8am-midnight, last elevator at 11pm; S B/D/F/M to 47th-50th Sts-Rockefeller Center). Crowning the GE Building, 70 stories above Midtown, its blockbuster vista includes one icon that you won't see from atop the Empire State Building – the Empire State Building.

TV comedy *30 Rock* gets its name from the GE Building, and the tower is the real-life home of NBC TV. Slated to reopen in late 2014, NBC Studio Tours leave from inside the NBC Experience Store, and include a sneak peak of Studio 8H, home to the legendary Saturday Night Live set. Advanced phone bookings are recommended. Check the website for tour recommencement updates. Across 49th St, opposite the plaza, is the glass-enclosed NBC Today show studio, broadcasting live from 7am to 11am daily.

Come the festive season, Rockefeller Plaza is where you'll find New York's most famous Christmas tree. In its shadow, Rink at Rockefeller Center is the city's most famous ice-skating rink.

NEED TO KNOW

Map p170; www.rockefellercenter.com; Fifth to Sixth Aves & 48th to 51st Sts; 24hr, times vary for individual businesses; S B/D/F/M to 47th-50th Sts-Rockefeller Center

Bus Terminal) The big pantless pig in a red jacket out front marks Hell's Kitchen's best divey mingler, with cheap pitchers of Rudy's two beers, half-circle booths covered in red duct tape, and free hot dogs. A mix of folks come to flirt or watch muted Knicks games as classic rock plays.

Entertainment

Midtown West & Times Square

Jazz at Lincoln Center — Jazz

Map p178 (☎ tickets to Dizzy's Club Coca-Cola 212-258-9595, tickets to Rose Theater & Allen Room 212-721-6500; www.jazzatlincolncenter.org; Time Warner Center, Broadway at 60th St; S A/C, B/D, 1 to 59th St-Columbus Circle) Perched high atop the Time Warner Center, Jazz at Lincoln Center consists of three state-of-the-art venues: the mid-sized Rose Theater; the panoramic, glass-backed Allen Room; and the intimate, atmospheric Dizzy's Club Coca-Cola. It's the last one you're likely to visit given its regular, nightly shows.

Carnegie Hall — Live Music

Map p178 (☎ 212-247-7800; www.carnegiehall.org; W 57th St at Seventh Ave, Midtown West; tours adult/child $15/5; ⏱ tours 11:30am, 12:30pm, 2pm & 3pm Mon-Fri, 11:30am & 12:30pm Sat, 12:30pm Sun Oct-May; S N/Q/R to 57th St-7th Ave) This legendary music hall may not be the world's biggest, nor grandest, but it's definitely one of the most acoustically blessed venues around. Opera, jazz and folk greats feature in the Isaac Stern Auditorium, with edgier jazz, pop, classical and world music in the hugely popular Zankel Hall.

Signature Theatre — Theater

Map p178 (☎ tickets 212-244-7529; www.signaturetheatre.org; 480 W 42nd St, btwn Ninth & Tenth Aves, Midtown West; S A/C/E to 42nd St-Port Authority Bus Terminal) Looking good in its Frank Gehry–designed home – complete with three theaters, bookshop and cafe – Signature Theatre devotes entire seasons to the body of work of its playwrights-in-residence, both past and present. To date, featured dramatists have included Tony Kushner, Edward Albee, Athol Fugard and Kenneth Lonergan. Aim to book shows one month in advance.

Playwrights Horizons — Theater

Map p178 (☎ tickets 212-279-4200; www.playwrightshorizons.org; 416 W 42nd St, btwn Ninth & Tenth Aves, Midtown West; S A/C/E to 42nd St-Port Authority Bus Terminal) An excellent place to catch what could be the next big thing, this veteran 'writers' theater' is dedicated to fostering contemporary American works. Notable past productions include Bruce Norris' Tony

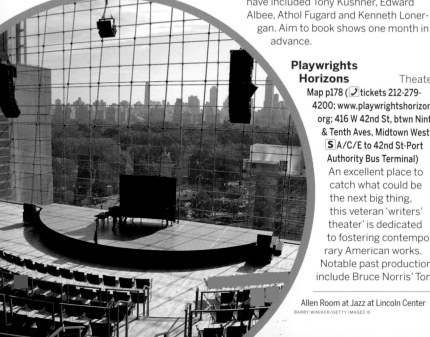

Allen Room at Jazz at Lincoln Center

BARRY WINIKER/GETTY IMAGES ©

award–winning *Clybourne Park*, as well as *I Am My Own Wife* and *Grey Gardens*, both of which moved on to Broadway.

Birdland Jazz, Cabaret

Map p178 (212-581-3080; www.birdlandjazz.com; 315 W 44th St, btwn Eighth & Ninth Aves, Midtown West; admission $20-50; 5pm-1am; ; S A/C/E to 42nd St-Port Authority Bus Terminal) This bird's got a slick look, not to mention the legend – its name dates from bebop legend Charlie Parker (aka 'Bird'), who headlined at the previous location on 52nd St, along with Miles, Monk and just about everyone else (you can see their photos on the walls). Covers run from $20 to $50 and the lineup is always stellar.

Caroline's on Broadway Comedy

Map p178 (212-757-4100; www.carolines.com; 1626 Broadway, at 50th St; S N/Q/R to 49th St, 1 to 50th St) You may recognize this big, bright, mainstream classic from comedy specials filmed here on location. It's a top spot to catch US comedy big guns and sitcom stars.

Second Stage Theatre Theater

Map p178 (Tony Kiser Theatre; tickets 212-246-4422; www.2st.com; 305 W 43rd St, at Eighth Ave, Midtown West; S A/C/E to 42nd St-Port Authority Bus Terminal) Second Stage is well known for debuting the work of talented emerging writers as well as that of the country's more established names. If you're after well-crafted contemporary American theater, this is a good place to find it.

Don't Tell Mama Cabaret

Map p178 (212-757-0788; www.donttellmamanyc.com; 343 W 46th St, btwn Eighth & Ninth Aves, Midtown West; 4pm-3am Mon-Thu, to 4am Fri-Sun; S N/Q/R, S, 1/2/3, 7 to Times Sq-42nd St) Piano bar and cabaret venue extraordinaire, Don't Tell Mama is an unpretentious little spot that's been around for more than 25 years and has the talent to prove it. Its regular roster of performers aren't big names, but true lovers of cabaret who give each show their all.

Madison Square Garden Stadium

Map p178 (www.thegarden.com; Seventh Ave btwn 31st & 33rd Sts, Midtown West; S 1/2/3 to 34th St-Penn Station) NYC's major performance venue – part of the massive complex housing Penn Station and the WaMu Theater – hosts big-arena performers, from Kanye West to Madonna. It's also a sports arena, with New York Knicks and New York Rangers games, as well as boxing matches and events such as the Annual Westminster Kennel Club Dog Show.

Shopping

Midtown East & Fifth Avenue

MoMA Design & Book Store Books, Gifts

Map p178 (www.momastore.org; 11 W 53rd St, btwn Fifth & Sixth Aves; 9:30am-6:30pm Sat-Thu, to 9pm Fri; S E, M to 5th Ave-53rd St) The flagship store at the Museum of Modern Art is a fab spot to souvenir shop in one fell swoop. Aside from stocking gorgeous books (from art and architecture tomes to pop culture readers and kids' picture books), you'll find art prints and posters, and one-of-a-kind knick-knacks. For furniture, lighting, homewares, jewelry, bags, and MUJI merchandise, head to the MoMA Design Store across the street.

Barneys Department Store

Map p170 (www.barneys.com; 660 Madison Ave, at 61st St, Midtown East; 10am-8pm Mon-Fri, to 7pm Sat, 11am-6pm Sun; S N/Q/R to 5th Ave-59th St) Serious fashionistas swipe their plastic at Barneys, respected for its spot-on collections of savvy labels such as Holmes & Yang, Kitsuné and Derek Lam. For (slightly) less expensive deals geared to a younger market, shop street-chic labels on the 8th floor.

Bergdorf Goodman Department Store

Map p170 (www.bergdorfgoodman.com; 754 Fifth Ave, btwn 57th & 58th Sts; 10am-8pm Mon-Fri, to 7pm Sat, noon-6pm Sun; S N/Q/R to 5th Ave-59th St, F to 57th St) Not merely loved for its Christmas windows (the city's best), plush BG leads the fashion race, its fashion director Linda Fargo considered an Anna Wintour of sorts. Drawcards include exclusive collections of Tom Ford and Chanel shoes, an expanded women's shoe department, and the biggest collection of Thom Browne clothing for men and women. The men's store is across the street.

Tiffany & Co Jewelry, Homewares

Map p170 (www.tiffany.com; 727 Fifth Ave, at 57th St; 10am-7pm Mon-Sat, noon-6pm Sun; S F to 57th St, N/Q/R to 5th Ave-59th St) Ever since Audrey Hepburn gazed longingly through its windows, Tiffany & Co has won countless hearts with its glittering diamond rings, watches, silver Elsa Peretti heart necklaces, crystal vases and glassware. Swoon, drool, but whatever you do, don't harass the elevator attendants with tired 'Where's the breakfast?' jokes.

FAO Schwarz Children

Map p170 (www.fao.com; 767 Fifth Ave, at 58th St; 10am-8pm Sun-Thu, to 9pm Fri & Sat; S 4/5/6 to 59th St, N/Q/R to 5th Ave-59th St) The toy store giant, where Tom Hanks played footsy piano in the movie *Big*, is number one on the NYC wish list of most visiting kids. Go on, indulge them!

Uniqlo Fashion

Map p170 (www.uniqlo.com; 666 Fifth Ave, at 53rd St; 10am-9pm Mon-Sat, 11am-8pm Sun; S E, M to Fifth Ave-53rd St) Uniqlo is Japan's answer to H&M and this is its showstopping 89,000-sq-ft flagship megastore. The forte here is affordable, fashionable, quality basics, from tees and undergarments, to Japanese denim, cashmere sweaters and super-light, high-tech parkas.

Dylan's Candy Bar Food & Drink

Map p170 (www.dylanscandybar.com; 1011 Third Ave, at 60th St, Midtown East; 10am-9pm Mon-Thu, to 11pm Fri & Sat, 11am-9pm Sun; S N/Q/R to Lexington Ave-59th St) Willy Wonka has nothing on this dental nightmare of giant swirly lollipops, crunchy candy bars, glowing jars of jelly beans, softball-sized cupcakes and a luminescent staircase embedded with scrumptious, unattainable candy. Stay away on weekends to avoid being pummeled by small, sugar-crazed kids. There's a cafe on the 2nd floor.

Time Warner Center

BARRY WINIKER/GETTY IMAGES ©

‹M›idtown West & ‹T›imes Square

Macy's Department Store

Map p178 (www.macys.com; 151 W 34th St, at Broadway; ⏲9am-9:30pm Mon-Fri, 10am-9:30pm Sat, 11am-8:30pm Sun; Ⓢ B/D/F/M, N/Q/R to 34th St-Herald Sq) Fresh from a much-needed facelift, the world's largest department store covers most bases, with fashion, furnishings, kitchenware, sheets, cafes, hair salons and even a branch of the Metropolitan Museum of Art gift store. It's more 'mid-priced' than 'exclusive', with mainstream labels and big-name cosmetics.

Housing Works Vintage

Map p178 (www.housingworks.org; 730-732 Ninth Ave, btwn 49th & 50th Sts, Midtown West; ⏲11am-8pm Mon-Sat, to 6pm Sun; Ⓢ C/E to 50th St) Welcome to the Hell's Kitchen branch of this much-loved thrift store, where Burberry shirts go for $25 and Joseph suede pants are yours for $40. While it's all about luck, the daily consignments mean a sterling find is never far off.

B&H Photo Video Electronics

Map p178 (www.bhphotovideo.com; 420 Ninth Ave, btwn 33rd & 34th Sts, Midtown West; ⏲9am-7pm Mon-Thu, to 1pm Fri, 10am-6pm Sun; Ⓢ A/C/E to 34th St-Penn Station) Visiting NYC's most popular camera shop is an experience in itself – it's massive and crowded, and bustling with black-clad (and tech-savvy) Hasidic Jewish salesmen. Your chosen item is dropped into a bucket, which then moves up and across the ceiling to the purchase area (which requires a second queue).

Time Warner Center Mall

Map p178 (www.theshopsatcolumbuscircle.com; Time Warner Center, 10 Columbus Circle; Ⓢ A/C, B/D, 1 to 59th St-Columbus Circle) A great add-on to an adventure in Central Park, the swank Time Warner Center has a fine line-up of largely upscale vendors including Coach, Stuart Weitzman, Williams-Sonoma, True Religion, Sephora and J Crew. For delectable picnic fare, visit the enormous **Whole Foods (www.wholefoodsmarket.com; Time Warner Center, 10 Columbus Circle; ⏲7:30am-11pm; Ⓢ A/C, B/D, 1 to 59th St-Columbus Circle)** in the basement.

Upper East Side

The Upper East Side has New York's greatest concentration of cultural centers. A long section of Fifth Ave north of 79th St has even been officially designated 'Museum Mile' and includes the grande dame that is the Metropolitan Museum of Art.

But it's not *all* highbrow museums: you'll also find plenty of seriously high-end shops. The neighborhood – whose residents, by the way, are in a never-ending contest with those of the Upper West Side just across the park – also includes many of the city's most exclusive hotels and residences (not to mention many of the city's most moneyed celebrities, from Woody Allen to Shirley MacLaine).

The side streets from Fifth Ave to Third Ave between 57th and 86th Sts feature some stunning town houses and brownstones. Walking through this area at night offers opportunities to see how the other half lives.

Upper East Side Highlights

Frick Collection (p205)

The wily and wealthy Henry Clay Frick, a Pittsburgh steel magnate, established a trust to open his private art collection as a museum. On display are paintings by Titian and Johannes Vermeer, and portraits by Gilbert Stuart, El Greco, Goya and John Constable. Perhaps the best asset here is that it is never crowded, providing a welcome break from the swarms of gawkers at larger museums.

Shopping (p208)

The Upper East Side isn't for amateurs. Madison Ave (from 60th St to 72nd St) features one of the globe's glitziest stretches of retail: the flagship boutiques of some of the world's top designers, including Gucci, Prada and Cartier. The neighborhood is also a good spot to hunt down designer deals at consignment shops.

Cartier, 5th Avenue

BEN HIDER/GETTY IMAGES ©

3 Neue Galerie (p198)

This showcase for German and Austrian art is a small gem among the Fifth Ave biggies, as it's an intimate but well-hung collection, featuring impressive works by Gustav Klimt, Paul Klee and Egon Schiele, housed in a former Rockefeller mansion with winding staircases and wrought-iron banisters. It also boasts a lovely, Viennese-style restaurant, Café Sabarsky (p204), on a corner that overlooks Central Park.

SYLVAIN SONNET/GETTY IMAGES ©

4 Guggenheim Museum (p196)

Inside the sculptural facade of the Frank Lloyd Wright building, the Guggenheim stages some of New York's best exhibitions. Its unique, spiraling design adds an unusual element: following the coiling pathways lined with art can be a meditative experience. Aside from cutting-edge shows, there's a strong collection of modern works, including iconic pieces by Van Gogh, Magritte and Pollack.

5 Metropolitan Museum of Art (p194)

Home to one of the greatest repositories of artwork on this planet, the Met simply staggers the imagination. The treasure trove spans many centuries, and its highlights include ancient Egyptian sarcophagi (and a full-size temple), works from ancient Greece, medieval treasures, European masters and paintings from the American school. The biggest challenge is where to begin.

On Location on the Upper East Side

The Upper East Side is ground zero for all things luxurious, especially the area that covers the blocks from 60th to 86th Sts between Park and Fifth Aves. A stroll around here is also a chance to explore Manhattan's most storied film sites, past film locations big and small.

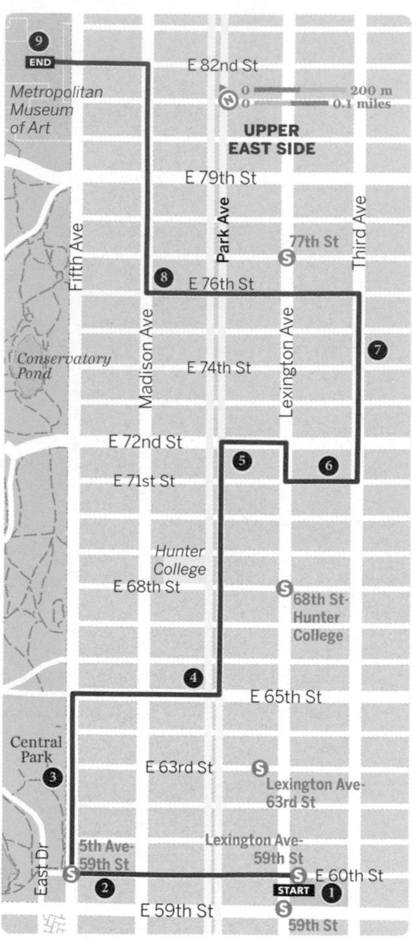

WALK FACTS

- **Start** Bloomingdale's
- **End** Metropolitan Museum of Art
- **Distance** 1.5 miles
- **Duration** Two hours

1 Bloomingdale's

Start outside the iconic department store, Bloomingdale's (p208), where Darryl Hannah and Tom Hanks shattered televisions in *Splash* (1984) and Dustin Hoffman hailed a cab in *Tootsie* (1982). Pop in to raid the racks for clothes and shoes from a who's who of US and global designers.

2 Copacabana

West of here, 10 60th St is the site of the now defunct Copacabana nightclub (now a health-food restaurant) that hosted Ray Liotta and Lorraine Bracco in *Goodfellas* (1990) and a coked-up lawyer played by Sean Penn in *Carlito's Way* (1993).

3 Central Park

Continue down 60th St until you hit Central Park (p216). The park has appeared in *The Royal Tenenbaums* (2001), *Ghostbusters* (1983), *The Muppets Take Manhattan* (1983), *Barefoot in the Park* (1967) and the cult classic *The Warriors* (1979).

4 John Malkovich's Apartment

Head up Fifth Ave and then turn right into E 65th St and walk until you reach Park Ave. At 620 Park Ave, on the corner of 65th St, you'll find the building that served as John Malkovich's apartment in Charlie Kaufman's *Being John Malkovich* (1999).

5 High-Rise

To the north at 114 72nd St is the high-rise where Sylvia Miles lured Jon Voight in *Midnight Cowboy* (1969).

6 Holly Golightly's Apartment

One block to the east and south is 171 E 71st St, a town house featured in one of the most famous movies to star New York: this was Holly Golightly's apartment in *Breakfast at Tiffany's* (1961).

7 JG Mellon

Continuing east to Third Ave, you'll find the restaurant JG Mellon at the corner of 74th St, a good spot for beer and burger – plus the site of a meeting between Dustin Hoffman and Meryl Streep in *Kramer vs. Kramer* (1979).

8 Carlyle

Heading west to Madison Ave, the tony Carlyle hotel stands at 35 76th St where Woody Allen and Dianne Wiest had a date from hell in *Hannah and Her Sisters* (1986). Notable guests in real life have included John and Jacqueline Kennedy, as well as Princess Diana.

9 Metropolitan Museum of Art

From the Carlyle, it's a short jaunt north and west to the Met (p194) at 82nd St and Fifth Ave, where Angie Dickinson had a fatal encounter in *Dressed to Kill* (1980) and Billy Crystal chatted up Meg Ryan in *When Harry Met Sally* (1989). End the tour by getting lost inside the museum's priceless collections.

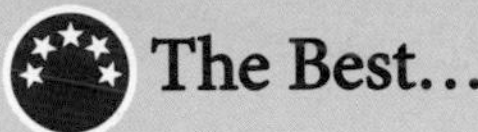

The Best...

PLACES TO EAT

James Wood Foundry English-inspired gastropub. (p206)

Café Sabarsky Well-rendered Austrian specialties are worth the wait. (p204)

ABV Buzzing space for delectable small plates and craft beers. (p205)

Tanoshi Humble-looking eatery serving outstanding sushi. (p206)

Café Boulud Top choice for Michelin-starred dining. (p207)

PLACES TO DRINK

Metropolitan Museum Roof Garden Café & Martini Bar Drinks with magical Central Park views. (p207)

Vinus and Marc Friendly, vintage-looking charmer with winning cocktails. (p207)

Bemelmans Bar Opulence for the upper crust. (p208)

FORMER MANSIONS

Frick Collection Henry K Frick's flamboyantly opulent home-cum-museum. (p205)

Neue Galerie Once a Rockefeller abode near the Met. (p198)

Cooper-Hewitt National Design Museum Billionaire Andrew Carnegie's 64-room home. (p201)

Central Park and the Upper East Side

…an Museum of Art

This sprawling encyclopedic museum, founded in 1870, houses one of the biggest art collections in the world. Its permanent collection has more than two million individual objects, from Egyptian temples to American paintings. Known colloquially as 'The Met,' the museum attracts almost six million visitors a year to its 17 acres of galleries – making it the largest single-site attraction in New York City. (Yup, you read that right: 17 acres.) In other words, plan on spending some time here. It is B-I-G.

212-535-7710

www.metmuseum.org

1000 Fifth Ave at 82nd St

suggested donation adult/child $25/free

10am-5:30pm Sun-Thu, to 9pm Fri & Sat

S 4/5/6 to 86th St

Egyptian Art

The museum has an unrivaled collection of ancient Egyptian art, some of which dates back to the Paleolithic era. Located to the north of the Great Hall, the 39 Egyptian galleries open dramatically with one of the Met's prized pieces: the Mastaba Tomb of Perneb (c 2300 BC), an Old Kingdom burial chamber crafted from limestone. From here, a web of rooms is cluttered with funerary stele, carved reliefs and fragments of pyramids. (Don't miss the irresistible quartzite sculpture of a lion cub in Gallery 103.) These eventually lead to the Temple of Dendur (Gallery 131), a sandstone temple to the goddess Isis that resides in a sunny atrium gallery with a reflecting pool – a must-see for the first-time visitor.

European Paintings

Want Renaissance? The Met's got it. On the museum's second floor, the European Paintings' galleries display a stunning collection of masterworks. This includes more than 1700 canvases from the roughly 500-year-period starting in the 13th century, with works by every important painter from Duccio to Rembrandt. In fact, everything here is, literally, a masterpiece. On the north end, in Gallery 615, is Vermeer's tender 17th-century painting *A Maid Asleep*. Gallery 608, to the west, contains a luminous 16th-century altar by Renaissance master Raphael. And in a room stuffed with works by Zurbarán and Murillo (Gallery 618), there is an array of paintings by Velázquez, the most extraordinary of which depicts the dashing Juan de Pareja. And that's just the beginning. You can't go wrong in these galleries.

Art of the Arab Lands

The newly renovated second-floor space comes with a very unwieldy name. The 'New Galleries for the Art of the Arab Lands, Turkey, Iran, Central Asia, and Later South Asia' are comprised of 15 incredible rooms that showcase the museum's extensive collection of art from the Middle East and Central and South Asia. In addition to garments, secular decorative objects and manuscripts, you'll find treasures such as a 12th-century ceramic chess set from Iran (Gallery 453) that is downright Modernist in its simplicity. There is also a superb array of Ottoman textiles (Gallery 459), a medieval-style Moroccan court (Gallery 456) and an 18th-century room from Damascus (Gallery 461).

American Wing

In the northwest corner, the recently revamped American galleries showcase a wide variety of decorative and fine art from throughout US history. These include everything from colonial portraiture to Hudson River School masterpieces to John Singer Sargent's unbearably sexy *Madame X* (Gallery 771) – not to mention Emanuel Leutze's massive canvas of *Washington Crossing the Delaware* (Gallery 760). The galleries are stacked around an interior sculpture court abutted by a pleasant cafe.

Rooftop

One of the best spots in the entire museum is the roof garden, which features rotating sculpture installations by contemporary and 20th-century artists. (Sol Lewitt, Jeff Koons and Andy Goldsworthy have all shown here.) But its best feature is the views it offers of the city and Central Park. It is also home to the **Roof Garden Café & Martini Bar** (p207), the best place in the museum for a sip – especially at sunset. The roof garden is open from April to October.

Seeing the Museum

A desk inside the Great Hall has audio tours in several languages ($7), while docents offer guided tours of specific galleries. These are free with admission. Check the website or information desk for details. If you can't stand crowds, avoid weekends.

Don't Miss
Guggenheim Museum

A sculpture in its own right, architect Frank Lloyd Wright's building almost overshadows the collection of 20th-century art it houses. Completed in 1959, the inverted ziggurat structure was derided by some critics, but it was hailed by others who welcomed it as a beloved architectural icon. Since it first opened, this unusual structure has appeared on countless postcards, TV programs and films.

212-423-3500

www.guggenheim.org

1071 Fifth Ave, at 89th St

adult/child $22/free, by donation 5:45-7:45pm Sat

10am-5:45pm Sun-Wed & Fri, to 7:45pm Sat

S 4/5/6 to 86th St

Abstract Roots

The Guggenheim came out of the collection of Solomon R Guggenheim, a New York mining magnate who began acquiring abstract art in his 60s at the behest of his art adviser, an eccentric German baroness named Hilla Rebay. In 1939, with Rebay serving as director, Guggenheim opened a temporary museum on 54th St titled Museum of Non-Objective Painting. (Incredibly, it had grey velour walls, piped-in classical music and burning incense.) Four years later, the pair commissioned Wright to construct a permanent home for the collection.

A Pink Guggenheim

Wright made hundreds of sketches and pondered the use of various materials for the construction of the museum. At one point, he considered using red marble for the exterior facade – a 1945 model sketch shows a pink building – but the color scheme was rejected.

Years in the Making

Like any development in New York City, the project took forever to come to fruition. Construction was delayed for almost 13 years due to budget constraints, the outbreak of WWII and outraged neighbors who weren't all that excited to see an architectural spaceship land in their midst. Construction was completed in 1959, after both Wright and Guggenheim had passed away.

Bring on the Critics

When the Guggenheim opened its doors in October 1959, the ticket price was 50 cents and the works on view included pieces by Kandinsky, Alexander Calder and abstract expressionists Franz Kline and Willem De Kooning.

The structure was savaged by the *New York Times*, which lambasted it as 'a war between architecture and painting in which both come out badly maimed.' But others quickly celebrated it as 'the most beautiful building in America.' Whether Wright intended to or not, he had given the city one of its most visible landmarks.

To the Present

The Guggenheim's vast collection includes works by Kandinsky, Picasso, Chagall and Jackson Pollock. In 1976, Justin Thannhauser donated a major trove of impressionist and modern works that included paintings by Monet, Van Gogh and Degas. Three years later, Guggenheim's niece Peggy left the museum key surrealist works, including pieces by René Magritte and Yves Tanguy. In 1992, the Robert Mapplethorpe Foundation bequeathed 200 photographs to the museum, making the Guggenheim the single-most important public repository of his work.

Visiting the Museum

The museum's ascending ramp is occupied by rotating exhibitions of modern and contemporary art. Though Wright intended visitors to go to the top and wind their way down, the cramped, single elevator doesn't allow for this. Exhibitions, therefore, are installed from bottom to top.

There are two good on-site food options: **The Wright** (☎212-427-5690; www.thewrightrestaurant.com; Guggenheim Museum, 1071 Fifth Ave, at 89th St; mains $23-28; ⏲11:30am-3:30pm Fri & Sun-Wed, to 6pm Sat; S 4/5/6 to 86th St), at ground level, a space-age eatery serving steamy risotto and classic cocktails, and **Cafe 3** (www.guggenheim.org; Guggenheim Museum, 1071 Fifth Ave, at 89th St; sandwiches $9-10; ⏲10:30am-5pm Fri-Wed; S 4/5/6 to 86th St), on the third floor, which offers sparkling views of Central Park and excellent coffee and light snacks.

The line to get in to the museum can be brutal. You'll save time if you purchase tickets online in advance.

Discover Upper East Side

Getting There & Away

- **Subway** The sole subway lines here are the 4/5/6 which travel north and south on Lexington Ave. A new stretch of subway track underneath Second Ave is expected to be completed by late 2016.
- **Bus** The M1, M2, M3 and M4 buses all make the scenic drive down Fifth Ave beside Central Park. The M15 is handy for getting around the far east side, traveling up First Ave and down Second. Crosstown buses at 66th, 72nd, 79th, 86th and 96th Sts take you across the park and into the Upper West Side.

Charles Engelhard Court, Metropolitan Museum of Art
STEVEN GREAVES/GETTY IMAGES ©

Sights

Metropolitan Museum of Art (p194)

Guggenheim Museum (p196)

Whitney Museum of American Art — Museum

Map p200 (☎212-570-3600; www.whitney.org; 945 Madison Ave, cnr 75th St; adult/child $20/free, by donation 6-9pm Fri; 11am-6pm Wed, Thu, Sat & Sun, 1-9pm Fri; S 6 to 77th St) The Whitney makes no secret of its mission to provoke, which starts with its imposing Brutalist building, a structure that houses works by 20th century masters Edward Hopper, Jasper Johns, Georgia O'Keeffe and Mark Rothko. In addition to rotating exhibits, there is a biennial on even years, an ambitious survey of contemporary art that rarely fails to generate controversy.

After inhabiting various locations downtown, the Whitney moved to its current Marcel Breuer–designed building in 1966. But, having outgrown these digs, it is set to move again. A new Renzo Piano–designed structure in the Meatpacking District was nearing completion as this book went to press. Located right next to the High Line (at Washington and Gansevoort Sts), the 200,000-square-foot space will open in 2015.

Neue Galerie — Museum

Map p200 (☎212-628-6200; www.neuegalerie.org; 1048 Fifth Ave, cnr E 86th St; admission $20, free 6-8pm 1st Fri of every month, children under 12 not admitted; 11am-6pm Thu-Mon; S 4/5/6 to 86th St) This restored Carrère and Hastings mansion from 1914 is a resplendent showcase for man and Austrian art, featuring works Paul Klee, Ernst Ludwig Kirchner and gon Schiele. In pride of place on the 2nd loor is Gustav Klimt's golden 1907 portrait of Adele Bloch-Bauer – which was acquired for the museum by cosmetics magnate Ronald Lauder for a whopping $135 million.

This is a small but beautiful place with winding staircases and wrought-iron banisters. It also boasts the lovely, street-level eatery, **Café Sabarsky** (p204). Avoid weekends if you don't want to deal with gallery-clogging crowds.

Jewish Museum — Museum

Map p200 (☎212-423-3200; www.jewishmuseum.org; 1109 Fifth Ave, at 92nd St; adult/child $15/free, Sat free, by donation 5-8pm Thu; ⊙11am-6pm Fri-Tue, to 8pm Thu; 👪; S 6 to 96th St) This New York City gem is tucked into a French-Gothic mansion from 1908, which houses 30,000 items of Judaica, as well as sculpture, painting and decorative arts. It hosts excellent temporary exhibits, featuring retrospectives on influential figures such as Art Spiegelman, as well as world-class shows on the likes of Marc Chagall, Édouard Vuillard and Man Ray among other past luminaries.

National Academy Museum — Gallery

Map p200 (☎212-369-4880; www.nationalacademy.org; 1083 Fifth Ave, at 89th St; adult/child $15/free; ⊙11am-6pm Wed-Sun; S 4/5/6 to 86th St) Co-founded by painter/inventor Samuel Morse in 1825, the National Academy Museum comprises an incredible permanent collection of paintings by figures such as Wlil Barnet, Thomas Hart Benton and George Bellows. It is housed in a beaux arts structure designed by Ogden Codman Jr and featuring a marble foyer and spiral staircase.

Temple Emanu-El — Synagogue

Map p200 (☎212-744-1400; www.emanuelnyc.org; 1 E 65th St, cnr Fifth Ave; ⊙10am-4:30pm Sun-Thu; S 6 to 68th St-Hunter College) Founded in 1845 as the first Reform synagogue in New York, this temple, completed in 1929, is now one of the largest Jewish houses of worship in the world. An imposing Romanesque structure, it is more than 175ft long and 100ft tall, with a brilliant, hand-painted ceiling that contains details in gold.

Museum of the City of New York — Museum

Map p200 (☎212-534-1672; www.mcny.org; 1220 Fifth Ave, btwn 103rd & 104th Sts; suggested admission adult/child $10/free; ⊙10am-6pm; S 6 to 103rd St) Situated in a colonial Georgian-style mansion, this local museum focuses solely on New York City's past, present and future. Don't miss the 22-minute film *Timescapes* (on the 2nd floor), which charts NYC's growth from tiny native trading post to burgeoning metropolis.

Asia Society & Museum (p201)
BARRY WINIKER/GETTY IMAGES ©

Upper East Side

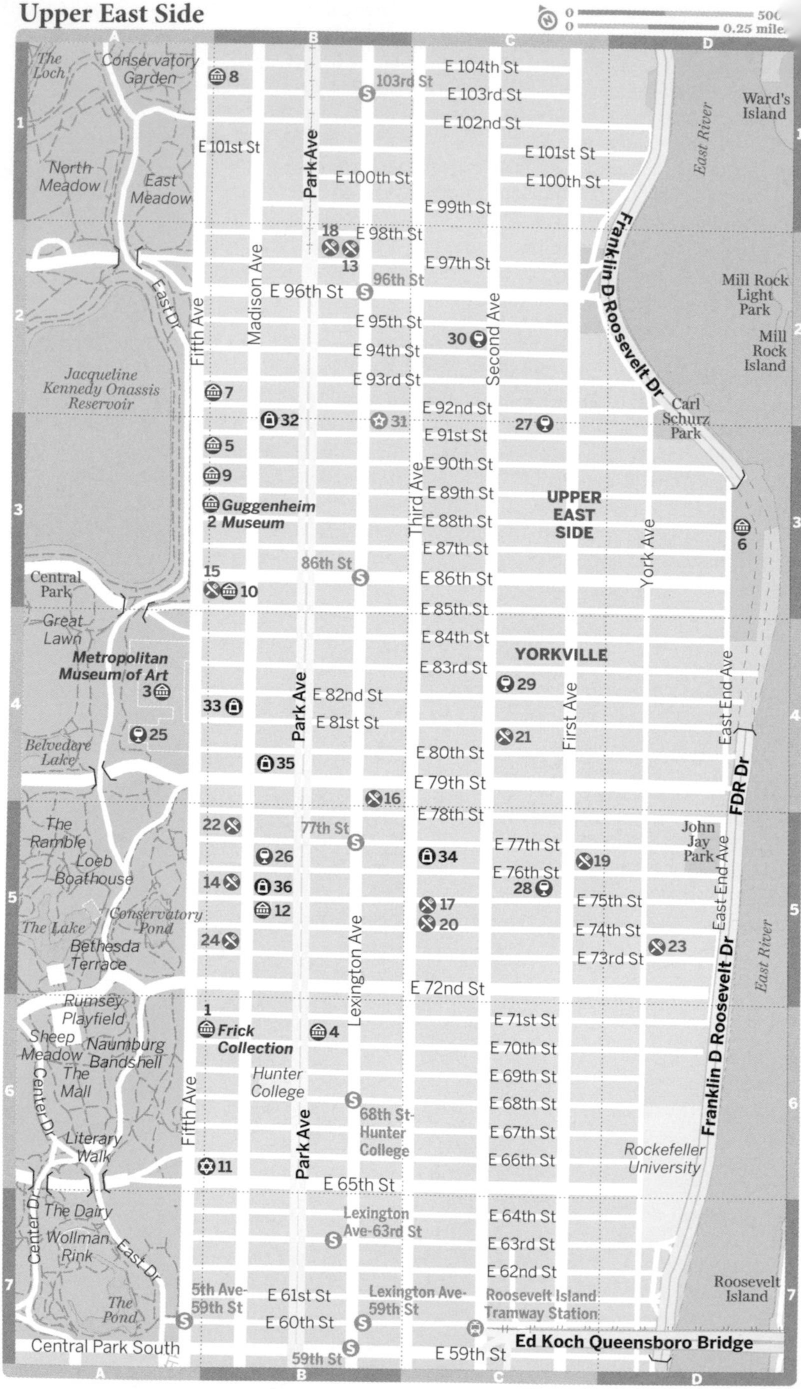

0 500 m
0 0.25 miles

The Loch
Conservatory Garden
North Meadow
East Meadow
East Dr
Jacqueline Kennedy Onassis Reservoir
Central Park
Great Lawn
Metropolitan Museum of Art
Belvedere Lake
The Ramble
Loeb Boathouse
Conservatory Pond
The Lake
Bethesda Terrace
Rumsey Playfield
Sheep Meadow
Naumburg Bandshell
The Mall
Center Dr
Literary Walk
The Dairy
Wollman Rink
The Pond
Central Park South
Fifth Ave
Madison Ave
Park Ave
Lexington Ave
Third Ave
Second Ave
First Ave
York Ave
East End Ave
E 104th St
E 103rd St
E 102nd St
E 101st St
E 100th St
E 99th St
E 98th St
E 97th St
E 96th St
E 95th St
E 94th St
E 93rd St
E 92nd St
E 91st St
E 90th St
E 89th St
E 88th St
E 87th St
E 86th St
E 85th St
E 84th St
E 83rd St
E 82nd St
E 81st St
E 80th St
E 79th St
E 78th St
E 77th St
E 76th St
E 75th St
E 74th St
E 73rd St
E 72nd St
E 71st St
E 70th St
E 69th St
E 68th St
E 67th St
E 66th St
E 65th St
E 64th St
E 63rd St
E 62nd St
E 61st St
E 60th St
E 59th St
103rd St
96th St
86th St
77th St
68th St-Hunter College
Lexington Ave-63rd St
Lexington Ave-59th St
5th Ave-59th St
59th St
Roosevelt Island Tramway Station
Ed Koch Queensboro Bridge
Hunter College
Rockefeller University
UPPER EAST SIDE
YORKVILLE
Franklin D Roosevelt Dr
FDR Dr
East River
Ward's Island
Mill Rock Light Park
Mill Rock Island
Carl Schurz Park
John Jay Park
Roosevelt Island
2 Guggenheim Museum
1 Frick Collection
3
4
5
6
7
8
9
10
11
12
13
14
15
16
17
18
19
20
21
22
23
24
25
26
27
28
29
30
31
32
33
34
35
36
A
B
C
D
1
2
3
4
5
6
7

Upper East Side

Don't Miss Sights

1 Frick Collection B6
2 Guggenheim Museum B3
3 Metropolitan Museum of Art A4

Sights

4 Asia Society & Museum B6
5 Cooper-Hewitt National Design Museum B3
6 Gracie Mansion D3
7 Jewish Museum B2
8 Museum of the City of New York B1
9 National Academy Museum B3
10 Neue Galerie B3
11 Temple Emanu-El B6
12 Whitney Museum of American Art B5

Eating

13 ABV B2
Cafe 3 .... (see 2)
14 Café Boulud B5
15 Café Sabarsky B3
16 Candle 79 .... B4
17 Candle Cafe C5
18 Earl's Beer & Cheese B2
19 James Wood Foundry C5
20 JG Melon C5
21 Sandro's C4
22 Sant Ambroeus B5
23 Tanoshi D5
24 Via Quadronno B5
Wright .... (see 2)

Drinking & Nightlife

25 Metropolitan Museum Roof Garden Café & Martini Bar A4
26 Bemelmans Bar B5
27 Drunken Munkey C3
28 JBird C5
29 Penrose C4
30 Vinus and Marc C2

Entertainment

31 92nd St Y B3
Frick Collection .... (see 1)

Shopping

32 Blue Tree B3
33 Crawford Doyle Booksellers B4
34 Housing Works Thrift Shop C5
35 Michael's B4
36 Zitomer B5

Asia Society & Museum — Museum

Map p200 (212-288-6400; www.asiasociety.org; 725 Park Ave, at E 70th St; admission $12, 6-9pm Fri mid-Sep–Jun free; 11am-6pm Tue-Sun, to 9pm Fri mid-Sep–Jun; S 6 to 68th St-Hunter College) Founded in 1956 by John D Rockefeller (an avid collector of Asian Art), this cultural center hosts fascinating exhibits (pre-Revolutionary art of Iran, retrospectives of leading Chinese artists, block prints of Edo-era Japan), as well as Jain sculptures and Nepalese Buddhist paintings. There are tours (free with admission) at 2pm on Tuesdays year-round and at 6:30pm Fridays (excluding summer months).

Gracie Mansion — Historic Building

Map p200 (tour reservations 311 or 212-639-9675; www.nyc.gov/gracie; East End Ave, at E 88th St; admission $7; tours 10am, 11am, 1pm & 2pm Wed; S 4/5/6 to 86th St) This Federal-style home served as the country residence of merchant Archibald Gracie in 1799. Since 1942, it has been where New York's mayors have lived – with the exception of megabillionaire Mayor Michael Bloomberg, who preferred his own plush, Upper East Side digs. The house has been added to and renovated over the years. To peer inside, you'll have to call ahead to reserve a spot on one of the 45-minute house tours.

The home is bordered by the pleasant, riverside Carl Schurz Park.

Cooper-Hewitt National Design Museum — Museum

Map p200 (212-849-8400; www.cooperhewitt.org; 2 E 91st St, at Fifth Ave; S 4/5/6 to 86th St) Part of the Smithsonian Institution in Washington, DC, this house of culture is the only museum in the country that's dedicated to both historic and contemporary design. The collection is housed in the 64-room mansion built by billionaire Andrew Carnegie in 1901. The museum closed for an extensive renovation and expansion, and is slated to reopen in 2014. Check the website for updates.

Metropolitan Museum of Art

PLAN OF ATTACK

Standing in the aptly named Great Hall, past the main entrance, head into the Egyptian galleries and make your way to the dramatic ❶ **Temple of Dendur**.

Stroll through the Charles Engelhard Court, a soaring sunlit atrium packed with American sculptures, and dip into the Arms and Armor galleries. See the meticulous craftsmanship of the 16th-century ❷ **Armor of Henry II of France**. The next room (Gallery 371) has four mounted fully armoured horsemen.

Head back into the American Wing and up to the second floor for a look at the ❸ **Washington Crossing the Delaware**. Also on the second floor is a jaw-dropping collection of European masters. Don't miss the Caravaggios in Gallery 621, in particular ❹ **The Denial of St Peter**.

Staying on the second floor, wind your way over to the Islamic Art galleries, where you'll find an elaborate ❺ **Mihrab**, or prayer niche; it's right next to a medieval-style Moroccan court with gurgling fountain (Gallery 456).

Nearby you'll find works by Monet, Renoir, Van Gogh and Gauguin. There are several masterpieces by Picasso, including the ❻ **Blind Man's Meal**.

Head downstairs and into Oceania exhibition halls for vivid tribal art from New Guinea and beyond. Have a look at tribal costumes such as the ❼ **Asmat Body Mask**; overhead is a ceiling lined with shields.

The Met has a trove of ancient Greek and Roman works. In the largest gallery you'll find the intricate marble sarcophagus, ❽ **Triumph of Dionysos and the Seasons**.

The Denial of Saint Peter Gallery 621
Painted in the final months of Caravaggio's short, tempestuous life, this magnificent work is a masterpiece of storytelling.

The Blind Man's Meal Gallery 830
Picasso's painting of a blind man at a table alludes to human suffering in general; the bread and wine also have undertones of Christian symbolism.

Mihrab (prayer niche) Gallery 455
One of the world's finest religious architectural decorations, this 8th-century piece from Iran was created by joining cut glazed tiles into a richly ornate mosaic.

Asmat Body Mask Gallery 354
A New Guinea costume like this was worn to represent the spirit of someone who recently died, and featured in ritual dances of the Asmat people.

Triumph of Dionysos and the Seasons Gallery 162
On this marble sarcophagus, you'll see the god Dionysos seated on a panther, joined by four figures representing (from left to right) winter, spring, summer and fall.

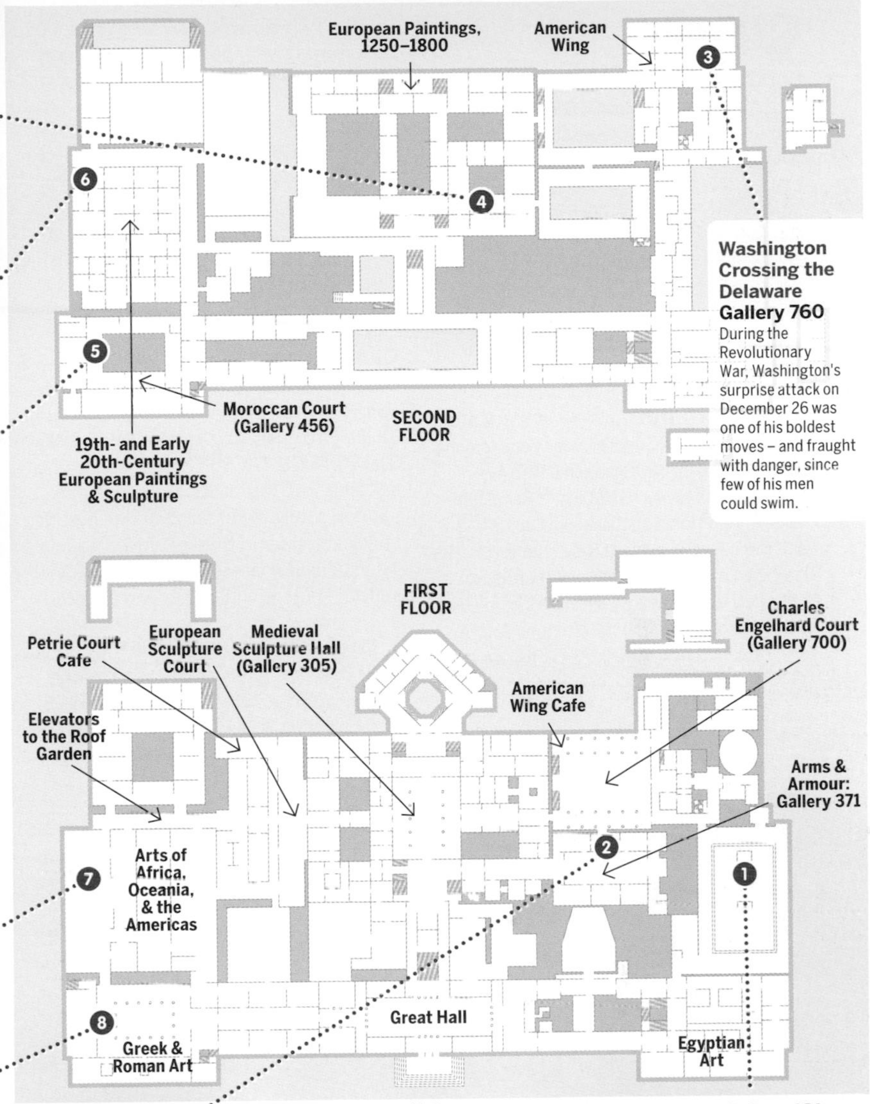

SECOND FLOOR

European Paintings, 1250–1800

American Wing

Moroccan Court (Gallery 456)

19th- and Early 20th-Century European Paintings & Sculpture

Washington Crossing the Delaware Gallery 760
During the Revolutionary War, Washington's surprise attack on December 26 was one of his boldest moves – and fraught with danger, since few of his men could swim.

FIRST FLOOR

Petrie Court Cafe

European Sculpture Court

Medieval Sculpture Hall (Gallery 305)

American Wing Cafe

Charles Engelhard Court (Gallery 700)

Elevators to the Roof Garden

Arms & Armour: Gallery 371

Arts of Africa, Oceania, & the Americas

Great Hall

Greek & Roman Art

Egyptian Art

Main entrance on Fifth Ave at 82nd St

Armor of Henry II of France Gallery 374
Look closely to see creatures, gods and warriors among the dense foliate scrolls, including Apollo chasing the nymph Daphne on the shoulders.

Temple of Dendur Gallery 131
One of the Met's must-see sights, this temple was built by order of Caesar Augustus. The Roman Emperor and ruler of Egypt had many temples built in honor of Egyptian deities.

Eating

Earl's Beer & Cheese American $

Map p200 (www.earlsny.com; 1259 Park Ave, btwn 97th & 98th Sts; grilled cheese $6-8; 4pm-midnight Mon & Tue, 11am-midnight Wed-Thu & Sun, to 2am Fri & Sat; S 6 to 96th St) Chef Corey Cova's tiny comfort-food outpost channels a hipster hunting vibe, complete with a giant deer in the woods mural and a mounted buck's head. Basic grilled cheese is a paradigm shifter, served with pork belly, fried egg and kimchi. Has great craft beers too.

Via Quadronno Cafe $

Map p200 (212-650-9880; www.viaquadronno.com; 25 E 73rd St, btwn Madison & Fifth Aves; sandwiches $8-15, mains $23-38; 8am-11pm Mon-Fri, 9am-11pm Sat, 10am-9pm Sun; ; S 6 to 77th St) A little slice of Italy that looks like it's been airlifted into New York, this cozy cafe-bistro has exquisite coffee, as well as a mind-boggling selection of sandwiches – one of which is stuffed with wild boar prosciutto and Camembert. There are soups, pastas and a very popular daily lasagna.

JG Melon Pub $

Map p200 (212-744-0585; 1291 Third Ave, at 74th St; burgers $10.50; 11:30am-4am; S 6 to 77th St) JG's is a loud, old-school, melon-themed pub that has been serving basic burgers on tea plates since 1972. It's a local favorite for both eating and drinking (the Bloody Marys are excellent) and it gets crowded in the after-work hours.

Candle Cafe Vegan $$

Map p200 (212-472-0970; www.candlecafe.com; 1307 Third Ave, btwn 74th & 75th Sts; mains $15-21; 11:30am-10:30pm Mon-Sat, to 9:30pm Sun; ; S 6 to 77th St) The moneyed, yoga set piles into this attractive vegan cafe serving a long list of sandwiches, salads, comfort food and market-driven specials. The specialty here is the house-made seitan. There is a juice bar and a gluten-free menu.

For a more upscale take on the subject, check out its sister restaurant, **Candle 79** Map p200 (212-537-7179; www.candle79.com; 154 E 79th St, at Lexington Ave; mains $19-24; lunch & dinner; ; S 6 to 77th St), two blocks away.

Sandro's Italian $$

Map p200 (212-288-7374; www.sandrosnyc.com; 306 E 81st St, near Second Ave; mains $20-40; 4:30-11pm Mon-Sat, to 10pm Sun; S 6 to 77th St) This neighborhood trattoria serves up fresh Roman dishes and homemade pastas by chef Sandro Fioriti. Specialties include crisp fried artichokes and sea urchin ravioli.

Café Sabarsky Austrian $$

Map p200 (212-288-0665; www.kg-ny.com/wallse; 1048 Fifth Ave, at E 86th St; mains $15-30; 9am-6pm Mon & Wed,

Apple strudel at Café Sabarsky

FRANCES M. ROBERTS/ALAMY ©

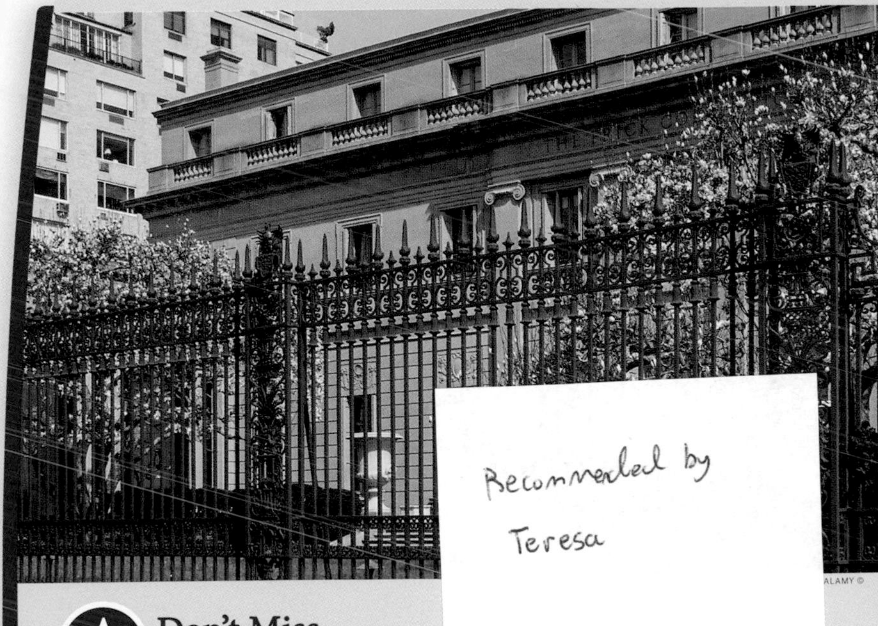

ALAMY ©

Don't Miss Frick Collection

This spectacular art collection sits in a mansion built by prickly steel magnate Henry Clay Frick, one of the many such residences that made up Millionaires' Row. The museum has more than a dozen splendid rooms that display masterpieces by Titian, Vermeer, Gilbert Stuart, El Greco and Goya.

This museum is a treat for a number of reasons. One, it resides in a lovely, rambling beaux-arts structure built from 1913–14 by Carrère and Hastings. Two, it is generally not crowded (one exception being during popular shows, such as a Vermeer and Rembrandt exhibit held in 2013). And, three, it feels refreshingly intimate, with a trickling indoor courtyard fountain and gardens that can be explored on warmer days.

Classical music fans will enjoy the frequent piano and violin concerts that take place on Sundays.

NEED TO KNOW

Map p200; ☎212-288-0700; www.frick.org; 1 E 70th St, at Fifth Ave; admission $20, by donation 11am-1pm Sun, children under 10 not admitted; ⏲10am-6pm Tue-Sat, 11am-5pm Sun; S 6 to 68th St-Hunter College

to 9pm Thu-Sun; ; ; S 4/5/6 to 86th St) The lines get long at this popular cafe, which evokes opulent turn-of-the-century Vienna. Expect crepes with smoked trout, goulash soup and creamed sptäzle. There is also a long list of specialty sweets, including a divine Sachertorte.

ABV Modern American **$$**

Map p200 (☎212-722-8959; 1504 Lexington Ave, at 97th St; mains $10-24; ⏲5pm-midnight Mon-Thu, 4pm-1am Fri, from 11am Sat & Sun; ; S 6 to 96th St) On the borderline of East Harlem, ABV draws a young, laid-back crowd who come for eclectic sharing plates (fish

Detour: Roosevelt: The Island Off the Island of Manhattan

Roosevelt Island, the tiny sliver of land that sits in the middle of the East River, has never had much to offer in the way of sights. For much of the 19th century, when it was known as Welfare Island, it was cluttered with hospitals, including a mental hospital and a crenellated small-pox ward. In the 1970s, a series of cookie-cutter apartment buildings were built along the island's only road. For years, the only things Roosevelt Island really had going for it were the good views of Manhattan and the picturesque ruins of the old small-pox hospital (which is under restoration and will eventually open to the public).

But the island hit the architectural map in 2012, when a five-acre **memorial** (Map p170; www.fdrfourfreedomspark.org; 9am-5pm Wed-Mon) FREE to President Franklin D Roosevelt opened on the southern tip. Designed by architect Louis Kahn in the 1960s, the monument was built as originally envisioned with only minor tweaks. A tapered lawn lined with linden trees leads down to the island's southern tip. As visitors walk toward the end of V-shaped lawn, they arrive at a small viewing platform, anchored with huge slabs of North Carolina granite. This final space perched over the river is 'the room', offering views of Manhattan through the narrow openings, with the UN building among the most prominently featured landmarks – a clear reference point between the president and one of his crowning achievements. It's a peaceful and sober monument, with many subtle hidden details.

The best way to get to Roosevelt Island is to take the picturesque four-minute aerial tram trip across the East River. Trams leave from the **Roosevelt Island Tramway Station** (212-832-4543; www.rioc.com/transportation.htm; 60th St, at Second Ave; one-way fare $2.25; every 15 min 6am-2am Sun-Thu, to 3am Fri & Sat). Otherwise, take the F train to the Roosevelt Island stop.

tacos, foie gras mousse, scallops, veal sweetbreads), wine ($9 to $12 per glass) and craft beers. Soaring ceilings and brick walls invite lingering, and there's live music on Monday nights (from 9pm), except during football season.

James Wood Foundry British **$$**
Map p200 (212-249-2700; 401 E 76th St, btwn First & York Aves; mains lunch $10-24, dinner $18-32; 11am-2am; ; S 6 to 77th St) Inside a narrow brick building that once housed an ironworks, the James Wood Foundry is a British-inspired gastropub serving first-rate beer-battered fish and chips, bangers and mash, lamb and rosemary pie and other temptations from the other side of the Atlantic. On warm days and nights, grab a table on the enclosed courtyard patio.

Tanoshi Sushi **$$$**
Map p200 (646-727-9056; 1372 York Ave, btwn 73rd & 74th Sts; 12-piece sushi $50; 6-10pm Tue-Sat; S 6 to 77th St) It's not easy to snag one of the 10 stools at this small, wildly popular sushi spot. The setting may be humble, but the flavors are simply magnificent, which might include Hokkaido scallops, Atlantic shad, seared salmon belly or mouth-watering uni (sea urchin). Only sushi is on offer and only *omakase* – the chef's selection of whatever is particularly outstanding that day. It's BYO beer, sake or what-not. Make reservations well in advance.

ant Ambroeus Cafe, Italian **$$$**
Map p200 (212-570-2211; www.santambroeus.com; 1000 Madison Ave, btwn 77th & 78th St; panini $12-18, mains $23-64; 7am-11pm; ; S 6 to 77th St) Behind a demure facade lies this dressy Milanese bistro and cafe that oozes old-world charm. Up front, a long granite counter dispenses rich cappuccinos, pastries and panini (grilled with the likes of parma ham and fontina), while the elegant dining room in the back dishes up northern Italian specialties such as breaded veal chop and saffron risotto. Don't bypass the famed gelato.

Café Boulud French **$$$**
Map p200 (212-772-2600; www.danielnyc.com/cafebouludny.html; 20 E 76th St, btwn Fifth & Madison Aves; mains $24-48; breakfast, lunch & dinner; ; S 6 to 77th St) This Michelin-starred bistro – part of Daniel Boulud's gastronomic empire – attracts a staid crowd with its globe-trotting French cuisine. Seasonal menus include classic dishes such as coq au vin, as well as more inventive fare such as scallop *crudo* (raw) with white miso. Foodies on a budget will be interested in the three-course, $43 prix fixe lunch.

Drinking & Nightlife

Metropolitan Museum Roof Garden Café & Martini Bar Cocktail Bar
Map p200 (www.metmuseum.org; 1000 Fifth Ave, at 82nd St; 10am-4:30pm Sun-Thu, to 8pm Fri & Sat, Martini Bar 5:30-8pm Fri & Sat May-Oct; S 4/5/6 to 86th St) Located within the Met, the roof garden's bar sits right above Central Park's tree canopy, allowing for splendid views of the park and the city skyline all around.

JBird Bar
Map p200 (212-288-8033; 339 E 75th St, btwn First & Second Aves; 5:30pm-2am Mon-Thu, to 4am Fri & Sat; S 6 to 77th St) This rare uptown gem serves craft cocktails and seasonal pub fare in a screen-free environment that feels more downtown than uptown. Grab a seat at the marble bar or (arrive early and) sink into a dark leather banquette.

Penrose Bar
Map p200 (212-203-2751; 1590 Second Ave, btwn 82nd & 83rd Sts; 3pm-4am Mon-Thu, noon-4am Fri, 10:30am-4am Sat & Sun; S 4/5/6 to 86th St) New in 2012, the Penrose brings a much-needed dose of style to the Upper East Side, with craft beers, exposed brick walls, vintage mirrors, floral wallpaper, reclaimed wood details and friendly bartenders setting the stage for a fine evening outing among friends.

Vinus and Marc Lounge
Map p200 (646-692-9015; 1825 Second Ave, btwn 95th & 94th Sts; 3pm-1am Sun-Tue, to 2am Wed & Thu, to 3am Fri & Sat; S 6 to 96th St) Red walls, gilt-edge mirrors, vintage fixtures and a long dark-wood bar sets the stage at this inviting new lounge in Yorkville. There's also good bistro fare (mussels, shrimp and grits, Angus beef tenderloin sandwich).

Drunken Munkey Lounge
Map p200 (338 E 92nd St, btwn First & Second Aves; 11am-2am Mon-Thu, to 3am Fri-Sun; S 6 to 96th St) This playful new lounge channels colonial-era Bombay with vintage wallpaper, cricket-ball door handles and jauntily attired waitstaff.

Money-Saving Tip

The Upper East Side is ground zero for all things luxurious, especially the area that covers the blocks from 60th to 86th Sts between Park and Fifth Aves. If you're looking for eating and drinking spots that are easier on the wallet, head east of Lexington Ave. First, Second and Third Aves are lined with less pricey neighborhood spots.

Bemelmans Bar Lounge

Map p200 (☎212-744-1600; www.thecarlyle.com/dining/bemelmans_bar; Carlyle Hotel, 35 E 76th St, at Madison Ave; ⏲noon-2am Mon-Sat, to 12:30am Sun; S 6 to 77th St) Sink into a chocolate leather banquette and take in the glorious 1940s elegance of this fabled bar – the sort of place where the waiters wear white jackets, a baby grand is always tinkling and the ceiling is 24-carat gold leaf. Show up before 9pm if you don't want to pay a cover (per person $15 to $30).

Entertainment

Frick Collection Classical Music

Map p200 (www.frick.org; 1 E 70th St, at Fifth Ave; admission $35; S 6 to 68th St-Hunter College) Once a month, this opulent mansion-museum hosts a Sunday concert that brings world-renowned performers such as cellist Yehuda Hanani and violinist Thomas Zehetmair.

92nd St Y Cultural Center

Map p200 (www.92y.org; 1395 Lexington Ave, at 92nd St; 👪; S 6 to 96th St) In addition to its wide spectrum of concerts, dance performances and literary readings, this nonprofit cultural center hosts an excellent lecture and conversation series. Playwright Edward Albee, cellist Yo-Yo Ma, funnyman Steve Martin and novelist Gary Shteyngart have all taken the stage.

Shopping

Bloomingdale's Department Store

Map p170 (www.bloomingdales.com; 1000 Third Ave, at E 59th St, Midtown East; ⏲10am-8:30pm Mon-Sat, 11am-7pm Sun; 📶; S 4/5/6 to 59th St, N/Q/R to Lexington Ave-59th St) Blockbuster 'Bloomie's' is something like the Metropolitan Museum of Art of the shopping world: historic, sprawling, overwhelming and packed with bodies, but you'd be sorry to miss it.

Housing Works Thrift Shop Vintage

Map p200 (202 E 77th St, btwn Second & Third Aves; ⏲11am-7pm Mon-Fri, 10am-6pm Sat, noon-5pm Sun; S 6 to 77th St) On good days, you might score a designer jacket, perfectly fitting jeans or a handbag bearing a high-

Bloomingdale's

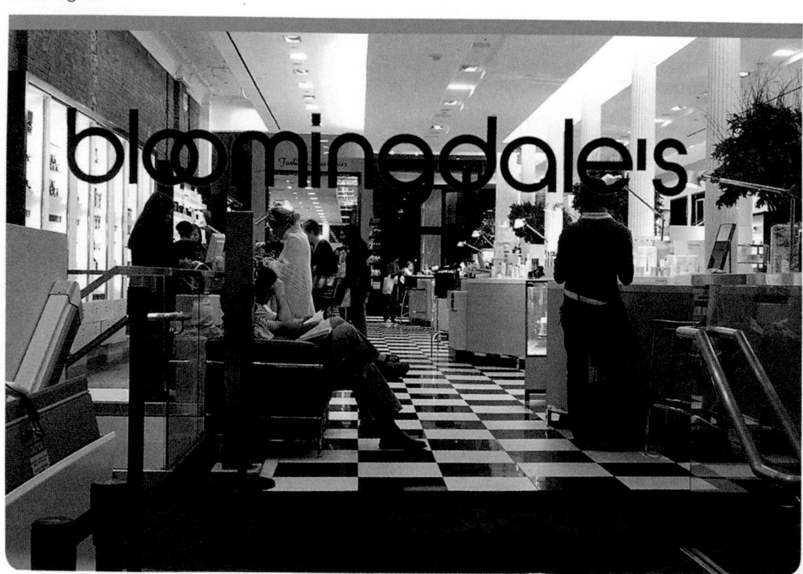

d label. There are also books, CDs and housewares. It gets crowded on weekends.

Michael's Clothing

Map p200 (www.michaelsconsignment.com; 2nd fl, 1041 Madison Ave, btwn 79th & 80th Sts; 9:30am-6pm Mon-Sat, to 8pm Thu; S 6 to 77th St) In operation since the 1950s, this is a vaunted Upper East Side resale store that is strong on high-end labels, including Chanel, Gucci and Prada. It's pricey, but cheaper than shopping the flagship boutiques on Madison Ave.

Crawford Doyle Booksellers Books

Map p200 (1082 Madison Ave, btwn 81st & 82nd Sts; 10am-6pm Mon-Sat, noon-5pm Sun; S 6 to 77th St) This genteel Upper East Side book shop invites browsing, with stacks devoted to art, literature and the history of New York – not to mention plenty of first editions. A wonderful place to while away a chilly afternoon.

Blue Tree Fashion, Homewares

Map p200 (www.bluetreenyc.com; 1283 Madison Ave, btwn 91st & 92nd Sts; 10am-6pm Mon-Fri, from 11am Sat & Sun; S 4/5/6 to 86th St) This charming (and expensive) little boutique, owned by actress Phoebe Cates Kline (of *Fast Times at Ridgemont High*) sells a dainty array of women's clothing, cashmere scarves, Lucite objects, whimsical accessories and quirky home design.

Zitomer Beauty

Map p200 (www.zitomer.com; 969 Madison Ave, btwn 75th & 76th Sts; 9am-8pm Mon-Fri, to 7pm Sat, 10am-6pm Sun; S 6 to 77th St) This multi-story retro pharmacy carries a treasure trove worth of high-end, all-natural skincare products, including brands such as Kiehl's, Clarins, Kneipp, Mustela and Ahava (made from rejuvenating Dead Sea minerals).

Upper West Side & Central Park

A sprawling park and high culture define this neighborhood's unique ecosystem.

Home to aging liberals, wealthy young families and an eclectic mix of actors and musicians, the Upper West Side stretches up along the western side of Central Park to Riverside Park, which runs along the Hudson River. Quaint residential blocks and bustling sections of Broadway have been hyperdeveloped into strips of high-rise condos, drugstore chains and banks. Much of the area is still an architectural wonderland, though, with everything from opulent apartment buildings to the redesigned Lincoln Center.

Designed as a leisure space for all New Yorkers, the vast and majestic Central Park is an oasis from the urban insanity. The lush lawns, cool forests, flowering gardens, glassy bodies of water, and meandering, wooded paths provide the dose of serene nature that New Yorkers crave.

Bow Bridge, Central Park
JAY LAZARIN/GETTY IMAGES ©

Upper West Side & Central Park Highlights

American Museum of Natural History (p227)

Kids of all ages will find something intriguing at the American Museum of Natural History, whether it's the stuffed Alaskan brown bear, the Star of India sapphire in the Hall of Minerals and Gems, the IMAX film on jungle life, or the skullcap of a pachycephalosaurus. Step inside the Rose Center for Earth & Space, a high-tech planetarium that traces the origins of the planets.

1

2

Lincoln Center (p228)

When it comes to the performing arts, few places can rival Lincoln Center. Spread among 16 acres, you'll find world-class opera, ballet, theater and cinema. Following a makeover completed in 2010, the complex is looking better than ever. Don't miss the illuminated facades by night or the summertime concerts.

BARRY WINIKER/GETTY IMAGES ©

New-York Historical Society (p220) 3

Dating back to the early 1800s, this cultural behemoth delves into the city's richly layered history. Fascinating temporary exhibits cover a wide range of topics, from oil paintings by artists of the Hudson River School to photographs of NYC during World War II. Works from the permanent collection feature a mix of artwork, textiles and furniture.

PATTI MCCONVILLE/GETTY IMAGES ©

4 Strawberry Fields (p217)

After the tragic murder of John Lennon in 1980, New York dedicated this peaceful oasis of greenery inside Central Park to his memory. Don't miss the 'Imagine' mosaic, where visitors sometimes leave flowers and other offerings in honor of the great peace advocate. The serene garden, with shrubs and tall elms, provides a meditative escape from the big-city bustle beyond.

5 Loeb Boathouse (p226 & p232)

Perched on the shores of the lake in the heart of Central Park, the historic Loeb Boathouse is one of the city's best settings for an idyllic meal and an escape from the urban madness. It is also an oft-filmed setting. There's no better romantic gesture or first date than renting a rowboat and powering your way around the nooks and crannies of the lake until you find a little corner all of your own.

Upper West Side & Central Park Walk

While real-estate developers have carpeted stretches of Broadway with charmless chains, the Upper West Side is still an architectural bonanza.

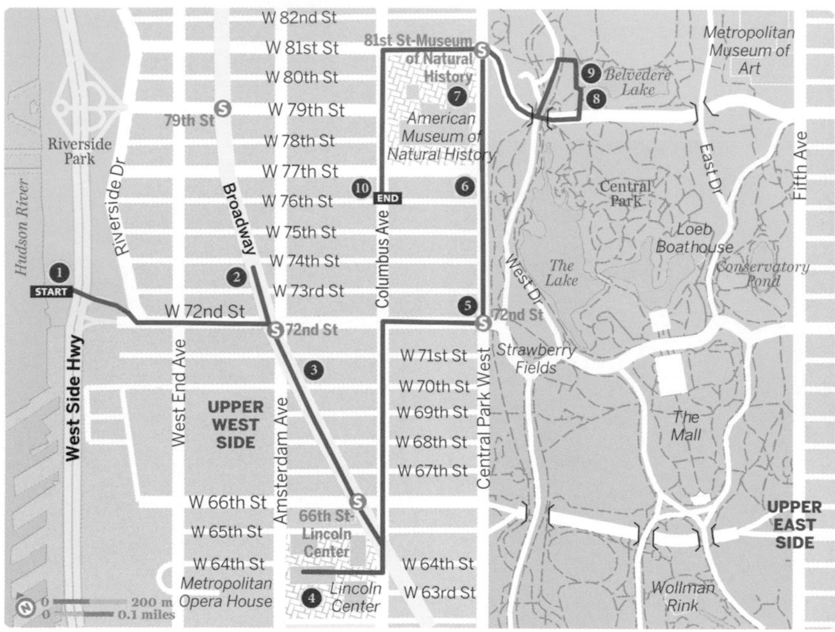

> **WALK FACTS**
> - **Start** Riverside Park
> - **End** Columbus Ave
> - **Distance** 2.3 miles
> - **Duration** One to two hours

1 Riverside Park

Begin your walk in Riverside Park (p221) – a lovely stretch of green on the western edge of the neighborhood. Be sure to visit the wonderful bronze statue of native New Yorker Eleanor Roosevelt, by sculptor Penelope Jencks, added to the park at 72nd St with some pomp and circumstance in 1996.

2 Ansonia

Walk east on 72nd St and turn left on Broadway, heading uptown to the grand and sophisticated Ansonia building between 73rd and 74th Sts.

3 Dorilton

Turn south on Broadway to 71st St to gaze at the Dorilton building, with an enormous entryway and beaux-arts magnificence.

4 Lincoln Center

Continue walking south on Broadway, heading downtown to 64th St and the grand entrance of the Lincoln Center (p228). Take a gander at the large and lovely Chagall paintings in the windows of the Metropolitan Opera House (p229).

Dakota

ad up Columbus Ave to 72nd St and turn ght, continuing east until you hit Central Park West. On your left is the grand Dakota building, used in the film *Rosemary's Baby*. It's also where John Lennon lived, and the site of his 1980 murder. Across the street, just inside Central Park, is Strawberry Fields (p217), a touching shrine to the late star.

6 New-York Historical Society

Continue up along Central Park West to 77th St for a fascinating collection of city ephemera (p220).

7 American Museum of Natural History

The American Museum of Natural History (p227) is one block north and filled with wildlife, geological and astronomical exhibits (it could take an entire day to see it all). At least gaze at the ethereal Rose Center for Earth & Space, on the 79th St side.

8 Belvedere Castle

Enter back into the park at 81st St and cross West Dr until you see the lovely 19th-century Belvedere Castle (p218), which rises up out of Vista Rock and provides breezy, beautiful views of the surrounding parkland; a great perch for a photo.

9 Delacorte Theater

Just on the other side of Turtle Pond is the Delacorte Theater (p218), home to summertime Shakespeare in the Park.

10 Columbus Ave

Head west out of the park to Columbus Ave, where you can stroll the bustling stretch of shops and eateries and get a nice sense of the rhythm of life. If you're up for a different sort of shopping experience, comb through the Greenflea (p232), one of the first open-air city markets.

The Best...

PLACES TO EAT

Gastronomía Culinaria First-rate Italian cooking in an inviting dining room. (p226)

Dovetail For foodies who are watching their dollars, the tasting menu is a bargain. (p229)

Barney Greengrass An Upper West Side classic famed for its lox, herring and sturgeon. (p226)

Jacob's Pickles Microbrews and upscale American comfort food. (p226)

PLACES TO DRINK

Ding Dong Lounge Popular with Columbia students and guests from nearby hostels for its beer-and-a-shot combo. (p229)

Barcibo Enoteca Near Lincoln Center, great for a pre-show glass of expertly curated Italian wine. (p229)

PLACES FOR LIVE PERFORMANCE

Metropolitan Opera House Top stars and mind-boggling costumes and sets. (p229)

Beacon Theatre Like a mini Radio City Music Hall, this renovated concert hall skews to classic rock. (p231)

Smoke Comfy lounge hosting excellent jazz. (p231)

Belvedere Castle
SCOTT DUNN/GETTY IMAGES

Don't Miss
Central Park

Comprising more than 800 acres of picturesque meadows, ponds and woods, it might be tempting to think that Central Park represents Manhattan in its raw state. It does not. Designed by Frederick Law Olmsted and Calvert Vaux, the park is the result of serious engineering: thousands of workers shifted 10 million cartloads of soil to transform swamp and rocky outcroppings into the 'people's park' of today.

Map p222

www.centralparknyc.org

59th & 110th Sts, btwn Central Park West & Fifth Ave

6am-1am

Strawberry Fields

This tear-shaped **garden** (Map p222; www.centralparknyc.org/visit/things-to-see/south-end/strawberry-fields.html; Central Park, at 72nd St on the west side; 🚻; Ⓢ A/C, B to 72nd St) serves as a memorial to former Beatle, John Lennon. The garden is composed of a grove of stately elms and a tiled mosaic that reads, simply, 'Imagine.' Find it at the level of 72nd St on the west side of the park.

Bethesda Terrace & the Mall

The arched walkways of **Bethesda Terrace**, crowned by the magnificent **Bethesda Fountain** (Map p222; at the level of 72nd St), pictured left, have long been a gathering area for New Yorkers of all flavors. To the south is the Mall (featured in countless movies), a promenade shrouded in mature North American elms. The southern stretch, known as **Literary Walk** (Map p222), is flanked by statues of famous authors.

Central Park Zoo

Officially known as the Central Park Wildlife Center (no one calls it that), this small **zoo** (Map p222; ☎212-861-6030; www.centralparkzoo.com; Central Park, 64th St, at Fifth Ave; adult/child $12/7; 🕑10am-5:30pm Apr-Nov, to 4:30pm Nov-Apr; 🚻; Ⓢ N/Q/R to 5th Ave-59th St) is home to snow monkeys, snow leopards and red pandas. Feeding times in the sea lion and penguin tanks make for a rowdy spectacle. (Check the website for times.)

The attached **Tisch Children's Zoo** (Map p222; www.centralparkzoo.com/animals-and-exhibits/exhibits/tisch-childrens-zoo.aspx; Central Park, at 65th & Fifth Ave), a petting zoo, has alpacas and mini-Nubian goats and is perfect for small children.

Conservatory Water & Around

North of the zoo at the level of 74th St is the Conservatory Water, where model sailboats drift lazily and kids scramble about on a toadstool-studded statue of Alice in Wonderland. There are Saturday story hours at the Hans Christian Andersen statue to the west of the water (at 11am from June to September).

Local Knowledge

Central Park

RECOMMENDATIONS FROM 'WILDMAN' STEVE BRILL, AUTHOR, NATURALIST, EDUCATOR AND TOUR GUIDE.

1 THE PARK'S IMPORTANCE

This was the first park designed to mimic nature rather than overly landscaped to resemble a formal garden – the centerpiece of this is the wooded area called the Ramble. Of course, it's since been much imitated. The hills and gradients of some parts of the park, which make it difficult to see very far, were conscious efforts to make the area seem more vast than it is.

2 ANIMALS & PLANTS

The animal life and abundance of intrinsically valuable plants are often overlooked by visitors. There are around 160 edible plants, almost as many with medicinal properties and 40 or so choice gourmet species of mushrooms including hen of the woods and chicken mushrooms.

3 FAVORITES

The red bud trees, one of the first flowering springtime plants found all over the park, are especially beautiful, as are the black locust plants whose white flowers smell like vanilla. There used to be a wild Kentucky coffee tree found just north of the boat house, but sadly it was destroyed in a recent thunderstorm. The roasted seeds taste like coffee, or you can mix them with a concoction of cocoa powder, dark chocolate etc to make delicious chocolate truffles.

4 JAZZ & CHESS

I love the jazz musicians who play near the Delacorte Theater on weekends. I head over there on lunch breaks and jam with them on my 'brillophone' – I cup my hands in front of my mouth and blow. Chess players should check out the area mid-park around 64th St. Of course, I enjoy the zoo, boating, and the simple feeling of peacefulness. And a big improvement is that smoking is no longer allowed.

Below: Central Park Lake & Belvedere Castle
Right: The Great Lawn

MEDIOIMAGES/PHOTODISC/GETTY IMAGES ©

TETRA IMAGES/GETTY IMAGES ©

Ramble

The **Great Lawn** (Map p222; Central Park, btwn 79th & 86th Sts; **S** B, C to 86th St) is a massive emerald carpet at the center of the park – between 79th and 86th Sts – and is surrounded by ball fields and London plane trees. (This is where Simon & Garfunkel played their famous 1981 concert.) Immediately to the southeast is the **Delacorte Theater** (Map p222; Central Park, enter at W 81st St), home to an annual Shakespeare in the Park festival, as well as **Belvedere Castle** (Map p222; 212-772-0210; Central Park, at 79th St; 10am-3pm Tue-Sun; ; **S** B, C, 1/2/3 to 72nd St) FREE, a lookout.

Further south, between 73rd and 79th Sts, is the leafy **Ramble** (Map p222; Central Park, mid-park from 73rd to 79th Sts), a popular birding destination (and legendary gay pick-up spot). On the southeastern end is the **Loeb Boathouse** (p226 and p232), home to a waterside restaurant that offers rowboat and bicycle rentals.

Jacqueline Kennedy Onassis Reservoir

The **reservoir** (Map p222; btwn East & West Drives; **S** B, C to 86th St) takes up almost the entire width of the park at the level of 90th street and serves as a gorgeous reflecting pool for the city skyline. It is surrounded by a 1.58-mile track that draws legions of joggers in the warmer months. Nearby, at Fifth Ave and 90th St, is a statue of New York City Marathon founder Fred Lebow, peering at his watch.

Conservatory Garden

If you want a little peace and quiet (as in, no runners, cyclists or boom boxes), the 6-acre Conservatory Garden serves as one of the park's official quiet zones. And it's beautiful, to boot: bursting with crab apple trees, meandering boxwood and, in the spring, lots of flowers. It's located at 105th St off Fifth Ave. Otherwise, you can catch maximum calm (and maximum bird life) in all areas of the park just after dawn.

Public Art in the Park

Scattered among the many natural sculptures otherwise known as trees is a host of wonderful, freestanding, crafted works of art. If you enter the park at the **Merchants' Gate** (Map p222; Columbus Circle), you'll see the mighty Maine Monument, a tribute to the sailors killed in the mysterious explosion in Havana Harbor in 1898 that sparked the Spanish-American War. Further east, toward the Seventh Ave entrance, there are statues of Latin America's greatest liberators, including José Martí, 'The Apostle of Cuban Independence' (history buffs will find Martí's proximity to the Maine Monument ironic, to say the least). Further east still, at the **Scholars' Gate** (Map p222; Fifth Ave at 60th St), there is a small plaza dedicated to Doris Chanin Freedman, the founder of the Public Art Fund, where you can see a new sculpture every six months or so.

At the **Conservatory Water** (Map p222), model sailboats drift lazily by and kids crawl over the giant toadstools of the **Alice in Wonderland statue** (Map p222). Replete with Alice of flowing hair and dress, a dapper Mad Hatter and mischievous Cheshire Cat, this is a Central Park treasure and a favorite with kids of all ages. Nearby is the Hans Christian Andersen statue, where Saturday story hour (11am from June to September) is an entertaining draw.

Birth of a Park

In the 1850s, the area was occupied by pig farms, a garbage dump, a bone-boiling operation and an African American village. It took 20,000 laborers 20 years to transform this terrain into a park. Today, Central Park has more than 24,000 trees, 136 acres of woodland, 21 playgrounds and seven bodies of water. It attracts more than 38 million visitors a year.

Discover Upper West Side & Central Park

Getting There & Away

- **Subway** On the Upper West Side, the 1, 2 and 3 subway lines are good for destinations along Broadway and points west, while the B and C trains are best for points of interest and access to Central Park. The park can be accessed from all sides, making every subway that travels north–south through Manhattan convenient. The A, C, B, D and 1 all stop at Columbus Circle at Central Park's southwestern edge, while the N, R or Q will leave you at the southeast corner. The 2 or 3 will deposit you at the northern gate in Harlem.
- **Bus** The M104 bus runs north–south along Broadway, and the M10 plies the scenic ride along the western edge of the park. Crosstown buses at 66th, 72nd, 79th, 86th and 96th Sts take you through the park to the Upper East Side. Note that these pick up and drop off passengers at the edge of the park – not inside.

Central Park
SYLVAIN SONNET/GETTY IMAGES ©

Sights

Central Park (p216)

Nicholas Roerich Museum Museum
Map p222 (www.roerich.org; 319 W 107th St, btwn Riverside Dr & Broadway; suggested donation $5; noon-5pm Tue-Fri, from 2pm Sat & Sun; S 1 to Cathedral Pkwy) This compelling little museum, housed in a three-story town house from 1898, is one of the city's best-kept secrets. It contains more than 200 paintings by the prolific Nicholas Konstantinovich Roerich (1874–1947), a Russian-born poet, philosopher and painter. His most remarkable works are his stunning depictions of the Himalayas, where he often traveled.

New-York Historical Society Museum
Map p222 (www.nyhistory.org; 2 W 77th St at Central Park West; adult/child $18/6, by donation 6-8pm Fri, library free; 10am-6pm Tue-Thu & Sat, to 8pm Fri, 11am-5pm Sun; S B, C to 81st St-Museum of Natural History) As the antiquated hyphenated name implies, the Historical Society is the city's oldest museum, founded in 1804 to preserve the city's historical and cultural artifacts. Its collection of more than 60,000 objects is quirky and fascinating and includes everything from George Washington's inauguration chair to a 19th-century Tiffany ice cream dish (gilded, of course).

Zabar's Market
Map p222 (www.zabars.com; 2245 Broadway, at 80th St; 8am-7:30pm Mon-Fri, to 8pm Sat, 9am-6pm Sun; S 1 to 79th St) A bastion of gourmet Kosher foodie-ism, this sprawling local market has been a neighborhood fixture

...ce the 1930s. And what a fixture it is: ...aturing a heavenly array of cheeses, ...meats, olives, caviar, smoked fish, pickles, dried fruits, nuts and baked goods, including pillowy fresh-out-of-the-oven knishes (Eastern European–style potato dumplings wrapped in dough).

American Folk Art Museum Museum

Map p222 (www.folkartmuseum.org; 2 Lincoln Sq, Columbus Ave, at 66th St; noon-7:30pm Tue-Sat, to 6pm Sun; S 1 to 66th St-Lincoln Center) FREE This tiny institution contains a couple of centuries' worth of folk and outsider art treasures, including pieces by Henry Darger (known for his girl-filled battlescapes) and Martín Ramírez (producer of hallucinatory *caballeros* on horseback). There is also an array of wood carvings, paintings, hand-tinted photographs and decorative objects. On Wednesday there are guitar concerts, and there's free music on Friday.

Riverside Park Outdoors

Map p222 (212-870-3070; www.riverside-parknyc.org; Riverside Dr, btwn 68th & 155th Sts; 6am-1am; ; S 1/2/3 to any stop btwn 66th & 157th Sts) A classic beauty designed by Central Park creators Frederick Law Olmsted and Calvert Vaux, this waterside spot, running north on the Upper West Side and banked by the Hudson River from 59th to 158th Sts, is lusciously leafy. Plenty of bike paths and playgrounds make it a family favorite.

From late March through October (weather permitting), a lively waterside restaurant, the **West 79th Street Boat Basin Café** **Map p222 (212-496-5542; www.boatbasincafe.com; W 79th St, at Henry Hudson Parkway; mains $11-19; lunch & dinner Apr-Oct, weather permitting; S 1 to 79th St)** serves a light menu at the level of 79th St. Two other outdoor cafes at the riverfront in the park include the **Hudson Beach Café** **Map p222 (www.hudsonbeachcafe.com; 105th St & Riverside Dr; mains around $14)** off 105th St and the **Pier i Café** **Map p222 (212-362-4450; www.piericafe.com; W 70th St & Riverside Blvd; mains $11-20; lunch & dinner; ; underground rail 1, 2, 3 to 72nd St)** at 70th St.

Eating

Le Pain Quotidien Sandwiches $

Map p222 (www.lepainquotidien.com; Mineral Springs Pavilion, off West Dr, Central Park; mains $10-16; 7am-9pm; ; underground rail B, C to 72nd St) Fresh salads and tartines (open-faced sandwiches) are to be found inside the airy Mineral Springs Pavilion, or outside if you are lucky enough to snag a terrace seat. Other Le Pain treats include beautiful berry tarts, draft beer and big cups (bowls, really) of café au lait (plus free wi-fi). You can also hit the take-out window and have a picnic on Sheep Meadow, just a few steps away.

Shake Shack Burgers $

Map p222 (www.shakeshacknyc.com; 366 Columbus Ave, btwn 77th & 78th Sts; burgers $4-9, shakes $5-7; 10:45am-11pm; ; S B, C, 1/2/3

Summer Happenings in Central Park

During the warm months, the park is home to countless cultural events, many of which are free. The two most popular are **Shakespeare in the Park** (www.shakespeareinthepark.org), which is managed by the Public Theater, and **SummerStage** (www.summerstage.org) FREE, a series of free concerts.

Shakespeare tickets are given out at 1pm on the day of the performance, but if you want to lay your hands on a seat, line up by 8am and make sure you have something to sit on and your entire group with you. Tickets are free and two per person; no latecomers are allowed in line.

SummerStage concert venues are generally opened to the public 1½ hours prior to the start of the show. But if it's a popular act, start queuing up early or you're not getting in.

Upper West Side & Central Park

Upper West Side & Central Park

to 72nd St) The 100% all-natural Angus beef burgers are hard to top, especially when paired with crispy curly fries and a rich, creamy milkshake – although there's also draft beer and wines by the glass or bottle. The portobello mushroom burger is no less satisfying.

Hummus Place — Middle Eastern $

Map p222 (www.hummusplace.com; 305 Amsterdam Ave, btwn 74th & 75th Sts; hummus from $8; lunch & dinner; ; S 1/2/3 to 72nd St) Hummus Place is nothing special in the way of ambience – about eight tables tucked just below street level, fronting a cramped, open kitchen – but it has got amazing hummus platters. They're served warm and with various toppings, from whole chickpeas to fava-bean stew with chopped egg. You'll also find tasty salads, couscous and stuffed grape leaves. Great value.

Fairway — Self-Catering $

Map p222 (www.fairwaymarket.com/store-upper-west-side; 2127 Broadway, at 75th St; 6am-1am; S 1/2/3 to 72nd St) Like a museum of good eats, this incredible grocery spills its lovely mounds of produce into its sidewalk bins, seducing you inside with international goodies, fine cooking oils, nuts, cheeses, prepared foods and, upstairs, an organic market and cafe (look for the stairs near the check-out).

Central Park

THE LUNGS OF NEW YORK

The rectangular patch of green that occupies Manhattan's heart began life in the mid-19th century as a swampy piece of land that was carefully bulldozed into the idyllic naturescape you see today. Since officially becoming Central Park, it has brought New Yorkers of all stripes together in interesting and unexpected ways. The park has served as a place for the rich to show off their fancy carriages (1860s), for the poor to enjoy free Sunday concerts (1880s) and for activists to hold be-ins against the Vietnam War (1960s).

Since then, legions of locals – not to mention travelers from all kinds of faraway places – have poured in to stroll, picnic, sunbathe, play ball and catch free concerts and performances of works by Shakespeare.

Loeb Boathouse
Perched on the shores of the Lake, the historic Loeb Boathouse is one of the city's best settings for an idyllic meal. You can also rent rowboats and bicycles and ride on a Venetian gondola.

Conservatory Garden
The only formal garden in Central Park is perhaps the most tranquil. On the northern end, chrysanthemums bloom in late October. To the south, the park's largest crab apple tree grows by the Burnett Fountain.

Jacqueline Kennedy Onassis Reservoir
This 106-acre body of water covers roughly an eighth of the park's territory. Its original purpose was to provide clean water for the city. Now it's a good spot to catch a glimpse of waterbirds.

Belvedere Castle
A so-called 'Victorian folly,' this Gothic-Romanesque castle serves no other purpose than to be a very dramatic lookout point. It was built by Central Park co-designer Calvert Vaux in 1869.

The park's varied terrain offers a wonderland of experiences. There are quiet, woodsy knolls in the north. To the south is the reservoir, crowded with joggers. There are European gardens, a zoo and various bodies of water. For maximum flamboyance, hit the Sheep Meadow on a sunny day, when all of New York shows up to lounge.

Central Park is more than just a green space. It is New York City's backyard.

FACTS & FIGURES

» **Landscape architects** Frederick Law Olmsted and Calvert Vaux

» **Year that construction began** 1858

» **Acres** 843

» **On film** Hundreds of movies have been shot on location, from Depression-era blockbusters such as *Gold Diggers* (1933) to the monster-attack flick *Cloverfield* (2008).

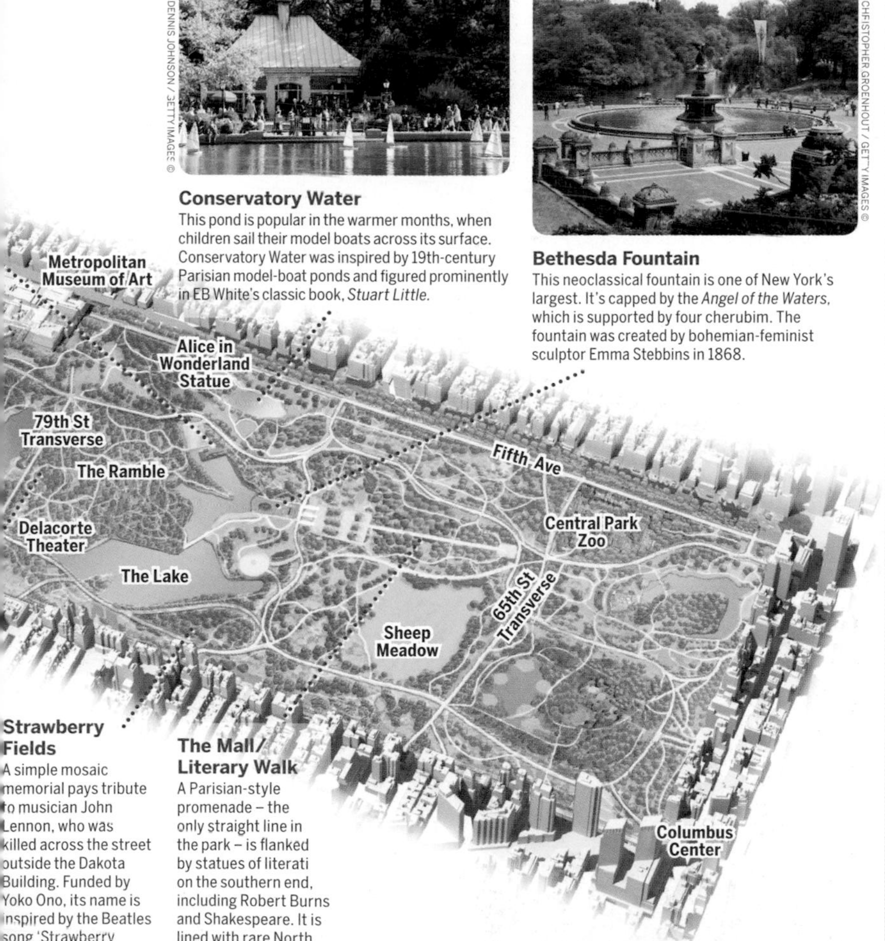

DENNIS JOHNSON / GETTY IMAGES ©

Conservatory Water
This pond is popular in the warmer months, when children sail their model boats across its surface. Conservatory Water was inspired by 19th-century Parisian model-boat ponds and figured prominently in EB White's classic book, *Stuart Little*.

CHRISTOPHER GROENHOUT / GETTY IMAGES ©

Bethesda Fountain
This neoclassical fountain is one of New York's largest. It's capped by the *Angel of the Waters*, which is supported by four cherubim. The fountain was created by bohemian-feminist sculptor Emma Stebbins in 1868.

Strawberry Fields
A simple mosaic memorial pays tribute to musician John Lennon, who was killed across the street outside the Dakota Building. Funded by Yoko Ono, its name is inspired by the Beatles song 'Strawberry Fields Forever.'

The Mall/ Literary Walk
A Parisian-style promenade – the only straight line in the park – is flanked by statues of literati on the southern end, including Robert Burns and Shakespeare. It is lined with rare North American elms.

Kefi Greek **$$**

Map p222 (www.kefirestaurant.com; 505 Columbus Ave, btwn 84th & 85th Sts; small sharing plates $7-10, mains $13-20; noon-3pm & 5-10pm Mon-Fri, from 11am Sat & Sun; ; S B, C to 86th St) This homey, whitewashed eatery run by chef Michael Psilakis channels a sleek taverna vibe while dispensing excellent rustic Greek dishes.

Jacob's Pickles American **$$**

Map p222 (212-470-5566; 509 Amsterdam Ave, btwn 84th & 85th; mains $14-21; 11am-2am Mon-Thu, to 4am Fri, 9am-4am Sat, to 2am Sun) Aside from briny cukes and other preserves, you'll find heaping portions of upscale comfort food, such as catfish tacos, wine-braised turkey leg dinner, and mushroom mac and cheese. The two dozen or so craft beers on tap showcase unique brews from New York, Maine and beyond.

Barney Greengrass Deli **$$**

Map p222 (www.barneygreengrass.com; 541 Amsterdam Ave, at 86th St; mains $9-20, bagel with cream cheese $5; 8:30am-6pm Tue-Sun; ; S 1 to 86th St) The self-proclaimed 'King of Sturgeon' Barney Greengrass serves up the same heaping dishes of eggs and salty lox, luxuriant caviar, and melt-in-your-mouth chocolate babkas that first made it famous when it opened a century ago. Pop in to fuel up in the morning or for a quick lunch; there are rickety tables set amid the crowded produce aisles.

Five Napkin Burger Bistro **$$**

Map p222 (212-333-4488; 2315 Broadway, at 84th St; mains $14-16; 11:30am-midnight; underground rail 1, 2, 3 to 86th St) This inviting spot always draws a crowd, with its juicy burgers and vaguely upmarket brasserie setting – comfy leather booths, big glass windows and outdoor seating in warm weather. Good beer and wine selections.

Peacefood Cafe Vegan **$$**

Map p222 (212-362-2266; www.peacefoodcafe.com; 460 Amsterdam Ave, at 82nd St; paninis $12-13, mains $10-17; 10am-10pm; ; S 1 to 79th St) This bright and airy vegan haven run by Eric Yu dishes up a popular fried seitan panino (served on homemade focaccia and topped with cashew, arugula, tomatoes and pesto), as well as pizzas, roasted vegetable plates and an excellent quinoa salad.

Burke & Wills Modern Australian **$$**

Map p222 (646-823-9251; 226 W 79th St, btwn Broadway & Amsterdam Ave; mains $17-28; 4pm-2am Mon-Fri, from noon Sat & Sun; S 1 to 79th St) New in 2013, this ruggedly attractive bistro and bar brings a touch of the outback to the Upper West Side. The menu leans toward Modern Australian pub grub: juicy kangaroo burgers with triple-fried chips, grilled prawns, kale cobb salad, merguez sausage sliders, and roasted cod with cauliflower, dates and pomegranate.

PJ Clarke's Pub **$$**

Map p222 (212-957-9700; www.pjclarkes.com; 44 W 63rd St, cnr Broadway; burgers $10-14, mains $18-42; 11:30am-1am; S 1 to 66th St-Lincoln Center) Right across the street from Lincoln Center, this red-checker-tablecloth spot has a buttoned down crowd, friendly bartenders and solid eats. If you're in a rush, belly up to the bar for a Black Angus burger and a Brooklyn Lager.

Gastronomía Culinaria Italian **$$**

Map p222 (212-663-1040; 53 W 106th St, btwn Columbus & Manhattan Aves; mains $14-23; 11:30am-10pm Sun-Thu, to 11pm Fri & Sat; S B, C, 1 to 103rd St) For locals, this tongue-twister of a restaurant is more often known as 'that great Italian restaurant on 106th St'. Run by a Roman chef, GC feels like a charming old-world trattoria, its narrow brick-walled dining room the backdrop to richly prepared dishes at reasonable prices.

Loeb Boathouse American **$$$**

Map p222 (212-517-2233; www.thecentralparkboathouse.com; Central Park Lake, Central Park, at 74th St; mains $24-47; restaurant noon-4pm & 5:30-9:30pm Mon-Fri, 9:30am-4pm & 6-9:30pm Sat & Sun; S A/C, B to 72nd St, 6 to 77th St) Perched on the northeastern tip of the Central Park Lake, the Loeb Boathouse, with its views of the Midtown skyline in

BRUCE YUANYUE BI/GETTY IMAGES ©

Don't Miss
American Museum of Natural History

Founded in 1869, this classic museum contains a veritable wonderland of some 30 million artifacts, along with a cutting-edge planetarium. From October through May, the museum is home to the Butterfly Conservatory, featuring 500-plus butterflies from around the globe. On the natural history side, the museum is perhaps best known for its Fossil Halls, containing nearly 600 specimens on view, including the skeletons of a massive mammoth and a fearsome Tyrannosaurus Rex.

There are plentiful animal exhibits, galleries devoted to gems, and an IMAX theater that plays films on natural phenomena. The Milstein Hall of Ocean Life contains dioramas devoted to ecologies, weather and conservation, as well as a beloved 94ft replica of a blue whale. At the 77th St Lobby Gallery, visitors are greeted by a 63ft canoe carved by the Haida people of British Columbia in the middle of the 19th century.

For the space set, the Rose Center For Earth & Space is the star of the show. With its mesmerizing glass box facade, home to space-show theaters and the planetarium, it is indeed an otherworldly setting. Every half-hour between 10:30am and 4:30pm, you can drop yourself into a cushy seat to view Dark Universe, which explores the mysteries and wonders of the cosmos.

Needless to say, the museum is a hit with kids, and as a result, it's swamped on weekends. Aim to go early on a weekday.

NEED TO KNOW

Map p222; ☎212-769-5100; www.amnh.org; Central Park West, at 79th St; suggested donation adult/child $22/12.50; ⏰10am-5:45pm, Rose Center to 8:45pm Fri, Butterfly Conservatory Oct-May; 👪; Ⓢ B, C to 81st St-Museum of Natural History, 1 to 79th St

JOHNNY STOCKSHOOTER/GETTY IMAGES ©

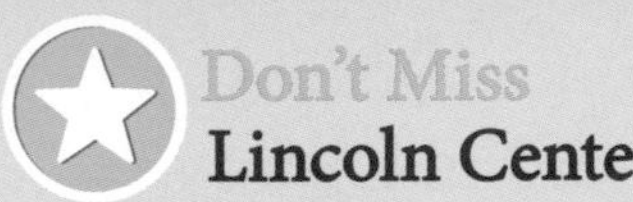

Don't Miss
Lincoln Center

This stark arrangement of gleaming Modernist temples contains some of Manhattan's most important performance spaces: Avery Fisher Hall (home to the New York Philharmonic), David H Koch Theater (site of the New York City ballet), and the iconic Metropolitan Opera House (pictured above), whose interior walls are dressed with brightly saturated murals by painter Marc Chagall. Various other venues are tucked in and around the 16-acre campus, including a theater, two film screening centers and the renowned Juilliard School.

Of the refurbished structures, there are a number that are worth examining, including Alice Tully Hall, now displaying a very contemporary translucent, angled facade, and the David Rubenstein Atrium, a public space offering a lounge area (free wi-fi), a cafe, an information desk and a ticket vendor plying day-of discount tickets to Lincoln Center performances. Free events are held here on Thursday evenings.

On any given night, there are at least 10 performances happening throughout Lincoln Center – and even more in summer, when Lincoln Center Out of Doors (a series of dance and music concerts) and Midsummer Night Swing (ballroom dancing under the stars) lure those who love parks and culture. For details on seasons, tickets and programming – which runs the gamut from opera to dance to theater to ballet – turn to the Entertainment section of this chapter.

Daily tours of the complex explore the Metropolitan Opera House, Revson Fountain and Alice Tully Hall and are a great way to get acquainted with the complex.

NEED TO KNOW

Map p222 ☎ 212-875-5456; http://lc.lincolncenter.org; Columbus Ave btwn 62nd & 66th Sts; public plazas free, tours adult/student $18/15; 👪; S 1 to 66th St-Lincoln Center

...istance, provides one of New York's ...st idyllic spots for a meal.

If you want to experience the location without having to lay out the bucks, a better bet is to hit the adjacent Bar & Grill (plates $16), where you can still get crab cakes and excellent views.

Café Luxembourg French **$$$**

Map p222 (☎212-873-7411; www.cafeluxembourg.com; 200 W 70th St, btwn Broadway & West End Ave; lunch mains $18-29, dinner mains $25-36; ⏰breakfast, lunch & dinner daily, brunch Sun; S1/2/3 to 72nd St) This quintessential French bistro is generally crowded with locals – and it's no mystery why: the setting is elegant, the staff friendly, and there's an outstanding menu to boot. The classics – salmon tartare, cassoulet and steak *frites* (fries) – are all deftly executed, and its proximity to Lincoln Center makes it a perfect pre-performance destination.

Dovetail Modern American **$$$**

Map p222 (☎212-362-3800; www.dovetailnyc.com; 103 W 77th St, cnr Columbus Ave; tasting menu $88, mains $36-58; ⏰5:30-10pm Mon-Sat, 11:30am-10pm Sun; 🌱; SA/C, B to 81st St-Museum of Natural History, 1 to 79th St) This Michelin-starred restaurant showcases its Zen-like beauty in both its decor (exposed brick, bare tables) and its delectable seasonal menus. On Mondays, chef John Fraser has a four-course vegetarian tasting menu ($58) that is winning over carnivores with dishes such as plump hen-of-the-woods mushrooms with d'anjou pears and green peppercorns.

Drinking & Nightlife

Barcibo Enoteca Wine Bar

Map p222 (www.barciboenoteca.com; 2020 Broadway, cnr 69th St; ⏰4:30pm-12:30am Mon-Fri, from 3:30pm Sat & Sun; S1/2/3 to 72nd St) Just north of Lincoln Center, this casual chic marble-table spot is ideal for sipping, with a long list of vintages from all over Italy, including 40 different varieties sold by the glass.

Dead Poet Bar

Map p222 (www.thedeadpoet.com; 450 Amsterdam Ave, btwn 81st & 82nd Sts; ⏰noon-4am; S1 to 79th St) This skinny, mahogany-paneled pub has been a neighborhood favorite for more than a decade, with a mix of locals and students nursing pints of Guinness.

Ding Dong Lounge Bar

Map p222 (www.dingdonglounge.com; 929 Columbus Ave, btwn 105th & 106th Sts; ⏰4pm-4am; SB, C, 1 to 103rd St) It's hard to be too bad-ass in the Upper West, but this former crack den turned punk bar makes a wholesome attempt by supplying graffiti-covered bathrooms to go with its exposed-brick walls.

Manhattan Cricket Club Cocktail Lounge

Map p222 (226 W 79th St, btwn Amsterdam Ave & Broadway; ⏰7pm-2am Tue-Sat; S1 to 79th St) Above the Aussie bistro **Burke & Wills** (p226), this elegant drinking lounge is modeled on the classy Anglo-Aussie cricket clubs of the early 1900s. Sepia-toned photos of batsmen and bowlers in action adorn the gold brocaded walls, while a mahogany-lined wall of books, Chesterfield sofas and an elaborate tin ceiling all create a fine setting for quaffing well-made but pricey cocktails (at $18 each).

Entertainment

Lincoln Center

In addition to the venues and companies listed below, the Vivian Beaumont Theater and the Mitzi E Newhouse Theater showcase works of drama and musical theater. Both of these have programming information listed on Lincoln Center's main website at http://lc.lincolncenter.org.

Metropolitan Opera House Opera

Map p222 (www.metopera.org; Lincoln Center, 64th St, at Columbus Ave; S1 to 66th St-Lincoln Center) New York's premier opera company, the Metropolitan Opera is the place to see classics such as *Carmen, Madame Butterfly* and *Macbeth,* not to mention

Wagner's *Ring Cycle*. The season runs from September to April.

You can get bargain-priced standing-room tickets ($17 to $25) starting at 10am on the day of the performance. (You won't see much, but you'll hear everything.) Two hours before shows on Monday through Thursday, 200 rush tickets are put on sale for starving artist types – just $20 for an orchestra seat (excluding galas and opening nights)! Line up early.

Film Society of Lincoln Center Cinema

(☎212-875-5456; www.filmlinc.com; S 1 to 66th St-Lincoln Center) The Film Society is one of New York's cinematic gems, providing an invaluable platform for a wide gamut of documentary, feature, independent, foreign and avant-garde art pictures. Films screen in one of two facilities at Lincoln Center: the new **Elinor Bunin Munroe Film Center** Map p222 (☎212-875-5601, film schedule 212-875-5600; www.filmlinc.com; Lincoln Center, 144 W 65th St; S 1 to 66 St-Lincoln Center), a more intimate, experimental venue, or the **Walter Reade Theater** Map p222 (☎212-875-5600; www.filmlinc.com; Lincoln Center, 165 W 65th St; S 1 to 66th St-Lincoln Center), with wonderfully wide, screening room–style seats.

New York Philharmonic Classical Music

Map p222 (www.nyphil.org; Avery Fisher Hall, Lincoln Center, cnr Columbus Ave & 65th St; 👪; S 1 to 66 St-Lincoln Center) The oldest professional orchestra in the US (dating back to 1842) holds its season every year at Avery Fisher Hall. Directed by Alan Gilbert, the son of two Philharmonic musicians, the orchestra plays a mix of classics (Tchaikovsky, Mahler, Haydn) and contemporary works, as well as concerts geared towards children.

New York City Ballet Dance

Map p222 (☎212-496-0600; www.nycballet.com; David H Koch Theater, Lincoln Center, Columbus Ave, at 62nd St; 👪; S 1 to 66th St-Lincoln Center) This prestigious company was

Left: Peacefood Cafe (p226); **Below:** Wollman Skating Rink (p233)
(LEFT) LONELY PLANET/GETTY IMAGES ©; (BELOW) STEVEN GREAVES/GETTY IMAGES ©

first directed by renowned Russian-born choreographer George Balanchine back in the 1940s. Today, the company has 90 dancers and is the largest ballet organization in the US, performing 23 weeks a year at Lincoln Center's David H Koch Theater. During the holidays the troop is best known for its annual production of *The Nutcracker*.

Upper West Side

Beacon Theatre Live Music

Map p222 (www.beacontheatre.com; 2124 Broadway, btwn 74th & 75th Sts; S 1/2/3 to 72nd St) This historic theater from 1929 is a perfect in-between-size venue, with 2600 seats (not a terrible one in the house) and a constant flow of popular acts, from Nick Cave to the Allman Brothers.

Cleopatra's Needle Club

Map p222 (www.cleopatrasneedleny.com; 2485 Broadway, btwn 92nd & 93rd Sts; ⏲ 4pm-late; S 1/2/3 to 96th St) Named after an Egyptian obelisk that resides in Central Park, this venue is small and narrow like its namesake. There's no cover, but there's a $10 minimum spend. Come early and you can enjoy happy hour (3:30pm to 6 or 7pm), when select cocktails are half-price.

Smoke Jazz

Map p222 (www.smokejazz.com; 2751 Broadway, btwn 105th & 106th Sts; ⏲ 5:30pm-3am Mon-Fri, 11am-3am Sat & Sun; S 1 to 103rd St) This swank but laid-back lounge – with good stage views from plush sofas – brings out old-timers and local faves, like George Coleman and Wynton Marsalis. Most nights there's a $10 cover, plus a $20 to $30 food and drink minimum. Purchase tickets online for weekend shows.

Symphony Space Live Music

Map p222 (☎ 212-864-5400; www.symphonyspace.org; 2537 Broadway, btwn 94th & 95th Sts; 👪; S 1/2/3 to 96th St) Symphony Space is a multidisciplinary gem supported by the local community. It often hosts three-day series that are dedicated to one musician, and has an affinity for world music, theater, film, dance and literature (with appearances by acclaimed writers).

Shopping

Greenflea Market

Map p222 (212-239-3025; www.greenfleamarkets.com; Columbus Ave, btwn 76th & 77th Sts; 10am-5:30pm Sun; S B, C to 81st St-Museum of Natural History, 1 to 79th St) One of the oldest open-air shopping spots in the city, this friendly, well-stocked flea market is a perfect activity for a lazy Upper West Side Sunday morning.

Westsider Books Books

Map p222 (www.westsiderbooks.com; 2246 Broadway, btwn 80th & 81st Sts; 10am-10pm; S 1 to 79th St) This great little shop is packed to the gills with rare and used books, including a good selection of fiction and illustrated tomes.

Westsider Records Music

Map p222 (212-874-1588; www.westsiderbooks.com/recordstore.html; 233 W 72nd St, btwn Broadway & West End Ave; 11am-7pm Mon-Thu, to 9pm Fri & Sat, noon-6pm Sun; S 1/2/3 to 72nd St) Featuring more than 30,000 LPs, this shop has got you covered when it comes to everything from funk to jazz to classical (plus spoken word, film soundtracks and other curiosities).

Century 21 Department Store

Map p222 (www.c21stores.com; 1972 Broadway, btwn 66th & 67th Sts; 10am-10pm Mon-Sat, 11am-8pm Sun; S 1 to 66th St-Lincoln Center) Exceedingly popular with fashionable locals and foreign travelers, the Century 21 chain is a bounty of season-old brand name and designer brands sold at steeply discounted prices.

Sports & Activities

Loeb Boathouse Kayaking, Cycling

Map p222 (212-517-2233; www.thecentralparkboathouse.com; Central Park, btwn 74th & 75th Sts; boating per hr $12, bike rentals per hr $9-15; 10am-dusk Apr-Nov; ; S B, C to 72nd St, 6 to 77th St) Central Park's boathouse has a fleet of 100 rowboats plus three kayaks available for rent from April to November. In the summer, there is also a Venetian-style gondola that seats up to six ($30 per 30 minutes). Bicycles are also available from April to November. Rentals require an ID and credit card and are weather permitting. Helmets included.

Bike & Roll Cycling

Map p222 (www.bikeandroll.com/newyork; Columbus Circle, at Central Park West; rentals per hr/day $14/44; 9am-7pm Mar-May, 8am-8pm Jun-Aug, 10am-4pm Sep-Nov; ; S A/C, B/D, 1/2 to

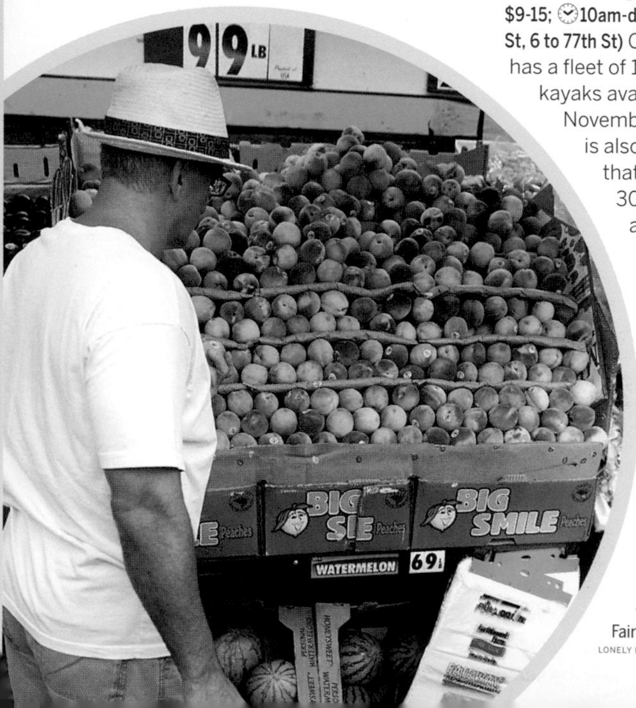

Fairway (p223)

9th St-Columbus Circle) At the southwestern entrance to the park, a small pop-up kiosk dispenses beach cruisers and 10-speeds for rides around Central Park. It also has child seats and tandem bikes.

Champion Bicycles Inc — Cycling

Map p222 (212-662-2690; www.championbicycles.com; 896 Amsterdam Ave, at 104th St; rentals per hr/day from $7/40; 10am-7pm Mon-Fri, to 6pm Sat & Sun; S 1 to 103rd St) This places stocks a variety of bikes for rent and has free copies of the helpful **NYC Cycling Map** (www.nyc.gov/bikes), which details several hundred miles of bike lanes around New York City.

Wollman Skating Rink — Ice Skating

Map p222 (212-439-6900; www.wollmanskatingrink.com; Central Park, btwn 62nd & 63rd Sts; adult Mon-Thu $11/Fri-Sun $18, child $6, skate rentals $8, lock rental $5, spectator fee $5; Nov-Mar; ; S F to 57 St, N/Q/R to 5th Ave-59th St) Larger than the Rockefeller Center skating rink, and allowing all-day skating, this rink is at the southeastern edge of Central Park and offers nice views. It's open mid-October through early April. Cash only.

HARLEM·LOVE
AMERICA
HAITI
CHINA
FINLAND
PERU
JAMAICA
PANAMA
Canada
JAPAN
GERMANY
MICHAEL
4 MICAEL
FOUR
ALPHA
BLONDY

Upper Manhattan & the Outer Boroughs

Upper Manhattan (p236)

The top half of Manhattan covers a lot of territory including an extravagant museum, a soaring cathedral and a vibrant neighborhood which is still a bastion of African-American culture.

Brooklyn (p240)

Historic 'hoods, hopping nightlife, gorgeous riverside parks and world-class museums – Brooklyn has everything the sophisticated and hip urbanite needs. Manhattan? Who needs it?

Queens (p247)

Throughout Queens' mighty ethnic and cultural sprawl are several top-flight museums. On the streets you'll find a cross section of humanity chattering in a million different languages. It's unmistakably New York.

Michael Jackson memorial, Harlem

Upper Manhattan

Harlem, a neighborhood soaked in history, remains one of the country's most fabled centers of African American life – it's where Cab Calloway crooned, where Ralph Ellison penned *Invisible Man* and where Romare Bearden pieced together his first collages. Like everywhere else in New York, however, Harlem is changing. National chains now blanket 125th St and of-the-moment eateries, luxury condos and young professionals (of all creeds and races) are moving in.

Just above the Upper West Side is Morningside Heights – a neighborhood covering the area between 110th and 125th Sts on the far west side, and a bedroom community for Columbia University. Nearby is the glorious Gothic-style Cathedral Church of St John the Divine, the largest place of worship in the US.

Inwood, at Manhattan's northern tip (from about 175th St), is a chilled-out residential zone with lovely parks and an extravagant must-see museum.

Getting There & Away

Subway Harlem's main drag – 125th St – is just one subway stop from the 59th St–Columbus Circle Station in Midtown on the A and D trains. Other areas of Harlem and northern Manhattan can be reached on the A/C, B/D, 1/2/3 and 4/5/6 trains.

Bus Dozens of buses ply the north–south route between Upper and Lower Manhattan along all the major avenues. The M10 bus provides a scenic trip along the west side of Central Park into Harlem. The M100 and the M101 run east to west along 125th St.

Taxi If yellow cabs are in short supply, look for bright green Boro Taxis which service Upper Manhattan, Queens and Brooklyn; they function by the meter, just like yellow cabs.

Sights

Cloisters Museum & Gardens — Museum

(www.metmuseum.org/cloisters; Fort Tryon Park; suggested donation adult/child $25/free; 10am-5pm; S A to 190th St) On a hilltop overlooking the Hudson River, the Cloisters is a curious architectural jigsaw made up of various European monasteries and other historic buildings. Built in the 1930s to house the Metropolitan Museum's medieval treasures, its frescoes, tapestries and paintings are set in galleries that sit around a romantic courtyard, connected by grand archways and topped with a Moorish terra-cotta roof. Among the museum's many rare treasures is the the beguiling 16th-century tapestry series *The Hunt of the Unicorn*.

Apollo Theater — Historic Building

(212-531-5300, tours 212-531-5337; www.apollotheater.org; 253 W 125th St at Frederick Douglass Blvd; tours weekdays/weekends $16/18; S A/C, B/D to 125th St) The Apollo has been Harlem's leading space for concerts and political rallies since 1914 and, with its gleaming marquee, is one of the neighborhood's most visible icons. Virtually every major African American artist in the 1930s and '40s performed here, including Duke Ellington and Billie Holiday. Decades on, this NYC landmark delivers a thriving program of music, dance, master classes and special events.

Its most famous event is the long-running Amateur Night – 'where stars are born and legends are made' – which takes place every Wednesday night. The wild and ruthless crowd is as fun to watch as the performers.

Studio Museum in Harlem — Museum

(212-864-4500; www.studiomuseum.org; 144 W 125th St at Adam Clayton Powell Jr Blvd, Harlem; suggested donation $7, free Sun; noon-9pm Thu & Fri, 10am-6pm Sat, noon-6pm Sun; S 2/3 to 125th St) This small cultural gem has been exhibiting the works of African American artists for more than four decades. While its rotating exhibition program is always

Upper Manhattan & the Outer Boroughs

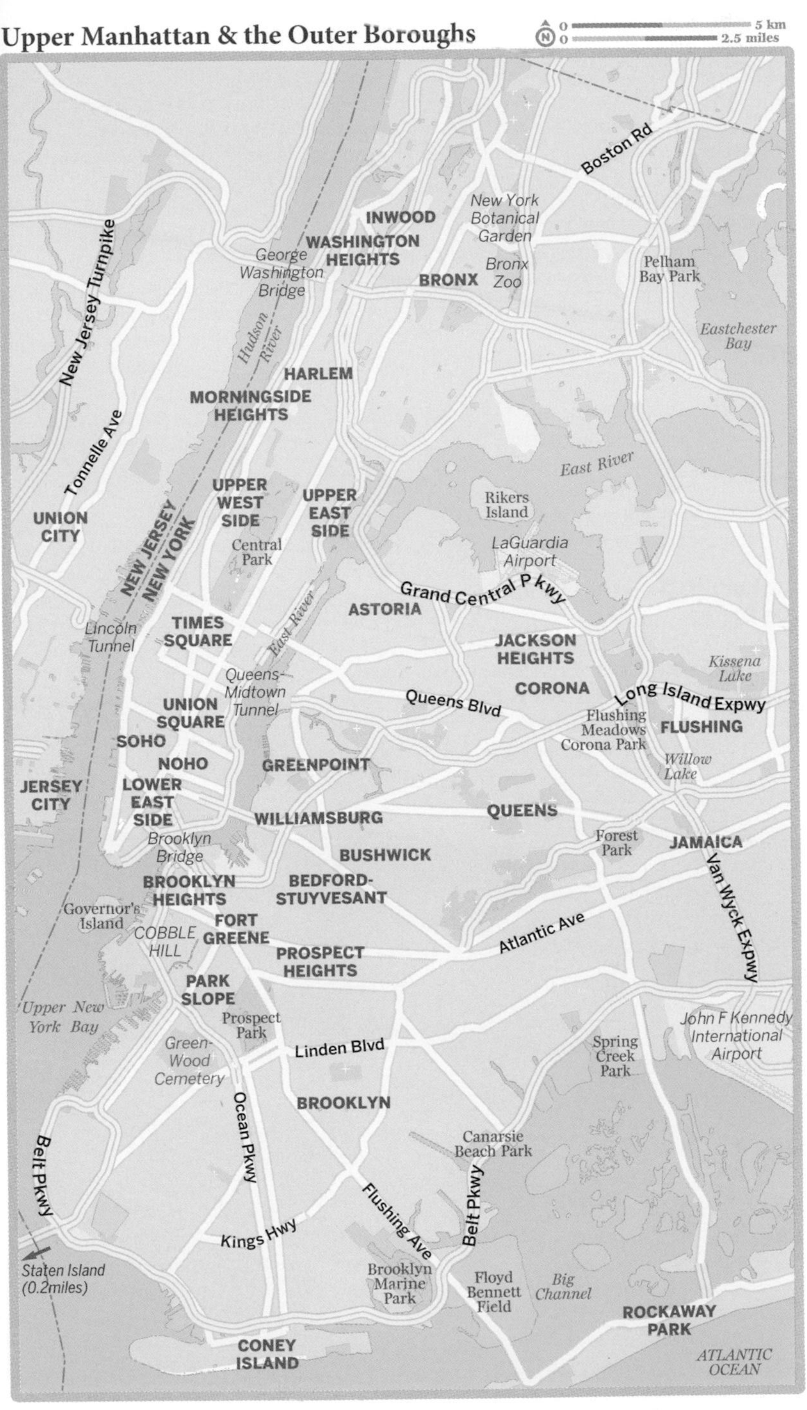

0 5 km
0 2.5 miles
Boston Rd
New York Botanical Garden
INWOOD
WASHINGTON HEIGHTS
George Washington Bridge
BRONX
Bronx Zoo
Pelham Bay Park
Eastchester Bay
New Jersey Turnpike
Hudson River
HARLEM
MORNINGSIDE HEIGHTS
Tonnelle Ave
East River
Rikers Island
UPPER WEST SIDE
UPPER EAST SIDE
UNION CITY
NEW JERSEY
NEW YORK
Central Park
LaGuardia Airport
Grand Central P kwy
ASTORIA
Lincoln Tunnel
TIMES SQUARE
East River
JACKSON HEIGHTS
Kissena Lake
Queens-Midtown Tunnel
Queens Blvd
CORONA
Long Island Expwy
UNION SQUARE
Flushing Meadows Corona Park
FLUSHING
SOHO
NOHO
GREENPOINT
Willow Lake
JERSEY CITY
LOWER EAST SIDE
WILLIAMSBURG
QUEENS
Brooklyn Bridge
Forest Park
JAMAICA
BUSHWICK
BROOKLYN HEIGHTS
BEDFORD-STUYVESANT
Van Wyck Expwy
Governor's Island
COBBLE HILL
FORT GREENE
Atlantic Ave
PROSPECT HEIGHTS
PARK SLOPE
Upper New York Bay
Prospect Park
John F Kennedy International Airport
Green-Wood Cemetery
Linden Blvd
Spring Creek Park
Ocean Pkwy
BROOKLYN
Belt Pkwy
Canarsie Beach Park
Flushing Ave
Belt Pkwy
Kings Hwy
Staten Island (0.2miles)
Brooklyn Marine Park
Floyd Bennett Field
Big Channel
ROCKAWAY PARK
CONEY ISLAND
ATLANTIC OCEAN

challenging, the museum is not just another art display center. It is an important point of connection for Harlem cultural figures of all stripes, who arrive to check out a rotating selection of shows, attend film screenings or sign up for gallery talks.

Yankee Stadium Stadium

(**☎718-508-3917, 718-293-6000; www.yankees.com; E 161st St at River Ave; tours $20; ⏰call for hrs; Ⓢ B/D, 4 to 161st St-Yankee Stadium)** The Boston Red Sox like to talk about their record of two World Series championships in the last 80 years, but the Yankees have won a mere 27 in that period. The team's magic appears to have moved with them across 161st St to the new Yankee Stadium, where they played their first season in 2009 – winning the World Series there in a six-game slugfest against the Phillies. The Yankees play from April to October.

Cathedral Church of St John the Divine Church

(**☎tours 212-932-7347; www.stjohndivine.org; 1047 Amsterdam Ave at W 112th St; suggested donation $10, highlights tour $6, vertical tour $15; ⏰7:30am-6pm; Ⓢ B, C, 1 to 110th St-Cathedral Pkwy)** The largest place of worship in the United States has yet to be completed – and probably won't be any time soon. But this storied Episcopal cathedral nonetheless commands attention with its ornate Byzantine-style facade, booming vintage organ and extravagantly scaled nave – twice as wide as Westminster Abbey in London.

If it is ever completed, the 601ft-long cathedral will rank as the third-largest church in the world, after St Peter's Basilica in Rome and Basilica of Our Lady of Peace at Yamoussoukro in Côte d'Ivoire.

Tours are offered at 11am and 1pm Saturdays and at 1pm Sundays. Vertical tours, which take you on a steep climb to the top of the cathedral (bring your own flashlight), are at noon and 2pm Saturdays.

Columbia University University

(**www.columbia.edu; Broadway at 116th St, Morningside Heights; Ⓢ 1 to 116th St-Columbia University)** FREE Founded in 1754 as King's College downtown, the oldest university in New York is now one of the premiere research institutions in the world. It moved to its current location (the site of a former insane asylum) in 1897, where its gated campus now channels a staid, New

Yankee Stadium

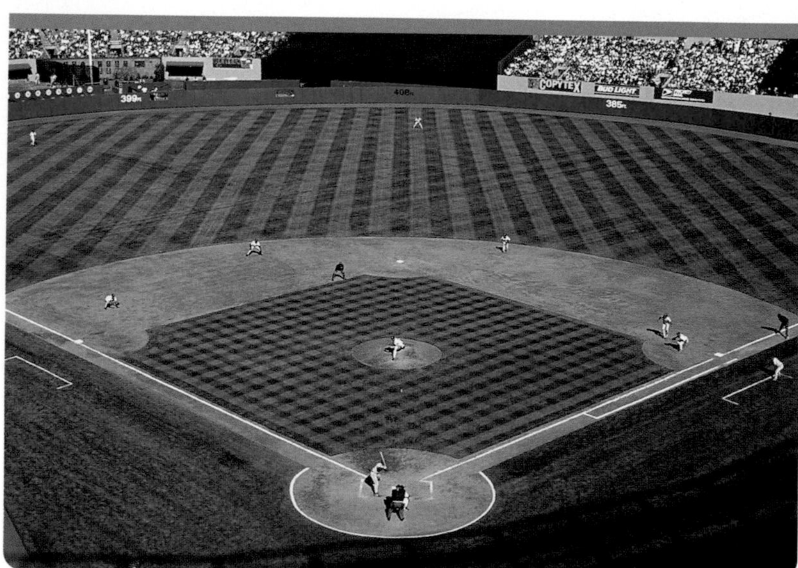

Full Pews: Gospel Church Services in Harlem

What started as an occasional pilgrimage has turned into a tourist-industry spectacle: entire busloads of travelers now make their way to Harlem every Sunday to attend a gospel service. The volume of visitors is so high that some churches turn people away due to space constraints. In some cases, tourists have been known to outnumber congregants.

Naturally, this has led to friction. Many locals are upset by visitors who chat during sermons, leave in the middle of services or show up in skimpy attire. Plus, for some, there's the uncomfortable sense that African American spirituality is something to be consumed like a Broadway show.

The churches, to their credit, remain welcoming spaces. But if you do decide to attend, be respectful: dress modestly (Sunday best!), do not take pictures and remain present for the duration of the service.

Sunday services generally start at 11am and can last for two or more hours. Below are just a few of the roughly five dozen participating churches.

Abyssinian Baptist Church (www.abyssinian.org; 132 W 138th St btwn Adam Clayton Powell Jr & Malcolm X Blvds; S 2/3 to 135th St) This famed congregation, now more than a century old, is the number one spot for foreign travelers (hence the separate tourist-seating section). It's so popular, in fact, that it offers a shorter Wednesday night service.

Canaan Baptist Church (www.cbccnyc.org; 132 W 116th St btwn Adam Clayton Powell Jr & Malcolm X Blvds; 👪; S 2/3 to 116th St) A neighborhood church, founded in 1932.

Convent Avenue Baptist Church (☎ 212-234-6767; www.conventchurch.org; 420 W 145th St at Convent Ave; S A/C, B/D or 1 to 145th St) Traditional baptist services since the 1940s.

Greater Hood Memorial AME Zion Church (www.greaterhood.org; 160 W 146th St btwn Adam Clayton Powell Jr & Malcolm X Blvds; 👪; S 3 to 145th) Also hosts hip-hop services on Thursdays at 6.30pm.

England vibe and offers plenty in the way of cultural happenings.

Eating & Drinking

Dinosaur Bar-B-Que Steakhouse **$$**
(www.dinosaurbarbque.com; 700 W 125th St at Twelfth Ave; meals $7-27; ⏰ 11:30am-11pm Mon-Thu, to 1am Fri & Sat, noon-10pm Sun; 📶; S 1 to 125th St) Jocks, hipsters, moms and pops: everyone dives into this honky-tonk rib bar for a rockin' feed. Get messy with dry-rubbed, slow-pit-smoked ribs, slabs of juicy steak, and succulent burgers, or watch the waist with the lightly seasoned grilled-chicken options.

Amy Ruth's Restaurant Southern **$$**
(www.amyruthsharlem.com; 113 W 116th St near Malcolm X Blvd; waffles $8.95-16.95, mains $12-22; ⏰ 11am-11pm Mon, 8:30am-11pm Tue-Thu, 8:30am-5am Fri, 7.30am-5am Sat, 7:30am-11pm Sun; S B, C, 2/3 to 116th St) This perennially crowded restaurant is *the* place to go for classic soul food, serving up fried catfish, mac'n'cheese and fluffy biscuits. But it's the waffles that are most famous – dished up 14 different ways, including with shrimp.

New Leaf Cafe Modern American **$$**
(☎ 212-568-5323; www.newleafrestaurant.com; 1 Margaret Corbin Dr, Inwood; lunch mains $12-20, dinner mains $18-30; ⏰ noon-3.30pm Mon, noon-9pm Tue-Thu, noon-10pm Fri, 11am-3.30pm & 6-10pm Sat, 11am-3.30pm & 6-9pm Sun; S A

to 190th St) Nestled into Fort Tryon Park, a short jaunt from the Cloisters Museum & Gardens (p236), this 1930s stone edifice feels like a distinguished country tavern. Settle in for seasonal produce made good in classic salads and pasta dishes, and regional seafood comforters including Maryland crab cakes. On sunny days, the outdoor patio is a perfect spot for brunch.

Red Rooster Modern American **$$$**
(www.redroosterharlem.com; 310 Malcolm X Blvd btwn 125th & 126th Sts, Harlem; mains $17-36; ⌚11:30am-10:30pm Mon-Fri, 10am-11pm Sat & Sun; S 2/3 to 125th St) Transatlantic super chef Marcus Samuelsson laces upscale comfort food with a world of flavors at his effortlessly cool, swinging brasserie. Here, mac'n'cheese joins forces with lobster, dirty rice gets the aged basmati treatment, and spectacular Swedish meatballs salute Samuelsson's home country. The prix-fixe lunch is a bargain at $25, and there's a soul-lifting Sunday gospel brunch in the basement supper club, **Ginny's** (p240).

Ginny's Supper Club Cocktail Bar
(www.ginnyssupperclub.com; 310 Malcolm X Blvd btwn 125th & 126th Sts; ⌚7pm-2am Thu, 6pm-3am Fri & Sat, Sun brunch sittings 10:30am & 12:30pm, closed Sun evening; S 2/3 to 125th St) Like something straight out of *Boardwalk Empire,* this roaring basement supper club is never short of styled-up punters sipping cocktails, nibbling on soul and global bites (from Red Rooster's (p239) competent kitchen), and grooving to sultry jazz, blues, or fat DJ beats. Highlights include Monday night's Rakiem Walker Project (an ensemble featuring Red Rooster staffers), and Sunday's life-affirming gospel brunch.

Bier International Beer Hall
(www.bierinternational.com; 2099 Frederick Douglass Blvd at 113th St; ⌚4pm-1am Mon, to 2am Tue-Thu, to 4am Fri, noon-4am Sat, noon-1am Sun; S B, C, 1 to 110th St-Cathedral Pkwy, 2/3 to 110th St-Central Park North) A fun, buzzing beer garden that peddles more than a dozen drafts and a full menu of eats to choose from. The truffle fries with Parmesan make a great accompaniment to the Bier Stiefel (beer in a boot glass).

Brooklyn

If Brooklyn were its own city, it'd be the fourth largest in the US. It is home to more than 2.5 million people and is a rambling 71 sq miles (easily three times larger than Manhattan); one set of subway lines services the north end of the borough, and another set travels to points south. So if you think you can see it all in a day, as the locals say: 'Fuhgeddaboudit!'

For day-trip purposes, it is best to pick a neighborhood and stick to it. South Brooklyn, especially brownstone-studded Brooklyn Heights, offers lots of history and great Manhattan views. Fans of vintage amusement parks should head to Coney Island. For the night owls, the trendy enclave of Williamsburg lies just a single subway stop from Manhattan and is loaded with bars and restaurants.

Getting There & Away

Subway Sixteen subway lines travel between Manhattan and Brooklyn, with an additional line (the G) connecting the Park Slope area of Brooklyn to Williamsburg and Queens. For southern Brooklyn, you'll want the A/C line that stops in Brooklyn Heights, downtown and Bed-Stuy. Park Slope and Coney Island are serviced by the D/F and the N/Q. Brooklyn Heights, downtown and Prospect Heights can be accessed by the 2/3 and the 4/5. In north Brooklyn, Bushwick and Williamsburg are reached primarily on the L.

Need to Know

- **Area code** ☎718
- **Location** Across the East River from Manhattan.
- **Tourist office** (☎718-802-3846; www.visitbrooklyn.org; 209 Joralemon St btwn Court St & Brooklyn Bridge Blvd; ⌚10am-6pm Mon-Fri; S 2/3, 4/5 to Borough Hall)

Sights

Brooklyn Bridge Park

Brooklyn Bridge Park — Park

(☎718-222-9939; www.brooklynbridgeparknyc.org; East River Waterfront, btwn Atlantic Ave & Adams St; 🕒6am-1am; 👪; Ⓢ A/C to High St, 2/3 to Clark St, F to York St) FREE This 85-acre park is one of Brooklyn's most talked-about new sights. Wrapping around a bend on the East River, it runs for 1.3 miles from Jay St in Dumbo to the west end of Atlantic Ave in Cobble Hill. It has revitalized a once-barren stretch of shoreline, turning a series of abandoned piers into public park land. There's also a few seasonal concessions (May to October), including wood-fired pizza, beer and Italian treats at **Fornino** (www.fornino.com; Pier 6, Brooklyn Bridge Park), which has a rooftop deck (it's a short stroll from the end of Atlantic Ave). A free seasonal ferry runs on weekends from Pier 6 to Governor's Island.

Empire Fulton Ferry State Park — Outdoors

(☎718-858-4708; www.nysparks.state.ny.us; 26 New Dock St; 🕒8am-dusk; Ⓢ A, C to High St, F to York St) On the water, set snugly between the bridges and backed by Civil War–era warehouses, the 9-acre Empire-Fulton Ferry State Park has a cozy lawn on the East River.

Jane's Carousel — Historic Site

(www.janescarousel.com; Brooklyn Bridge Park, Empire Fulton Ferry, Dumbo; tickets $2; 🕒11am-7pm Wed-Mon, to 6pm Nov-Apr; 👪; Ⓢ F to York St) Behold the star attraction of Empire Fulton Ferry State Park: a vintage carousel built by the Philadelphia Toboggan Company back in 1922.

It is the first carousel to be placed on the National Register of Historic Places. Housing this treasure is an acrylic glass pavilion designed by Pritzker Prize–winning architect Jean Nouvel. Do not miss.

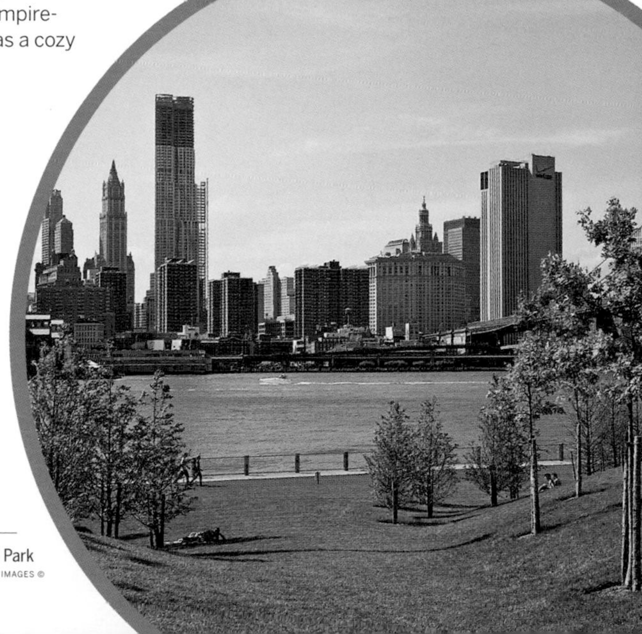

Brooklyn Bridge Park
BARRY WINIKER/GETTY IMAGES ©

Brooklyn Heights Promenade — Lookout

(btwn Orange & Remsen Sts; 🕒24hr; 👪; Ⓢ 2/3 to Clark St) All of the neighborhood's east–west lanes (such as Clark and Pineapple Sts) lead to the neighborhood's number-one attraction: a narrow park with breathtaking views of Lower Manhattan and New York Harbor. Though it hangs over the busy Brooklyn–Queens Expressway (BQE), this little slice of urban perfection is a great spot for a sunset walk.

Brooklyn Museum — Museum

(☎718-638-5000; www.brooklynmuseum.org; 200 Eastern Pkwy; suggested admission $12; 🕒11am-6pm Wed & Fri-Sun, to 10pm Thu; Ⓢ 2/3 to Eastern Pkwy-Brooklyn Museum) This encyclopedic museum is housed in a five-story, 560,000-sq-ft beaux arts building designed by McKim, Mead & White. Today, the building houses more than 1.5 million

BARRY WINIKER/GETTY IMAGES ©

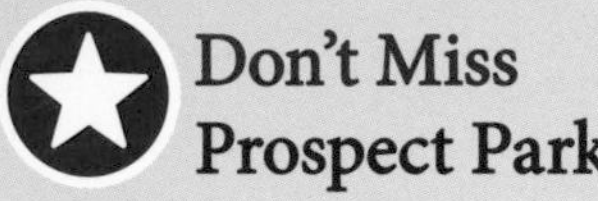

Don't Miss Prospect Park

The creators of the 585-acre Prospect Park – Frederick Law Olmsted and Calvert Vaux – considered this an improvement over their other New York project, Central Park. Created in 1866, Prospect Park has many of the same features. It's gorgeous, with a long meadow running along the western half, filled with soccer, football, cricket and baseball players (and barbecuers). Much of the rest is dotted with hilly forests and there's a lovely boathouse (pictured above) on the east side. Many more visitors come to bike, skate or just lounge around. There are also free concerts at the Prospect Park Bandshell (near the 9th St and Prospect Park West entrance).

NEED TO KNOW

718-965-8951; www.prospectpark.org; Grand Army Plaza; 5am-1am; S 2/3 to Grand Army Plaza, F to 15th St-Prospect Park

objects, including ancient artifacts, 19th-century period rooms, and sculptures and paintings from across several centuries.

Brooklyn Botanic Garden Gardens **(www.bbg.org; 1000 Washington Ave, at Crown St; adult/child $10/free, free Tue & 10am-noon Sat; around 8am-6pm Tue-Fri, from 10am-6pm Sat & Sun; ; S 2/3 to Eastern Pkwy-Brooklyn Museum)** One of Brooklyn's most picturesque attractions, this 52-acre garden is home to thousands of plants and trees, as well as a Japanese garden where river turtles swim alongside a Shinto shrine.

A network of trails connects the Japanese garden to other popular sections devoted to native flora, bonsai trees, a wood covered in bluebells and a rose garden.

Coney Island & Brighton Beach

Located about an hour by subway from Lower Manhattan, these two beachside neighborhoods sit side by side, facing the Atlantic. Brighton Beach, to the east, is quieter, with coffee shops and grocery stands that display signs in Cyrillic, catering to the large Ukrainian and Russian population. Coney Island, a mile to the west, is brassier with carnival rides and boardwalk bars and a surreal parade of humanity.

The two communities are connected by a boardwalk that runs along the beach, the best see-and-be-seen spot in Brooklyn during the steamy summer months.

Luna Park Amusement Park
(Cyclone roller coaster; www.lunaparknyc.com; Surf Ave, at 10th St; late Mar-Oct; ; S D/F, N/Q to Coney Island-Stillwell Ave) Luna Park is one of Coney Island's most popular amusement parks and contains one of its most legendary rides: the Cyclone ($8), a wooden roller coaster that reaches speeds of 60mph and makes near-vertical drops. (Way scarier than anything at Universal Studios.)

Williamsburg

Williamsburg is essentially a college town without a college – it's New York's of-the-moment Bohemian magnet, drawing slouchy, baby-faced artists, musicians, writers and graphic designers. Once a bastion of Latino working-class life, it's become a prominent dining and nightlife center – and, as a result, has attracted plenty of young urban professionals (and their attendant condo towers). It may not be full of major museums and picturesque architecture, but Williamsburg nonetheless offers plenty to do.

Most of the neighborhood is located along the East River waterfront, to the north of the Williamsburg Bridge. Bedford Ave serves as the main drag, with clusters of side-by-side cafes, boutiques and restaurants tucked into the area between N 10th St and Metropolitan Ave.

Brooklyn Flea Market Flea Market
(www.brooklynflea.com; East River Waterfront, btwn 6th & 7th Sts, Williamsburg; 10am-5pm Sun, Apr-Dec; S L to Bedford Ave) On Sundays in the summer and fall, you can get market action at this large outdoor space. You'll find plenty of vintage furnishings, retro clothing and bric-a-brac, not to mention an array of lobster rolls, *pupusa* (corn tortillas filled with cheese, beans, meat or vegetables), tamales, chocolate and much more.

Eating & Drinking

Brooklyn Bridge Park

Juliana's Pizzeria **$$**
(19 Old Fulton St, btwn Water & Front Sts; pizza $16-30; 11:30am-11pm; S A/C to High St) The legendary 80-something pizza maestro Patsy Grimaldi makes a triumphant return to Brooklyn, with Juliana's (named after his late mother), which opened in 2012.

AlMar Italian **$$**
(718-855-5288; 111 Front St, btwn Adams & Washington Sts, Dumbo; mains $14-26; 8am-10:30pm Mon-Thu, to 11pm Fri, 9am-11pm Sat, 10am-5pm Sun; ; S F to York St; A/C/E to High St) This welcoming Italian eatery serves breakfast, lunch and dinner in a homey, wood-lined space in Dumbo. The small, inviting bar is an ideal spot to sip wine and nibble on olives.

Brooklyn Museum

Cheryl's Global Soul Cafe **$$**
(www.cherylsglobalsoul.com; 236 Underhill Ave, btwn Eastern Pkwy & St Johns Pl, Prospect Heights; sandwiches $8-14, mains $15-25; 8am-4pm Mon, to 10pm Tue-Sun; ; S 2/3 to Eastern Pkwy-Brooklyn Museum) Around the corner from the Brooklyn Museum and the Brooklyn Botanic Garden, this homey brick-and-wood favorite serves up fresh, unpretentious cooking that draws on a world of influences. Expect everything from sake-glazed salmon with jasmine rice to exceptional homemade quiche to a long list of tasty sandwiches. There are veggie options, as well as kid-friendly mac 'n' cheese or fish and chips.

Below: Japanese gate, Brooklyn Botanic Garden (p242); **Right:** Williamsburg
(BELOW) BEN KLAUS/GETTY IMAGES ©; (RIGHT) MICHAEL MARQUAND/GETTY IMAGES ©

Tom's Restaurant Diner **$**
(☎718-636-9738; 782 Washington Ave, at Sterling Pl, Prospect Heights; ⏰6am-4pm; Ⓢ2/3 to Eastern Pkwy-Brooklyn Museum) Open since 1936, this diner looks like grandma's cluttered living room and delivers good, greasy-spoon cooking just three blocks from the Brooklyn Museum. Breakfast is served all day and it's a deal: two eggs, toast and coffee with home fries or grits comes to $4. If you want to go old school, order an egg cream (milk, soda and chocolate syrup).

Coney Island & Brighton Beach

Nathan's Famous Hot Dogs **$**
(1310 Surf Ave cnr Stillwell Ave, Coney Island; hot dogs from $4; ⏰breakfast, lunch & dinner till late; Ⓢ D/F to Coney Island-Stillwell Ave) The hot dog was invented in Coney Island in 1867 – which means that eating a frankfurter is practically obligatory when you're here. The best place to do it is at Nathan's Famous, which has been around since 1916. The hot dogs are the real deal and the clam bar is tops in summer.

Varenichnaya Russian **$**
(☎718-332-9797; 3086 Brighton 2nd St, Brighton Beach; mains around $10; ⏰lunch & dinner; Ⓢ B, Q to Brighton Beach) This small, family-run hideaway serves up consistently fresh dumplings from a variety of former Soviet Bloc countries. There are *pelmeni* (Siberian meat dumplings), *vareniki* (Ukrainian ravioli) and *mantis* (Uzbek lamb dumplings). The borscht is divine, as are the sturgeon and lamb kebabs.

Totonno's Pizzeria **$$**
(☎718-372-8606; 1524 Neptune Ave, cnr 16th St, Coney Island; pizza $17-20; ⏰noon-8pm Wed-Sun; 🚫; Ⓢ D/F, N/Q to Coney Island-Stillwell Ave) The toppings menu is slim (check the board above the open kitchen), but this is the kind of pie that doesn't need lots of overwrought decoration: coal-fired dough

is topped with mozzarella first, followed by tomato sauce, so your crust never gets soggy. A place of pilgrimage, complete with real-deal New York attitude.

Williamsburg

Rye Modern American **$$**
(☎718-218-8047; 247 S 1st St, btwn Roebling & Havemeyer Sts; mains $16-28; ⏰6-11pm Mon-Fri, from noon Sat & Sun; S L to Lorimer St, J/M to Marcy Ave) A Williamsburg throwback, this inviting spot with a long mahogany bar channels an early 1900s vibe. The menu is small but well executed with choices such as Long Island duck breast, braised short ribs and pan-roasted skate, plus classics including mac 'n' cheese, pork-belly sandwiches and raw bar selections (oysters, shrimp cocktail). Great cocktails.

Marlow & Sons Modern American **$$**
(☎718-384-1441; www.marlowandsons.com; 81 Broadway, btwn Berry St & Wythe Ave; mains lunch $13-16, dinner $17-27; ⏰8am-midnight; S J/M/Z to Marcy Ave, L to Bedford Ave) The dimly lit, wood-lined space feels like an old farmhouse cafe, which hosts a buzzing nighttime scene as diners and drinkers crowd in for oysters, tip-top cocktails and a changing menu of locavore specialties (smoked pork loin, crunchy crust pizzas, carmelized turnips, fluffy Spanish-style tortillas). Brunch is also a big draw, though prepare for lines.

Maison Premiere Cocktail Bar
(www.maisonpremiere.com; 298 Bedford Ave, btwn 1st & Grand Sts, Williamsburg; ⏰4pm-2am Sun-Wed, to 4am Thu-Sat; S L to Bedford Ave) We kept expecting to see Dorothy Parker stagger into this old-timey place, which features an elegant bar full of syrups and essences, suspendered bartenders and a jazzy soundtrack to further channel the French Quarter New Orleans vibe.

A raw bar doles out delicious oysters, while there's more serious dining (and an outdoor patio) behind the bar.

Spuyten Duyvil Bar

(www.spuytenduyvilnyc.com; 359 Metropolitan Ave, btwn Havemayer & Roebling, Williamsburg; from 5pm Mon-Fri, from noon Sat & Sun; S L to Lorimer St, G to Metropolitan Ave) This low-key Williamsburg bar looks like it was pieced together from a rummage sale. But the beer selection is excellent, the locals from various eras are chatty and there's a decent sized patio with leafy trees that is open in good weather.

Entertainment

Brooklyn Bowl Live Music

(718-963-3369; www.brooklynbowl.com; 61 Wythe Ave, btwn 11th & 12th Sts; 6pm-2am Mon-Thu, to 4am Fri, noon-4am Sat, noon-2am Sun; S L to Bedford Ave, G to Nassau Ave) This 23,000-sq-ft venue inside the former Hecla Iron Works Company combines **bowling (lane rental per hr $40-50, shoe rental $5)**, microbrews, food and groovy live music. In addition to the live bands that regularly tear up the stage, there are NFL game days, karaoke and DJ nights. Aside from weekends (noon to six pm), it's age 21 and up.

Bell House Live Music

(www.thebellhouseny.com; 149 7th St, Gowanus; 5pm-4am; ; S F, G, R to 4th Ave-9th St) A big, old venue in the mostly barren neighborhood of Gowanus, the Bell House features live performances, indie rockers, DJ nights, comedy shows and burlesque parties. The handsomely converted warehouse has a spacious concert area, plus a friendly little bar in the front room with flickering candles, leather armchairs and 10 or so beers on tap.

Music Hall of Williamsburg Live Music

(www.musichallofwilliamsburg.com; 66 N 6th St, btwn Wythe & Kent Aves, Williamsburg; show $15-35; S L to Bedford Ave) This popular Williamsburg music venue is *the* place to see indie bands in Brooklyn. (For many groups traveling through New York, this is their one and only spot.) It is intimate and the programming is solid.

Warsaw Live Music

(www.warsawconcerts.com; Polish National Home, 261 Driggs Ave, at Eckford St, Greenpoint; S L to Bedford Ave, G to Nassau Ave) A burgeoning New York classic, this stage is in the Polish National Home, with good views in the old ballroom, for bands ranging from indie darlings (The Dead Milkmen) to legends (George Clinton). Polish ladies serve *pierogis* (dumplings) and beers under the disco balls.

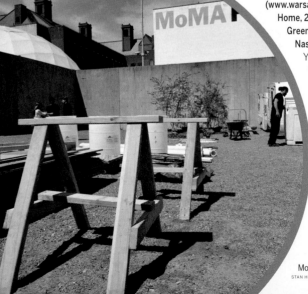

MoMA PS1

STAN HONDA/GETTY IMAGES ©

Brooklyn Academy of Music Performing Arts

(BAM; www.bam.org; 30 Lafayette Ave, at Ashland Pl, Fort Greene; ; S D, N/R to Pacific St, B, Q, 2/3, 4/5 to Atlantic Ave) Founded in 1861, BAM is the country's oldest performing arts center and supplies New York City with its edgier works of modern dance, music and theater. The complex contains a 2109-seat opera house, an 874-seat theater and the four-screen Rose Cinemas. Its stage has showcased Mercer Cunningham retrospectives, contemporary African dance and avant-garde interpretations of Shakespeare.

Bargemusic Classical Music

(www.bargemusic.org; Fulton Ferry Landing, Brooklyn Heights; tickets $35-45; ; S A/C to High St) The chamber-music concerts held on this 125-seat converted coffee barge (built c 1899) are a unique, intimate affair. Performances of classical favorites are hosted four days a week throughout the year. Enjoy Beethoven as you gently float and bob on the river. There are free children's concerts on some Saturdays.

Queens

Of the city's five boroughs, Queens is top dog in size and runner-up in head count. Anywhere else, it would be a major city in its own right. So where to begin?

Assuming it's not Tuesday or Wednesday (when most of the galleries are closed), start your explorations in Long Island City (LIC). A quick subway ride from Midtown, it's packed with contemporary art musts including MoMA PS1 and the lesser-known Fisher Landau Center for Art.

Spend some time in neighboring Astoria, taste-testing its ethnic delis and nosh spots, downing Czech beers at the Bohemian Hall & Beer Garden, and spending a few happy hours at the impressive Museum of the Moving Image.

Further out, Flushing (home to NYC's biggest Chinatown) merits a half-day at least. If you're short on time, spend the morning exploring the area around Main St and Roosevelt Ave, chow down freshly made dumplings, then spend the afternoon in neighboring Corona, dropping your jaw over the giant scale model of NYC at Queens Museum of Art.

Getting There & Away

Subway Twelve lines service Queens. Useful lines from Manhattan include the N/Q/R and M to Astoria, the 7 to Long Island City, Jackson Heights, Sunnyside, Woodside, Corona and Flushing, and the A to Rockaway Beach. The E and J/Z lines reach Jamaica, while the G directly connects Long Island City to Brooklyn (including Williamsburg).

Train Long Island Rail Road (LIRR) has a useful connection from Manhattan's Penn Station to Flushing.

Bus Useful routes include the M60, which runs from La Guardia Airport to Harlem and Columbia University in Manhattan, via Astoria.

Need to Know

- **Area code** ☎718
- **Location** Across the East River from Manhattan
- **Tourist office** (www.itsinqueens.com)

Sights

MoMA PS1 Gallery

(www.momaps1.org; 22-25 Jackson Ave, at 46th Ave, Long Island City; adult/child $10/free, admission free with MoMA ticket, Warm Up party admission online/at venue $15/18; noon-6pm Thu-Mon, Warm Up parties 3-9pm Sat Jul-early Sep; S E, M to 23rd St-Ely Ave; G to 21st; 7 to 45th Rd-Court House Sq) This smaller, hipper relative of Manhattan's Museum of Modern Art is a master at hunting down fresh, bold contemporary art and serving it up in a Berlin-esque, ex-school locale. Expect more than 50 exhibitions a year, exploring anything from Middle Eastern video art to giant mounds of thread. Best of all, admission is free with your MoMA ticket – so hold on tight!

Museum of the Moving Image Museum

(www.movingimage.us; 36-01 35th Ave, at 37th St, Astoria; adult/child $12/6, admission free 4-8pm Fri; 10:30am-5pm Wed & Thu, to 8pm Fri, 11:30am-7pm Sat & Sun; S M/R to Steinway St) Fresh from a $65-million upgrade, this super-cool complex is now one of the world's top film, television and video museums. State-of-the-art galleries show off the museum's collection of 130,000-plus TV and movie artifacts, including Robert De Niro's wig from *Taxi Driver*, Robin Williams' space suit from *Mork & Mindy* and the creepy stunt doll used in *The Exorcist*.

Queens Museum Museum

(QMA; www.queensmuseum.org; flushing Meadows Corona Park, Queens; adult/child $8/free; noon-6pm Wed-Sun; S 7 to 111th St) The recently expanded Queens Museum is one of the city's most unexpected pleasures. Its most famous drawcard is the Panorama of New York City, a gob-smacking 9335-sq-ft miniature New York City, with all buildings accounted for and a 15-minute dusk-to-dawn light simulation of a New York day. The museum also hosts top-notch exhibitions of modern art, from contemporary photography to site-specific installations.

Flushing Meadows Corona Park Park

(www.nycgovparks.org/parks/fmcp; Grand Central Pkwy; S 7 to Mets-Willets Point) The area's biggest attraction is this 1225-acre park, built for the 1939 World's Fair and dominated by Queens' most famous landmark, the stainless steel **Unisphere** (the world's biggest globe, 120ft high and weighing 380 tons). Facing it is the former New York City Building, now home to the highly underrated Queens Museum.

Also nearby is the **Arthur Ashe Stadium**, and the rest of the **USTA Billie Jean King National Tennis Center** (718-760-6200; www.usta.com; Flushing Meadows Corona Park, Queens; S 7 to Mets-Willets Pt). Head west on the pedestrian bridge over the Grand Central Pkwy to find a few more attractions, including the **New York Hall of Science** (718-699-0005; www.nysci.org; 47-01 111th St; adult/child $11/8; admission free 2pm-5pm Fri & 10-11am Sun Sep-Jun, daily late Aug-early Sep ; 9:30am-5pm Mon-Fri, 10am-6pm Sat & Sun Apr-Aug, closed Mon Sep-Mar; S 7 to 111th St).

Unisphere, Flushing Meadows Corona Park

SCULPTURE: GILMORE DAVID CLARKE; IMAGE: BARRY WINIKER/GETTY IMAGES ©

Eating & Drinking

M. Wells Dinette — Canadian $$

(www.magasinwells.com; MoMA PS1, 22-25 Jackson Ave, Long Island City; mains $9-29; ⏲noon-6pm Thu-Mon; Ⓢ E, M to 23rd St-Ely Ave; G to 21st; 7 to 45th Rd-Court House Sq) Just like being back at school (but with better grub), this cultish nosh spot sits inside school-turned-art gallery MoMA PS1. Desk-like tables face the open kitchen, where Québécois head chef Hugue Dufour gives regional ingredients a gutsy French-Canadian makeover.

Feast on the likes of frisée salad with duck hearts, smoked egg and fried bread, cleverly paired with a small, interesting selection of wines by the glass.

Golden Shopping Mall — Chinese $

(41-28 Main St, flushing; meals from $3; Ⓢ 7 to Flushing-Main St) A chaotic jumble of hung ducks, airborne noodles and greasy laminated tables, Golden Mall's basement food court dishes up fantastic hawker-style meals.

Two must-tries are the lamb dumplings from Xie Family Dishes (stall 38) – best dipped in a little black vinegar, soy sauce and chili oil – and the spicy cumin lamb burger at Xi'an Famous Foods next door.

Taverna Kyclades — Greek $$

(☎718-545-8666; www.tavernakyclades.com; 33-07 Ditmars Blvd, at 33rd St, Astoria; mains $11-35; ⏲noon-11pm Mon-Sat, to 10pm Sun; Ⓢ N/Q to Astoria-Ditmars Blvd) Fresh seafood is its forte, shining through in simple classics such as succulent grilled octopus and fried calamari. The grilled fish dishes are testament to the adage that 'less is more,' while the *saganaki* (pan-fried cheese) is sinfully good.

Bohemian Hall & Beer Garden — Beer Hall

(www.bohemianhall.com; 29-19 24th Ave, btwn 29th & 31st Sts, Astoria; ⏲5pm-1am Mon-Thu, to 3am Fri, noon-3am Sat, noon-1am Sun; Ⓢ N/Q to Astoria Blvd) Easily one of NYC's great happy drinking grounds, this outdoor beer garden is especially brilliant when the weather is warm. The mouthwatering list of cold Czech imports on draft are served with Czech accents, as are the schnitzels, goulash and dumplings. On some warm nights, folk bands set up (with occasional cover charge of $5 or so); arrive early to ensure a spot.

New York City In Focus

Manhattan at night

New York City Today

Not even Hurricane Sandy's vicious slap can stop America's biggest, boldest metropolis

housing
(% of population)

0.05

Renters | Homeowners | Homeless (documented)

if New York City were 100 people

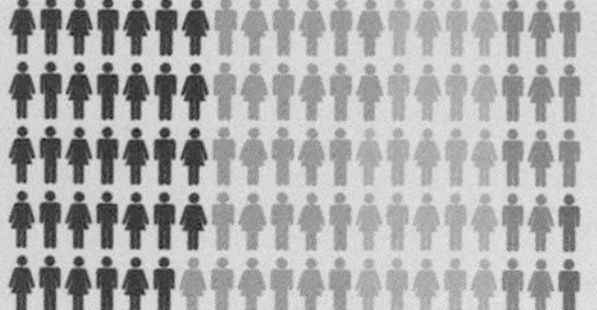

34 would be Caucasian
28 would be Hispanic/Latino
23 would be African American
13 would be Asian
2 would be Other

population per sq mile

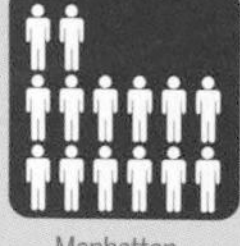

Manhattan

New York State

≈ 5000 people

Williamsburg Bridge

After the Storm

She may have given it her best shot, but superstorm Hurricane Sandy failed to defeat NYC. Since it raged through the city in October 2012, more than $1 billion worth of response and recovery work has commenced or been completed. Full recovery is a slow and steady process. As of 2014, work was still being carried out on damaged parts of the city, among them Battery Park, Ellis Island and South Street Seaport. What is certain, though, is that NYC is back, stronger and smarter than ever before.

WTC: From Zero to Hero

After more than a decade of sputters, spats and ballooning costs, the mammoth World Trade Center redevelopment is finally sprinting towards the finish line. While 2006 saw the completion of the 52-story 7 World Trade Center tower, September 2011 witnessed the opening of the National September 11 Memorial, its two giant reflecting pools attracting

MICHAEL MARQUAND/GETTY IMAGES ©

more than 10 million visitors since its debut. October 2013 debuted the 72-story, Fumihiko Maki-designed 4 World Trade Center skyscraper, and in spring 2014, the National September 11 Memorial Museum opened its doors to the public, thanks in part to a $15 million push from Michael Bloomberg. Also scheduled for completion in 2014 is the 104-story One World Trade Center, the Western Hemisphere's tallest skyscraper. The tower will offer visitors the city's most enviable vantage point when its observation decks debut in 2015. In the same year, architect Santiago Calatrava's ambitious rail-and-retail complex – the WTC Transportation Hub – will also open at the site. Ground Zero is reborn.

New Mayor in Town

NYC swung to the left with the election of mayor Bill de Blasio in November 2013, the city's first Democrat mayor since 1989. The 52 year old is also NYC's first white mayor with an African American spouse. It was a fact not lost on de Blasio in his election campaign TV commercials, which showcased his interracial family to a city which has had a population dominated by people of African American, Latino and Asian descent since the 1980s. His campaign also tapped into growing concerns about education, housing affordability and growing economic inequality, with promises to, among other things, bump up taxes to fund universal pre-school and reform then-mayor Michael Bloomberg's controversial 'stop and frisk' policy. It was a campaign that served de Blasio well on election day, as the self-proclaimed progressive beat Republican candidate Joseph J Lhota by a breathtaking 49-point margin.

Pedal Power

New York's aim for a cleaner, greener future took another step forward in May 2013 with the launch of Citi Bike, its hugely popular bike-sharing program. By the end of the year, 4 million trips covering 8 million miles had been made, with over 80,000 people forking out the $95 for an annual membership. Yet not everyone is peddling smiles. Many residents resent the addition of Citi Bike kiosks on their streets, calling them eyesores. In fact, almost 45% of the original kiosk locations across the city were altered to appease disapproving locals. Despite these protests, there is no stopping America's largest bike-sharing scheme. In late 2013, plans were announced for an extra 4000 bikes across the city, boosting the total fleet to 10,000. No doubt NYC's bar-hopping punters (some of the bikes' most regular users) will be toasting to that.

History

Rose Main Reading Room, New York Public Library (p168)

SHOBEIR ANSARI/GETTY IMAG

This is the tale of a city that never sleeps, of a kingdom where tycoons and world leaders converge, of a place that's seen the highest of highs and the most devastating of lows. Yet through it all, NYC continues to reach for the sky (both figuratively and literally). And to think it all started with $24 and a pile of beads...

Encounters

About 11,000 years before the first Europeans arrived, the Lenape foraged, hunted and fished the regional bounty. European explorers muscled in, touching off decades of raids on Lenape villages. Dutch West India Company employee Henry Hudson arrived in 1609, and in 1624 the company sent 110 settlers to begin a trading post. They settled in Lower Manhattan and called their colony New Amsterdam. In 1626 the colony's first gov-

AD 1500

About 15,000 Native Americans live in 80 different sites around the region.

ernor, Peter Minuit, offered to buy Manhattan's 14,000 acres from the Lenape for 60 guilders ($24) and some glass beads. The Lenape agreed, possibly thinking the exchange was about rent and permission to hunt, fish and trade. By the time peg-legged Peter Stuyvesant arrived to govern the colony in 1647, the Lenape population had dwindled to about 700.

In 1664 the English arrived in battleships. Stuyvesant avoided bloodshed by surrendering without a shot. King Charles II renamed the colony after his brother the Duke of York. New York became a prosperous British port and the population rose to 11,000 by the mid-1700s; however, colonists started to become resentful of British taxation.

The Best... Places to Learn About NYC's History

1 Ellis Island (p54)

2 Lower East Side Tenement Museum (p110)

3 Museum of the City of New York (p199)

4 New-York Historical Society (p220)

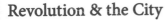

Revolution & the City

By the 18th century the economy was so robust that the locals were improvising ways to avoid sharing the wealth with London, and New York became the stage for the fatal confrontation with King George III. Revolutionary battle began in August of 1776, when General George Washington's army lost about a quarter of its men in just a few days. He retreated, and fire engulfed much of the colony. But soon the British left and Washington's army reclaimed their city.

In 1789 the retired general found himself addressing crowds at Federal Hall, gathered to witness his presidential inauguration. Alexander Hamilton, as Washington's secretary of the treasury, began rebuilding New York and working to establish the New York Stock Exchange.

Population Bust, Infrastructure Boom

There were setbacks at the start of the 19th century: the bloody Draft Riots of 1863, cholera epidemics, tensions among 'old' and 'new' immigrants, and poverty and crime in Five Points, the city's first slum. But the city prospered and found resources for mighty public works. Begun in 1855, Central Park was a vision of green reform and a boon to real estate speculation, and it offered work relief when the Panic of 1857

1625–26
The Dutch West India Company imports slaves from Africa for fur trade and construction work.

1646
The Dutch found the village of Breuckelen on the eastern shore of Long Island.

1784
Alexander Hamilton founds America's first bank, the Bank of New York, with holdings of $500,000.

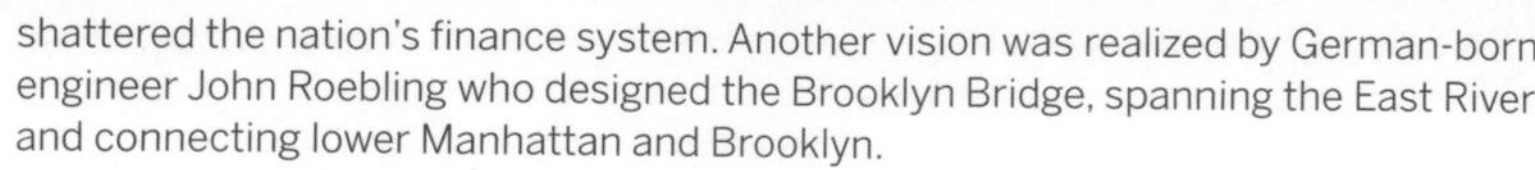

shattered the nation's finance system. Another vision was realized by German-born engineer John Roebling who designed the Brooklyn Bridge, spanning the East River and connecting lower Manhattan and Brooklyn.

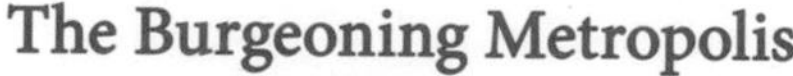

The Burgeoning Metropolis

By the turn of the 20th century, elevated trains carried a million people a day in and out of the city. Rapid transit opened up areas of the Bronx and Upper Manhattan. Tenements were overflowing with immigrants arriving from southern Italy and Eastern Europe, who increased the metropolis to about three million.

Newly wealthy folks – boosted by an economy jump-started by financier JP Morgan – built splendid mansions on Fifth Ave. Reporter and photographer Jacob Riis illuminated the widening gap between the classes, leading the city to pass much-needed housing reforms.

1898: Boroughs Join Manhattan

After years of governmental chaos caused by the 40 independent municipalities around the area, 1898 saw the ratification of the Charter of New York, which joined the five boroughs of Brooklyn, Staten Island, Queens, the Bronx and Manhattan into the largest city in America.

Factory Conditions, Women's Rights

Wretched factory conditions in the early 20th century were illuminated when the 1911 Triangle Shirtwaist Company fire killed 146 women workers trapped behind locked doors. The event led to sweeping labor reforms. Nurse and midwife Margaret Sanger opened the first birth-control clinic in Brooklyn and suffragists held rallies to obtain the vote for women.

The Jazz Age

James Walker was elected mayor in 1925 – a time when jazz ruled; Babe Ruth reigned at Yankee Stadium; and the Great Migration from the South led to the Harlem Renaissance, when the neighborhood became the center of African American culture and society, producing poetry, music, art and an innovative attitude that continues to influence and inspire. Harlem's nightlife attracted the flappers and gin-soaked revelers that marked the complete failure of Prohibition.

1811

Manhattan's grid plan is developed by Mayor DeWitt Clinton, reshaping the city.

1825

The Erie Canal, an engineering feat, is completed, influencing trade and commerce in New York.

1853

The State Legislature authorizes the allotment of public lands for what will later become Central Park.

rd Times

e stock market crashed in 1929 and e city dealt with the Great Depression through grit, endurance, rent parties, militancy and public works projects. Texas-born, Yiddish-speaking Mayor Fiorello LaGuardia worked to bring relief in the form of New Deal–funded projects.

WWII brought troops to the city, ready to party in Times Square before shipping off to Europe. Converted to war industries, factories hummed, staffed by women and African Americans who had rarely before had access to good, unionized jobs. With few evident controls on business, Midtown bulked up with skyscrapers after the war.

Beat Poets & Gays

The 1960s ushered in an era of legendary creativity and anti-establishment expression, with many of the key figures centered in Greenwich Village. Writers such as Beat poets Allen Ginsberg and Jack Kerouac gathered in coffeehouses to exchange ideas and find inspiration, often in the form of folk music from burgeoning stars, including Bob Dylan. The environment was ripe for rebellion – a task gay revelers took on with gusto, finding their political strength and voice in fighting a police raid at the Stonewall Inn in 1969.

Enter Robert Moses

Working with LaGuardia to usher the city into the modern age was Robert Moses, an urban planner who influenced the physical shape of the city more than anyone else in the 20th century. He was the mastermind behind the Triborough and Verrazano-Narrows Bridges, Jones Beach State Park, the West Side Hwy and the Long Island Pkwy system – plus endless highways, tunnels and bridges, which shifted this mass-transit area into one largely dependent on the automobile.

'Drop Dead'

By the early 1970s deficits had created a fiscal crisis. President Ford refused to lend federal aid – summed up by the *Daily News* headline 'Ford to City, Drop Dead!' Massive layoffs decimated the working class; untended bridges, roads and parks reeked of hard times.

The traumatic '70s – which reached a low point in 1977 with a citywide blackout and the existence of serial killer Son of Sam – drove down rents, helping to nourish an alternative culture that transformed the former industrial precincts of SoHo and Tribeca into energized nightlife districts.

1863

Civil War Draft Riots erupt; order is restored by the Federal Army.

1886

The Statue of Liberty's pedestal is completed and a dedication ceremony held.

1919

The Yankees acquire slugger Babe Ruth from Boston, leading to their first championship.

September 11

On September 11, 2001, terrorists flew two hijacked planes into the World Trade Center's Twin Towers, turning the complex into dust and rubble and killing nearly 2800 people. Downtown Manhattan took months to recover from the fumes wafting from the ruins, as forlorn missing-person posters grew ragged on brick walls. While recovery crews coughed their way through the debris, the city mourned the dead amid constant terrorist alerts and an anthrax scare. Shock and grief drew people together in a determined effort not to succumb to despair.

Out of the Ashes

While the stock market boomed for mu of the 1980s, neighborhoods struggled with the spread of crack cocaine; the city reeled from the impact of addiction, crime, and AIDS. Squatters in the East Village fought back when police tried to clear a big homeless encampment, leading to the Tompkins Square Park riots of 1988. In South Bronx, a wave of arson reduced blocks of apartments to cinders. But amid the smoke, an influential hip-hop culture was born there and in Brooklyn.

Still convalescing from the real-estate crash of the late 1980s, the city faced crumbling infrastructure, jobs leaking south and Fortune 500 companies leaving for suburbia. Then the dot-com market roared in, turning the New York Stock Exchange into a speculator's fun park and the city launched a frenzy of building and partying unparalleled since the 1920s.

With pro-business, law-and-order Rudy Giuliani as mayor, the dingy and destitute were swept from Manhattan's yuppified streets to the outer boroughs, leaving room for Generation X to live the high life. Giuliani grabbed headlines with his campaign to stamp out crime, even kicking the sex shops off notoriously seedy 42nd St.

The Naughts in New York

The 10 years after 9/11 were a period of rebuilding – both physically and emotionally. In 2002 Mayor Michael Bloomberg began the unenviable task of picking up the pieces of a shattered city. Much to Bloomberg's pleasure, New York did see a ton of renovation and reconstruction, especially after the city hit its stride with spiking tourist numbers in 2005. By the latter part of Bloomberg's second term as mayor, the entire city seemed to be under construction, with luxury high-rise condos sprouting up in every neighborhood.

Soon the economy buckled under its own weight in what has largely become known as the Global Financial Crisis. The city was paralyzed as the cornerstones of the business world were forced to close shop. Although hit less badly than many pockets of the country, NYC still saw a significant dip in real-estate prices and many cranes turned to frozen monuments of a broken economy.

1931

The Empire State Building becomes the world's tallest skyscraper.

1945

The United Nations, headquartered on Manhattan's east side, is established.

1961

Nineteen-year-old folk singer Bob Dylan arrives in NYC.

In 2011 the city commemorated the 10th anniversary of the 9/11 attacks with the opening of a remembrance center and a half-built Freedom Tower – a new corporate behemoth – that loomed overhead.

Superstorm Sandy

New York's resilience would be tested again in 2012 by superstorm Hurricane Sandy. On October 29, cyclonic winds and drenching rain pounded the city, causing severe flooding and property damage in all five boroughs, including to the NYC subway system, Hugh L Carey Tunnel and World Trade Center site. A major power blackout plunged much of Lower Manhattan into surreal darkness, while trading at the New York Stock Exchange was suspended for two days in its first weather-related closure since 1888.

In the neighborhood of Breezy Point, Queens, a devastating storm surge hindered the efforts of firefighters confronted with a blaze that reduced over 125 homes to ashes. The fire went down as one of the worst in NYC's history, while the storm itself claimed 44 lives in the city alone.

New York Stock Exchange (p59)

1988
Crowds of squatters riot when cops attempt to forcibly remove them from East Village's Tompkins Square Park.

2001
On September 11, terrorist hijackers fly two planes into the Twin Towers, killing nearly 2800 people.

2013
Brooklyner Bill de Blasio is elected, becoming New York's first Democratic mayor in two decades.

Family Travel

Path along the East River near Brooklyn Bridge

WAYNE FOGDEN/GETTY IMAGE

New York City has loads of activities for young ones, including imaginative playgrounds and leafy parks where kids can run free, plus lots of kid-friendly museums and sights. Most kids love sunny boat rides on the harbor and gazing at dinosaurs and other wondrous beasts at the Natural History Museum. Other highs: carousel rides, roller coasters and boardwalk fun out at Coney Island.

Parks & Playgrounds

Central Park

More than 800 acres of green space, a lake that can be navigated by rowboat, a carousel, a zoo and a massive statue of Alice in Wonderland. Heckscher playground, near Seventh Ave and Central Park South, is the biggest and best of Central Park's 21 playgrounds.

Prospect Park

Brooklyn's hilly 585-acre Prospect Park has abundant amusement for kids, including a zoo, hands-on playthings at Lefferts Historic House and a new ice-skating rink that becomes a water park in summer.

Sights & Activities

Museums, especially those geared toward kids such as the Children's Museum of the s and the American Museum of Natural History, are ways great places, as are children's theaters, movie heaters, book and toy stores and aquariums. The city is dotted with vintage carousels; rides cost from $2 to $3.

The boat ride to the Statue of Liberty offers the opportunity to chug around New York Harbor and get to know an icon that most kids only know from textbooks.

The city has a number of zoos. The best, by far, is the Bronx Zoo; otherwise, if you're pressed for time, the Central Park Zoo will keep the tots entertained.

With hot dogs, vintage rollercoasters and an open stretch of beach, Coney Island is just what the doctor ordered if the family is in need of some fun in the sun.

Transportation

The biggest pitfalls tend to revolve around public transportation, as a startling lack of subway-station elevators will have you lugging strollers up and down flights of stairs (though you can avoid the turnstile by getting buzzed through an easy-access gate); visit the **MTA website** (http://web.mta.info/accessibility/stations.htm) to find a guide to subway stations with elevators. Regarding fares, anyone over 44 inches is supposed to pay full fare, but the rule is rarely enforced.

Not for Parents

For an insight into New York City aimed directly at kids, pick up a copy of Lonely Planet's *Not for Parents: New York*. Perfect for children aged eight and up, it opens up a world of intriguing stories and fascinating facts about New York's people, places, history and culture.

Babysitting

While most major hotels (and a handful of boutique-style places) offer onsite babysitting services – or can at least provide you with referrals – you could also turn to a local childcare organization. **Baby Sitters' Guild** (☎212-682-0227; www.babysittersguild.com), established in 1940 specifically to serve travelers staying in hotels with children, has a stable of sitters who speak a range of 16 languages. All are carefully screened, most are CPR-certified and many have nursing backgrounds; they'll come to your hotel room and even bring games and arts-and-crafts projects. Another good option is **Pinch Sitters** (☎212-260-6005; www.nypinchsitters.com). Both will set you back about $22 per hour.

Need to Know

- **Change Facilities** Not common in bars and restaurants.
- **Useful Website** Find helpful tips in **Time Out New York Kids** (www.timeout.com/new-york-kids).
- **Strollers** Not allowed on buses unless folded up.
- **Transportation** Subway stairs can be challenging with strollers; taxis are exempt from car-seat laws.

Food & Drink

Greenmarket Farmers Market (p148), Union Square

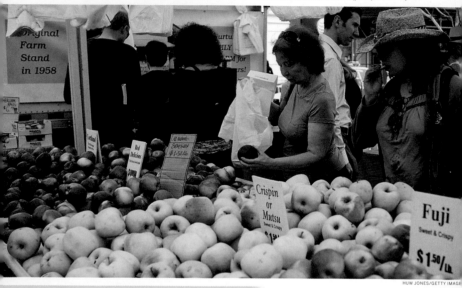

HUW JONES/GETTY IMAGES

In a city with over 20,000 restaurants, New York is a city of staggering options when it comes to dining. From inspired iterations of world cuisine, to quintessentially local bites, New York City's dining scene is infinite, all-consuming and a proud testament to the kaleidoscope of citizens that call the city home. Meanwhile new trends and ever-changing appetites fuel a culinary culture ever on the cusp of reinvention.

Specialties

Unlike California, the South or the Southwest, New York is never really referred to as having one defining cuisine. Try asking for some 'New York food,' for example, and you could wind up getting anything from a hot dog, a South Indian feast or a Gallic $220 seven-course tasting menu at Daniel on the Upper East Side. Cuisine in this multicultural town is global by definition, and constantly evolving by its very nature.

That said, it's the food items with the longest histories that folks usually have in mind when they refer to New York City specialties. Those at the top of the list – bagels and slices of pizza – were introduced by Eastern European Jews and Italians, because those groups were among the earliest waves of immigrants. But egg creams (milk, soda water and chocolate syrup), cheesecake and hot dogs (just to name a few) are also old-school NYC staples.

oing Global

ne range of global cuisine you'll find in NYC is amazing. Get ready to dive your chopsticks into some authentic Cantonese or Korean; sop up Ethiopian with a spongy shred of *injera* bread; pull apart a fresh lobster with your bare hands; chase Turkish meze, Spanish tapas or Mexican *torta* sandwiches with a glass of raki, sherry or *mezcal*, respectively.

Keep in mind that while plenty of tourists descend on Manhattan's Little Italy and Curry Row, you'll find more authenticity in the outer boroughs, where the latest waves of immigrants have settled and continue to arrive.

The Best... Global Dining Experiences

1 RedFarm (p127)

2 Rosemary's (p127)

3 Danji (p177)

4 Cafe Mogador (p104)

5 Veselka (p104)

6 Tía Pol (p133)

Urban Farm to Table

Having perfected the fast, New York City is rediscovering the slow. In recent years, a growing number of city rooftops, backyards and community gardens have been transformed into urban farms, turning America's biggest concrete jungle into an unlikely food bowl. While you can expect to find anything from organic tomatoes atop Upper East Side delis to beehives on East Village tenement rooftops, the current queen of the crop is **Brooklyn Grange** (http://brooklyngrangefarm.com), an organic farm covering two rooftops in Long Island City and the Brooklyn Navy Yards. At 108,000 sq ft, it's purportedly the world's biggest rooftop farm, growing everything from carrots and beans to 40 varieties of tomatoes. Collaborators include dining hotspots such as Brooklyn's Marlow & Sons, where the menus proudly showcase this homegrown goodness.

To Market, to Market

Don't let the concrete streets fool you – New York City has a thriving greens scene that comes in many shapes and sizes. At the top of your list should be the Chelsea Market, which is packed with gourmet goodies of all kinds – both shops (where you can assemble picnics) and food stands (where you can eat on-site).

Many neighborhoods in NYC have their own green market. One of the biggest is the Greenmarket Farmers Market in Union Square, open four days weekly throughout the year. Check **Grow NYC** (www.grownyc.org) for a list of the other 50-plus markets around the city.

The best market for noshers (rather than cook-at-home types) is the weekend Brooklyn Flea, with dozens of food vendors. In summer, also check out **Smorgasburg** (www.smorgasburg.com) – the food-only component of Brooklyn Flea.

Also popular are high-end market-cum-grocers such as Eataly and Whole Foods.

Need to Know

- **Price ranges** The following price symbols indicate the average cost of a main dish, exclusive of tax and tip:
  - **$** less than $12
  - **$$** $12–$25
  - **$$$** more than $25
- **Tipping** New Yorkers tip between 15% and 20% of the final price of the meal. You needn't tip for takeaway, though it's polite to drop a dollar or two in the tip jar at the register.
- **Reservations** Popular restaurants abide by one of two rules: either they take reservations and you need to plan in advance (even weeks or months early for the real treasures) or they only seat patrons on a first-come basis, in which case you should eat early to avoid the impossibly long lines.
- **Useful Websites** Find the latest restaurant openings and trends on **Grub Street** (www.newyork.grubstreet.com), **NY Eater** (ny.eater.com) and **Gothamist** (www.gothamist.com). **Open Table** (www.opentable.com) provides a click-and-book reservation service for a wide spread of restaurants around town.

Food Truck City

Skip the bagel- and hot-dog-vending food carts. These days, there's a new mobile crew in town dishing up high-end treats and unique fusion fare. These trucks ply various routes, stopping in designated zones throughout the city – namely around Union Square, Midtown and the Financial District – so if you're looking for a particular grub wagon, it's best to follow them on Twitter.

Here are a few of our favourites:

- **Kimchi Taco** (http://kimchitacotruck.com)
- **Red Hook Lobster Pound** (twitter.com/lobstertruckny)
- **Korilla BBQ** (www.twitter.com/korillabbq)
- **Calexico Cart** (www.calexico.net)
- **Wafels & Dinges** (www.twitter.com/waffletruck)
- **Van Leeuwen Ice Cream** (www.twitter.com/VLAIC)

The Arts

Avery Fisher Hall at the Lincoln Center (p228)

RUDI VON BRIEL/GETTY IMAGES ©

The sheer number of performance venues is testament to this city's great love for the arts. How to take it all in? Don't even try. Instead, pick your favorite medium – classical music, jazz or ballet, for example – and see a few shows. Or see a little of everything: a poetry reading one night, followed by an indie film or an opera, with an off-Broadway show thrown in for good measure.

Music

This is the city where jazz players including Ornette Coleman, Miles Davis and John Coltrane pushed the limits of improvisation in the '50s. It's where various Latin sounds – from cha-cha-cha to rumba to mambo – came together to form the hybrid we now call *salsa*; where folk singers Bob Dylan and Joan Baez crooned protest songs in coffee houses; and where bands such as the New York Dolls and the Ramones tore up the stage in Manhattan's gritty downtown. And it was the cultural crucible where hip-hop was nurtured and grew – then exploded.

The city remains a magnet for musicians to this day. The local indie-rock scene is especially vibrant: groups like the Yeah Yeah Yeahs and Animal Collective all emerged out of New York; Williamsburg is at the heart of the scene.

Theater

Big, splashy Broadway shows are most often associated with NYC's entertainment scene. But Broadway shows refer strictly to productions staged in the 40 official Broadway theaters – lavish early-20th-century jewels surrounding Times Square.

Off-Broadway (more adventurous, less costly theater playing to smaller houses) and off-off-Broadway (even edgier, more affordable performances housed in theaters for crowds of less than 100) are both big businesses here.

Comedy

The comedy scene is divided between the big-name, big-ticket clubs and the more experimental and obscure places. Check out the **Upright Citizens Brigade Theatre**, the **Magnet Theater** (www.magnettheater.com) and the **PIT** (People's Improv Theater; www.thepit-nyc.com).

The Best... Alternative Performance Spaces

1 Amore Opera (p115)

2 Joyce Theater (p139)

3 Don't Tell Mama (p185)

Classical Music & Opera

Lincoln Center houses the main halls of Alice Tully, Avery Fisher and the Metropolitan Opera House. The smaller Carnegie Hall is just as beloved a venue, offering piano concerts as well as eclectic alt-folk and world music. At the Brooklyn Academy of Music (BAM), the country's oldest academy for the performing arts, you'll find opera, theater and dance.

Dance

Dance fans are spoiled for choice in this town, which is home to both the New York City Ballet and the American Ballet Theatre. Another key venue dedicated to dance is the Joyce Theater, which stages acclaimed contemporary productions by dance companies from every corner of the globe.

Painting & Visual Arts

Today, the arts scene is mixed and wide-ranging. The major institutions – the Metropolitan Museum of Art, the Museum of Modern Art, the Whitney Museum, the Guggenheim Museum and the Brooklyn Museum – show major retrospectives covering everything from Renaissance portraiture to contemporary installation. The New Museum of Contemporary Art, on the Lower East Side, is more daring.

The gallery scene is equally diffuse, with more than 1500 galleries around the city. Chelsea is the epicenter of the scene, though you'll also find dozens of galleries in the Lower East Side and in the Upper East Side.

Architecture

100 Eleventh Avenue (left) and the IAC Building (right)

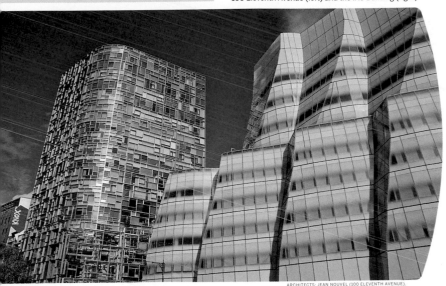

ARCHITECTS: JEAN NOUVEL (100 ELEVENTH AVENUE), FRANK GEHRY (IAC BUILDING); BARRY WINIKER/GETTY IMAGES ©

New York's architectural history is a layer cake of ideas and styles – one that is literally written on the city's streets. Graceful Federal-style buildings, ornate beaux-arts palaces and revival works (Greek, Gothic, Romanesque and Renaissance) are all part of the cityscape. And, in recent years, there has been the addition of the torqued forms of deconstructivist architects. For the architecture buff, it's a goldmine.

Architecture in the Early Republic

Some of New York's first notable buildings date from the early 1800s, when the so-called Federal style emerged. Works featured classical touches: slim, columned entrances, triangular pediments at the roof line and rounded fanlights over doors and windows. City Hall, built in 1812, owes its French form to émigré architect Joseph François Mangin and its Federal detailing to American-born John McComb Jr.

Greek, Gothic & Romanesque: The Revivals

Starting in the late 1830s, simple Georgian and Federalist styles started to give way to more ornate structures that employed Gothic and Romanesque elements. Among the most resplendent are St Patrick's Cathedral

(1853–79), which took over an entire city block at Fifth Ave and 51st St, and the perpetually under-construction Cathedral Church of St John the Divine (1911–), in Morningside Heights.

Beaux Arts

At the turn of the 20th century, New York entered a gilded age. Public buildings grew ever more extravagant in scale and ornamentation. Gleaming white limestone began to replace all the brownstone, first stories were elevated to allow for dramatic staircase entrances, and buildings were adorned with sculptured keystones and Corinthian columns.

Classics include the central branch of the New York Public Library (1911) designed by Carrère and Hastings, the 1902 extension of the Metropolitan Museum of Art by Richard Morris Hunt, and Warren and Wetmore's stunning Grand Central Station (1913), which is capped by a statue of Mercury, the god of commerce.

The Best... New York's Must-See Structures

1 Brooklyn Bridge (p66)

2 Chrysler Building (p169)

3 Grand Central Terminal (p174)

4 Empire State Building (p166)

5 Guggenheim Museum (p196)

6 New Museum of Contemporary Art (p103)

Reaching Skyward

By the time New York settled into the 20th century, elevators and steel-frame engineering had allowed the city to grow up – literally. This period saw a building-boom of skyscrapers, starting with Cass Gilbert's neo-Gothic 57-story Woolworth Building (1913).

Others soon followed. In 1930, the Chrysler Building, the 77-storey, art-deco masterpiece designed by William Van Alen, became the world's tallest structure. The following year, the record was broken by the Empire State Building, a clean-lined, art-deco monolith crafted from Indiana limestone.

Bring on the Starchitects

New York has seen the arrival of daring recent additions, including Norman Foster's trailblazing Hearst Tower (2006), a glass tower zigzagging its way out of a 1920s sandstone structure in Midtown. Frank Gehry's post-structuralist New York by Gehry (2011) is a rippling 76-floor apartment tower in Lower Manhattan. Other arresting designs, including Gehry's IAC Building (2007), a billowing white-glass structure that resembles the fluttering sails of a ship, and Renzo Piano's New York Times Building (2007), a 52-story building armored in ceramic rods. Renzo is also behind the Whitney Museum's new home in the Meatpacking District; a boldly asymmetrical structure due for completion in 2015. Also in the works is Santiago Calatrava's luminous design for the WTC Transportation Hub.

Shopping

Barneys department store (p185), Madison Ave

INGOLF POMPE/GETTY IMAGES ©

Shopping here isn't just about collecting pretty, fanciful things. It's also about experiencing the city in all its variety and connecting to New York's many subcultures. There are shops for lovers of chess, street art, artist monographs, Danish things, handmade jewelry, Ukrainian handicrafts, old-fashioned toys, vintage boots and New York State wine. This is just the beginning and there really is no end.

Fashion & Couture

The 'Gold Coast' along Madison Ave is a 40-block stretch of big-name designers: Armani, Kors, Ferragamo, Bulgari, Prada and many more. The few thrift shops that populate this area have, as you can imagine, waiting lists to inspect the merchandise. These stores get last year's cast-offs from the well-heeled, and the working-class girls line up waiting to buy.

In the Meatpacking District, the aura is a little less rarefied, but the focus is still on high-end fashion. Edgier, more youthful names such as Malandrino, Miele and McQueen are all the rage.

Downtown in Nolita and Tribeca is where almost-but-not-quite discovered young models like to browse; the flashy boutiques are more willing to take a chance on the latest European and Asian imports.

Bargain & Souvenir Seeking

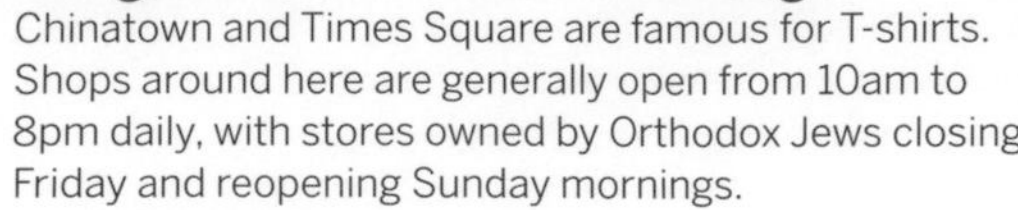

Chinatown and Times Square are famous for T-shirts. Shops around here are generally open from 10am to 8pm daily, with stores owned by Orthodox Jews closing Friday and reopening Sunday mornings.

While clothing sales happen year-round, sample sales are held frequently, mostly in the huge warehouses in the Fashion District of Midtown or in SoHo.

Flea Markets & Vintage Adventures

As much as New Yorkers gravitate towards all that's shiny and new, it can be infinitely fun to rifle through closets of unwanted wares and threads. The most popular flea market is the Brooklyn Flea, housed in all sorts of spaces throughout the year.

The East Village is the city's de facto neighborhood for secondhand clothes stores – the uniform of the unwavering legions of hipsters. For antiques and assorted ephemera from the past (records, artwork, books, home furnishings, toys) don't miss the sprawling Antiques Garage Flea Market held on weekends in Chelsea or the affiliated Hell's Kitchen Flea Market.

The Best... Stores

1 Century 21 (p232)

2 Strand Book Store (p140)

3 Barneys (p185)

4 Housing Works Thrift Shop (p140)

5 B&H Photo Video (p187)

6 ABC Carpet & Home (p154)

Best Shopping Strips

- **West Broadway** SoHo is one big shopping mall, with high-end fashion well represented.
- **Mott St** Between Houston and Broome Sts in Nolita, it has lovely little clothing, shoe and accessory shops.
- **Orchard St** Between Houston and Grand Sts are edgy fashions and urban style.
- **E 9th St** Between Second Ave and Ave A is a good intro to the vintage stores and curio shops of the East Village.
- **Bleecker St** Between Bank and W 10th Sts, running south from Abingdon Sq, Bleecker St is sprinkled with eye-catching storefronts and boutiques selling trendy apparel.
- **Fifth Ave** Between Central Park and Rockefeller Center, this commercial strip is the El Dorado of shopping, with Tiffany's, Bergdorf Goodman and many others.
- **Madison Ave and 72nd** Gateway to the bejeweled storefronts of the Upper East Side.
- **Bedford Ave** Between N 4th and N 10th Sts, Bedford Ave has alternative fashions, record stores and lots of flashy-trashy stuff.

Gay & Lesbian New York City

Gay-pride rainbow flags, Greenwich Village

ROGER GAESS/GETTY IMAGES ©

The future has arrived in NYC: men seek out other men using apps, drag queens are so 'out' that they're practically 'in,, and gay wedding bells are chiming. It may not always be perfect, but few cities make being queer so utterly fabulous. The West Village, Chelsea and Hell's Kitchen are a few pivotal destinations in the city's ever-evolving gay nightlife.

Drinking & Nightlife

This is one category that is unapologetically separated from the straight version – probably because gay bars hold such an important place in gay history, as they used to be the only places where being out was free and easy. You'll find endless options here and watering holes that appeal to all sorts of subcultures, from pierced and tattooed baby dykes to aging circuit boys.

Note that places come and go very quickly – especially nightclubs – only to reopen a few weeks later under a new moniker; some parties are only one-night affairs. Visit the websites of some of the community's favorite roving weekly or monthly bashes to see what's next or try one of the following online resources:

- **Next Magazine** (www.nextmagazine.com) Online version of the ubiquitous print guide to all things gay in NYC.
- **Gayletter** (www.gayletter.com) An e-newsletter about what's on.

- **Get Out! (getoutmag.com)** A handy print (and online) guide to all things queer in town.
- **Metrosource (www.metrosource.com)** Glossy entertainment mag available in many shops.
- **Time Out New York (www.timeout.com/newyork)** Features a good events section.

Promoters

One of best ways to dial into the party hotline is to follow the various goings-on of your favorite promoter. Here are some of ours:

- **Josh Wood** (www.joshwoodproductions.com)
- **Rafferty Mazur Events** (www.raffertymazurevents.com)
- **Spank** (www.spankartmag.com)
- **Daniel Nardicio** (www.danielnardicio.com)
- **Erich Conrad** (www.twitter.com/zigzaglebain)

The Best... Gay Nightspots

1 Eastern Bloc (p112)

2 Marie's Crisis (p135)

3 Stonewall Inn (p136)

4 Barracuda (p137)

5 G Lounge (p136)

6 Industry (p182)

Weeknight Revelry

Weekdays are the new weekend. Here in the Big Apple, any night of the week is fair game to paint the town rouge – especially for the gay community, who attack the weekday social scene with gusto. Wednesdays and Thursdays roar with a steady stream of parties, and locals love raging on Sundays (especially in summer).

Gay Pride

Gay Pride (www.nycpride.org) is a month-long celebration in June of the city's longstanding and diverse queer communities, and an apt description of New York's gay and lesbian lifestyle: unabashedly out and empowered in a city noted for its overachievers.

Gay & Lesbian by Neighborhood

- **Greenwich Village, Chelsea and the Meatpacking District** The original flavor of gay New York still shines as a rainbow beacon.
- **East Village & Lower East Side** Slightly grittier, sweatier, grungier versions of the West Side haunts.
- **Union Square, Flatiron District and Gramercy** Hosts a spillover of gay venues from the East Village, West Village and Chelsea.
- **Midtown** Midtown West's Hell's Kitchen neighborhood is the 'new Chelsea' (read: 'Hellsea'), with an ever-expanding booty of gay and gay-friendly shops, bars, nosh spots and clubs.
- **Brooklyn** Multiculti borough with gays of every ilk, and diverse watering holes peppered throughout.

Survival Guide

Times Square (p162)

SYLVAIN SONNET/GETTY IMAGES ©

Sleeping

Accommodations Types

B&BS & FAMILY-STYLE GUESTHOUSES

Offer mix-and-match furnishings and some serious savings (if you don't mind some Victorian styles or eating breakfast with strangers).

BOUTIQUE HOTELS

Usually have tiny rooms decked out with fantastic amenities and at least one celebrity-filled basement bar, rooftop bar or hip, flashy eatery on-site.

CLASSIC HOTELS

Typified by old-fashioned, small-scale European grandeur; these usually cost the same as boutiques and aren't always any larger.

EUROPEAN-STYLE TRAVELERS' HOTELS

Have creaky floors and small but cheap and clean (if chintzily decorated) rooms, often with a shared bathroom.

HOSTELS

Functional dorms (bunk beds and bare walls) that are nonetheless communal and friendly. Many have a backyard garden, kitchen and a pretty lounge that make up for the soulless rooms.

PRIVATE APARTMENTS

We can all thank little Plaza-dweller Eloise for conjuring up fanciful dreams of hanging one's hat in a luxury New York City hotel room, but these days, finding a place to sleep in the city that never does is hardly restricted to the traditional spectrum of lodging.

Websites like **Airbnb** (www.airbnb.com) are providing a truly unique – and not to mention economical – alternative to the wallet-busting glitz and glam. Selling 'unique spaces' to tourists looking for their home away from home, they offer locals the opportunity to rent out their apartments while they're out of town, or lease a space (be it a bedroom or pull-out couch) in their home. Airbnb is an undeniable hit in NYC, where space comes at a premium and obscenely high real-estate prices act as quite the incentive for locals to supplement their housing income.

Costs

The average room is over $300 a night, with some seasonal fluctuations (lowest in January and February, highest in September and October), and plenty of options both below and above (especially above) this rate. When you get your bill, the hotel will also tack on a 14.75% room tax and a $3.50 per night occupancy tax.

If you're looking to find the best room rates, then flexibility is key – weekdays are often cheaper. If you are visiting over a weekend, try for a business hotel in the Financial District, which tends to empty out when the work week ends.

Need to Know

PRICE RANGES

Prices in this guide represent the standard range in rates at each establishment, regardless of the time of year.

- **$** less than $150
- **$$** $150–$350
- **$$$** more than $350

BREAKFAST

Breakfast is not included in the price of the room unless specified in the review. Many hotels do, however, include breakfast.

RESERVATIONS

Reservations are essential – walk-ins are practically impossible and rack rates are almost always unfavorable relative to online deals. Reserve your room as early as possible.

TIPPING

Always tip your maid – leave $3 to $5 per night in an obvious location with a note. Porters should receive a dollar or two, and service staff bringing items to your room should be tipped accordingly as well.

…s also worth checking …the slew of members-only …bsites, such as **Jetsetter** (www.jetsetter.com), that offer discounted rates and 'flash sales' (limited time only sales akin to Groupon) for their devotees. Flash sales are a great way to scoop up discounted beds when planning a holiday at the last minute.

Useful Websites

Lonely Planet (www.lonelyplanet.com) Lots of accommodations reviews; it's also possible to book your room online here.

Kayak (www.kayak.com) Simple all-purpose search engine.

Hotel Tonight (www.hoteltonight.com) An app with great deals but only for booking after noon or even later on the night you want to check in.

Where to Stay

NEIGHBORHOOD	FOR	AGAINST
SoHo & Chinatown	Shop to your heart's content right on your doorstep	Crowds (mostly tourists) swarm the commercial streets of SoHo almost all day
East Village & Lower East Side	Funky and fun, the area feels the most quintessentially 'New York' to visitors and Manhattanites alike	Not tons to choose from when it comes to hotel sleeps
Greenwich Village, Chelsea & the Meatpacking District	Brilliantly close to everything in a thriving, picturesque part of town that almost has a European feel	High prices for traditional hotels, but reasonable for B&Bs; rooms are sometimes on the small side
Union Square, Flatiron District & Gramercy	Convenient subway access to anywhere in the city; you're also steps away from the Village and Midtown in either direction	Prices are high and there's not much in the way of neighborhood flavor
Midtown	In the heart of the postcard version of NYC: skyscrapers, museums, shopping and Broadway shows	One of the most expensive areas in the city – and expect small rooms; Midtown can often feel touristy and impersonal
Upper West Side & Central Park	Convenient access to Central Park and the Museum of Natural History	It can be a long subway ride to the livelier eating and drinking options of downtown
Brooklyn	Better value for money; great for exploring NY's most creative neighborhoods	It can be a long subway ride to Midtown and points north

Best Places to Stay

NAME	NEIGHORHOOD	REVIEW
SOLITA SOHO $$	SoHo & Chinatown	Great for soaking up the flavor of Chinatown ar Little Italy. Good last-minute deals online.
NOLITAN HOTEL $$$	SoHo & Chinatown	Situated between SoHo and the Village, rooms l like they're ready to be photographed for the ne CB2 catalog.
BOWERY HOTEL $$$	East Village & Lower East Side	A symbol of the new downtown, combining old-fashioned elements with modern elegance; includes a happening bar and Italian eatery.
HOTEL ON RIVINGTON $$	East Village & Lower East Side	This 20-floor hotel looks like a shimmering new Shanghai building with glass-walled rooms and enviable views over the East River.
EAST VILLAGE BED & COFFEE $	East Village & Lower East Side	A quirky, arty, offbeat B&B with colorful, themec private rooms and great amenities; each floor h shared common and kitchen spaces.
BLUE MOON HOTEL $$	East Village & Lower East Side	You'd never guess that this quaint, welcoming b guesthouse – full of colors, detailed moldings, marble baths – was once a tenement.
EAST VILLAGE B&B $	East Village & Lower East Side	A popular and stylish oasis for sapphic couples in the East Village with exposed brickwork, wooc floors and modern art.
JADE HOTEL $$	Greenwich Village, Chelsea & the Meatpacking District	This 113-room boutique hotel has heritage style just steps from the great dining scene of the Village.
HÔTEL AMERICANO $$	Greenwich Village, Chelsea & the Meatpacking District	Perfectly polished rooms with a carefully curate selection of minimalist and muted furniture.
STANDARD $$$	Greenwich Village, Chelsea & the Meatpacking District	A wide, boxy, glass tower that straddles the High Line with floor-to-ceiling windows, glossy wood-framed beds and marbled bathrooms.
CHELSEA PINES INN $$	Greenwich Village, Chelsea & the Meatpacking District	With its five walk-up floors coded to the rainbow flag, the Chelsea Pines welcomes guests of all stripes.
MARITIME HOTEL $$	Greenwich Village, Chelsea & the Meatpacking District	This white tower dotted with portholes has beer transformed into a marine-themed luxury inn by hip team of architects.
CHELSEA LODGE $	Greenwich Village, Chelsea & the Meatpacking District	Housed in a landmark brownstone in Chelsea's lovely historic district, this European-style lodge a super deal, with well-kept rooms.
JANE HOTEL $	Greenwich Village, Chelsea & the Meatpacking District	The tiny 50ft rooms have been recently renovat and outfitted for modern travelers and there's a gorgeous communal lobby/lounge.
GRAMERCY PARK HOTEL $$$	Union Square, Flatiron District & Gramercy	Has dark-wood paneling and sumptuous furnishir in the rooms, celebrity-studded bars, and a guest-only rooftop terrace.

CTICALITIES	BEST FOR
☎ 212-925-3600; www.solitasohohotel.com; 159 Grand St, at Lafayette St; r from $289; ❄ 📶; S N/Q/R, J/Z, 6 to Canal St	Affordable style
☎ 212-925-2555; www.nolitanhotel.com; 30 Kenmare St, btwn Elizabeth & Mott Sts; r from $358; ❄ 📶 🐾; S J/Z to Bowery, 6 to Spring St, B/D to Grand St	Good-value style
☎ 212-505-9100; www.theboweryhotel.com; 335 Bowery, btwn 2nd & 3rd Sts; r from $395; ❄ @ 📶; S F/V to Lower East Side-Second Ave, 6 to Bleecker St	Well-heeled hipsters
☎ 212-475-2600; www.hotelonrivington.com; 107 Rivington St, btwn Essex & Ludlow Sts; r from $311; 📶; S F to Delancey St, J/M/Z to Essex St, F to Second Ave	Downtown panoramas
☎ 917-816-0071; www.bedandcoffee.com; 110 Ave C, btwn 7th & 8th Sts; s/d with shared bath from $130/140; ❄ 📶; S F/V to Lower East Side-Second Ave	Homey, personal charm
☎ 212-533-9080; www.bluemoon-nyc.com; 100 Orchard St, btwn Broome & Delancey Sts; r incl breakfast from $210; ❄ 📶; S F to Delancey St, J/M to Essex St	Feeling like a neighborhood resident
☎ 212-260-1865; evbandb@juno.com; Apt 5-6, 244 E 7th St btwn Aves C & D; r $150-175; S F/V to Lower East Side-Second Ave	Peace and quiet
☎ 212-375-1300; www.thejadenyc.com; 52 W 13th St; r from $260; ❄ 📶	Boutique elegance
☎ 212-216-0000; www.hotel-americano.com; 518 W 27th St, btwn Tenth & Eleventh Aves; r from $255; S A/C/E to 23rd St	Design geeks
☎ 212-645-4646; www.standardhotels.com; 848 Washington St, at 13th St; r from $355; ❄ 📶; S A/C/E to 14th St, L to Eighth Ave	Wannabe exhibitionists
☎ 212-929-1023, 888-546-2700; www.chelseapinesinn.com; 317 W 14th St, btwn Eighth & Ninth Aves; r incl breakfast from $209; ❄ 📶; S A/C/E to 14th St, L to Eighth Ave	Gay and lesbian central
☎ 212-242-4300; www.themaritimehotel.com; 363 W 16th St, btwn Eighth & Ninth Aves; r from $220; S A/C/E to 14th St, L to Eighth Ave	Staying in a luxury *Love Boat*
☎ 212-243-4499; www.chelsealodge.com; 318 W 20th St btwn Eighth & Ninth Aves; s/d from $130/140; ❄ 📶; S A/C/E to 14th St, 1 to 18th St	Homey value
☎ 212-924-6700; www.thejanenyc.com; 113 Jane St, btwn Washington St & West Side Hwy; r with shared bath from $99; P ❄ 📶; S L to Eighth Ave, A/C/E to 14th St, 1/2 to Christopher St-Sheridan Sq	Living like a luxury sailor
☎ 212-920-3300; www.gramercyparkhotel.com; 2 Lexington Ave, at 21st St; r from $349; ❄ 📶; S 6 to 23rd St	Living like a Spanish grandee

NAME	NEIGHORHOOD	REVIEW
HOTEL 17 $$	Union Square, Flatiron District & Gramercy	On a leafy residential block, this popular eigh floor town house has rooms with basic furnish exuding old New York with cheap prices.
ANDAZ FIFTH AVENUE $$$	Midtown	Youthful and hip, the Andaz has sleek rooms wit NYC-inspired details, a 'secret' basement bar, locavore restaurant, and talks by guest artists.
ACE HOTEL $$$	Midtown	A hit with cool creatives, rooms are best describe as upscale bachelor pads, and the hipster-packec lobby is fun.
YOTEL $$	Midtown	This uber-cool 669-room futuristic-looking opti bases its rooms on airplane classes; all cabins feature floor-to-ceiling windows with killer views
IVY TERRACE $$	Midtown	A seriously charming B&B with spacious, Victori inspired rooms.
NIGHT $$	Midtown	In the glare of Times Square's neon, Night is dar and decadent, from the rocker-glam entrance, t the sleek-and-sexy black-and-white rooms.
BELVEDERE HOTEL $$	Midtown	This 1928 art-deco original has been given a glorious modern makeover; bathrooms are bigg than many boutique hotel rooms.
POD 51 $	Midtown	This affordable hot spot has a range of room typ most barely big enough for the bed.
GERSHWIN HOTEL $$	Midtown	This raffish, pop-art-themed veteran has small, simply designed rooms with comfy beds near th buzzing Flatiron District.
HOTEL BEACON $$	Upper West Side & Central Park	Adjacent to the Beacon Theatre, this hotel offers a winning mix of attentive service, comfortable rooms and good location.
HOTEL BELLECLAIRE $$	Upper West Side & Central Park	A landmark beaux-arts building (plenty of litera lore) with contemporary rooms in a variety of siz and configurations.
JAZZ ON THE PARK HOSTEL $	Upper West Side & Central Park	This hostel is generally a good bet, with clean dorm a cafe/TV lounge and three terrace sitting areas.
WYTHE HOTEL $$	Brooklyn	Industrial-chic rooms set in a converted 1901 factor Great brasserie on the ground floor, and a top-floor bar for sunset cocktails and Manhattan skyline view
KING & GROVE $$	Brooklyn	Appealing, minimalist rooms with great amenitie excellent restaurant, saltwater pool and an uppe level bar with jaw-dropping views.
NEW YORK LOFT HOSTEL $	Brooklyn	A young bohemian crowd flocks to this Bushwick locale. Loads of activities on offer, making it a go spot to meet other travelers.

CTICALITIES	BEST FOR
212-475-2845; www.hotel17ny.com; 225 E 17th St, btwn Second & Third Aves; $91-181; ; S N/Q/R, 4/5/6 to 14th St-Union Sq, L to Third Ave	Good-value old-world charm
212-601-1234; http://andaz.hyatt.com; 485 Fifth Ave, at 41st St, Midtown East; d from $380; ; S S, 4/5/6 to Grand Central-42nd St, 7 to Fifth Ave	Uber-chicness
212-679-2222; www.acehotel.com/newyork; 20 W 29th St, btwn Broadway & Fifth Ave, Midtown East; r $199-799; ; S N/R to 28th St	Social media types
646-449-7700; www.yotel.com; 570 Tenth Ave, at 41st St, Midtown West; r from $149; ; S A/C/E to 42nd St-Port Authority Bus Terminal, 1/2/3, N/Q/R, S, 7 to Times Sq-42nd St	*The Jetsons* fanatics
516-662-6862; www.ivyterrace.com; 230 E 58th St, btwn Second & Third Aves, Midtown East; r $249-390; ; S 4/5/6 to 59th St; N/Q/R to Lexington Ave-59th St	Couples
212-835-9600; www.nighthotelny.com; 132 W 45th St, btwn Sixth & Seventh Aves, Midtown West; r from $180; ; S B/D/F/M to 47th-50th Sts-Rockefeller Center	Feeling like you're sleeping in an Anne Rice novel
888-468-3558, 212-245-7000; www.belvederehotelnyc.com; 319 W 48th St, btwn Eighth & Ninth Aves, Midtown West; r $199-599; ; S C/E to 50th St	Classical luxury
866-414-4617; www.thepodhotel.com; 230 E 51st St, btwn Second & Third Aves, Midtown East; r from $89; ; S 6 to 51st St, E/M to Lexington Ave-53rd St	Hip Midtown affordability
212-545-8000; www.gershwinhotel.com; 7 E 27th St at Fifth Ave; r from $245; @; S N/R, 6 to 28th St	Slacker types
212-787-1100, reservations 800-572-4969; www.beaconhotel.com; 2130 Broadway, btwn 74th & 75th Sts; d $230-350, ste $300-450; ; S 1/2/3 to 72nd St	Families and convenience
212-362-7700; www.hotelbelleclaire.com; 250 W 77th St, at Broadway; d $150-370, ste $310-600; ; S 1 to 79th St	Good value for location
212-932-1600; www.jazzhostels.com; 36 W 106th St, btwn Central Park West & Manhattan Ave; dm $44-70, d $125-200; ; S B, C to 103rd St	Central Park budget
718-460-8000; wythehotel.com; 80 Wythe Ave, at N 11th St, Williamsburg; r $205-600;	Hipsters
718-218-7500; www.kingandgrove.com; 160 N 12th St, btwn Bedford Ave & Berry St, Williamsburg; d $175-360; ; S L to Bedford, G to Nassau	Jetsetters
718-366-1351; www.nylofthostel.com; 249 Varet St, btwn Bogart & White Sts, Bushwick; dm $60-75; @; S L to Morgan Ave	Urban pioneers

Transport

Arriving in New York City

With its three bustling airports, two train stations and a monolithic bus terminal, New York City rolls out the welcome mat for the more than 50 million visitors who come to take a bite out of the Big Apple each year.

Direct flights are possible from most major American and international cities. Figure six hours from Los Angeles, seven hours from London and Amsterdam, and 14 hours from Tokyo. Consider getting here from within the US by train instead of car or plane to enjoy a mix of bucolic and urban scenery en route, without unnecessary traffic hassles, security checks and excess carbon emissions.

Flights, tours and rail tickets can be booked online at lonelyplanet.com/bookings.

John F Kennedy International Airport

John F Kennedy International Airport (JFK; ☎718-244-4444; www.panynj.gov), 15 miles from Midtown in southeastern Queens, has eight terminals, serves millions of passengers annually and hosts flights coming and going from all corners of the globe.

Taxi

A yellow taxi from Manhattan to the airport will use the meter; prices (often about $60) depend on traffic – it can take 45 to 60 minutes. From JFK, taxis charge a flat rate of $52 to any destination in Manhattan (not including tolls or tip); it can take 45 to 60 minutes for most destinations in Manhattan.

Vans & Car Service

Shared vans, like those offered by **Super Shuttle Manhattan** (www.supershuttle.com), cost around $20 to $25 per person, depending on the destination. If traveling *to* the airport from NYC, car services have set fares from $45.

Express Bus

The **NYC Airporter** (www.nycairporter.com) runs to Grand Central Station, Penn Station or the Port Authority Bus Terminal from JFK. The one-way fare is $16.

Train

From the airport, take the AirTrain ($5, as you exit) to Jamaica Station. From there, LIRR trains go frequently to Penn Station in Manhattan. It's about a 20-minute journey from station to station. One-way fares cost $7 ($10 at peak times).

Subway

If money is tight, the subway is the cheapest, but slowest, way of reaching Manhattan. From the airport, hop on the AirTrain ($5, payable as you exit) to Sutphin Blvd-Archer Ave (Jamaica Station) to reach the E, J or Z line (or the Long Island Rail Road). To take the A line instead, ride the AirTrain to Howard Beach station. The E train to Midtown has the fewest stops. Expect the journey to take at least 90 minutes to Midtown.

LaGuardia Airport

Used mainly for domestic flights, **LaGuardia** (LGA; ☎718-533-3400; www.panynj.gov) is smaller than JFK but only eight miles from midtown Manhattan; it sees about 26 million passengers per year.

Taxi

A taxi to/from Manhattan costs about $42 for the approximately half-hour ride.

Car Service

A car service to LaGuardia costs about $35.

Express Bus

The NYC Airporter costs $13.

Subway/Bus

It's less convenient to get to LaGuardia by public transportation than the other airports. The best subway link is the 74 St–Broadway station (7 line, or the E, F, M and R lines at the connecting Jackson Hts Roosevelt Ave station) in Queens, where you can pick up the new Q70 Express Bus to the airport (about 10 minutes to the aiport).

Newark Liberty International Airport

About the same distance from Midtown as JFK (16 miles), **Newark's airport** (EWR; ☎973-961-6000; www.panynj.gov) brings many New Yorkers out for flights (there's

...ne 36 million passengers annually).

Car Service

A car service runs about $45 to $60 for the 45-minute ride from Midtown – a taxi is roughly the same. You'll have to pay $13 to get into NYC through the Lincoln (at 42nd St) and Holland (at Canal St) Tunnels and, further north, the George Washington Bridge, though there's no charge going back through to New Jersey. There are a couple of cheap tolls on New Jersey highways, too, unless you ask your driver to take Highway 1 or 9.

Subway/Train

NJ Transit runs a rail service (with an AirTrain connection) between Newark airport (EWR) and New York's Penn Station for $12.50 each way. The trip takes 25 minutes and runs every 20 or 30 minutes from 4:20am to about 1:40am. Hold onto your ticket, which you must show upon exiting at the airport.

Express Bus

The Newark Liberty Airport Express has a bus service between the airport and Port Authority Bus Terminal, Bryant Park and Grand Central Terminal in Midtown ($16 one way). The 45-minute ride goes every 15 minutes from 6:45am to 11:15pm and every half hour from 4:45am to 6:45am and 11:15pm to 1:15am.

Port Authority Bus Terminal

For long-distance bus trips, you'll leave and depart from the world's busiest bus station, the **Port Authority Bus Terminal** (Map p178; ☎212-564-8484; www.panynj.gov; 41st St at Eighth Ave; S A, C, E, N, Q, R, 1, 2, 3, & 7), which sees nearly 70 million passengers pass through each year. Bus companies leaving from here include the following:

Greyhound (☎800-231-2222; www.greyhound.com) Connects New York with major cities across the country.

Peter Pan Trailways (☎800-343-9999; www.peterpanbus.com) Daily express service to Boston (one way $18–32), Washington, DC ($16–25) and Philadelphia ($12–16).

ShortLine Bus (☎201-529-3666, 800-631-8405; www.coachusa.com) Goes to northern New Jersey and upstate New York (Rhinebeck for $25.30, Woodbury Common for $21).

Penn Station

Train

Penn Station (33rd St, btwn Seventh & Eighth Aves; S 1/2/3/A/C/E to 34th St-Penn Station) The departure point for all Amtrak trains, including the Metroliner and Acela Express services to Princeton, NJ, and Washington, DC (note that both these express services will cost twice as much as a normal fare). All fares vary, based on the day of the week and the time you want to travel. There is no baggage-storage facility at Penn Station.

Climate Change & Travel

Every form of transport that relies on carbon-based fuel generates CO_2, the main cause of human-induced climate change. Modern travel is dependent on aeroplanes, which might use less fuel per kilometer per person than most cars but travel much greater distances. The altitude at which aircraft emit gases (including CO_2) and particles also contributes to their climate change impact. Many websites offer 'carbon calculators' that allow people to estimate the carbon emissions generated by their journey and, for those who wish to do so, to offset the impact of the greenhouse gases emitted with contributions to portfolios of climate-friendly initiatives throughout the world. Lonely Planet offsets the carbon footprint of all staff and author travel.

Long Island Rail Road (LIRR; www.mta.nyc.ny.us/lirr) The Long Island Rail Road serves over 300,000 commuters each day, with services from Penn Station to points in Brooklyn and Queens, and on Long Island. Prices are broken down by zones. A peak-hour ride from Penn Station to Jamaica Station (en route to JFK via AirTrain) costs $9.50 if you buy it at the station (or a whopping $16 onboard!).

New Jersey Transit (☎800-772-2287; www.njtransit.com) Also operates trains from Penn Station, with services to the suburbs and the Jersey Shore.

New Jersey PATH (800-234-7284; www.panynj.gov/path) Another option for getting into NJ's northern points, such as Hoboken and Newark. Trains ($2.50) run from Penn Station along the length of Sixth Ave, with stops at 33rd, 23rd, 14th, 9th and Christopher Sts, as well as at the reopened World Trade Center site.

Bus

A growing number of budget bus lines operate from locations just outside Penn Station:

BoltBus (877-265-8287; www.boltbus.com) Owned by Greyhound, BoltBus is notable for its free wi-fi (which occasionally actually works). Buses travel from New York to Philadelphia, Boston, Baltimore and Washington, DC. Prices range from $10 to $27, with better deals the earlier you buy (even $1 deals sometimes!). Buses depart from W 33rd between 11th and 12th Aves. If you're heading to Philadelphia, Baltimore or DC, buses also depart downtown, from Sixth Ave between Grand and Watts Sts. Buy tickets online.

megabus (877-462-6342; us.megabus.com) Also offering free (sometimes functioning) wi-fi and similar rates, megabus travels between New York and Boston, Washington, DC and Toronto, among other destinations.

Grand Central Station

The last line departing from Grand Central Terminal, the

Metro-North Railroad (212-532-4900; www.mta.info/mnr) serves Connecticut, Westchester County and the Hudson Valley.

Getting Around New York City

Once you've arrived in NYC, getting around is fairly easy. The 660-mile subway system is cheap and (reasonably) efficient and can whisk you to nearly every hidden corner of the city. There are also buses, ferries, trains, pedicabs and those ubiquitous yellow taxis (though don't expect to see many available when it's raining) for zipping around and out of town when the subway simply doesn't cut it.

The sidewalks of New York, however, are the real stars in the transportation scheme – this city is made for walking. Increasingly, it's also made for bicycles, with the addition of hundreds of miles of new bike lanes and greenways over the last few years.

S Subway & Buses

The New York subway's 660-mile system, run by the **Metropolitan Transportation Authority** (MTA; 718-330-1234; www.mta.info), is iconic, cheap ($2.50 for a SingleRide, $2.25 if using MetroPass), round-the-clock and easily the fastest and most reliable way to get around the city.

It's a good idea to grab a free map, available from any attendant. When in doubt, ask someone who looks like they know what they're doing. They may not, but subway confusion (and consternat[ion]) is the great unifier in this diverse city.

MetroCards for Travelers

New York's classic subway tokens now belong to the ages: today all buses and subways use the yellow-and-blue **MetroCard** (718-330-1234; www.mta.info/metrocard), which you can purchase or add value to at one of several easy-to-use automated machines at any station. You can use cash or an ATM or credit card. Just select 'Get new card' and follow the prompts. Tip: if you're not from the US, when the machine asks for your zip code, enter 99999. The card itself costs $1.

You then select one of two types of MetroCard. The 'pay-per-ride' is $2.50 per ride, though the MTA tacks on a 5% bonus on MetroCards over $5. (Buy a $20 card, and you'll receive $21 worth of credit). If you plan to use the subway quite a bit, you can also buy an 'unlimited ride' card ($30 for a seven-day pass). These cards are handy for travelers – particularly if you're jumping around town to a few different places in one day. Note that the MetroCard works for buses as well as subways (and offers free transfers between them).

Taxi

Hailing and riding in a cab are rites of passage in New York – especially when you get a driver who's a neurotic speed demon, which is often. (A word of advice: don't forget to buckle your seatbelt.)

…he **Taxi Limousine & …mmission** (TLC; ☎311), …e taxis' governing body, …as set fares for rides (which can be paid with credit or debit card). It's $2.50 for the initial charge (first one-fifth of a mile), 50¢ each additional one-fifth mile as well as per 60 seconds of being stopped in traffic, $1 peak surcharge (weekdays 4pm to 8pm), and a 50¢ night surcharge (8pm to 6am), plus a new NY State surcharge of 50¢ per ride. Tips are expected to be 10% to 15%, but give less if you feel in any way mistreated – and be sure to ask for a receipt and use it to note the driver's license number.

The TLC keeps a Passenger's Bill of Rights, which gives you the right to tell the driver which route you'd like to take, or ask your driver to stop smoking or turn off an annoying radio station. Also, the driver does not have the right to refuse you a ride based on where you are going.

To hail a cab, look for one with its roof light on. It's particularly difficult to score a taxi in the rain, at rush hour and around 4pm, when many drivers end their shifts.

Private car services are a common taxi alternative in the outer boroughs. Fares differ depending on the neighborhood and length of ride, and must be determined beforehand, as they have no meters. Though these 'black cars' are quite common in Brooklyn and Queens, never get into one if a driver simply stops to offer you a ride – no matter what borough you're in. A couple of car services in Brooklyn include **Northside** (☎718-387-2222; 207 Bedford Ave) in Williamsburg and **Arecibo** (☎718-783-6465; 170 Fifth Ave at Degraw St) in Park Slope.

Boro Taxis

In 2013, light green Boro Taxis began operating in the outer boroughs and Upper Manhattan. These allow folks to hail a taxi on the street in neighborhoods where yellow taxis rarely roam. These have the same fares and features as yellow cabs, and are a good

Subway Cheat Sheet

A few tips for understanding the madness of the New York underground:

NUMBERS, LETTERS, COLORS

Color-coded subway lines are named by a letter or number, and most carry a collection of two to four trains on their tracks. For example, the red-colored line in Manhattan is the 1, 2, 3 line; these three separate trains follow roughly the same path in Manhattan, then branch out in the Bronx and Brooklyn.

EXPRESS & LOCAL LINES

A common mistake is accidentally boarding an 'express train' and passing by a local stop you want. Know that each color-coded line is shared by local trains and express trains; the latter make only select stops in Manhattan (indicated by a white circle on subway maps).

GETTING IN THE RIGHT STATION

Some stations – such as SoHo's Spring St station on the 6 line – have separate entrances for downtown or uptown lines (read the sign carefully). Also look for the green and red lamps above the stairs at each station entrance; green means that it's always open, while red means that particular entrance will be closed at certain hours, usually late at night.

LOST WEEKEND

All the rules switch on weekends, when some lines combine with others, some get suspended, some stations get passed, others get reached. Check the MTA website (www.mta.info) for weekend schedules.

way to get around the outer boroughs (from say Astoria to Williamsburg, or Park Slope to Red Hook).

Boro Taxi drivers are reluctant (but legally obligated) to take passengers into Manhattan as they aren't legally allowed to take fares going out of Manhattan south of 96th St.

Ferry

East River Ferry (**www.eastriverferry.com**) runs year-round commuter service connecting a variety of locations in Manhattan, Queens and Brooklyn. **New York Water Taxi** (**212-742-1969; www.nywatertaxi.com; hop-on-hop-off service 1-day $26**) has a fleet of zippy yellow boats that provide hop-on, hop-off service around Manhattan and Brooklyn. Another bigger, brighter ferry (this one's orange) is the commuter-oriented Staten Island Ferry (p71), which makes constant free journeys across New York Harbor.

Tours

There are dozens upon dozens of organized tours around the city. The following are a few favorites.

Boat

Circle Line Boat Tours
Map p178 (212-563-3200; www.circleline42.com; pier 83, 42nd St at Twelfth Ave; cruises $30-40; S A/C/E to 42nd-Port Authority) The classic Circle Line guides you through all the big sights from the safe distance of a boat that circumnavigates the five boroughs.

Bus

Gray Line (**212-397-2620; www.newyorksightseeing.com; $44-60**) The most ubiquitous guided tour in the city, Gray Line is responsible for bombarding New York streets with the red double-decker buses that locals love to hate. Really, though, for a comprehensive tour of the big sights, it's a great way to go.

Cycling

Bike the Big Apple
(**877-865-0078; www.bikethebigapple.com; tours incl bike & helmet around $95**) Bike the Big Apple, recommended by NYC & Company (the official tourism authority of New York City and operators of www.nycgo.com), offers ten set tours.

Walking

Municipal Art Society **Map p178 (212-935-3960; www.mas.org; 111 W 57th St; tours adult/child $20/15; S F to 57th St)** Various scheduled tours focusing on architecture and history.

Specialist

Sidetour (**www.sidetour.com; tours $50-60**) Sidetour offers unique, off-the-beaten path experiences for those who want to delve deep into NYC. The range of experiences on offer is vast: you can attend a jazz jam in a Brooklyn brownstone, take an ethnic food walk around Astoria, take a renegade art tour through the Met or the galleries of Chelsea or explore the urban art of the Lower East Side.

Foods of New York (**212-913-9964; www.foodsofny.com; tours $52-65**) The official foodie tour of NYC & Company offers various three-hour tours that help you eat your way through gourmet shops in either Chelsea or the West Village.

On Location Tours (**212-683-2027; www.screentours.com; tours around $45**) This company offers four tours – covering *Sex and the City*, *The Sopranos*, general TV and movie locations, and movie locations in Central Park – that let you live out your entertainment-obsessed fantasies.

Wildman Steve Brill
(**914-835-2153; www.wildmanstevebrill.com; sliding scale up to $20**) New York's best-known naturalist – betcha didn't know there were any! – has been leading folks on foraging expeditions through city parks for more than 20 years.

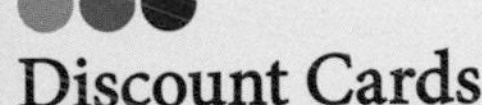

Discount Cards

The following discount cards offer a variety of perks and passes to some of the city's must-sees.

Downtown Culture Pass www.downtownculturepass.org

New York CityPASS www.citypass.com

Explorer Pass www.nyexplorerpass.com

The New York Pass www.newyorkpass.com

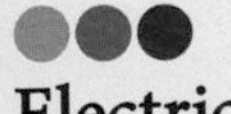

Electricity

120V/60Hz

120V/60Hz

Emergency

Police, Fire, Ambulance (☎ 911)

Poison Control (☎ 800-222-1222)

Internet Access

It is rare to find accommodations in New York City that do not offer wi-fi, though it isn't always free. Public parks with free wi-fi include the High Line, Bryant Park, Battery Park, Tompkins Square Park and Union Square Park.

Internet kiosks can be found at the scatter of **Staples** (www.staples.com) and **FedEx Kinko's** (www.fedexkinkos.com) locations around the city. Also try Apple stores (www.apple.com).

New York Public Library (☎ 212-930-0800; www.nypl.org/branch/local; E 42nd St, at Fifth Ave; S B, D, F or M to 42nd St-Bryant Park) Offers free internet access for laptop toters and half-hour internet access via public terminals at almost all of its locations around the city. Visit the website for more information.

NYC Wireless (www.nycwireless.net) A local free wi-fi activist group that has an online map of free access points, which requires sign-in.

Money

US dollars are the only accepted currency in NYC. While debit and credit cards are widely accepted, it's wise to have a combination of cash and cards.

ATMs

Automatic teller machines are on practically every corner. You can either use your card at banks – usually in a 24-hour-access lobby, filled with up to a dozen monitors at major branches – or you can opt for the lone wolves, which sit in delis, restaurants, bars and grocery stores, charging fierce service fees that go as high as $5.

Opening Hours

Standard business hours are as follows:

Banks 9am-6pm Mon-Fri, some also 9am-noon Sat

Businesses 9am-5pm Mon-Fri

Restaurants Breakfast: 6am to noon, lunch: 11am to around 3pm, dinner: 5pm to 11pm. Sunday brunch (often served on Saturdays too) lasts from 11am until 4pm.

Bars 5pm-4am

Clubs 10pm-4am

Shops 10am to around 7pm on weekdays, 11am to around 8pm Saturdays, and Sundays can be variable – some stores stay closed while others keep weekday hours. Stores tend to stay open later in the neighborhoods downtown.

Public Holidays

New Year's Day January 1

Martin Luther King Day Third Monday in January

Presidents' Day Third Monday in February

Easter March/April

Memorial Day Late May

Gay Pride Last Sunday in June

Independence Day July 4

Labor Day Early September

Rosh Hashanah and Yom Kippur Mid-September to mid-October

Halloween October 31

Thanksgiving Fourth Thursday in November

Christmas Day December 25

New Year's Eve December 31

Safe Travel

Crime rates in NYC are still at their lowest in years. There are few neighborhoods remaining where you might feel apprehensive, no matter what time of night it is (and they're mainly in the outer boroughs). Subway stations are generally safe, too, though some in low-income neighborhoods, especially in the outer boroughs, can be dicey. There's no reason to be paranoid, but it's better to be safe than sorry, so use common sense: don't walk around alone at night in unfamiliar, sparsely populated areas, especially if you're a woman. Carry your daily walking-around money somewhere inside your clothing or in a front pocket rather than in a handbag or a back pocket, and be aware of pickpockets particularly in mobbed areas, like Times Square or Penn Station at rush hour.

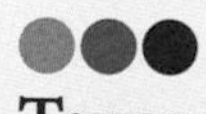

Taxes

Restaurants and retailers never include the sales tax – 8.875% – in their prices, so beware of ordering the $4.99 lunch special when you only have $5 to your name. Several categories of so-called 'luxury items,' including rental cars and dry-cleaning, carry an additional city surcharge of 5%, so you wind up paying an extra 13.875% in total for these services. Clothing and footwear purchases under $110 are tax-free; anything over that amount has a state sales tax of 4.5%. Hotel rooms in New York City are subject to a 14.75% tax, plus a flat $3.50 occupancy tax per night. Since the US has no nationwide value-added tax (VAT), there is no opportunity for foreign visitors to make 'tax-free' purchases.

Telephone

Phone numbers within the USA consist of a three-digit area code followed by a seven-digit local number. If you're calling long distance, dial ☎1 + the three-digit area code + the seven-digit number. To make an international call from NYC, call ☎011+ country code + area code + number. When calling Canada, there is no need to use the 011.

Area Codes

No matter where you're calling within New York City, even if it's just across the street in the same area code, you must always dial ☎1 + the area code first.

Operator Services

Local directory ☎411

Municipal offices and information ☎311

National directory information ☎1-212-555-1212

Operator ☎0

Toll-free number information ☎800-555-1212

Time

New York City is in the Eastern Standard Time (EST) zone – five hours behind Greenwich Mean Time, two hours ahead of Mountain Standard Time (including Denver, Colorado) and three hours ahead of Pacific Standard Time (San Francisco and Los Angeles, California). Almost all of the USA observes daylight-saving time: clocks go forward one hour from the second Sunday in March to the first Sunday in November, when the clocks are turned back one hour.

Tourist Information

In person, try one of the five official bureaus (the Midtown office is the shining star) of **NYC & Company** (212-484-1222; www.nycgo.com):

Midtown (Map p178; 212-484-1222; www.nycgo.com; 810 Seventh Ave btwn 52nd & 53rd Sts; 8:30am-6pm Mon-Fri, 9am-5pm Sat & Sun; S B/D, E to 7th Ave)

Times Square (Map p178; 212-484-1222; Seventh Ave btwn 46th & 47th Sts, Times Square; 9am-7pm; S 1/2/3, 7, N/Q/R to Times Sq)

Lower Manhattan (Map p60; 212-484-1222; City Hall Park at Broadway; 9am-6pm Mon-Fri, 10-5pm Sat & Sun; S R/W to to City Hall)

Chinatown (Map p86; 212-484-1222; cnr Canal, Walker & Baxter Sts; 10am-6pm; S J/M/Z, N/Q/R/W, 6 to Canal St)

Practicalities

- **Newspapers** The **New York Post** (www.nypost.com) is known for screaming headlines, conservative political views and its popular Page Six gossip column. The **New York Times** (www.nytimes.com) – the gray lady – has become hip in recent years, adding sections on technology, arts and dining out. The legendary **Village Voice** (www.villagevoice.com), owned by national alternative-newspaper chain New Times, has less bite but still plenty of bark. The intellectual daily **Wall Street Journal** (www.wallstreetjournal.com) focuses on finance, though its new owner, media mogul Rupert Murdoch, has ratcheted up the general coverage to rival that of the *Times*.

- **Magazines** Those that give a good sense of the local flavor include: **New York Magazine** (www.nymag.com), a weekly magazine with feature stories and great listings about anything and everything in NYC, with an indispensable website; **New Yorker** (www.newyorker.com), the highbrow weekly that covers politics and culture through its famously lengthy works of reportage, and also publishes fiction and poetry; and Time Out New York (p272), a weekly magazine whose focus is on mass coverage, plus articles and interviews on arts and entertainment.

- **Radio** An excellent programing guide can be found in the *New York Times* entertainment section on Sunday. Our top pick is **WNYC93.9FM and 820AM** (820-AM & 93.9-FM; www.wnyc.org). NYC's public radio station is the local NPR affiliate, offering a blend of national and local talk and interview shows, with a switch to classical music in the day on the FM station.

- **Smoking** Smoking is strictly forbidden in any location that's considered a public place; this includes subway stations, restaurants, bars, taxis and parks.

Borough Tourism Portals

Outer boroughs have a special tourism website:

Bronx ilovethebronx.com

Brooklyn visitbrooklyn.org

Queens discoverqueens.info

Staten Island statenislandusa.com

Neighborhood Tourism Portals

In addition to each borough, many of the city's most popular neighborhoods have their own websites (either official or 'unofficial') dedicated to exploring the area.

Lower East Side www.lowereastsideny.com

Chinatown www.explorechinatown.com

Upper East Side www.uppereast.com

Soho www.sohonyc.com

Williamsburg www.freewilliamsburg.com

Travelers with Disabilities

Federal laws guarantee that all government offices and facilities are accessible to the disabled. For information on specific places, you can contact the mayor's **Office for People with Disabilities** (212-639-9675; 9am-5pm Mon-Fri), which will send you a free copy of its *Access New York* guide if you call and request it.

Another excellent resource is the **Society for Accessible Travel & Hospitality** (SATH; 212-447-7284; www.sath.org; 347 Fifth Ave at 34th St, New York, USA, Suite 605; 9am-5pm; M34 to 5th Ave, M1 to 34th St, S 6 to 33rd St), which gives advice on how to travel with a wheelchair, kidney disease, sight impairment or deafness.

For detailed information on subway and bus wheelchair accessibility, call the **Accessible Line** (511; http://web.mta.info/accessibility/) or visit www.mta.info/mta/ada for a list of subway stations with elevators or escalators. Also visit the NYC & Company website (p287); search for 'accessibility.'

Visas

The USA Visa Waiver Program (VWP) allows nationals from 37 countries to enter the US without a visa, provided they are carrying a machine-readable passport. For the updated list of countries included in the program and current requirements, see the **US Department of State** website (http://travel.state.gov/visa).

If you are a citizen of a VWP country, you do not need a visa only if you have a passport that meets current US standards and you have gotten approval from the Electronic System for Travel Authorization (ESTA) in advance. Register online with the Department of Homeland Security (https://esta.cbp.dhs.gov/esta) at least 72 hours before arrival; once travel authorization is approved, your registration is valid for two years. The fee, payable online, is $14.

Behind the Scenes

Our Readers

Many thanks to the travelers who wrote to us with helpful hints, useful advice and interesting anecdotes: Tora Aarberg, Isabelle Bourgey, Elena Casás Barrela, Carla de Beer, Bern Marcowitz, Jenn Pryor, Katrin Sosnick, Rebecca Wilkinson, Michael Zohn.

Author Thanks

Regis St Louis

Many thanks to Cristian Bonetto for his fine work on *New York City 9*, and to all the friends and colleagues who provided helpful tips for this book.

Acknowledgments

Climate map data adapted from Peel MC, Finlayson BL & McMahon TA (2007) 'Updated World Map of the Köppen-Geiger Climate Classification', *Hydrology and Earth System Sciences*, 11, 1633–44.

New York City Subway Map (c) 2014 Metropolitan Transport Authority. Used with permission.

Illustration on p224-5 by Javier Zarracina.

Cover photographs

Front: New York City skyline, Tony Shi Photography/Getty.

Back: Grand Central Terminal, dbimages/Alamy.

This Book

This 3rd edition of Lonely Planet's *Discover New York City* guidebook was researched and written by Regis St Louis and Cristian Bonetto. The previous edition was written by Michael Grosberg, Cristian Bonetto, Carolina Miranda and Brandon Presser. This guidebook was commissioned in Lonely Planet's Oakland office, and produced by the following:

Destination Editor Dora Whitaker
Product Editor Anne Mason
Book Designer Clara Monitto
Senior Cartographer Alison Lyall
Assisting Editors Katie Connolly, Elizabeth Jones, Kate Mathews, Katie O'Connell, Monique Perrin
Cover Researcher Naomi Parker
Thanks to Ryan Evans, Larissa Frost, Genesys India, Jouve India, Claire Naylor, Karyn Noble, Lyahna Spencer

SEND US YOUR FEEDBACK

We love to hear from travelers – your comments keep us on our toes and help make our books better. Our well-traveled team reads every word on what you loved or loathed about this book. Although we cannot reply individually to your submissions, we always guarantee that your feedback goes straight to the appropriate authors, in time for the next edition. Each person who sends us information is thanked in the next edition, the most useful submissions are rewarded with a selection of digital PDF chapters.

Visit **lonelyplanet.com/contact** to submit your updates and suggestions or to ask for help. Our award-winning website also features inspirational travel stories, news and discussions.

Note: We may edit, reproduce and incorporate your comments in Lonely Planet products such as guidebooks, websites and digital products, so let us know if you don't want your comments reproduced or your name acknowledged. For a copy of our privacy policy visit lonelyplanet.com/privacy.

Index

See also separate subindexes for:
- Eating p294
- Drinking & Nightlife p296
- Entertainment p297
- Shopping p297
- Sports & Activities p298

Sights 000
Map pages 000

I

J

K

L

M

N

Sights 000
Map pages 000

U

V

Sights 000
Map pages 000

W

Y

Z

Eating

A

B

C

D

E

F

Drinking & Nightlife

Sights 000
Map pages 000

Entertainment

Shopping

Sports & Activities

Sights 000
Map pages 000

NOTES

NOTES

NOTES

How to Use This Book

These symbols give you the vital information for each listing:

- Telephone Numbers
- Opening Hours
- Parking
- Nonsmoking
- Air-Conditioning
- Internet Access
- Wi-Fi Access
- Swimming Pool
- Vegetarian Selection
- English-Language Menu
- Family-Friendly
- Pet-Friendly
- Bus
- Ferry
- Metro
- Subway
- Tram

All reviews are ordered in our authors' preference, starting with their most preferred option. Additionally:

Sights are arranged in the geographic order that we suggest you visit them, and within this order, by author preference.

Eating and Sleeping reviews are ordered by price range (budget, midrange, top end) and within these ranges, by author preference.

Look out for these icons:

- ★ Must-visit recommendation
- FREE No payment required
- A green or sustainable option

Our authors have nominated these places as demonstrating a strong commitment to sustainability – for example by supporting local communities and producers, operating in an environmentally friendly way, or supporting conservation projects.

Map Legend

Sights
- Beach
- Buddhist
- Castle
- Christian
- Hindu
- Islamic
- Jewish
- Monument
- Museum/Gallery
- Ruin
- Winery/Vineyard
- Zoo
- Other Sight

Activities, Courses & Tours
- Diving/Snorkelling
- Canoeing/Kayaking
- Skiing
- Surfing
- Swimming/Pool
- Walking
- Windsurfing
- Other Activity/Course/Tour

Sleeping
- Sleeping
- Camping

Eating
- Eating

Drinking
- Drinking
- Cafe

Entertainment
- Entertainment

Shopping
- Shopping

Information
- Post Office
- Tourist Information

Transport
- Airport
- Border Crossing
- Bus
- Cable Car/Funicular
- Cycling
- Ferry
- Monorail
- Parking
- S-Bahn
- Taxi
- Train/Railway
- Tram
- Tube Station
- U-Bahn
- Underground Train Station
- Other Transport

Routes
- Tollway
- Freeway
- Primary
- Secondary
- Tertiary
- Lane
- Unsealed Road
- Plaza/Mall
- Steps
- Tunnel
- Pedestrian Overpass
- Walking Tour
- Walking Tour Detour
- Path

Boundaries
- International
- State/Province
- Disputed
- Regional/Suburb
- Marine Park
- Cliff
- Wall

Population
- Capital (National)
- Capital (State/Province)
- City/Large Town
- Town/Village

Geographic
- Hut/Shelter
- Lighthouse
- Lookout
- Mountain/Volcano
- Oasis
- Park
- Pass
- Picnic Area
- Waterfall

Hydrography
- River/Creek
- Intermittent River
- Swamp/Mangrove
- Reef
- Canal
- Water
- Dry/Salt/Intermittent Lake
- Glacier

Areas
- Beach/Desert
- Cemetery (Christian)
- Cemetery (Other)
- Park/Forest
- Sportsground
- Sight (Building)
- Top Sight (Building)

Our Story

A beat-up old car, a few dollars in the pocket and a sense of adventure. In 1972 that's all Tony and Maureen Wheeler needed for the trip of a lifetime – across Europe and Asia overland to Australia. It took several months, and at the end – broke but inspired – they sat at their kitchen table writing and stapling together their first travel guide, *Across Asia on the Cheap*. Within a week they'd sold 1500 copies. Lonely Planet was born.

Today, Lonely Planet has offices in Franklin, London, Melbourne, Oakland, Beijing and Delhi, with more than 600 staff and writers. We share Tony's belief that 'a great guidebook should do three things: inform, educate and amuse'.

Our Writers

REGIS ST LOUIS

Coordinating Author, East Village & Lower East Side, Greenwich Village, Chelsea & the Meatpacking District, Upper East Side, Upper West Side & Central Park

A Hoosier by birth, Regis grew up in a sleepy riverside town where he dreamed of big-city intrigue and small, expensive apartments. In 2001, he settled in New York, which had all that and more. Based in Boerum Hill, Brooklyn, Regis is a full-time travel writer and has contributed to more than 40 Lonely Planet titles, including *New York City*, *USA* and *Washington, DC*.

Read more about at:
lonelyplanet.com/thorntree/profiles/regisstlouis

CRISTIAN BONETTO

Lower Manhattan & the Financial District, SoHo & Chinatown, Union Square, Flatiron District & Gramercy, Midtown, Upper Manhattan & the Outer Boroughs

Planet-roaming Cristian has played both visitor and local in New York City, a place he has been obsessed with since his *Sesame Street* diaper days. From mainstream Midtown to the far-flung corners of outer Queens, the one-time TV and theater scribe has explored countless corners of the city, his musings appearing in newspapers, magazines and online publications across the world. He also tweets at twitter.com/cristianbonetto.

Published by Lonely Planet Publications Pty Ltd
ABN 36 005 607 983
3rd edition – Oct 2014
ISBN 978 1 74220 897 8

10 9 8 7 6 5 4 3 2 1
Printed in China